D0986987

The French Presence in Cochinchina and Cambodia

Rule and Response (1859–1905)

Map 1. The Indochinese Peninsula (adapted from "Cambodia-Laos-Vietnam," Service Géographique de l'Indochine, 1938).

The French Presence
in Cochinchina
and Cambodia

Rule and Response

(1859–1905)

By MILTON E. OSBORNE

For Robert A. Silano
Best personal wishes
Milton Osborne

Cornell University Press

ITHACA AND LONDON

Washington DC
April 2000.

Copyright © 1969 by Cornell University

All rights reserved. Except for brief quotations in a review, this book, or parts thereof, must not be reproduced in any form without permission in writing from the publisher. For information address Cornell University Press, 124 Roberts Place, Ithaca, New York 14850.

First published 1969

Standard Book Number 8014-0512-2

Library of Congress Catalog Card Number 78-87021

PRINTED IN THE UNITED STATES OF AMERICA
BY VAIL-BALLOU PRESS, INC.

For Gwynneth Janet Osborne
and in memory of
George Davenport Osborne

Preface

This study seeks to appraise the impact of the alien French colonial presence in Cochinchina [1] and Cambodia during a period of fifty significant years, from the late 1850's to the first decade of the twentieth century. While in both regions the French desire to carry out a colonial civilizing mission produced a certain unity of policy, the comparison is chiefly one of contrasts. Not only were there fundamental social differences between Cochinchina and Cambodia, but the French methods of government in each region also differed.

For both Cochinchina and Cambodia the period treated in this study has suffered from historical neglect. The conquest of Viet-Nam has been analyzed in considerable detail, but remarkably little attention has been given to the various developments which followed upon that conquest. Neglect of nineteenth-century Cambodia has been even greater.

Archives in London, Paris, Phnom Penh, and Saigon were consulted in the preparation of this study. In addition, the rare holdings of libraries, particularly in Paris, were used to supplement official manuscript records. Wherever possible, interviews with Cambodian, Vietnamese, and French informants who had a special knowledge of the period were added to written sources. Lacunae remain: English, French, and Vietnamese sources were used, but little nineteenth-century Vietnamese material gives the point of view of those Vietnamese in Cochinchina who opposed the French. Until about 1900, printed material in *quoc-ngu* was published almost exclusively by the French administration and French Catholic missions. For Cambodia, the existence of Cambodian royal records

---

[1] For an explanation of the term Cochinchina see the Note on Usage and Transcription.

must remain a supposition only; if they exist, they could not be used. French records and French translations of Cambodian material in the Cambodian archives had to supply the main framework for the study of that country. I have tried to tell my story with due regard for two regions that cannot provide their own sources by which to compare and assess French statements. In Cambodia and Cochinchina, as in so many Southeast Asian countries, the indigenous records that would be the ideal point of departure do not exist.

In preparing this study I received help and encouragement from many persons and institutions, for which I wish to express my sincere gratitude.

Before the exact nature of my intended project was decided, Professor J. M. Ward and Professor Marjorie Jacobs of the Department of History, University of Sydney, provided me with an opportunity to carry out research in Saigon in early 1963. This was a valuable starting point.

My debt to Professors O. W. Wolters, G. McT. Kahin, and M. W. Young of Cornell University is great indeed. Support from the Southeast Asia Program and the Cornell Graduate School allowed me to study at Cornell. Both for my research in Europe and Southeast Asia and for financial support during 1967, I am indebted to funds granted by the Carnegie Corporation of New York through the London-Cornell Project at Cornell University. The Cornell Graduate School also contributed to the cost of my period overseas.

In the United Kingdom I was helped by the staff of the India Records Office, London.

In France I was given every assistance by the Archives Nationales de France; the Archives Nationales de France, Section Outre-Mer; the Archives du Ministère des Affaires Etrangères; the Archives de la Marine; and the Service Historique de l'Armée de Terre, Section Outre-Mer. The Société des Missions Etrangères kindly permitted me to examine their printed records. Both with matters related to my work and with personal advice, M. Philippe Devillers provided kind guidance while I was in Paris.

The Cambodian government permitted me to consult the Archives Nationales du Cambodge while I was working in Phnom Penh, and for this I am grateful.

In Viet-Nam my thanks go to the staff of the Archives of the Republic of Viet-Nam, Van-Kho Viet-Nam Cong-Hoa, who made great efforts to assist me at a time when other concerns pressed upon them. I also acknowledge the kindness of M. Charles Truong-Vinh-Tong, who allowed me to consult the papers of his grandfather, Pétrus Truong-Vinh-Ky, in the Pétrus Ky Museum, Saigon. The Director and staff of the Archeological Institute, the Vien Khoa-Co, Saigon, also permitted me to consult material relating to Pétrus Ky held in that institution.

Both in Cambodia and Viet-Nam I was helped and advised by persons who would prefer that their names not appear in a public document. My thanks to them is no less sincere.

I owe a general debt of gratitude to my fellow graduate students at Cornell, who so often provided helpful comments and criticisms of my work.

My final thanks are to Professor J. D. Legge of Monash University, who, in reading the original and longer manuscript on which this study is based, made many helpful suggestions for revision.

In acknowledging the help of so many individuals and institutions, I must emphasize that I alone am responsible for the statements made and the views expressed.

MILTON E. OSBORNE

Monash University
January 1969

Contents

Illustrations

Maps

Note on Usage and Transcription

Cochinchina. No wholly satisfactory term exists for the portion of Viet-Nam that the French called *Cochinchine.* The region was composed of six Vietnamese provinces in the pre-French period: Gia-Dinh, Bien-Hoa, Dinh-Tuong (My-Tho), Long-Ho (Vinh-Long), An-Giang (Chau-Doc), and Ha-Tien. Various Vietnamese names have been applied to this area, but none is particularly well known outside Viet-Nam. At times it has been called Nam-Ky, Gia-Dinh, and Nam-Bo, the last essentially a Vietnamese Communist usage. In the circumstances, Cochinchina appears the best term, particularly since it is the one used almost exclusively in nineteenth-century literature.

Annamite and Vietnamese. Under French rule, the inhabitants of Viet-Nam were called Annamites, from the Chinese name for Viet-Nam, An-Nam (Pacified South). The words *An-Nam* and *Annamite* are regarded as pejorative in modern Viet-Nam, and in this study the inhabitants of Viet-Nam are termed Vietnamese. In quotations, however, the French usage of Annamite(s) is preserved. When the term Annam is used in the text, it refers to central Viet-Nam, for under French colonial rule Viet-Nam was divided into three regions: Tonkin in the north, Annam in the center, and Cochinchina in the south.

Transcription of Vietnamese words and names. With the exception of such well-known place names as Saigon and Cholon, Vietnamese toponyms are presented in their hyphenated Vietnamese form; thus, My-Tho, and not Mytho. No attempt has been made with either toponyms or personal names to render the diacritics and tone marks which are an essential part of the Vietnamese written language.

Transcription of Cambodian words and names. A variety of transcriptions exists for Cambodian words and personal names. In the case of Cambodian words—chiefly titles—I have followed the most common usage. I have, however, elected not to include the French accents sometimes placed above vowels in transcriptions of Cambodian words. These accents are of limited value in what is, in any event, an imperfect rendering of the Cambodian language. Cambodian personalities are identified by the most frequently used transcription of their name.

Collaborateurs. The important group of Vietnamese who worked with the French in Cochinchina are referred to as *collaborateurs* in this study. This was the term used by the French in the nineteenth century. The English word *collaborator* has too many opprobrious associations that did not accompany the French use of the term in Cochinchina.

Abbreviations

AF	Archives Nationales de France
AOM	Archives Nationales de France, Section Outre-Mer
AAE	Archives du Ministère des Affaires Etrangères (Quai d'Orsay)
AM	Archives de la Marine
AC	Cambodian archives
AVN	Vietnamese archives
BAVH	*Bulletin des Amis de Vieux Hue*
BEFEO	*Bulletin de l'Ecole Française d'Extrême-Orient*
BOCF	*Bulletin Officiel de la Cochinchine Française;* in 1863 this publication superseded the *Bulletin de l'Expédition de Cochinchine,* for which the same abbreviation is used.
BSEI	*Bulletin de la Société des Etudes Indochinoises*
FA	*France-Asie*

Part I

BACKGROUND

I

The Setting

Where the Mekong River divides to form its rich delta, centuries of cultural collision give meaning to the much-abused term "Indochina." Here two outposts, the one of an Indianized, the other of a Sinicized, political system—Cambodia and Viet-Nam—met in irreconcilable conflict. By the early nineteenth century, Viet-Nam appeared to be the political and cultural victor. From the first moment of sustained conflict between the two states, in the middle of the seventeenth century, the Vietnamese had demonstrated a greater vigor and a more persistent resilience. Uncertain relations with China and internal political divisions proved less decisive than the state-supported and individually undertaken expansion of the Vietnamese population towards the fertile lands of the south. Moreover, Cambodia was under attack from Siam as well as Viet-Nam. If one may risk a retrospective hypothesis, there is every reason to suppose that, without French colonial penetration, the contest in the soft underbelly of Indochina would have ceased to be one between Cambodia and Viet-Nam and have become instead a battle between Viet-Nam and Siam. In the first few decades of the nineteenth century, it was already little short of this.[1]

Thus, the arrival of the French at the end of the 1850's occurred during a period of great political turbulence in the Indochinese region. The Cambodian court possessed only a memory of former greatness. Its survival owed more to the preoccupations of its stronger neighbors than to any efforts that it could mount on its own behalf. Viet-Nam had been split by rivalries between two great seigneurial houses, based in the north and south, and by a major rebellion, which, during the last decades of the eighteenth century, successfully usurped power throughout most of Viet-Nam. In Siam a new ruling dynasty, the Chakri, had assumed power in

1782. It was concerned with achieving internal stability and with the perennial problem of relations with Burma. From the early nineteenth century, however, Viet-Nam was unified under the Emperor Gia-Long, and Siam's position was sufficiently strong for it to devote greater energy to extending its authority to the east, both in Cambodia and in Laos. The political map of the Southeast Asian region stretching across modern Thailand, Cambodia, and Viet-Nam, in the first half of the nineteenth century, showed a pitifully weak Cambodia wedged between two expanding and powerful states.

No general descriptions exist of Cambodia during the early years of the nineteenth century. The various chronicles provide an account of the most important political events, but not of the society as a whole, nor of the countryside. Cambodia's territory had shrunk to even smaller limits than those it possesses today. Siam controlled the provinces of Battambang and Siemreap, or Angkor, in the west, and Vietnamese encroachments extended over most of modern South Viet-Nam and along the Gulf of Siam to Kampot. In the extreme northeast, effective Cambodian authority went little beyond the modern town of Kratie. Above this point, the Laotian principality of Champassak exerted a tenuous control. At best, the Cambodian court could be regarded as the shaky master of the lowland regions south of the Great Lake and Kratie, with a shifting and porous border against Viet-Nam on a line running roughly from Kampot to Tay-Ninh.

Within this restricted region, a small population of Khmers clustered along the main waterways, the Mekong, the Bassac, and the Tonlé Sap, and the innumerable minor tributaries of those larger rivers. The population probably did not exceed one million.[2] It was largely agricultural and pastoral, exploiting the areas about settlements but leaving immense forested areas uncultivated. On the fringes of this plains society there were minority groups, many with ethnic affinities to the majority population, who maintained varying relationships with the lowlanders. The hill peoples provided slaves, forest products, and, from time to time, manpower for the armies of Cambodian rulers.

The majority population had a clear ethnic unity, reinforced by a common language and a national religion: Therevada Buddhism. The importance of this national religion to the Cambodian people is a major, if at times shadowy, theme throughout their history in the nineteenth century. Vietnamese persecution of Buddhist monks and monasteries was a major factor in the Cambodian revolt against Vietnamese rule in the 1840's. Ang Duong, the last Cambodian king before the French protectorate, strongly encouraged the growth of Buddhism. It was surely not by chance that when, in 1851, an inscription was erected to record Ang Duong's return to Cambodia and the defeat of the Vietnamese, the site chosen was a monastery destroyed in the wars.[3] Buddhism, the village pagoda, and its monks provided continuity in the Khmer state.

National unity, however, was a fragile thing. Cambodians in border regions showed no reluctance to move from control by Cambodian officials if that control became too harsh and arbitrary. For the population living near regions controlled by Siam and Champassak, crossing the border did not bring major changes in the style of government or in religious belief. In the southeast, however, the alternative authority was exercised by the wholly alien Vietnamese.

The strongest unifying force was the Cambodian king. Broad generalizations about the role of kingship in the Indianized states of Southeast Asia are always open to qualification, yet the king of Cambodia had great symbolic significance. He was the center of the kingdom, just as his capital was a symbolic representation of the Hindu-Buddhist heaven at the center of the universe. Even without temporal power, the king remained a semidivine being for his people, the ultimate source of the country's well-being, an absolute ruler with the power of life and death over even the highest officials within his realm.[4] Successive palace revolts and the great power held by regional officials could not completely eliminate the force of the king's appeal for his subjects. The office, rather than any individual incumbent, remained the central focus for national interest.[5]

However, the realities of power placed severe limitations on the king's authority unless he was of outstanding caliber. He shared the administration of the kingdom with his royal relatives and with the senior officials. In the Cambodian polity there were usually two, and sometimes three, other royal figures who had territorial responsibility. The *abjoreach* was a former king who had abdicated, usually to ensure his choice of a successor. When this post was occupied, the *abjoreach* held precedence after the king. Next important was the *obbareach*, the heir presumptive to the throne. This title was normally given either to the younger brother of a ruling king or to one of his sons. The final member of the royal family with territorial responsibilities was the queen mother. In the nineteenth century Cambodia was composed of fifty-six provinces. Of these, the king controlled the administration of forty-one, seven were allotted, in theory, to the *abjoreach,* five to the *obbareach,* and three to the queen mother.[6] This was the theory of government, not always the practice. The position of *abjoreach,* for instance, was filled during the early nineteenth century by a brother of the king, and the nomination of princes to this and other posts ceased to be the right of the Cambodian ruler and came, instead, to depend on the choice of the king of Siam, the ruler of Cambodia's suzerain.

Other members of the Cambodian royal family had special titles and accompanying responsibilities. In general, however, these specialized titles are not of importance for the present study. One exception is the title *prea-keu-fea,* normally a designation given by a king to his favored son. This did not assure succession to the throne, but it was a powerful aid for a candidate who bore the title. More important than a detailed listing of the multiple titles within the royal family is the essential picture of a large, and often factious, group. Royalty was not a permanent hereditary right. As in Siam, a system of declining dignities brought the extinction of the personal status of royalty after five generations. Even following this change of status, those who could prove royal descent had special privileges. Because of the existence of widespread royal polygamy, the Cambodian court housed a mass of princes of varying status, and many of these felt that they had some claim to the throne.

So far as it is possible to describe any procedure as normal in a state racked by internal and external conflict over a period of centuries, the normal procedure on a king's death was for a new ruler to be chosen on the recommendation of the five great officials of the kingdom. These five officials, or ministers, met with the chief civil and religious dignitaries of the kingdom. The aim of the meeting was consensus, with the ministers seeking to place before the most important elements of the court the name of a prince who would receive general support. The procedure illustrates the power of nonroyal officials in Cambodia and also explains much of the rivalry that existed among members of the royal family. A king frequently sired many sons from many wives. These half brothers felt little fraternal affection. Their mothers not infrequently intrigued, each hoping to see her son placed on the throne. Such an elective monarchy might theoretically ensure the most able and popular succession. In practice it bred and encouraged conflict.

Such a situation placed considerable power in the hands of the five great ministers of the court. These were the *chaufea* or *akhamohasena,* the prime minister, the *youmreach*, minister of justice, the *veang*, minister of the palace, the *kralahom*, minister of the navy, and the *chacrey*, or minister of war. In addition to the duties attached to their titles, these ministers had general authority over an individual apanage, a section of the kingdom that was their special concern. It was a further reflection of the checks and balances of the Cambodian state system that these apanages were not single blocs of territory but instead were made up of provinces scattered all over the kingdom. Within the provinces there were governors, *chau-muong*, whose status varied according to the importance of their province.

Outside the royal family and the official community were the peasants, who made up the mass of the population. They lived at the whim of their superiors, subject to *corvées,* demands for military service, and, in times of stability, to substantial taxation. The frequent appearance in Cambodian history of leaders who could arouse the population to rebellion provides an index of the state of the peasantry. Their deepest loyalty was to their god-king, but they could be readily persuaded to follow others who claimed the same regal attributes. At best their life was untroubled in a rich agricultural country. At worst they were buffeted by wars and exploited by officials.

Below the free peasantry were those who, either temporarily or in perpetuity, were legally bound to a life of servitude. The word slave has so many connotations in the western world that the difference between the slaves of Cambodia and those, say, of the American South must be underlined. Of the three classes of slaves, two were a part of society and not outside it. These were the debt slaves and the slaves of the state. The first were private persons who engaged themselves to meet a debt by giving up their freedom and working for the creditor. In theory, at least, their condition was subject to change once a debt had been met or an agreed period had elapsed. Not uncommonly, these persons formed an integral part of the household to which they were attached. The slaves of the state were frequently prisoners of war or criminals. Most important, they filled menial positions within the royal court. It was these slaves, too, who gathered the valuable cardamom seeds which the ruler used as tribute. Only the third group of slaves, assembled from less civilized tribal groups, had no hope of ultimate freedom. The position of these men and women was, indeed, similar to the slave in western society.[7]

The turbulence of Cambodian history in the eighteenth and nineteenth centuries made for a situation in which power was either solidly with the ruler or largely with the major provincial officials. A king who was an outstanding leader in war or who had the firm support of an outside power could exercise significant authority. This was true for the last king to reign free from French direction, King Ang Duong. When a weak monarch was on the throne, the provincial officials exercised power without real check, unless it was imposed by foreign invaders from Siam or Viet-Nam. This gave little encouragement to political stability. It may very well be that the aura of piety and good government surrounding the memory of King Ang Duong's reign was the result of the contrast with earlier decadence. Ang Duong was, in fact, severely limited by lack of both real power and money, but he reigned in comparative peace and had no patience for brutal or flagrantly corrupt officials.[8]

Just how low the Cambodian kingdom had sunk before the arrival of the French is revealed in a brief résumé of the principal events during the first five decades of the nineteenth century.[9] Siamese influence in Cambodia had been strong throughout the eighteenth century, with Cambodia frequently little more than a vassal state. King Ang Eng, who had succeeded to the throne in 1779, was crowned in Bangkok in 1794 and sent into Cambodia with the support of a Siamese army. When Ang Eng died in 1796, Siam did not approve the elevation of another Cambodian prince until 1806. This was King Ang Chan. These two kings acknowledged their vassalage to Siam by an annual tribute, a practice that appears to have first taken place between 1719 and 1722. As insurance for the correct behavior of the Cambodian king, the ruler of Siam held important members of the Cambodian royal family in Bangkok. Although they had places of honor in the court, they were still hostages.

Despite Ang Chan's tributary relationship with the Bangkok court, he turned to Viet-Nam in 1811, when he was unable to overcome the opposition of one of his own brothers who had fled from the court and seemed bent on rebellion. The decision to seek Vietnamese aid led to conflict between Siam and Viet-Nam, with Cambodia as the marching ground. After a series of engagements, the Vietnamese withdrew their forces and took the king with them. His half brothers, Ang Em and Ang Duong, deserted the ruler and turned to Bangkok. This period confirmed Cambodia's dual vassalage to both Siam and Viet-Nam. Although owing support chiefly to the Vietnamese, Ang Chan continued to send annual tribute to Bangkok. His tribute to Hue was sent triennially. Backed by Viet-Nam, Ang Chan re-established himself at Oudong, the Cambodian capital just to the north of modern Phnom Penh, while his brothers remained in Bangkok.

An uneasy calm persisted until Ang Chan's death in 1834. Vietnamese control in the Cambodian court was sufficiently strong at this period to prevent the succession passing to any of the dead king's brothers, who were still living in Bangkok. King Ang Chan had left no sons of his own, and under Vietnamese pressure the court's choice for a successor fell on a princess, Ang Mey. She was a *reine fainéante,* nothing more.

The almost total control exercised over Cambodia by the Vietnamese at this period set the stage for a struggle by Siam to regain its influence over Cambodian affairs and by Ang Duong to gain the throne. The Vietnamese, following the stern policies of the Emperor Minh-Menh, attempted to change the face of Cambodia. Vietnamese provincial administration was substituted for Cambodian, and an attempt was made to impose Vietnamese patterns of dress on the Cambodians. It is difficult to exaggerate the searing effect of the Vietnamese occupation. Pagodas were desecrated and monks persecuted. Those members of the royal family who had remained in Cambodia were increasingly subject to pressure. By acting against Buddhism and the royal family, the Vietnamese struck at the vital roots of the Khmer state. King Ang Duong's later desperate effort to rebuild the state faced not only a lack of finance but also a people worn down by an alien occupation that had sought to erase all that was distinctively Cambodian. Fifty years later, the memory of the period was still strong in Cambodian minds. The intolerable abuses of the occupation finally sparked an uprising of the Cambodian population. At the same time, the Siamese, under General Bodin, undertook a series of campaigns to reassert their suzerainty.

Accompanying Bodin in his campaigns was Ang Duong, now in his late forties. In 1835, 1840, and 1841, by three different wives, Ang Duong had sired three male children who became the chief actors in the Cambodian drama during the protectorate period. These sons were Norodom, Sisowath, and Si Votha, whose relationship as half brothers partially explains their later bitter rivalry. These princes were too young to participate in Bodin's long campaign against the Vietnamese. Norodom was only eleven years old when, in 1846, a peace treaty was finally negotiated between Siam and Viet-Nam. This brought Ang Duong to the throne and recognized Siamese influence as preponderant in the Cambodian court.

Nevertheless, when Ang Duong was crowned in 1847, it was by the representatives of Siam and Viet-Nam, reflecting Cambodia's tributary relationship to both countries.

Ang Duong's reign has been idealized in modern Cambodia, because it was the last before the imposition of the French protectorate. Yet, even allowing for the judgments of national pride, there can be no doubt that he was the first Cambodian king in many generations to use his prestige to benefit the kingdom more than his own person. Within the limitations surrounding his power, he strove to regenerate the kingdom. He built roads, notably a great road linking the royal capital, Oudong, with the seaport of Kampot. He ordered a revision of the country's legal code, decreed sumptuary laws, and laid down a simplified hierarchy for the members of the royal family. He took an interest in foreign trade and personally promoted the use of Kampot as a port from which a state-financed junk could trade with Singapore. In a telling comment on Ang Duong's association with this port, Pavie noted that "his frequent presence contributed not a little to the liveliness of the country and to the enthusiasm of business." [10]

In pursuing these efforts, Ang Duong must frequently have reflected on the contrast between his own power and that of his Siamese neighbor. After many years of residence in Siam, Ang Duong knew that state well. His association with the Siamese general, Bodin, was much more than a matter of necessity. As a testimony to his friendship and respect for Bodin, Ang Duong set up a statue to the general, after his death in 1848, within the royal palace at Oudong.[11] Although it has generally been accepted that the Thommayut sect of Buddhism was introduced into Cambodia as late as 1864, there is a continuing oral tradition that the introduction took place earlier, during Ang Duong's reign.[12] If true, this reflects both Ang Duong's concern for religious austerity and his close links with the Bangkok court.

Looking beyond his immediate frontiers, the king sought, in the early 1850's, to regularize trade with Singapore. Although he did not seek any political arrangement with the British colony, he hoped to gain British assistance in repressing the pirates that troubled the coast of the Gulf of Siam. He also demonstrated his interest in modern knowledge by ordering his Singapore representatives to obtain dies for striking coins, a lathe, a barometer, and other mechanical goods.[13] His awareness of the outside world led to his efforts to establish an ill-defined relationship with France, an attempt that led ultimately to the imposition of the French protectorate.

Given the limitations that surrounded Ang Duong's exercise of power, there is some risk in describing his reign as a high point in Cambodian history. It stood out as a time of relative calm after many decades of internal strife and external assault. It was notable because of the energy that the king displayed, in contrast to the self-interested preoccupations of his recent predecessors on the throne. But the kingdom remained weak and a prey to its neighbors. The survival of Cambodia must have seemed a matter for speculation, rather than for certainty, through most of Ang Duong's lifetime. His efforts to revitalize the kingdom faced the constant difficulty of a grave lack of funds. In the closing years of his life he faced renewed internal rebellion, and after his death his sons showed no indication that they had learned that the division of its leadership posed a fatal threat to Cambodia. Ang Duong showed that energy on the part of the king could still reform the administration of the kingdom and spark activity among the officials of the court, but one man's efforts could not overcome the massive problems facing Cambodia.

Cambodia survived, in tenuous fashion and dependent on the good will of its neighbors. In direct contrast, Viet-Nam entered the nineteenth century under a vigorous ruler whose goal of national unity was achieved during his lifetime. The geographical framework of Viet-Nam has encouraged a process of emigration throughout its history. The country's heartland is in the Red River Valley, but over the centuries the government extended its power down the coast. Not far south of the Red River, the littoral narrows and remains narrow until, many hundreds of miles to the south, the land levels out and one enters the rich plain of the Mekong Delta. Between the deltas of the north and the south the topography imposes strict limits on the number of persons who can gain a liveli-hood. This is not the only explanation of the migratory theme in Vietnamese history. The organization of Vietnamese society into rigid communal units, in which a sharp distinction was made be-tween "registered" members of the communal or village unit and those who were not, seems to have encouraged rather than lessened the nomadic tendency of the people. Vietnamese law took an unfavorable view of "vagabonds" and "wanderers," but the presence of a floating population living outside areas under the firm control of the government, and constantly moving the frontier further south, is one of the most distinctive facets of Vietnamese history.[14]

But despite the legal injunctions recorded against those who did not accept their allotted place within society, the authorities in Viet-Nam did not always oppose the extension of settlement. In-deed, the reverse was true under the Nguyen dynasty, which con-trolled the southern section of Viet-Nam first as virtually indepen-dent lords of the land and later, after 1802, assumed power over the whole of the country as the ruling family. From the middle of the seventeenth century onwards, with the ancient kingdom of Champa virtually destroyed, Vietnamese settlers, soldiers, ad-venturers, and criminals moved into the Mekong River Delta with the approval of the Nguyen. Such an extension of settlement had obvious advantages to the Vietnamese authorities, for it pro-vided a buffer against the weakening Cambodian kingdom to the west. Vietnamese acceptance of a request by Chinese refugees to settle in the delta region, in the late seventeenth century, was partly prompted by fear of the consequences of refusal. At the same time, it further reflects the wish to secure a reliable frontier to the south.[15] In direct contrast to the rulers of the Indianized states such as Cambodia, those who controlled Viet-Nam firmly believed in well-defined borders. This did not mean that such a border was immediately established in Cochinchina. The celebrated Vietnam-ese administrative handbook that gives a history and description of the southern regions, the *Gia-Dinh Thong-Chi,* emphasizes how slowly the south developed throughout the eighteenth century.[16]

The freedom permitted the settlers, combined with the relatively scant population of Cochinchina, resulted in a markedly different settlement pattern in the south of the country from that of the north and the center. In these older regions of Vietnamese settlement, the people clustered in village communities, population oases in the agricultural plains. Normally, the village or commune was sheltered behind a thick bamboo hedge. This was a physical representation of the social and political situation: by tradition, the authority of the central government ceased at the village limits.[17] By contrast, in Cochinchina, settlement spread out along waterways, so, while the village unit was preserved for administrative purposes, it was a less closely knit group.[18]

This lack of social cohesion was a notable feature of the south. The *Gia-Dinh Thong-Chi* observes that following the accession of Gia-Long in 1802, an attempt was made to exert greater government control. But even when this was done, the taxes demanded of Vietnamese living farther to the north were higher than those required of the southern population.[19] The government clearly chose to be less rigorous in what was still a frontier region. The atmosphere of this frontier region is conveyed in several ways in the *Gia-Dinh Thong-Chi*. The mandarins adhered rigidly to proper modes of behavior and followed the models of China in a way that parallels the insistence of European colonizers on the preservation of metropolitan standards, however inappropriate these might be for climate or locale.[20] Meanwhile, the nonofficial population did not hesitate to adopt Cambodian words from the earlier inhabitants in the region, a practice that suggests a degree of fluidity impossible in older parts of Viet-Nam.[21]

During the Tay-Son rebellion from 1771 to 1802, the embattled Nguyen and their supporters often took refuge in the south of Viet-Nam. Nguyen-Anh, who became the Emperor Gia-Long, depended on the inhabitants of the region for troops to man his army. His contact with Cochinchina helps to explain Gia-Long's later leniency towards it. Although his reign was marked by efforts to impose a unified system of administration throughout Viet-Nam, his readiness to tolerate lower taxes in the south has already been noted. He gave considerable discretionary power to a former comrade-in-arms, Le-Van-Duyet, who governed the entire Cochinchinese region as a separate fief, not yet broken down into regular provincial administrative units. Gia-Long remembered his debts. In a similar fashion he never forgot the part played by such French adventurers as Chaigneau and Vannier in his fight to regain the throne.[22]

It is customary to dwell on Gia-Long's reign in any consideration of the general history of Viet-Nam. He not only brought political unity to a country that had been effectively divided for centuries; he also undertook a series of reforms of the state's government. He established new supervisory bodies in the central administration; a new legal code was proclaimed; the army was trained with some approximation to western standards; and the emperor devoted much energy to the construction of strong citadels in strategic points of the kingdom. To encourage education, a national academy was built in the imperial city of Hue.[23]

Yet if Gia-Long's place is assured in the general history of Viet-Nam, it may be that his successor, Minh-Menh, was the more important figure for the south, if not indeed for the whole of Viet-Nam. Gia-Long had to restore unity to a shattered country. Minh-Menh placed his imprint on an already unified state. His chief concern was to build a solid administrative framework for the country. It was under Minh-Menh that the imperial literary examinations began again in the capital at Hue. Late in his reign he introduced measures to pay mandarins for their service in money and rice, abandoning the earlier procedure of rewarding mandarins with land grants. A land and population survey was carried out in Cochinchina in his reign, the last important survey before the arrival of the French, and one on which they based their taxation calculations for many years.[24]

With his concern for centralization, Minh-Menh had little sympathy for the freedom that his father had accorded Marshal Le-Van-Duyet. The position of the eunuch general was so strong, however, that it was not until after his death, in 1832, that the Vietnamese emperor brought the Cochinchinese region within the new, unified administrative system for the whole of Viet-Nam. The curbing of regional power associated with this reform was a major reason for the subsequent Khoi revolt, provoked by the late marshal's adopted son, Le-Van-Khoi. Minh-Menh believed that missionaries and Vietnamese Christians were implicated in this revolt, and they suffered in the harsh repression that followed. He had already proscribed the Christian religion in 1825, but his actions against Christians, up to this point, had been measured. The deaths of priests and believers at the time of the Khoi revolt were martyrdoms to which advocates of French intervention could later appeal.[25]

Towards the end of his life, Minh-Menh showed a sudden interest in extending contacts with the outside world. His policy previously had been to turn his and his countrymen's backs to the West. Deeply steeped in Confucian scholarship, he believed that the knowledge to be gained from the Chinese classics was sufficient to meet the problems confronting Viet-Nam. His estimation appeared justified through most of his life. If there is a tendency by Vietnamese historians to overemphasize the success of the Nguyen, before the French intervened, it is nevertheless true that great steps were taken towards a truly unitary state. When this is kept in mind, the blindness of Minh-Menh and the hesitations of his successors and their advisers are thrown into a more understandable perspective. The one initiative that Minh-Menh took towards closer ties with the West was made, however, at a time when France, the chief object of a Vietnamese embassy sent to Europe, was uninterested in establishing relations.[26]

After Minh-Menh's death, the next two emperors, Thieu-Tri and Tu-Duc, maintained the institutions that he had worked so hard to perfect. Regional discontent was still present, but in the far south the population seemed more concerned with the daily business of cultivating the rich lands available to them than with questioning the authority of Hue. Moreover, not only had Minh-Menh installed a regular administrative system in the area, he had also encouraged colonization by military groups (*don-dien*) in which colonizers subject to military discipline combined westward expansion with a readiness to act for the government in time of war. In the 1840's the *don-dien,* which had proved successful but had not been used extensively, were given further encouragement. Through exempting members of these colonies from taxation for seven years, the organizations attracted many poorer persons.[27]

The administrative system imposed in Cochinchina was a model of pyramidal bureaucracy. It took Chinese forms as a point of departure, but its character was determined by Vietnamese conditions.[28] The fact that Viet-Nam was so much smaller than China brought some differences. Those who had gained the doctoral degree in the state examinations entered the civil service at a higher level than was the case in China. Some bureaucratic attitudes, it seems, were different, so that, unlike in China, service in the capital was esteemed over service in the provinces.

Inherent in the system was the assumption that all power devolved from the emperor, the son of heaven: *hoang-de* in formal usage, a term that conjures up the glory of courts and imperial power; less formally, *vua.* Gia-Long had, through force of circumstances, gone out among his people. This was not the case with his successors, who lived the bulk of their lives in the beauty and secrecy of the imperial city in Hue, *dai-noi,* the "great within," a miniature version of the Forbidden Palace of Peking. Here the emperor was advised and assisted in the dispatch of his country's business by the elite of the mandarinal bureaucracy.[29] Surrounded by architectural and bureaucratic formalism, the emperor could readily believe that the wisdom of Confucian learning provided the essential answers to the demands of life.

Below the emperor, his ministers, and the court officials was the provincial administration. Following Minh-Menh's reforms there was no longer any place for provincial functionaries with power extending beyond two provinces. The distance of Cochinchina from the central administration, however, led to the appointment of a *kinh-luoc,* a title variously translated as viceroy or commissioner-general, who had general supervisory control over the whole of the southern region. The essence of the provincial system, in its usual form, lay in the organization within the *tinh,* or province. At the head of each *tinh* was a *tong-doc,* whose responsibility extended to all affairs. Except in the most unusual circumstances, he controlled military as well as civil officials. Beneath the governor came the subordinate provincial officials, who administered the province as a whole. There was a mandarin with responsibility for finances, the *bo-chanh* or *quan-bo;* a mandarin in charge of justice, the *an-sat* or *quan-an;* and the province's chief educational officer, the *doc-hoc.* In charge of military matters was a military mandarin, the *lanh-binh.* Just as Hue centralized all power in the kingdom, so did all affairs within the province pass under the scrutiny of the *tong-doc.*

The smallest units within this administrative framework of the central bureaucracy were the *phu,* prefecture, and *huyen,* or subprefecture. At the head of the first was a *tri-phu,* and of the second a *tri-huyen.* The prefix *tri,* meaning chief, is frequently omitted, so that it is normal to refer to a *phu* or *huyen* and mean the official rather than the administrative unit. The older authorities, such as Luro, understood each mandarin filling the position of *phu* to have some authority over a number of *huyen.* Writing after considerable study of the question, Schreiner concluded that although a *huyen* was subordinate to a *phu,* each was essentially independent of the other. They enjoyed considerable individual reponsibility in general administration and less important judicial matters.[30]

The *huyen* occupied the base of the mandarinal administrative pyramid. From this point on, administration lay in the hands of men who represented the prosperous or respected nonofficial population. Within each *huyen* there were a number of *tong,* or cantons. Responsibility for the administration of these units was the concern of the canton chiefs, the *cai-tong,* or simply *tong.* These men were extensions of the communal administration, the fundamental unit in official Vietnamese society and one that guarded its prerogatives jealously. The commune (*xa*) was normally made up of a number of hamlets linked by a common tutelary god and founder. The spiritual center of the commune was the *dinh,* a communal meeting place—still built on stilts, suggesting an ancestral memory of the time before the Vietnamese adopted the Chinese style of building directly on the ground. While it had clear responsibilities to the central administration, the *xa* controlled its own affairs. Its members were divided into two broad categories: those registered on the tax rolls, and those who were not. Only the former had the right to participate in governing the commune. The registered persons were the more prosperous members of the village community, but all were not expected to contribute to expenses in the same degree. In theory, at least, less wealthy persons paid smaller taxation contributions than did the wealthy. A poor scholar would be subsidized by his less well-educated fellow villagers.[31]

The commune, as a whole, tendered tax to the central government. The amount of taxation was a matter for discussion between the local mandarin and the commune's representatives. But once the amount had been determined, the commune decided just how it would raise the funds required. Making all essential decisions within the commune was the council of notables, *huong-chuc*. Among early commentators on Vietnamese institutions, ink ran like water as different observers gave their interpretation of the role of each notable within the commune council. The most important point to be remembered, however, is that whatever the superficial similarities, the communal council was not comparable with western municipal bodies.

The first French observers made this error. They saw officials within the village who appeared to have similar duties to those within a French municipal commune. They looked for, and found, a mayor. In doing this they made a fundamental mistake, for although the commune council did have an official with executive duties that approximated those of a French mayor, his standing and his power of decision were in no way the same. The council of notables was, in fact, divided into two groups, the great notables and the lesser notables, and it was among the second group that the "mayor," the *thon-truong* or *xa-truong*, was found. Very briefly, the great notables were the decision-making members of the council; the lesser notables were those who carried out decisions. Membership on the council, particularly at the level of the great notables, implied a high standing within the village community.

These were usually men who had prospered through their land-holdings. Their high status reflected both their personal success and the prestige that they gained through representing the commune in its relations with higher authority. It was from the ablest members of these village councils that the canton chiefs were drawn.

The self-contained nature of the commune and the power reserved to its administrators reveal one of the basic tensions within Vietnamese society. The emperor in Hue was the ruler of all the people and venerated as an almost divine person upon whom heaven had bestowed its mandate. But the emperor's mandarin servants did not have this special character. They could earn respect if they were honest, fair, and learned, but their demands for taxes had to be discussed and negotiated with the commune. While they lacked the learning of the classically trained mandarin, the village notables had the assurance of their position and of wealth. In the Cochinchinese region, in particular, the richness of the countryside resulted in active and able persons gaining considerable agricultural wealth. The nineteenth-century Vietnamese geographer Phan-Huy-Chu, in his description of Gia-Dinh Province, written about 1821, emphasized the prosperity of the region and of many of its inhabitants.[32] Finally, it was not uncommon for a former mandarin to spend his old age as a member of the council of notables in his ancestral village, assured of respect and prestige as the result of his scholarly accomplishments.

If there was a difference between the interests of the commune and the state at one level, there was also an important link between the two as the result of the special character of the mandarinal bureaucracy. In contrast to the courts and administrations of Indianized Southeast Asia, the Vietnamese officials did not, theoretically, hold their positions through any hereditary right. Emphasis must be placed on the difference between this theory and actual practice. In theory, the mandarinate was open to all who could justify their entrance through successful completion of state-sponsored examinations. These examinations culled the most competent scholars from the whole of the country, gradually eliminating candidates by successive examinations at higher standards until only the most competent entered the most exacting test of all, the examinations in the imperial capital. Those who hoped to rise within the mandarinate would normally have completed the examination that entitled them to the designation *cu-nhan,* a title variously translated as the equivalent of a *licence* or of a doctorate.

As with various societies, the theory of a bureaucracy of merit was balanced by the fact of many families developing the character of hereditary public servants. It was not surprising that the sons of mandarins should have better opportunities to obtain the education essential for advancement. There are instances where members of one family occupied important mandarinal posts over many generations.[33] The sons of mandarins serving at Hue naturally had a better opportunity to attend the national school, the *quoc-tu giam,* established in Hue in 1821. Despite the difference between theory and practice, it was still possible for a scholar with no mandarinal connections to rise on the basis of merit. He could move from the enclosed world of his family commune to the imperial world of Hue. When this happened, it was a matter of the greatest pride for his village.[34] Once a member of the mandarinate, an official could hope through ability and influence to rise through the nine grades into which the institution was divided and to serve, finally, in the court.[35]

The quality of the Vietnamese mandarins provided the first French commentators with one of their most contested points of dispute. Those who admired Vietnamese society as an alternative to the society of the West were inclined to argue that, according to Vietnamese standards, the mandarinate was in many ways an admirable institution. Even Luro, one of the most sympathetic of these observers, did not deny that there were aspects of the system unacceptable to a European, but he believed that in its emphasis on merit and training in the Confucian classics the mandarinate provided an effective bureaucracy attuned to the people. The opposing arguments can be easily imagined: the mandarins were the spearhead of the persecution of Vietnamese Christians; they were dishonest and accepted bribes in legal cases; their learning was unproductive repetition, wholly irrelevant to the problems of the modern world.

Modern observers have difficulty making any final satisfactory assessment. Doubtless there was dishonesty, but whether the corruption was greater or less than that of western administrations is impossible to say. We can only judge the effectiveness of a mandarin's training for the problems posed by the aggressive onrush of western colonialism. As a whole, the Vietnamese mandarinate proved ill equipped for the challenge of the West. Some in the court at Hue urged the emperor to expand contacts with the West, but the majority did not favor this. The failure of the tradition-oriented court and its servants to provide any viable alternative to submission to the French partially explains the persistent rejection of the past and of Confucian learning that characterizes much of twentieth-century Vietnamese writing on politics.

Much research remains to be done on the Vietnamese mandarinate, on mobility within it, and on the training of its members. The extent to which the inculcation of Confucian ethics was given a specially Vietnamese slant is an unanswered question. Many of the judgments made on the teaching of Chinese classics in Viet-Nam seem to be based more on extrapolation from Chinese models than on any firm attempt to discover the reality in Viet-Nam. Yet some provisional judgment must be made on the importance of traditional Vietnamese education and its effect on the population. Whatever the gaps in our knowledge, and however brief the present summary, traditional Vietnamese education, with its stress on the Chinese classics and the precepts of Confucius, was of the greatest importance to the precolonial society.

The most outstanding student of Vietnamese religion, Father Léopold Cadière, argued cogently that Confucianism cannot be considered a religion in Viet-Nam. He saw it rather as a code of behavior linked with the worship of spirits that constituted the true religion of Viet-Nam. For Cadière, Buddhism was even less significant in Vietnamese life. Whereas Confucianism was linked with the primary religious concern of both the state and the population at large, Buddhism was a secondary concern.[36] In short, religious belief for the Vietnamese of the south, as for the remainder of their countrymen, encompassed a matrix of beliefs. The secondary nature of Buddhism explains its limited importance in the period under study, yet accounts for the occasional appearance of Buddhist monks at the head of rural unrest.

All fair-minded commentators on Viet-Nam have stressed the importance of moral training in the traditional system of education.[37] Instruction in the Chinese classics in the earliest years of a child's learning meant that morality was taught side by side with the more practical education in reading Chinese characters. As an advanced student, a Vietnamese scholar would master the Four Classics, called in Vietnamese the *Tu-Thu,* which collated the precepts of Confucius and his disciples, and the other works of the Confucian canon.[38] The values that this education praised were of moral behavior, the correct fulfillment by each individual of his role in society. No better demonstration of the significance attached to moral behavior exists than the consistent concern for morality in education that emerges from the statements of those Vietnamese who chose to work closely with the French in Cochinchina. Separated from their countrymen by a geographic division and from their past by the slow but certain elimination of traditional education, the principal *collaborateurs* still called for instruction that stressed morality as much as learning and so would provide an educated population free from vice.

The moral man was the good man, the mandarin who was as a father to his family in his relations with the population, a relationship sufficiently rare for a mass of popular sayings to arise criticizing the corruption of mandarins. The failure of many mandarins to represent the highest ideal of Confucius, a moral life devoid of self-interest, did not prevent intense admiration for those officials who did conform to the ideal. Such a man was Phan-Thanh-Gian, a great mandarin from the south of Viet-Nam whose closing years figure importantly in later pages of this study. His ability and his morality were widely known and admired in his own day. He was an exemplar and a living justification of the theoretical possibility of the humblest child within the kingdom becoming one of the greatest officials within the land.[39]

The only substantial town in the south was Saigon, with a population thought to have been well in excess of one hundred thousand.[40] The rest of the population, spread thin across the land, farmed and migrated to new areas. The open frontier and the recent pattern of settlement loosened the ties of traditionalism. But in the period before the French, the imperial net was drawn closer about the southernmost provinces. Minh-Menh had insisted that they be administered on a pattern with the rest of Viet-Nam. The mandarins sent south from Hue cleaved to Chinese ideals of behavior. Land surveys and taxation were slowly being more strictly controlled, and the regional examination system was in force in the decades preceding the French conquest. One well-informed Vietnamese writer, describing the examination system in an article prepared early in the twentieth century, estimated that three to four thousand candidates presented themselves for the preliminary examination (*khoa*) administered at the provincial level. At the triennial examinations organized by the central government for the Cochinchinese region, the *thi-huong*, four or five thousand persons sought to obtain the titles of *tu-tai* (bachelor) or *cu-nhan*. Of these candidates, perhaps sixteen would gain the distinction of *cu-nhan*, which opened the way to a mandarinal career. Up to four hundred would gain the lesser distinction.[41] These numbers suggest that Cohinchina's representation within the mandarinate as a whole would have been small in relation to its population for many years, even if the French had not arrived.

Yet, however delicately balanced the Vietnamese state may have been in the middle of the nineteenth century, the Cochinchinese region was distinctly more Vietnamese by the 1850's than it had ever been before. In using such a description, it is important to distinguish between the fact of Vietnamese settlement in the south and the effectiveness of central control. Without firm control, the Vietnamese settler appears to have been a more malleable person, readily adopting new words from those whom he regarded as barbarians, or *moi*. The assertion of control from Hue brought him within the Vietnamese fold. Increasingly the Vietnamese of Cochinchina in the late 1840's and 1850's would have found evidence of a pervasive government presence. Whether honest or corrupt in his administration, the mandarin was a firm reminder of the central government's authority and a repository of administrative knowledge and leadership.

Within this region one group resisted the integration that was slowly overtaking the bulk of the Vietnamese population: the small Christian minority, aptly described by later French observers as foreigners in their own land. Considerable attention has been given to the Catholic presence in the southern sections of Viet-Nam because of the close connection between Bishop Pigneau de Béhaine and the efforts of Nguyen-Anh, later Gia-Long, to regain control of southern and central Viet-Nam from the Tay-Son rebels. Bishop Pigneau was instrumental in recruiting the French military adventurers, such as Chaigneau, who played a significant part in Gia-Long's victories.[42] The persecution of Christians under Minh-Menh was among the most insistent reasons for pressure by the French Catholic Church on the French government to intervene in Viet-Nam.

Catholic missionary effort in the Cochinchinese region, however, was never particularly successful. This was not merely a result of the persecutions under Minh-Menh, for the rate of conversions remained extremely slow after French control of Cochinchina was complete and virtually unchallenged. This situation contrasts with developments in northern Viet-Nam. The explanation may lie, in part, in the geographic and demographic differences between the north and south. In the north the limited area of arable land and the slow but persistent growth of population pressure created opportunities for missionary priests, who were prepared to act not merely as evangelists for their faith but also as community leaders. At the simplest level, and this again is only a partial explanation, many of the converts in the north could be described as "rice Christians." The open frontier and the agricultural abundance of the south of Viet-Nam provided less successful ground for missionary endeavor. The opportunity for a priest to act as a community leader was constantly undermined by the nomadic tendencies of the Vietnamese settlers in Cochinchina.

When due account is taken of these facts and of the persecutions that erupted during the reign of Minh-Menh and his successors, the very survival of the Catholic population of Cochinchina is a surprise. Catholics lived in constant fear of retribution from the Vietnamese government. Father Bouillevaux, a Missions Etrangères priest who worked in Cochinchina in the late 1840's, has left us a description of the furtive life that he led. During the daylight hours he scarcely dared to emerge from the homes that sheltered him. Because of their fear of punishment, his Christian Vietnamese hosts would only take him under their roofs for a limited period.[43]

These persecutions probably provide some explanation for the survival of Catholic groups in Viet-Nam despite indifference and proscription. Like so many religious groups before them, convinced believers were encouraged, rather than deterred, by the difficulties under which they had to practice their faith. Still, there were probably no more than twenty thousand Vietnamese Christians in Cochinchina in the period just before the French arrived, out of a total population of two million.[44] One notable contribution of the missionaries, which was to play a vital role following the establishment of a French colonial presence, was the development of a system for writing the Vietnamese language in Roman letters. The transcription that the missionaries devised came to be known as *quoc-ngu,* the national language. The ability of Catholic Vietnamese to use this script was an important reason for the heavy dependence that the French placed on this group in the early postconquest years.

It was into this new, still partly settled, and less than fully integrated region of Viet-Nam that the French presence came, and into the decaying state of Cambodia that this presence spilled over once a permanent base had been established at Saigon. The reasons for French entry into both Cochinchina and Cambodia have been examined in considerable detail by a number of writers.[45] Only the briefest outline of the course of events is therefore required in this study, where the focus is directed essentially at the period of interaction between an established French presence and the existing indigenous society.

The French entry upon the Far Eastern stage was part of a widespread European imperial expansion in the nineteenth century. Possibly the most distinctive feature of the growth of French influence was the extremely active role played by missionaries and by their supporters in France. But evangelistic fervor alone did not stir the French government, not even that of Napoleon III, whose wife, Eugénie, was one of the strongest supporters of the missionary lobby. It took the additional elements of imperial ambition and commercial opportunity to convince the French authorities in Paris that an expedition should be mounted against Viet-Nam.

The decision came slowly. As the result of intermittent persecution of Catholic missionaries in Viet-Nam, Church representatives in France sought to have the government take a firm line with the Emperor of Viet-Nam. Support was given to this point of view by the Ministry of the Navy, where many regretted the loss of France's first colonial empire in the eighteenth century and yearned for a new empire in the East, where the perfidious British were already consolidating their interests. The Montigny mission of 1856 is taken by many as the real prelude to the French advance into Viet-Nam. Although this diplomatic mission was chiefly concerned with French interests in Siam, it came to have importance for Viet-Nam and Cambodia also. French Catholic missionaries had been active in Cambodia even though it had proved almost impossible to gain converts. Bishop Miche reported that the only sure way to advance Christianity was for missionaries to purchase the freedom of slaves, who would then become converts.[46] But this lack of success had not prevented Miche from seeking to involve France in Cambodia. In 1853 he had written, allegedly on King Ang Duong's behalf, to the French emperor. This letter offered Ang Duong's homage but did not seek protection.[47] When, in 1856, Montigny called in at Kampot, on the Cambodian coast, to pick up Bishop Miche to act as an interpreter for the discussions that he hoped to have at Hue, the envoy and the missionary seem to have agreed on the necessity of persuading Ang Duong to enter into some relationship with France.

The details of Montigny's sojourn in Kampot, with the efforts by the French countered by the Siamese officials' concern to assert their ruler's rights over Cambodia, provide a farcical *tableau*. It is sufficient to note that Ang Duong did not make any clear call for protection. A letter that he sent to Napoleon following Montigny's visit expressed the hope that France might arrange for the return of Cambodian territories held by the Vietnamese. It did not offer to submit to French control in return.[48]

From Cambodia, Montigny went on to Viet-Nam. The atmosphere of farce continued, for he arrived so late at Tourane (modern Da-Nang) that the French ships that were to reinforce his exhortation to the Vietnamese not to persecute missionaries had already departed. A foreboding of tragedy, however, tinged the farce. Before Montigny arrived, French ships had shelled forts in Tourane in an effort to intimidate the Vietnamese and so to prevent them from persecuting missionaries. The Vietnamese court might have taken this as a warning of the need to make some future adjustment to the French. Because of Montigny's late arrival, French prestige sank to a low ebb, and despite the earlier shelling it appeared to the Hue court that they could ignore the interests of the European powers.

The mandarins were wrong. The pace of Western imperialist activity in China was accelerating, with France seeking desperately to gain a share of expected rich markets. In Paris commercial expectation and imperial ambition were added to the hopes of the Church. This blending of interests resulted in two developments of capital importance for the commencement of French colonial endeavor in Viet-Nam. First, France joined with Britain, in 1857, in asserting the position of the European powers dealing with China. A series of incidents had brought conflict between the Chinese imperial authorities and European traders and missionaries. The execution of a French missionary led to the decision in Paris that France should take part in a joint expedition with Britain.[49]

Secondly, while French forces were committed to this venture, there was an important change in attitudes in Paris. Originally as the result of missionary initiative, the French government once again considered the question of intervention in Viet-Nam. A Committee on Cochinchina—the term used in this case to describe the whole of Viet-Nam—was established, and for reasons of religion, trade, and imperial prestige a strong recommendation was made to establish some form of protectorate over Viet-Nam, which would assure French interests of all sorts there. With Napoleon III convinced of the rightness of the Committee's decisions, the die was cast for French intervention.[50]

Again, there is ample published commentary on the slow progress of the French forces once they were committed to Viet-Nam in 1858.[51] It was soon apparent that major difficulties attended an attempt to assume a position at Tourane. Divergences quickly developed between the military leadership and the missionaries. The help that the missionaries had promised from Vietnamese Christians, eager to demonstrate their gratitude to those who came to defend their faith, was not forthcoming. The weakness of the Vietnamese army and its lack of modern equipment with which to face the French and Spanish soldiers—for a small Spanish force had joined the crusade to uphold the Catholic faith—was a factor in French favor. But it was offset to a considerable extent by the remarkably firm organization of the Vietnamese mandarins, who showed themselves well able to control the population in a time of crisis, and by the costly toll of lives that the Vietnamese climate and tropical diseases exacted from the invaders.

Unable to make substantial progress at Tourane, the French next looked to the south and to Saigon. In contrast to Tourane, this site seemed worth holding. It was already an important trade center, and the French naval observers also reacted to the undoubted richness of the land they saw about them, convinced that it offered the prospect of profitable European settlement. Although a French position was established at Saigon in 1859, the expeditionary troops could do little more than hold on to the area immediately about their camp until major reinforcements were provided in late 1860.

A decisive battle in February 1861 secured the French position in Saigon and led to the conclusion, in 1862, of a treaty between France and the court of Hue which accepted the French presence in the eastern provinces of Cochinchina. The Emperor Tu-Duc, who had assumed the Vietnamese throne in 1848, was beset by the defeat of his troops, interruption of the normal rice shipments from the French-controlled southern regions, and the insurrection mounted by a scion of the Le family, which had once ruled Viet-nam. These threats left him little alternative but to accept the French treaty. He later tried to have it substantially revised.

While attention in France was directed towards the events in Viet-Nam, some thought was being given to France's position towards Cambodia. Discussion of Cambodia became a faint, at times inaudible, counterpoint to the major theme of Viet-Nam. Disputes between the naval commanders of the French forces in Viet-Nam and the missionaries diminished the effect of Catholic appeals for action. Nevertheless, Bishop Miche, based in a mission station near the royal court at Oudong, continued to urge the establishment of some French relationship with Cambodia. His urgings intensified as he saw the destruction wrought on mission property in the unsettled conditions following King Ang Duong's death. More important to the naval commanders in Saigon and their superiors in Paris, however, was the issue of Cambodia's relationship with Siam, for if Siam controlled Cambodia it could provide an opportunity for British interference. Here again Ang Duong's death raised important issues, since it was followed by the same sort of fraternal squabbling that so often in the past had provided an opportunity for Siam to interfere to assert its will in Cambodia.

Even before Ang Duong's death, Cambodia had once more shown its restive character. The king's devotion and energy were insufficient to put down all the challenges to his authority, and in 1858 he had to face a rebellion from Chams and Malays living in the southeast of his kingdom. He next conceived a plan of attacking areas of Cochinchina, to take advantage of the difficulties that the Vietnamese faced because of the French invasion. Before this could be done, he died, in 1860. The Cambodian court elected

Norodom as his successor. Earlier, in 1856, Ang Duong had indicated his preference for this son by asking the King of Siam to grant him the title of *obbareach*. This appointment was balanced, to some extent, by the appointment of Sisowath as *prea-keu-fea*. Norodom's selection was not a surprise to the Cambodian court, but it displeased his half brothers Sisowath and Si Votha. After vainly endeavoring to gain his aims at court, Votha went into open dissidence as an opponent to Norodom's throne.

In the years 1860 and 1861 the Cambodian royal family came close to totally destroying its patrimony. The country was torn by rebellion. Not only were there the partisans of Norodom and Votha, but also other rebel groups and bandits. Sisowath, without openly avowing his dissidence, did nothing to help Norodom. Before the end of 1861, Norodom abandoned the capital at Oudong for the comparative safety of Battambang, and in 1862 he fled to Bangkok. Just as his father before him, Norodom was brought back to Cambodia and restored to the throne by the Siamese. Sisowath, at the King of Siam's behest, went to Bangkok. Once again, Cambodia was a vassal state.

This situation increasingly worried the French authorities in Saigon. The Mekong was already exercising its fatal attraction over the French, who hoped to find in it a route to the trade riches of China. Much of the great river ran through Cambodia. That the river debouched in Cochinchina would have little value if a hostile power restricted navigation further upstream. French suspicions of British behavior in Siam allowed observers in Saigon to conjure up, both for themselves and for the authorities in Paris, visions of conspiring British agents at the Bangkok court who would urge the Siamese to assert their power over Cambodia, to France's disadvantage.[52]

At the same time, the French were concerned over the extent to which Vietnamese bands opposing the French position in Cochinchina received assistance and sanctuary in Cambodia. Out of these dual concerns came a slowly arrived at decision to extend a French protectorate over Cambodia. The legal justification, which became a French defense for their actions, was that Viet-Nam had

suzerainty over Cambodia. France now claimed to have succeeded
to those rights. Against Norodom's own wishes and the desperate
maneuvering of the Siamese, the French authorities finally concluded a protectorate treaty with Norodom in August 1863.[53]

In the space of five years, therefore, France had assumed a colonial role in both Cochinchina and Cambodia. Its presence in Cambodia was termed "protection," and its initial aims were limited,
but it was not long before the intruders controlled a great deal
more than Cambodia's foreign policy. Despite the deliberation that
had preceded French involvement in Viet-Nam, the first administrators there were very ill informed on the nature of the society
into which they had intruded. French knowledge of Cambodia was
even slighter. The decision to establish a colonial position in Viet-
Nam was conscious and deliberate: Cochinchina was impaled on a
trident of French missionary zeal, imperial ambition, and commercial hope. The entry into Cambodia came as an afterthought.
Although the same administrators were involved in both regions,
the societies with which they now came in contact were radically
different. These societies and their distinctive characteristics
shaped the history of interaction during the years that followed.

2

The Civilizing Missioners

Whatever the gaps in their knowledge of the region, the early French administrators in Cochinchina and Cambodia carried with them the great, sustaining conviction that their presence was both right and necessary. At a time when imperial action was closely linked with the evangelical ambitions of the French Catholic missionaries, many felt that France's colonial efforts were God-ordained. For others, smarting still at the loss of the first French colonial empire and jealous of British colonial expansion, the French presence in the Far East offered the prospect of *gloire* long denied and of economic advantage in the expanding industrial economy of the nineteenth century. For almost all, since this was the nineteenth century, a faith in progress and the moral superiority of the white man confirmed their actions as a promise of a better, more civilized life for the "native people." [1]

These convictions, or at least some of them, have been shared by the French writers who have chronicled the French conquest of Viet-Nam and French control of Cambodia. The trend was most marked in the literature before the First World War, but it persisted long after.[2] Many distortions of the actual historical process have resulted from this concern with conquest and the assumption of superiority. On the broadest level, French accounts of their own colonial history have provided a near caricature of "Europe-centric" writing, and in doing so they have disguised the very real interaction that did occur, in Cochinchina in particular and in Cambodia to a lesser extent, between the European intruders and the inhabitants of the regions into which they came.

Other issues have dominated French consideration of the history of Viet-Nam and Cambodia in the nineteenth century and the early twentieth. Instead of an assessment of the interaction between colonizers and colonized, there has been a major concern with the supposed differences between the colonial policies of assimilation and association. Recent studies of French colonial theory have shown the very considerable confusion that accompanied the use of these terms.[3] Broadly, the terms were supposed to reflect the contrast between colonial policies that emphasized the introduction of forms of government approximating those used in France and an indirect form of government that built upon existing indigenous institutions.

The confusion inherent in the discussion, and the fact that theory seldom accorded with the facts of administration in the colonies, made argument over these conflicting theories a false debate. But in any consideration of the history of Cochinchina, it is important to note that there was controversy over what policies should be followed. The controversy's existence has obscured the fact that a more fundamental belief in assimilation governed almost all French activities in Indochina. This can be demonstrated by brief reference to the discussions of the early twentieth century. Leading officials expressed nostaligic admiration for the supposed advantages of the policy of association followed by the early admiral-governors of Cochinchina and then abandoned by the civil regime introduced in 1879. In speeches before the Colonial Council, the Lieutenant Governor of Cochinchina, Rodier (1902–1906), lamented the policies that had forced the Vietnamese to adopt French legal practice, brought substantial change to the Vietnamese commune, and placed the learning of French and *quoc-ngu* above the preservation of traditional education. Rodier blamed these policies on the decision to stress assimilation that accompanied the implementation of civil government in 1879.[4]

Criticism of this sort had some basis in fact. Like later French writers, however, Rodier tended to place more weight on the policies proposed by the earliest French administrators than on the actual developments that took place.[5] It is true that the decision to appoint a civil governor, in 1879, represented a departure from earlier practice. Up to that date the head of France's colony in Viet-Nam had always been a naval officer. By the end of the seventies it was thought that the colony had reached sufficient maturity for a civilian administrator to be placed at its head. But despite the first civil governor's brief to institute a policy of assimilation, the realities of the Cochinchinese situation had already made it difficult to pursue any real program of indirect rule. Moreover, even among those Frenchmen who between the early 1860's and 1879 had spoken enthusiastically of the benefits of association, there was a strong belief in the ultimate value of assimilating the Vietnamese into a society that, in important respects, approximated their own. This underlying concept was vitally important in relations between the French and those whom they ruled.

The history of Cochinchina and Cambodia from the 1860's to the first decade of the twentieth century reveals an important record of continuities in the concepts underlying administrative decisions. Trends set in the first years of contact persisted through the succeeding four or five decades and beyond. These trends emerged from interaction between the administrators and the administered. To some extent, the interaction was marked by negative contributions on the part of both the Vietnamese of Cochinchina and the Cambodians. In Cochinchina, the withdrawal of the mandarins following the establishment of French power had as an almost inevitable consequence the introduction of direct administration. In a system of government that relies upon a mandarinal bureaucracy, no one else is trained to assume an official role. In Cambodia, great restrictions placed on King Norodom's power by the generally weak condition of the country time and again forced him to acquiesce to French demands for change and prevented assertion of the king's point of view. Not all developments, however, were marked by this pattern of French direction and Cochinchinese or Cambodian acceptance. The role of the pro-French Vietnamese—most, but not all, Catholics—in the development of *quoc-ngu* in Cochinchina was of the utmost importance. In Cambodia the existence of factions within the royal court, a centuries-old theme, was exploited but not created by the protectorate.

Nevertheless, the particular conditions in Cochinchina and Cambodia—the first deprived of its traditional bureaucracy, the

second saved from even further reduction of its territory and
power by the arrival of the French—ensured that French decisions
triumphed over local resistance in most major issues. Because of
this, the underlying preconceptions that marked French activity in
the Indochinese region are of particular interest. Cochinchina was
not acquired, nor policies executed there, as a result of an historical
accident, in the way that some historians describe the early development of British territorial interests in India. The establishment
of a protectorate over Cambodia may have been seen as a strategic
corollary to events in Cochinchina, but before long it seemed desirable to urge Cambodia towards nineteenth-century French standards of behavior. In short, a dominant theme of colonial theory,
in both Cochinchina and Cambodia, was the belief in a French
mission civilisatrice. That actions frequently fell short of the high
standards implied in this phrase should scarcely be surprising. The
very assumption of a moral superiority that licensed individuals of
one nation to enlighten those of another paved the way for the use
of force and coercion to ensure that the advocate of civilization
had his way. The dual standard involved in such actions is obvious
from the standpoint of the mid-twentieth century, not that of the
participants. At this time men of the West had few doubts concerning their right and duty to lead the world.[6]

The early administrators in Cochinchina and Cambodia were
young and articulate. Naval officers for the most part, they committed to print a mass of theoretical and practical justification for
their policies. Examination of archival sources shows that the spirit
of their printed material was matched by the tone of their official
correspondence. Outstanding among these younger men were
Garnier and Luro, the first venerated as a martyr among the advocates of a forward policy in French colonial endeavors after his
early death in Hanoi, the second a more scholarly analyst of Vietnamese social institutions who made the first important critique of
the French presence in Cochinchina. Philastre, an accomplished
orientalist, was another outstanding member of the early administrative corps. Within the administration he was a judicious but firm
critic of many of the programs instituted by the French, yet his

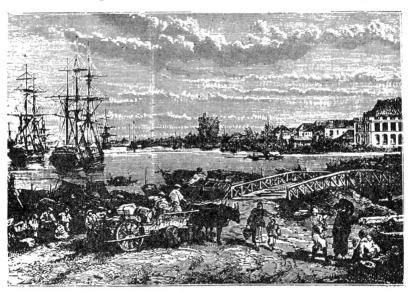

I. The Saigon waterfront in the late 1860's (from F. Garnier, *Voyage d'exploration en Indo-Chine*, Paris, 1885).

conviction that there was a need for a French presence in Cochin-china did not flag. Moura, Aymonier, and Pavie, all associated at one time with Cambodia, believed in France's duty to urge others towards an attainable goal of civilization. These were some of the more important subordinate officials. The views of Bonard and La Grandière, both of them admirals and governors, and of Le Myre de Vilers, Thomson, and Doumer among the civil leadership testify to the continuing importance of a sense of mission in the years af-ter the end of military control.

Once a French presence had been firmly implanted in Saigon and its environs, the immediate problem arose of finding a way to administer the territory under French control. The solution of Ad-miral Bonard (1861–1863), which has led to his characterization as an advocate of association, was to follow as closely as possible the structure of the Vietnamese bureaucracy and to use Vietna-mese officials whenever possible. But there were basic contradic-tions in his policy. In the field of education, he tried to rally Vietnamese administrators to the French side by setting up an examination system that would approximate to the traditional triennial examinations,[7] while at the same time he advocated the teaching of *quoc-ngu* and the extension of French education. For, in the words of a decision printed in the *Bulletin Officiel*, "the extension of French education is of the first necessity for the future of Cochinchina." [8] Bonard, like so many of his contemporaries and successors in Cochinchina, viewed the traditional Vietnamese use of Chinese characters for official announcements with extreme disfavor. In a long dispatch defending the temporary use of the Gia-Long legal code, he simultaneously attacked the use of Chinese characters as a barrier to progress:

It will only be with time and perseverance, above all so long as the only means for communicating ideas is this official language *Chinese*, *incompatible* with all progress, that it will be possible to achieve any marked result.

The development of Franco-Annamite schools which will substitute alphabetic writing for characters is the surest way of arriving at change: after a generation it must be hoped that one will be able to communicate ideas of progress and humanity in a language that all the Franco-Annamite people will understand.[9]

Bonard's successor, La Grandière (1863–1868), was above all an activist. Under La Grandière, the three western provinces of Cochinchina, not ceded to France in the treaty concluded with Hue in 1862, were seized. His proclamation, issued after the ratification of the 1862 treaty, showed his belief in the elevated role which a French Cochinchina could play. It was a "land forever French, open to the civilization, the riches, and the fertile ideas of Europe, which will radiate over neighboring countries." [10] When he found that the administrative system instituted by Bonard was unable to operate because of the poor caliber of the Vietnamese recruited to serve in it, he changed the system to give a much greater role to French administrators. He believed that Christianity and French advancement marched hand in hand, and like Bonard he was a mortal enemy of Chinese characters. During his governance a *quoc-ngu* newspaper, *Gia-Dinh Bao,* was founded to assist in the propagation of the romanized transcription of Vietnamese.

If La Grandière was a particularly forceful advocate of his point of view, the spirit of his successors was little different. Admiral Ohier (1868–1869), during his limited period as temporary governor of Cochinchina, strove to eliminate the use of the Vietnamese legal code and to substitute the French penal code as a step towards civilization. Increased efforts were made through the 1870's to abolish the use of Chinese characters in all official documents. There is little, therefore, to support the picture of "patient and measured" approaches to assimilation during the period of military rule. That some changes came slowly, such as the use of *quoc-ngu* for all official documents, demonstrates not a decision to move slowly but the resistance that the governors faced as they attempted to complete their programs in the existing social conditions. The swifter rate of change in the years of civil government reflected the preparatory nature of the years of military rule rather than a change in aims.

The spirit of the early years was exemplified by the younger officers who arrived in Cochinchina at the time of the expeditionary force's victory or shortly after and frequently stayed to take up positions as administrators. They were keen students of colonial practice, noting the successes and failures of French and British policies in India, and Dutch policies in the East Indies. Garnier was the most famous of these men, but there were many others who shared his views. La Grandière's aide-de-camp, Ansart, gave his view of the situation in Cochinchina in a long letter to the governor in April, 1863. He saw France as having redeemed the Vietnamese peasants from the mandarins, "an aristocracy of scholars, a collection of ill-mannered men and pedants . . . excessively formal and bureaucratic to a supreme degree." [11] But the opportunity was open to France to give Cochinchina, and the Cochinchinese, civilization through the true foundation of that state of life, Christianity. In a curious blend of idealism and Machiavellian practicality, he observed that the Vietnamese who had embraced Christianity, and they alone, could not return to the *status quo ante*. It was upon these Christians that the French should base their moral reforms.

It is, however, with Garnier and Rieunier, both of whom chose to publish their views under pseudonyms, that one finds the purest distillation of the combined spirit of imperial ambition and civilizing responsibility. These two naval officers wrote as propagandists for the extension of French control over the three western provinces as well as convinced advocates of the civilizing mission.

Francis Garnier had moved directly from naval service to the embryonic French administrative service in Cochinchina. Anglophobic, eager for French glory, he is best known for his participation in the famous Mekong expedition and for his heroic death in Hanoi in 1873. His published contributions to the study of the Indochinese region as a whole mark him as a man of immense energy. It is clear that when he writes of the Vietnamese and their inadequacies, he does so with conviction. This is apparent from his pseudonymous pamphlet *La Cochinchine française en 1864:*

From the material point of view, all the reforms undertaken which, in the minds of their authors, ought to excite the admiration and the gratitude of the population, have only excited its astonishment. . . . Unable to reason, without the capacity to appreciate the real import of the works accomplished in their country, the Annamites are only able to think of attributing them to a means of exploitation, to a desire to create a reason for another tax. . . .[12]

It was equally clear to Garnier that France, "this generous nation . . . has received from Providence a higher mission, that of emancipation, of bringing into the light and into liberty the races and people still enslaved by ignorance and despotism." [13] Garnier's appeals to glory, profit, and the responsibilities of civilized men made a heady mixture. Their force is apparent in the anguish that Garnier's death excited amongst the French population of Saigon and in the vicious attacks launched against his colleague Philastre, who was vilified for having negotiated a treaty with the Vietnamese authorities, after Garnier's death, which did not advance

French commercial interests in Tonkin and so was seen as unworthy of Garnier's efforts.[14]

Rieunier, who had served in Cochinchina under Admiral Bonard, vied with Garnier as an enunciator of the classic statement linking economic aims with the bestowal of the benefits of civilization on an underprivileged people:

Since the last distant expeditions, France can dream of again finding overseas not only the activity necessary to its commerce, for the development of its industry and the creation of outlets for the future, but it can also begin again the noble civilizing mission that has always given it such a high place in the world.[15]

To these views were joined the pronouncements of the official newspaper of Cochinchina, the *Courrier de Saigon.* Reflecting official opinion, its editorials record the almost constant official optimism that surrounded discussion of French colonial endeavor and the advantages that French rule offered to the Vietnamese. The Vietnamese were reported to have "rallied without hesitation to the cause of civilization." [16] The annexation of the three western provinces was welcomed:

It is a new step of civilization amidst the most isolated and least known people of Asia; it is a token of peace for the neighboring nations, it is also an assurance of security for all the merchants who already appreciate the liberal institutions of our establishment.[17]

Some of the most articulate proponents of France's civilizing presence in Cochinchina were the Catholic missionaries. The high point of cooperation between the secular authorities and the representatives of the Church came at the very beginning of the protracted conquest of Cochinchina. Quarrels and disillusionment soon dissipated the atmosphere of mutual trust. It became clear that the missionaries, particularly Bishop Pellerin, wished to exert greater influence over policy decisions than was acceptable to the early admirals.[18]

Nevertheless, there was a considerable degree of mutual dependence between the missionaries and the administrators. The quality of the early interpreters and minor officials who came from the

Vietnamese Catholic ranks was generally low.[19] But it was the outstanding Catholic Vietnamese who played such a large role in disseminating *quoc-ngu* and directed police action against those resisting the colonial power. For the first two decades of the colony's existence, the principal efforts in education were made by Catholic teaching orders through their schools in Saigon. Moreover, priests and officials held the same view of France's mission, as may be grasped from an extract from a speech by the director of the Saigon Seminary: "You wish then that this country might be Christian; once Christian it will be French. The instinct even of the Annamites alerts them to this mysterious correlation. . . . This country, moreover, is Christian." [20]

The priests' judgments of the Vietnamese as a people, too, are indistinguishable from those of the lay population. Vietnamese were "childish and improvident" and remained so throughout their lives.[21] Bishop Depierre, the apostolic vicar of Cochinchina, summarized French efforts in 1898:

The precise honor of our country is to place intellectual culture and moral progress above any other preoccupations. Instead of exploiting its subjects and pressuring them to death, as is still done in the Indies and to some extent throughout the Anglo-Saxon world, Frenchmen have always made it a point of honor to bring to the nations in which they establish themselves their ideas, their civilization, and their faith.[22]

A conviction of the rightness of their actions was an essential support in the difficult conditions under which the early French administrators lived in Cochinchina and Cambodia. Sudden death was not unusual, as an examination of the obituary notices in the *Courrier de Saigon* clearly shows. To question the utility and the correctness of French actions demanded a particularly strong personality. Indeed, even the most thoughtful and acute critics questioned method rather than principle. The outstanding critical commentators on French actions in Cochinchina, Luro and Philastre, were no exception. Both began their careers in the navy, transferred to the Service of Native Affairs in Cochinchina, and were closely associated with the long debate in the sixties and seventies as to the form and character of the judicial system that the French administration should maintain in its colonial possession.

Luro's fame came from his role as director of the Collège des Stagiaires in Saigon between 1874 and 1876.[23] This short-lived institution aimed at giving a complete course in administration, to prepare future French administrators for duty in Cochinchina. In one year students were expected to master the Vietnamese language, written both in *quoc-ngu* and in characters, and complete courses in traditional Vietnamese administration, botany, and practical construction, as well as one on Cambodia that covered the country's language, history, and geography.[24] The brevity of the Collège's existence seems not unconnected with the workload required of the students.

Luro presented the most important course, traditional Vietnamese administration, himself. The text of his lectures contains invaluable information on Viet-Nam and deals with the organization of the commune, relations between the village authorities and the representatives of the central power, taxation, and justice.[25] Although Luro included much of the material contained in his lectures in the posthumously published *Le Pays d'Annam*, the latter does not compare with the *Cours d'administration annamite* for depth of analysis. Many later writers on Cochinchina have drawn on Luro as a source of information about the region. It is seldom, however, that a French writer indicates the extent of Luro's criticisms and their fundamental character. The publication of sections of Luro's private correspondence, as well as comments revealed by archival sources, suggest that the observations in his lectures were formed after an initial enthusiasm had given way to disillusion with the policies followed in Cochinchina.

First and foremost, in his estimation, the French administration had followed the wrong path in seeking to teach the Vietnamese French rather than urging the French administrators who came into contact with the Vietnamese to learn the language of the country:

Gentlemen, the origin of all these errors [Luro had by this stage of his course reviewed most of the failings of the French administration] is that it was estimated that one could teach a people to forget its language and its customs in a few years. . . . The idea was supported that it was easier to force two million inhabitants to learn French, than to require the administrators to learn Annamite.[26]

The belief that it was possible to teach the Vietnamese to speak French had been one of the central features of all the governors' policies up to the time when Luro wrote and continued to be so for a considerable period afterwards. The use of a romanized script to write Vietnamese was long seen as merely a transitional step towards the final achievement of fluent French among a substantial segment of the population. Luro saw *quoc-ngu* as an abomination that divorced the Vietnamese from the values of Confucian thought, taught through characters.[27] As for the extension of French, its use was current only in the lowest classes of society, the "boys" and prostitutes.

He was an undisguised admirer of at least the theory of traditional Vietnamese administration. It remains arguable whether his estimation of the mandarins was just, but in contrast to so many of his countrymen, Luro saw the shades, instead of merely the blacks and the whites, of Vietnamese society. His estimate that the Vietnamese employed by the French were less capable than the traditional mandarins was, at the time he wrote, most certainly correct. Less easy to judge is his conclusion that under the French the Vietnamese paid more tax than had been the case previously. It seems probable that he was correct.

Even Luro's admiration for what had gone before had its limits, since to admire too much would have been to deny the desirability of the French presence. This he most certainly did not do. Luro sought perfection in the French administration. Thus, he spoke in 1875 against the early extension of French territory in Viet-Nam, arguing that there was a need to consolidate France's position:

I do not wish the extension of territory, so long as our administration has not reached a level of perfection which is complete; so long as our domination will only be accepted by force. . . . I dream of conquest by peace and good administration, by the propagation of our civilization, convinced by this maxim of the Chinese philosophers: "The wise man does not seek an empire, and the empire comes to him." [28]

Such observations ran against the current of colonial opinion, and Luro did not live much longer to defend his thesis. He died in 1877 from an illness contracted in Cochinchina, and the Collège that he had directed did not survive after 1878. The quality of the students had varied greatly, and the demands of the course, taught in the difficult climate of Saigon, had proved too much for many of the trainees. A lack of enthusiasm among the senior members of the colonial administration and mixed feelings in the home ministry combined to bring the venture to an end.

The doubts of Luro's colleague Philastre were possibly even more fundamental.[29] This scholarly administrator is remembered by students of Viet-Nam for his enormous undertaking, the translation of the Gia-Long code from Chinese characters into French. The size of this work has overshadowed Philastre's more routine tasks within the colony as an inspector of native affairs and as head of the Office of Native Justice. It is in the correspondence that emerged from Philastre's tenure of these positions, during the sixties and seventies, that one must seek for his observations on the development and mistakes of French policy. In a long memoir prepared in 1873, Philastre attacked the whole basis on which official estimations of the situation in Cochinchina were made:

It has become fashionable to shout out, in all manner of ways, that the Annamite population happily saw us come to deliver it from the oppression which weighed upon it and which it detested.

To say that the Annamites like all our reforms and are proud to live under our domination.

That has been said, said again, written, printed in all fashions, so well that these mistakes have become articles of faith and are generally believed in very good faith.

We have thus reached the point of talking and acting in an atmosphere of convention where our illusions and our desires are taken for reality.

The extraordinary resistance, sometimes violent, sometimes passive in nature, day by day more hateful, which is opposed to us by all classes of the people, is stronger today than at any time since the conquest. It requires, nevertheless, that we open our eyes.

We have proclaimed unceasingly that we respect the customs and the institutions of the conquered people. It was in proclaiming this respect that we required our enemies to lay down their arms, and we pitilessly violate these customs and institutions. . . .

The Annamites are very much aware of this situation, and I do not fear to affirm it, although with pain, to respect the truth, that far from progressing in the spirit of the population, we are less and less well regarded by the Annamites for whom we are no more than adventurers with an unrestrained greed, incapable of governing a people. *This is their own estimation.*[30]

Philastre shared with Luro an opposition to the implementation of *quoc-ngu,* seeing the suppression of writing in Chinese characters as reflecting the whole approach of the French administration, which mistrusted "the methods and the necessities of the Annamite people." [31] The sharpness of his criticisms earned Philastre the opposition of his superiors. His erudition was not questioned, nor his dedication, but the validity of his outlook most certainly was. He was, in the view of his superior, the director of the interior, "a profound admirer of the Annamites, of their institutions, and above all of Chinese characters. Also, he has nothing but rather bitter criticism for all measures of the local administration which bring any change to these holy traditions." [32]

Despite his criticisms and reservations, Philastre was not wholly divorced from the preconceptions of his generation. He respected the best in Vietnamese society, but he noted that the lack of competent Vietnamese administrators made it incumbent upon the French authorities to involve themselves in the administration of justice: "Only the European can spread, by example, the ideas of absolute justice which are the principal force of European civilization and which must, in a few years, raise up the Annamite people from the state of moral degradation into which they have fallen." [33]

Developments in Cochinchina have been the focus for discussion so far. The French colony was uppermost in any discussion of France's role in the Far East. From it were expected to come the

agricultural riches to finance the heavy cost of the colonial administration. By contrast, Cambodia was a buffer zone against suspected and exaggerated British influence in Siam, a commercial
backwater. Only a handful of Frenchmen lived in Phnom Penh before the end of the nineteenth century, with the notable exception
of the 1885–1886 period, when a rising threatened France's control
over the protected state. This handful believed no less ardently in a
civilizing mission, but the Frenchmen who observed Cambodia
from Oudong and Phnom Penh had fewer hopes for the regenera-
tion of the Cambodian population or even the Cambodian court,
which was constantly described in terms of mixed amusement, irri-
tation, and not infrequently contempt.

The early years of French-Cambodian contact were relatively
tranquil. France could enforce its viewpoint and did so, but
French force could also work to Norodom's advantage by suppressing revolts against the king's authority. Noninterference in the
internal administration of the kingdom was a policy honored in
theory, if not always observed in fact, during the first ten or twelve
years of the protectorate. In such a situation the French representative observed the country but did little to change it. He viewed it
with the values and prejudices of his colleagues in Cochinchina.
Doudart de Lagrée set the tone for commentary on Norodom with
the description, which occurs over and over again in his private letters, of the monarch as a *roitelet,* a kinglet, a petty ruler.[34] Moura,
who was French representative in Cambodia over an eleven-year
period, was irritated by Norodom's lack of interest in administration [35] and played an active role in attempting to block Norodom's
influence over the selection of his successor to the throne.

Notwithstanding earlier intentions of preserving a limited role in
Cambodia, French officials came to believe that maintenance of
their control over the country was endangered by the existing administrative system. Frequent risings against Norodom's authority,
which at times appeared to pose a very real threat of overthrowing
the French protégé, were attributed to faults in the king's administration. In recommending changes, Moura and the governors of
Cochinchina, who had final authority over French policy until

1887, had the achievement of French control as their primary concern. Their duty to the Cambodian population was not, however, absent from their thinking. Admiral Duperré's view that the government of Cambodia was "detestable" was a judgment of values as well as of administrative shortcomings.[36]

By the mid-seventies, discussion had already opened on deposing Norodom and replacing him with a figure more sympathetic to French views. Two substantial reports were forwarded by the governor of Cochinchina to the minister of the colonies giving the views of Moura and Aymonier, then serving as Moura's assistant.[37] Both reports condemn Norodom's government; both men expressed regret that such an advanced nation as France should allow the continuance of slavery. For Aymonier, it was a scandal that France should support, by the force of its arms, such a "ferocious" ruler as Norodom.

Restrained espousal of the civilizing mission in respect of Cambodia in the early period may have reflected the limited role that the missions and commerce played in the country. The maneuverings of Bishop Miche had been of the utmost importance in the accomplishment of the 1863 treaty of protection, but he was not optimistic about the opportunities in Cambodia for converting the population. His assessment was correct, and the *Lettre commune* of the Missions Etrangères throughout the nineteenth century stresses that Catholic missionary effort in Cambodia was confined almost entirely to the Vietnamese minority settled there. French commercial interests in Cambodia were limited in nature. It is doubtful if any of the small number of merchants can be described as "typical," but the most notorious of them, Frederic Thomas Caraman, has left an evaluation of Cambodians that accords with official expressions of French superiority. "If," Caraman wrote, "one must judge by Stobée's aphorism that 'it is by his customs that one can judge a free man,' it must be recognized that the Khmer people are found wanting, since they are born, live, and die in slavery."[38]

As was the case for Cochinchina, the official press in Saigon provides further indication of attitudes towards France's role in Cambodia. Fallen from their "antique splendor," the Cambodians, "this restless and demoralized people," had only found peace under the protection of France.[39] More positively, "One could not admire too greatly the providential role that has been reserved for France in relation to the debris of this population, so unfortunate and so worthy of concern, which will henceforth exist in peace under its protection." [40] Ensuring Cambodian acceptance of much wider French authority was the dominant theme of Cambodian history in the final two decades of the nineteenth century.

In both Cambodia and Cochinchina there were important continuities in the concepts underlying French rule throughout the nineteenth century. But the institution of civil control in 1879 was a second act in the drama, with a new backdrop. By the time Governor Le Myre de Vilers (1879–1883) arrived to take up his appointment in Cochinchina, it was clear that French power in the colony was firmly established.[41] In contrast to the admirals who had preceded him, he had fewer restrictions on his freedom of action. The sixties had been a period of experiment and innovation in which the home government's policy was at times uncertain.[42] The Franco-Prussian War at the beginning of the seventies had been another restraint.[43] On the other hand, Le Myre de Vilers assumed his post with a long background of administrative experience in both France and Algeria and a strong brief to establish civil institutions in the colony which would favor policies of assimilation. In succeeding years the growth of a colonial lobby in the French parliament and continuing development of French commercial interests throughout the Indochinese region gave impetus to those many policies likely to "Frenchify" the indigenous population.

The governorships of Le Myre de Vilers and Thomson (1883–1885) and the governor generalship of Doumer (1897–1902) must be the foci for any consideration of developments in the Indochinese region between 1880 and 1905. In Doumer's case, it should be noted, he had less interest in the individual components of the Indochinese region than in organizing an effective over-all administrative and economic control. The importance of these men came from the impact of their policies on both the rulers and the ruled. Moreover, apart from these senior officials, the limited length of time that other governors and governors general spent in the Indochinese states prevented their leaving any firm imprint on policy.

It was under Le Myre de Vilers that a Colonial Council was established in Cochinchina, which, while firmly dominated by French representatives, did have six Vietnamese members. His instructions had observed that this elected institution could not exclude indigenous representation, for "in excluding the natives from all participation in affairs, it would not correspond sufficiently to the goal of assimilation which we have in view." [44] The same instructions encouraged the program of sending young Vietnamese from Cochinchina to France, since their brief acquaintance with the metropole would enable them to return to their own country "in some way impregnated with our national genius, informed of the causes and effects of our civilization." [45] Increasingly, from Le Myre de Vilers' governorship onwards, French standards were taken as the only ones proper to apply when judging what policy should be applied in Cochinchina. Le Myre de Vilers ended the uncertainty that had accompanied the administration of justice for so long with a firm decision in favor of applying the French penal code.[46]

Increasingly, too, following the institution of civil rule, there was evidence of greater preoccupation in France with the philosophical issues of the nation's role as a colonial power. This was not absent from the dispatches and instructions sent from France before 1879, but after that date one senses a greater consciousness of this issue. In a particularly striking example, a ministerial dispatch of 1881 to Le Myre de Vilers considered the transformation that the French presence in Cochinchina had brought to the rural population. The dispatch recognized that this presence had contributed to the dislocation of the traditional Vietnamese society:

This is a phenomenon which should not surprise us and which is common to all societies in the process of transformation. As you have remarked yourself, it is the natural substitution, in some sense fatal, of modern individualism for primitive collectivism. There can be no question of acting against such a state of affairs, which is the inevitable consequence of the development of civilization.[47]

Not surprisingly, the eighties saw the first instances of Vietnamese being granted French citizenship and the foundation of the Alliance Française, which, through teaching French, hastened the establishment of French control over the indigenous peoples of her colonies.[48]

Le Myre de Vilers' successor, Thomson, pursued basically the same policies in Cochinchina. In Cambodia, on the other hand, he accelerated the tendency towards interference in the affairs of the kingdom, which culminated in the June 1884 convention, which Norodom signed under pressure and which began a period of active and concerted resistance to the French. Thomson's immediate motive in forcing Norodom to conclude the new convention was closely linked with French policies aimed at controlling all Cambodian revenues and so reducing the cost of French activities in the kingdom. Thomson was firmly convinced of the moral need for reforms within Cambodia. There is no cant in Thomson's observation that the reforms announced after the 1884 convention were "necessary in the interests of the Cambodian people." Cambodian laws were to be permitted to operate, he observed, "so far as they are compatible with the eternal principles of law and progress which alone make nations happy, great, and free." [49]

Surveys of French activity in Indochina have always dwelt at length on Paul Doumer. His energy in pursuing the economic development of the region, his articulate defense of his policies in a major volume of *souvenirs,* and his later fame as president of the French Republic have all contributed to the interest that his work has aroused. Presiding over the administration of the colony of Cochinchina and the protectorates of Cambodia, Annam, and Tonkin, Doumer acted with an absolute conviction of the rightness of his, and France's, role in Viet-Nam:

In the Annamite who is devoted to her, and bound to her more closely each day, France has a perfect instrument for the great economic and political role which she can claim in Asia. The Annamese empire reached its greatest point a century ago when it was directed by Frenchmen. Now it has become an integral part of France; with the empire modernized, the new Indochina can reach a prosperity and a glory about which the ancestors of our present subjects could not have dared dream.⁵⁰

As recipients of French civilization, the Vietnamese had the opportunity to advance, always within the French orbit and always under French direction.

To stress the existence of a belief in France's civilizing role is in no way to deny the more venal preoccupations of the period. Apart from the assumption of the correctness of French dominance, the noisy demands of the commercial and settler groups were a perpetual background to discussion of policy in Cochinchina. Often in the Colonial Council debates scant consideration was given to the feelings of the Vietnamese members. An unofficial French member could remark in 1882, "We are in a conquered country where we have a right to remain, maintaining ourselves as masters of the population." ⁵¹ Any suggestion in this elected body that Vietnamese might obtain a majority of votes met with strong French resistance.⁵² The Saigon newspapers, while providing a vehicle for pronouncements on the civilizing mission, generally supported the positions of the unofficial members of the French community in calling for greater control over the local population and the introduction of measures to benefit the commercial and planting interests in the colony.

The fact remained that a French administrator in Cochinchina, if not in Cambodia, could look for and find Vietnamese who provided reassurance that the civilizing mission was both right and practicable. The best known of this Vietnamese colonial elite, and in many ways its most outstanding member, was Pétrus Truong-Vinh-Ky. Trained by Catholic missionaries, he had an extraordinary capacity for languages, which assured him of a variety of positions within the colonial administration. The extent to which he identified himself with the over-all role of France in Indochina emerges from his observations on French rights to the territories on the left bank of the Mekong River, in modern Laos. Ky argued strongly in favor of the view that France had become the successor state to the Hue court in matters of foreign affairs and by virtue of this had clear rights to the territory in dispute. He urged that the Vietnamese court should be told to demand tribute from such states as Luang Prabang and to occupy forts that Hue had formerly maintained in the Laotian regions. This would be an assertion of French rights:

These are, Monsieur le Gouverneur *par interim,* the convictions which my considerable experience in these countries and my devotion to France give me. I have believed it my duty to give them to you, although they are matters of a political nature, because I am personally persuaded that in doing so I serve equally my native land and the great French fatherland.[53]

Ky was outstanding in his qualifications and in the role that he played in the nineteenth century. He was not alone, however, in holding views of the sort expressed in this quotation. Despite the humiliations to which they were exposed in the Colonial Council, the Vietnamese members frequently delivered themselves of statements concerning France and its role in Cochinchina in very much the same tone. When the Catholic Bishop Mossand suggested that the emphasis upon instruction in French, demanded by the colonial administration, produced the Vietnamese least loyal to France, a Vietnamese member of the Council, Diep-Van-Cuong, protested: "These words come from the pen of the head of the Catholic Church in Cochinchina . . . and constitute an accusation of very great gravity against all Annamites who, like myself, have received the benefits of French civilization." [54]

There was, in fact, very real respect accorded the limited, but significant, new Vietnamese elite on the part of the members of the official establishment, if not always by the *colons.* Tran-Ba-Loc, a Catholic Vietnamese who rallied to the French cause early in the sixties, may not emerge as a particularly attractive figure in a twentieth-century world accustomed to concepts of nationalism; his family had suffered persecution under the rule of the mandarins and in return he became a relentless punisher of those who opposed the French. But in his own time, and in the conditions that prevailed, he was regarded by the French colonial authorities as one of their most trusted Vietnamese associates and an exemplar of virtues that others of Loc's countrymen should imitate.[55] Similar comments may be made about such a figure as Do-Huu-Phuong, whose sons became officers in the French military forces and who adopted a European way of life.[56] These men were the proof that France's goals of inculcating civilization were possible.

Yet these members of the elite represented a very small minority indeed, and the question may still be posed: Was France's colonial endeavor in Cochinchina and Cambodia qualitatively different from that of the British in Malaya or the Dutch in Indonesia? Did not Sir Frank Swettenham refer to the British forward movement in Malaya "to put a stop to a disgraceful state of affairs" as a "duty inspired from motives of humanity alone"? [57] It may be difficult to develop a case for Cambodia. Certainly concepts of civilizing the Khmer, of effectively bringing pressure on Norodom and his court to institute reforms, were in harmony with the philosophy underlying much of the activity in Cochinchina. But in contrast to the Vietnamese region across the frontier, the French officials in Cambodia never had sufficient personnel to effect changes of the sort that they attempted and achieved in Cochinchina. Although the pretense of indirect rule had, in fact, been abandoned by the end of the nineteenth century, the theory that Cambodia was a protectorate was honored to the extent that French interference stopped short of the mass of the people.

This, then, was what was so particular about the development of Cochinchina. The belief in a mission did stimulate the French administration in Cochinchina to extend its influence among the population as widely as possible. The aim was not merely to ensure stability in the colony. Much more positively, programs were undertaken to bring the admittedly ill-defined benefits of French civilization to the population at large, particularly through education. The belief in reform, combined with the social vacuum created by the withdrawal of the indigenous bureaucracy, brought about the total involvement of a new and alien bureaucracy in the affairs of Cochinchina. The early attempt to preserve a judicial system along traditional lines foundered on the twin rocks of the difficulty of enforcing a legal code unfamiliar to those called upon to enforce it and a growing assumption that it was unworthy of a French colonial administration to perpetuate a legal system so radically different from its own.

In the Vietnamese commune changes came more slowly and were sometimes of such a subtle nature that the French observers were apparently unable to perceive that their policies were bound to bring change. Administration in this sphere showed a strange reverse application of the French commitment to the superiority of their way of life. The superficial similarities of the Vietnamese commune to the French municipal system led to many false assumptions. There was an early belief that, a "mayor" having been identified and invested with similar reponsibilities to those of a French *maire,* the problem of administering Vietnamese villages had been solved. Vietnamese requests that "mayors" should receive payment for performing the duties required by the French administration were rejected because it was not normal for a French municipal officer to receive payment for the duties of office.[58]

Involvement in the administration of justice and in the affairs of the previously largely autonomous communes, fundamental as these matters were, took second place to the involvement and interaction that followed upon French educational policies. The majority of French administrators believed that a French system of education could be introduced into Cochinchina and that teaching in *quoc-ngu* would be an effective step towards this goal. For this reason Chinese characters were banned from official publications and documents. It was for this reason, also, that by the 1880's discussions among educational theorists in Cochinchina were less concerned about the dangers of suppressing the moral education that accompanied traditional education and more with whether a transition should be made to the use of French alone. No less a personality than Etienne Aymonier, Director of the Ecole Coloniale in Paris, advocated this latter step, seeing *quoc-ngu* as an impediment to scientific progress and a barrier to the total gallicization of the Vietnamese.[59]

This was the philosophic background to the French element in the history of Cochinchina and Cambodia during the first forty years of the colonial experience. It had vital importance because of the peculiar weaknesses of the regions to which the French first came in Southeast Asia and because of the zeal with which the French administrators adhered to their beliefs. This study will not attempt to decide whether a colonial relationship that involved such constant theorizing and a genuine commitment to a goal that went beyond administrative utility was "better" or even more "successful" than the more pragmatic colonial policies. It is possible, however, to note briefly the essential failure of French policy, making that judgment in its own terms.

In Cochinchina, and to an extent also in Cambodia, French administrators sought to fashion an elite in their own image. Because of their policies, they achieved some remarkable approximations of this goal. Yet, within the colonial situation, no matter how closely an individual approached the French ideal, even if he were naturalized and possessed French citizenship, he was unable to move completely into the French world. This possibility was open in France, but not in Cochinchina or Cambodia. A routine administrative enquiry from the beginning of the twentieth century and the reply to it provide a commentary. In November 1903 the minister of the colonies wrote to the governor general of Indochina to obtain information on the salaries paid to indigenous members of the French administration. The minister's particular concern was to know how many indigenous employees received annual salaries in excess of one thousand five hundred francs. In reply, the governor general noted that while a limited number did receive salaries above this figure, none earned more than two thousand francs annually. No French employee of the colonial administration earned less than two thousand francs.[60]

Part II

COCHINCHINA

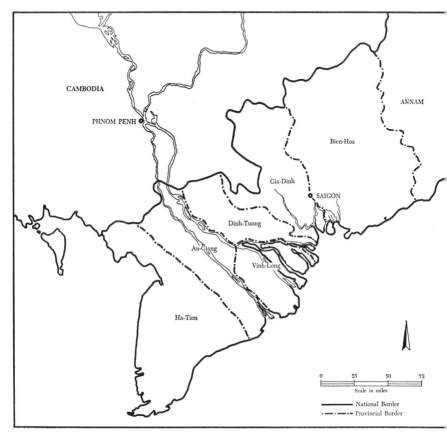

Map 2. Cochinchina, showing precolonial provincial divisions.

3

Establishment of an Administrative and Legal Framework (1859–1879)

The critical event that shaped developments in Cochinchina throughout the nineteenth century and beyond was the withdrawal of the Vietnamese mandarins in the face of the new, intrusive French presence. Neither the Hue court nor the mandarins themselves would work with the European newcomers at this stage. The withdrawal left the French officials with two choices: either they could attempt to replace the traditional scholarly administrators with those Vietnamese who accepted the French presence, or they could assume the task of administration themselves. No exact figure is available for the number of mandarins who withdrew from the south of Viet-Nam. The exodus took place in stages, officials of the eastern provinces (Gia-Dinh, Bien-Hoa, and My-Tho) leaving their posts in the period up to 1861, and officials of the western provinces (Vinh-Long, Chau-Doc, and Ha-Tien) remaining until the French takeover in 1867. For the eastern provinces alone, the loss of trained officials must have been no less than seven *phu* (prefects) and sixteen *huyen* (subprefects), as well as more senior supervisory mandarins and a host of ancillary officials.[1]

The opportunity for withdrawal seized by the mandarins was not available to the ordinary, nonofficial population, including the officers of the communes and cantons who had no mandarinal training. In contrast to the majority of the mandarins, these were men of the south. But they were not competent in matters of administration and justice. Trained to deal with the internal matters of villages and groups of villages, they were strangers to the wider field of provincial administration.

French territorial control extended slowly. At first it encompassed little more than the area about the French military position around Saigon. It was not until the Vietnamese army had been forced from their camp at Khi-Hoa, in February 1861, that a larger area was available for the first French essays at administration. Still the expansion was slow. Disorder continued in the area adjacent to Saigon, and French administrators found themselves isolated in the countryside as the non-Catholic villagers responded to the urgings of the mandarins and deserted their lands. Throughout 1862, particularly in December, there were a series of substantial risings against French rule. The extent of Hue's involvement in armed resistance to the French remains unclear. Following the French success at Khi-Hoa, the Hue court entered into protracted negotiations with the invaders. It disavowed those Vietnamese who continued to fight against the French and sought a French withdrawal from Cochinchina through diplomacy.[2]

The evidence concerning Hue's involvement in resistance to the French, much of it from French sources, is contradictory. Although the French alleged that one of the most notable of the insurgent leaders fighting against them, Truong-Dinh, was receiving support from Hue, Dinh's own letters and manifestoes strongly denied court support.[3] The scale of the risings in December 1862 certainly suggests an organized concerted effort, backed by Hue. This judgment, however, is based on inference, not on certain fact. After the failure of the 1862 risings, Hue had little active part in the repeated risings in the south. The reasons for this lack of involvement must be the concern of other studies. The personality of the Vietnamese emperor and the effectiveness of his bureaucracy will need to be analyzed in detail in order to arrive at a firm answer. Noninvolvement in practical ways did not mean the end of interest, and there seems some reason to accept the French allegation that the sporadic risings against their control of Cochinchina received the clandestine approval of Hue for many years.[4]

Such clandestine approval could not stop the growth of French power. The June 1862 treaty between Viet-Nam and France had surrendered the eastern provinces of Cochinchina to the invaders but had left the western provinces under the control of Hue. While the Vietnamese court sought to achieve modifications of the treaty, the enthusiastic naval officers who made up the administrative corps in Cochinchina fixed their gaze on the remaining three provinces to the west. As negotiations continued through 1863 the Vietnamese court could still hope that a permanent French presence in Cochinchina might be avoided by the payment of a heavy financial indemnity to the French government and the granting of commercial rights similar to the treaty port provisions in China. The French occupation of the eastern provinces of Cochinchina geographically separated the court at Hue from a section of its territory. At best, this was a vexing interference; at worst, an intolerable violation of Vietnamese sovereignty.

Vietnamese resentment, however, could not match the propaganda efforts of French naval officers to overcome the French government's vacillations towards Cochinchina. The admiral-governors in Saigon pronounced the six provinces of Cochinchina an essential unity, and more junior officers, such as Garnier and Rieunier, wrote public pamphlets to add weight to their superiors' official recommendations.[5] The advance came under Admiral La Grandière, the activist governor of the colony who left a firm imprint on some of the most important of the colony's administrative practices. Undeterred by recommendations of caution from his home ministry, he pursued his own independent policy, which was designed to ensure that all Cochinchina would be French. In January 1865 he described in a private letter the manner in which he believed the western provinces would fall to France:

We will work on the mandarins, and if the fruit does not fall by itself we will shake the tree; let us know how to be patient. My intention is to maintain the treaty of 1862 up to the point where circumstances give us the right to tear it up by way of reprisal.[6]

La Grandière was convinced that the Chinese inhabitants of the western provinces wanted to live under French control, a prospect that augured well for commerce. Just as importantly, in La Grandière's estimations, many of the attacks on French positions and against Vietnamese *collaborateurs* throughout 1866 were mounted from the west.

Carrying out his own diplomatic policy, La Grandière urged the Vietnamese court to cede the western provinces. A hesitant approval from Paris for a policy of expansion, given in early 1867, was followed by a further call for caution. But La Grandière, acting on his own initiative, decided that the time for discussion had passed. In a series of well-coordinated operations, French units occupied the administrative centers of the three western provinces between 20 and 25 June 1867. The action was bloodless. La Grandière had warned the chief Vietnamese official, Phan-Thanh-Gian, that he intended to occupy the provinces, either peacefully or by force, some days before the occupation took place. The aged mandarin, aware of the impossibility of resisting the French without an army to match French arms, presented no defense against the new invasion.[7] Established in the new territory, Admiral La Grandière addressed the Vietnamese population through a proclamation that combined routine self-congratulation with faith in France's civilizing mission:

The mandarins have seen the old instrument of routine despotism fall apart in their hands. They have understood that the sympathy and confidence of the people draws them away from the mandarins and to us, and it is necessary to bow before the prestige exercised over the intelligent and long oppressed race [the Vietnamese] by a civilization based on religion, justice, and power.[8]

The seizure of the provinces was a sad end to the long mandarinal career of Phan-Thanh-Gian. The first Vietnamese from the Cochinchinese region to win high honors in the imperial examinations at Hue, his career, even in his own lifetime, exemplified the best in the traditional system of the mandarinate. He had taken part in the Vietnamese mission to France in 1863, which sought to reverse the terms of the 1862 treaty and which, for a period, seemed to promise success for Hue's aims. His role in the loss of

the three western provinces seems likely to be debated for some
time. It is certainly too simple to argue that his failure to offer
armed resistance to the French was nothing more than a derelic-
tion of national duty. Vietnamese policy, right up to the seizure of
the western provinces, was conceived within the most cautious
framework. Support for those armed bands opposing the French
was more often moral than material. So long as there seemed any
possibility that the French would abandon their territorial gains,
the Hue court appears to have striven to avoid outright confrontation. Phan-Thanh-Gian had been an instrument of this policy. His
final assessment that there could be no useful resistance to the
force of French arms seems realistic, but it led to his posthumous
disgrace at Hue, following his suicide in August 1867.[9]

The occupation of the western provinces placed the whole of the
rich southern section of Viet-Nam within French hands. Cochinchina was still sparsely settled, but its importance as a rice-
producing region was already apparent. By forbidding rice exports
to the rice-deficit areas of Viet-Nam in the center and north, the
French created major difficulties for the Hue court, and this was
openly admitted by the Vietnamese ambassadors when they sought
to bargain with the French in Saigon in 1861.[10] Control of the
western provinces removed a major base for armed action against
the French. Now the frontier to the east of Bien-Hoa marked the
end of Vietnamese society operating with a mandarinal bureaucracy and owing allegiance to Hue. As had happened in 1861 and
1862 in the eastern provinces, the mandarins from the west withdrew following the French arrival.[11]

The events of 1867 represented the last territorial aggrandizement until the sustained French expansion of the 1880's. The broad
territorial limits of Cochinchina were established for the remainder of the colonial period. The colony's quite separate character, as opposed to the protectorates established over Tonkin and
Annam, was formed during the nineteenth century. Once geographical unity of the south had been obtained, the way was open
for accelerated social, economic, and political change. Armed resistance to the French was never totally suppressed, but for the

remainder of the nineteenth century it never seriously threatened the French administration of Cochinchina.

The impact of French occupation on the inhabitants of Cochinchina must be deduced from a relatively limited number of sources. The views of the *collaborateurs* may be easily found, but the spirit of those who continued to fight against the French after Hue had withdrawn its forces is more difficult to discover. Some of the best indications of the feelings of these Vietnamese are in the appeals made by Truong-Dinh, perhaps the most notable of the military leaders who fought on after official Viet-Nam had accepted a partial French presence in the south of the country. Truong-Dinh called on the population to join his fight against the French and stressed the separateness of the two nations. Dispirited by his lack of resources, he nevertheless saw no alternative to resistance against the barbarians who usurped his ruler's authority.[12] Modern writings on Viet-Nam frequently cite a particularly striking statement of this feeling of separateness that underlay continuing resistance to the French. The unknown author of a manifesto circulated in the Go-Cong region wrote: "As the horse and the buffalo differ between themselves, so do we differ by our language, our writing, and our customs."[13]

Rejection of all that French rule stood for and an unwillingness to involve himself in any way with the French also marked the life of the famous blind poet Nguyen-Dinh-Chieu, whose verses praised those who resisted the French.[14] Many other Vietnamese in Cochinchina shared the hopes of the early opponents of the French that the newcomers would leave and permit the country to return to its own traditions. As late as 1864, even those Vietnamese who supported the French were concerned lest the new administration should suddenly depart.[15] It would have been natural for those who opposed the French to hold such a hope for a considerable period, but without aid from Hue the sporadic risings had no hope of success.

Incidents of armed opposition to the French in Cochinchina continued throughout the sixties and seventies. Often the underlying motivations of the Vietnamese participants are difficult to judge. Much of the opposition seems to have been fundamental: the reaction of peasants against a foreign presence that contributed to unstable conditions in the countryside. One characteristic expression of this was the formation of a secret society, which banded its members together for self-help and occasional acts of violence.[16] Another reaction was the sudden birth of small religious sects led by "inspired" monks who rallied their credulous followers with promises of wealth and glory. Such was the case in My-Tho, in 1878, where a monk gathered followers to his banner and spoke of assuming the throne of southern Viet-Nam.[17]

Between the dedicated opponents and the loyal supporters of French rule lay the bulk of the population. It is impossible to document the reactions of the Vietnamese peasantry in any detail. The groups of peasants who joined in risings against the French throughout the nineteenth century probably reflect the social disintegration that accompanied colonial rule rather than a commitment to particular political values. There is some evidence, however, that some scholarly Vietnamese, despite their distaste for French rule, preferred it to what they saw as the mistakes of the mandarins. Such a person was the anonymous author of the *Tho Nam Ky* (*Letter from Cochinchina*), a long poem written in Chinese characters and *chu-nom* (a demotic rendering of Vietnamese using Chinese characters) and translated into French by Michel Duc Chaigneau, the son of Gia-Long's French associate. The author leaves no doubt of his critical view of the mandarins:

The mandarins are philosophers, men of genius, heroes,
And they consider us as grass and wood;
But they are more capable of beating us with well-applied canes than
     of conquering the French.
We are like birds
Which place themselves with security on great trees, but who mistrust
     those who only offer them a precarious retreat.
A forewarned bird avoids traps and lakes;
A prudent fish flees from fishing lines, nets, and fishtraps.

Indeed, who is not attached to his native land?

But when the flood has reached right to the roots of the tree, the tree
    is overthrown and the current carries it along.

Alas, let us moderate our love for the fatherland;

The wind of the West has blown lightly over us and made us shiver
    and tremble.

         .   .   .   .   .

Let us offer our homage to the striking power of the French;

Friendly people of the four seas are one people under heaven.

Let us make our farewells to the fatherland and unite with the French.[18]

Finally there were the true believers in the worth of the new
alien administration. Some of their names have already been cited in
discussion of the concept of a civilizing mission. The most famous
of the nineteenth-century *collaborateurs,* Truong-Vinh-Ky, began
acting as an interpreter in 1860, and Paulus Huynh-Tinh-Cua,
sometimes judged to have had an even greater influence than Ky in
the propagation of *quoc-ngu,* was active as an interpreter and
translator from a similarly early period.[19] But interpreters were
not the only Vietnamese associates sought by the French administration. Efforts were made to recruit Vietnamese who would fight
for the French against the forces of Hue and against insurgents
once the main Vietnamese army was no longer opposing the
French. At first, even Vietnamese Catholics were reluctant to engage in battle on the newcomers' behalf. As it became apparent
that the French administration would be permanent, there were
fewer recruiting problems. The composition of the first militia
forces raised by the French was heavily Catholic, and the most
notable Vietnamese military leaders fighting for the French in the
early 1860's were either born Catholics or converts.[20]

The best known was Tran-Ba-Loc, a Catholic by birth. His military capacities not only earned him the gratitude of a colonial administration beset by periodic insurgency well into the third
decade of its existence, but also led to his occupying a special position as an adviser on problems of administration and policy.[21] A
native of Cochinchina, Loc was born in Long-Xuyen. Like so many
of his southern compatriots, his father had been born to the north

of Cochinchina. The father had moved south after a disagreement with his family and there married a Christian woman, subsequently becoming a convert himself. As a Christian he was subject to persecution, despite having qualified as a *tu-tai,* or bachelor, in the state examinations. Loc was born in 1839 and raised as a Christian. He learned to use *quoc-ngu* in a mission school and narrowly escaped punishment by the imperial authorities after he was denounced for teaching *quoc-ngu;* the transcription was closely linked with outlawed Christianity in the official mind. With such a background, and on the advice of a missionary who worked for the French administration, Loc moved his family into an area under French control shortly after the arrival of the expeditionary force. Once there, he enlisted in the newly created indigenous militia. His undoubted energy now turned to the repression of the enemies of the French and of his religion. For his employers he was "active, devoted, zealous, and highly intelligent," a man who "always rendered the greatest service." [22]

As well known as Loc, in their own time, were two Vietnamese without a Catholic background, Tran-Tu-Ca and Do-Huu-Phuong, who also served the French with great devotion. Phu (Prefect) Ca (for so his name appears in most nineteenth-century references) had been a notable in a village close to Saigon when the confrontation took place between the French army and that of the Hue court. Before the French succeeded in breaking the Vietnamese blockade of Saigon, Ca had been commended for his devotion to the Vietnamese cause. Once the blockade had been overcome and the French attack against Khi-Hoa had succeeded, Ca changed sides. He entered the French service, became a Catholic, and by 1865 had been decorated with the Legion of Honor. Thereafter he was regarded as one of the colony's most trusted servants.[23]

The same uncertainty concerning the motivations that led him to join the French attaches to Do-Huu-Phuong. His father had no mandarinal position, but he was probably a man of some wealth, a *ba-ho*. Through his mother he was connected with a mandarinal family. Like Ca, his change of allegiance came after the Vietnamese were defeated at Khi-Hoa. From that point his association with the French was complete, and his activity as a leader of militia forces rivalled that of Tran-Ba-Loc.[24] For those southern Vietnamese who had adopted Christianity, alliance with the French administration was a natural step. Such an association was encouraged by the missionary priests and, once French power was clearly established, guaranteed protection from reprisals from Hue. The extent to which Catholic Vietnamese were separated from their fellow countrymen is shown in Paulin Vial's account of a meeting in 1862 between French representatives and envoys of the Vietnamese court led by Phan-Thanh-Gian. One of those who accompanied the French was Tran-Tu-Ca. He, with two other Vietnamese in the French employ, saluted the mandarins sent from Hue in the traditional fashion of prostration. Phan-Thanh-Gian and his companions, Vial reports, flushed with anger at seeing the Vietnamese who worked for the invaders. But this anger disappeared when it was explained that Ca and the other employees were Christians. In the minds of the mandarins, those of their countrymen who had adopted Christianity had passed outside the pale.[25]

But Ca, in 1861, had not been a Catholic. The same was true for Phuong. There are, however, some hints of their motives for joining the French. The account of Ca's elevation to the membership of the Legion of Honor refers to him as a "property owner." The extent of his holdings is, unfortunately, not clear. Phuong's father, too, was probably a man of some wealth. This is the implication of his honorific *ba-ho*. There is thus the suggestion that a hope of preserving their wealth played a part in the decision of these *collaborateurs*. In his often acute observations, Vial noted that, aside from the Christians who had an obvious reason for association with the French, a number of property-owning notables sought protection for their possessions under the French. They remembered the troubled and uncertain years of the thirties when so much of Cochinchina had been in revolt against the central authorities. These same property owners had suffered as a result of the incursions by Siamese forces during the nineteenth century, when the Vietnamese court appeared powerless to render assistance. It seems likely that Ca and Phuong fell within the group that Vial describes.[26]

None of the Vietnamese *collaborateurs* noted so far possessed the training in traditional administration essential for an understanding of the system of government that had existed before the French arrival. Truong-Vinh-Ky was knowledgeable about his country and its history, but his comments on administration are extremely general in character. Tran-Ba-Loc was frequently consulted on major policy issues, but his observations, too, consist chiefly of general criticism of malpractices at the village level under the *ancien régime*. Probably the closest to possessing the background of the traditional administrator among those who worked for the French was Ton-Tho-Tuong. His name remains well known in Viet-Nam, in direct contrast to the limited importance accorded him in French histories of Cochinchina. Vietnamese know him for his part in the poetic exchange in which Tuong, as a supporter of the French, opposed his beliefs to those of Phan-Van-Tri, a scholar who was an uncompromising enemy of French rule. Tuong was unusual in being a member of a family that had held important posts within the mandarinate. His grandfather had played a significant role in Gia-Long's campaigns. Tuong's father had passed the examination to become a *cu-nhan* and had administered provinces in the center of Viet-Nam. These antecedents had not ensured Tuong's success within the traditional system. His application for honorary rank as a descendant of a civil mandarin was denied by the court at Hue, and his attempts to advance his position by the traditional examinations failed.[27] It would be an oversimplification to see these reverses as Tuong's sole motive for joining the French administration in 1862, but it would be unrealistic not to accord them some weight.

Once an auxiliary of the French, he was entrusted with a number of important responsibilities. Tuong accompanied the Vietnamese mission to Paris in 1863 for discussion of the 1862 treaty, and in the late sixties and seventies he worked with French officials who dealt with justice as it affected the Vietnamese population of

II. Tran-Ba-Loc, who wrote of his relations with the French, "If I have served France to this day, it has been so as to be able to cover the object of my affections with the shadow of my influence" (from P. Doumer, *L'Indo-Chine française: Souvenirs,* Paris, 1905).

Cochinchina. Estimates of his capacity in this work are contradictory.[28] Despite his poetic output he remains an ill-defined figure, the exceptional case of a Vietnamese from a solidly official background who joined the French invaders at the beginning of their rule in Cochinchina.

These were the best-known and most able of the *collaborateurs*. Below them were a growing number of interpreters and petty clerks. All observers agree that the ability of these minor employees was poor. Catholic Vietnamese who had been taught *quoc-ngu* and some Latin, but not French, were able to play only a restricted part in French attempts during the early years to find some satisfactory way of communicating with the population. As for the character of many of the interpreters, Pallu de la Barrière stigmatizes them as "catechists sacked by their bishops for misconduct, who under a Latin [Christian] name presented a summary of the deception, the prevarication, and the corruption of Asia." [29]

A decade later French judgments were little less critical. Philastre, the scholarly administrator and expert in Vietnamese legal matters, observed that Vietnamese employed by the French far too often took advantage of their position to achieve material gain.[30] Luro, perhaps the ablest student of Vietnamese administration among the early officials, was more damning in his comments. He asserted:

Our new officials, both through instruction and education, are, in general, infinitely inferior to the old [mandarins]. They are not in the least scholars nor imbued with Confucian doctrine. In the first years of conquest one takes men of goodwill that one finds in one's hands. Fidelity counts more than capacity . . . many would not have been given employment as simple clerks formerly.[31]

This was his public assessment. In a private letter Luro dwelt on the tendency of the Vietnamese employed by the French to gamble away their substance so that they were constantly impoverished and ready to extort money from the population.[32]

Finally one must attempt an assessment of the French administrators. The admiral-governors of Cochinchina left sufficient documentary material to suggest their characters and their major policy preoccupations, and these will emerge in the more detailed examination of particular issues. The men in the field are not so clearly defined. The bulk of the early administrators continued to be recruited from the ranks of the military well into the seventies. Although we have considerable information on such men as Luro, Philastre, and Father Legrand de La Liraye, a missionary who served within the French administration, these men were not only the best known but also the most able of the administrators. There were many others whose talents it is now difficult to gauge. It would be extremely interesting to know more about the linguistic capacities of these early figures, for this would suggest how much they understood the customs and interests of those whom they administered. A review of the individual dossiers of the inspectors of native affairs, the title given to those Frenchmen responsible for provincial administration, is not of great assistance, since there is no standard method used for assessing linguistic capacity. Comments on linguistic skills were haphazard.[33] It is only in such remarks as those made by Luro in a letter to Philastre in 1868 that some impression of the linguistic abilities of the inspectors may be gained. Luro, it is clear, had very considerable doubts about his colleagues' capacity to carry out administration without an interpreter.[34]

In a colony in which Frenchwomen were few in number, concubinage was a common arrangement for the inspectors, particularly those posted to the more distant rural areas. This outraged Catholic authorities, but critical Church comment seems to have had little effect on the Frenchmen involved in such alliances. In contrast to other colonial situations in Southeast Asia, there is little to suggest that the acquisition of a Vietnamese concubine served as an introduction to the language and customs of the country. Instead, there are hints that a Vietnamese woman who accepted the role of concubine to a French official learned a smattering of French.[35]

The most important attempt to ensure the steady development of a well-trained body of French provincial officials serving in Cochinchina was the establishment in 1874 of the Collège des

Stagiaires. This institution, under Luro's direction, for a brief period in the seventies offered the prospect of French administrators entering upon their service in the field trained in all the branches of knowledge essential to their success. The short life of the institution did not end the hope that Frenchmen serving in Cochinchina would be competent in the Vietnamese language and trained in an understanding of Vietnamese customs, but the hope survived only as an ideal. The ideal faced erosion as the number of administrators increased and as efforts to encourage the use of French widened.[36]

By the end of the seventies, both official pressure and the inclinations of the administrators brought increasing emphasis on the use of French in all dealings with the Vietnamese population of Cochinchina. Outstanding scholars of the language and customs of the people remained; Auguste Landes was one. But after nearly twenty years of French control over Cochinchina, one no longer senses the driving enthusiasm that marked the careers of the earliest French administrators and resulted in some of the most important published studies of the region. Administration became more routine within a framework that was constantly reinforced to provide the maximum use of French methods and the maximum adherence to French ideals.

These, then, were the principal human factors that played a part in the French efforts to establish an administration in Cochinchina. Enthusiastic naval officers, convinced of the great role that France was to play in its new colony, set out to administer an alien population with totally different cultural values. Within that population they found a limited number of convinced supporters and an important segment that, even after peace had been officially established, continued to show its unreadiness to accept French control. The mass of the population lay between these two extremes, unready to risk their lives in battle against a stronger foe, but confused and uncertain in the face of the new, powerful invaders. During the first four years of the French presence in Cochinchina, French administrative policy wavered between direct and indirect government. The exigencies of the military situation led to the first attempt at total replacement by French officials of the mandarins who had fled from Gia-Dinh Province, while conserving as much as possible of the structure of the Vietnamese commune. This initial essay was followed by an effort to use Vietnamese officials in all but the most senior supervisory positions. Finally, the pattern of French administrators filling all positions above the cantonal level was implemented.

The swing from one system of administration to another reflected both the personalities of the individual governors and the adjustments to rapidly changing conditions. Admiral Charner had been instructed by Paris to maintain the Vietnamese system of administration in the annexed territory but to substitute French officials for the mandarins. These instructions accorded with his own wishes, but the lack of interpreters and the difficulty for a Frenchman of administering in Vietnamese fashion, particularly in matters of justice, soon became clear.[37] Charner's successor, Bonard, was equally convinced of the value of indirect rule, with Frenchmen occupying only the most senior positions. His support for such a policy stemmed from his admiration for indirect rule policies instituted elsewhere by Britain and from his belief that the use of Vietnamese officials would mean a lower expenditure. His support of indirect rule in no sense meant that he did not wish to see substantial social change in Cochinchina. He was a supporter of *quoc-ngu* as a weapon to undermine the Confucian ethic associated with the teaching of Chinese characters, and he regarded the expansion of Catholicism as an essential for the colony's progress.[38]

Admiral Bonard could not avoid the difficulties that Charner had encountered in seeking to institute his administrative program. If it had been difficult to find interpreters to assist French officials, how much more difficult was it to find competent Vietnamese to fill provincial posts that had formerly required training and qualification in examinations sponsored by the Vietnamese court. From the very beginning of the Bonard experiment, this prime difficulty was manifest. He hoped that mandarins would come to serve the French, but even his enthusiastic reports could not disguise the fact that Frenchmen continued to be closely involved in all levels of provincial administration and that capable Vietnamese officials were exceptional.[39]

As with many other aspects of French policy in Cochinchina, the administrative policies established by Bonard's successor, Admiral de La Grandière, set the pattern for many years to come. After a short period in 1863 and 1864 in which La Grandière allowed a mixed system of administration to continue, with some regions administered entirely by Frenchmen and others by a combination of French and Vietnamese officials, he acted in 1864 to eliminate Vietnamese participation in the administrative process.[40] All aspects of regional administration were placed in the hands of French inspectors of native affairs, and henceforth Vietnamese occupied auxiliary positions only. These inspectors, each responsible for about twenty thousand persons, dealt with matters of civil administration such as taxation, rendered justice, and supervised the activities of the Vietnamese employed by the French administration. The Vietnamese, in the case of the more senior employees, were still called by Vietnamese titles, but though these terms persisted throughout the nineteenth century, the duties of their recipients in no sense approximated those of the traditional *phu* or *huyen*.

La Grandière's decisions were modified in succeeding years, but his program set the essential pattern. It was accepted by the end of 1864 that no qualified substitutes could be found to replace the mandarins who had withdrawn from the regions occupied by the French. Having acknowledged this fact, the French administration was firmly set on a path of direct administration that brought increasingly close interaction between the Vietnamese population and their alien rulers. There could be no doubt about the subordinate status of the Vietnamese who worked for the French. It was now up to the colonizers to demonstrate that they could successfully involve themselves in such complex matters as justice, tax collection, and education.

Within the over-all problem of general administration, no issue was to prove more difficult than the establishment of a legal system for Cochinchina. Here again the withdrawal of the mandarins left a vacuum that was hard, if not impossible, to fill. The discovery of copies of the Vietnamese legal code during the conquest provided the opportunity for Aubaret to effect the translation on which French administrators relied for most of the period up to 1880. For the early years, however, the delay in translation and the subsequent problems of using it were, to a considerable extent, academic. In the face of almost unceasing armed resistance that posed varying degrees of threat to the French position, the French administrators did not hesitate to make legal decisions on the basis of expediency. Execution of rebels or suspected rebels or their deportation to Poulo Condore, which was soon used as a place of detention for the opponents of the French, were countenanced because of the unsettled conditions that prevailed.[41]

Despite this justice rendered more with a view to the preservation of power than to legal niceties, there was, from an early date, considerable discussion as to the form that a legal system should take in Cochinchina. Initially there was a wide acceptance of the principle that justice for the Vietnamese should be based as far as possible on Vietnamese law. The difficulties of such a decision were not fully recognized. There was optimism that Aubaret's translation would provide a Frenchman with all the necessary information to assume the duties of a Vietnamese mandarin. The difficulties of interpreting a code of laws radically different in spirit from French law were minimized, if not ignored altogether. While French power extended little farther than their military positions about Saigon, Admiral Charner sought to establish a system of justice that would rely, in part, on Vietnamese assessors who would assist French officials in trying cases. This, and a subsequent decision to seek the aid of cantonal chiefs and village notables in the rendering of justice were without success. Without the mandarins there were no Vietnamese available to interpret legal matters.[42]

To this state of uncertainty Admiral Bonard came with his conviction that the preservation of the legal system was desirable, in fact integral, for the preservation of the Vietnamese system of administration. Yet Bonard's comments on the Vietnamese legal code indicate the doubts that operated in the minds of so many of his

successors and finally led to the complete abolition of the Vietnamese code in penal matters. It was not merely that certain punishments provided in the code were repugnant to a nineteenth-
century Frenchman. More disturbing was the philosophy involved.
The code, he noted,

had as its aim to terrify, by fear of the gravest punishments, all those
who it appeared could cause the slightest damage to the absolute
authority of the king, first of all, then his family and relatives, to the
power of the husband over his wife and children, of the master over his
slaves, and finally of the mandarins, both military and civil, over their
subordinates and those whom they administered.[43]

Bonard observed that only time could bring ideas of progress to a
society based on such concepts. His aim was a judicial system
under which Vietnamese judges would hear cases and hand down
judgments, subject to the supervisory control of Frenchmen in
more serious matters. But it is far from clear if such a system ever
functioned properly. The available evidence in the archives suggests that in the region about My-Tho, at least, some Vietnamese
did act as judges for a brief period in 1862 and 1863. By the following year, however, this practice had generally ceased.[44]

When Admiral de La Grandière replaced Bonard he showed
impatience with the linguistic barrier, which hampered relations
between French and Vietnamese, and he distrusted the capacity of
the latter to play any substantial role within the colonial administration. Justice, his letters indicate, was a matter of too much importance to be discharged by Vietnamese subordinates. Presaging
the tone of the later protracted debates about justice in Cochinchina, he found fault with the fact that there was no separate
compilation of laws to govern civil matters that could be used
alongside the Gia-Long code translated by Aubaret.[45]

Despite these reservations, La Grandière inaugurated a system
of justice in 1864 that, in spirit at least, accorded with the judicial
program proposed by Bonard. By the decree of 25 July 1864,
strong theoretical support was given to the maintenance of a Vietnamese system of justice. Vietnamese law, at this stage still known

only in the abridged version of the Gia-Long code translated by Aubaret, was held to apply to all Vietnamese except those who lived in areas under the jurisdiction of French law, such as Saigon. There were the additional exceptions that French law applied when a Vietnamese entered into a contractual arrangement with a Frenchman or under the provisions of French law, and whenever a case before the courts involved a European.

Moreover, Article 12 of the decree provided that the "native tribunals established by the Annamite code are maintained." [46] This decree had a strange history. Apparently it provided for the continued use of Vietnamese law and for the use of Vietnamese judges in the first degree of jurisdiction. These judgments were to be reviewed, it is true, by French officials, but the decree seemed to guarantee continued Vietnamese participation in the judicial process. Yet only four years later Philastre could comment that the "Annamites have been totally excluded from the rendering of justice." [47] The lack of qualified Vietnamese was again the critical factor. There was scarcely any other outcome possible with a colonial situation in which not only did the rulers have an all-embracing belief in the virtues of their own society, but also the ruled could no longer provide the advocates to defend their traditional practices and values.

The evolution of a system of colonial justice in Cochinchina thus provides one of the most interesting, and largely neglected, examples of the clash between Vietnamese tradition and French conviction in the absolute superiority of western, more particularly French, standards. In a region frequently disturbed by armed risings against the government, it is not surprising that the administration of justice was far from regular. Yet the achievement of regularity by a system based on either French or Vietnamese principles, according to the prejudices of a particular commentator, was one of the most discussed goals of French officials in Cochinchina.

There is some evidence of continuing involvement in judicial or semijudicial matters by Vietnamese employees of the French administration. Although major matters came to the inspectors' attention, Vietnamese officials did not hesitate to arbitrate disputes informally. The informality of these efforts is stressed by the observation that whenever such attempts at arbitration failed, the Vietnamese employees who had tried to arbitrate seldom kept records or were able to provide information to help settle the case.[48] One later observer, Governor Le Myre de Vilers, suggested that the naval officers administering the colony in the 1860's misunderstood the meaning of the 1864 decree and assumed that Frenchmen making use of Vietnamese forms constituted "native tribunals." [49] This may have been so. Some weight must also be given to the possibility that many French administrators welcomed the opportunity to sit in judgment within their administrative region and would have resented Vietnamese subordinates playing any significant part in the judicial process. Questions of the separation of powers, which dominated later judicial discussion, would have been academic for a lone Frenchman in an isolated section of the colony who was concerned to demonstrate that he represented the new and powerful government in Saigon.

As for judgment by the Vietnamese code, the difficulties of carrying out this principle soon became apparent. Within less than a decade of the 1864 decree, there was a severe shortage of copies of Aubaret's translation, and the records in Saigon reveal the plaintive cry of an inspector at Sa-Dec who telegraphed: "I am excessively embarrassed. Have several judgments both civil and criminal in suspense because I do not have the Annamite code to be able to render judgment. Beg you to do all possible to try and send me a copy." [50] Where copies did exist, administrators found that Aubaret's incomplete translation, which did not include the commentaries of the original, was difficult to interpret and did not always cover the issues brought before them. Even those with some background of legal training encountered this problem. In this situation the simplest path to follow was the application of French law, possibly modified by the administrator's own judgment of what was proper to an individual situation.[51] Le Myre de Vilers leaves a macabre picture of the extremes to which such an ill-defined system could lead when an inspector's inclinations were toward harshness. Close to death from dysentery himself, one inspector handed down summary judgment of death from his *chaise percée*.[52]

While men such as Luro and Philastre sought to improve the system by ensuring greater Vietnamese participation, others argued for total change. In response to a long and critical commentary on the legal situation that Philastre prepared in 1868, the *procureur impérial* of Cochinchina asked whether the time had not come for the implementation of French penal justice throughout the colony.[53] This view received strong backing during the interim governorship of Admiral Ohier (1868–1869), a stereotype of the Frenchmen who wanted to substitute French practice for Vietnamese tradition. Among the mass of Ohier's correspondence, there is the constant theme of the need for greater French involvement in the affairs of their Vietnamese subjects. In matters of law he wrote frequently of his hopes to see the complete substitution of the French penal code for the Vietnamese code then in use, and, he assured the officials in Paris, his personal desires to see such a change had the full support of the inspectors of native affairs within the colony.[54] Ohier felt passionately that France could play an outstanding role in Cochinchina. His reports show his unflagging enthusiasm for all aspects of administration. They also reveal a readiness to overlook facts that ran contrary to his own assessments. Ohier stated his views on justice succinctly in a dispatch during November 1868. Making a general report on the year 1868, Ohier expressed a desire to see French justice used in Cochinchina: "It is our social order which must exist in the colony —our penal code which is the safeguard of our social order must exist without challenge." [55]

Conforming to this position, Ohier in January 1869 set up a committee to consider the question of substituting the French penal code for the Vietnamese code.[56] The committee was composed of five Frenchmen, including Philastre, and three Vietnamese. Two of the Vietnamese were familiar figures: Ton-Tho-Tuong, then *phu* of Saigon and using the name Ba-Tuong, and Do-Huu-Phuong, the reliable *huyen* of Cholon. The third Vietnamese member was Johannes Lieu, an interpreter who had been connected with the

French administration from early in the conquest. Of these Vietnamese, Philastre observed, only Tuong had any knowledge of the code used before the French arrived, and his knowledge was "approximate." Lieu, the interpreter, had great difficulty in translating exchanges since he had no knowledge of traditional Vietnamese law, and Tuong did not speak French. Only Philastre among the French could speak Vietnamese and knew anything of the Gia-Long code. The Vietnamese members could not read the French penal code. Facing this impasse, Philastre obtained a recess of the committee and translated the French penal code into Vietnamese. It remained clear, Philastre noted, that the other French members of the committee had made up their minds that a wholesale substitution was necessary and that the Vietnamese members thought only in terms of altering certain articles of the Vietnamese code, notably those connected with brutal punishments, while preserving the bulk of the code's provisions.

At some length, Philastre argued that the Aubaret translation of the Vietnamese code was faulty as well as being incomplete through the omission of the commentaries. Aubaret founded his translation, Philastre claimed, on the translation of the Chinese legal code made earlier by Sir George Staunton. The Aubaret translation gave the impression that the Vietnamese legal code was excessively concerned with punishment. The contrary concern was present, Philastre argued, in both the Chinese and the Vietnamese view of legal matters. These errors had given French officials a false concept of Vietnamese justice. Philastre noted the fundamental problem: the criticisms of the Vietnamese code expressed by the French members of the committee turned on the fact that the Vietnamese legal code was different from the French penal code. This was true, Philastre readily agreed, but this did not make the Vietnamese code any less precious to the Vietnamese.

Without Philastre's energetic defense of the Vietnamese point of view, the French penal code might have been substituted for the Vietnamese code early in the seventies. The Vietnamese members of the committee had little chance of convincing the Frenchmen of the justice of their attitude, even if they had been better acquainted with the matter under discussion. Arguing for the need to know more of the Vietnamese code before any drastic change was made, Philastre prevented the institution of the French penal code during Ohier's governorship and that of his successor, Admiral Cornulier-Lucinière (1870–1871). Admiral Dupré's appointment as governor (1871–1874) brought a more sympathetic understanding of Philastre's arguments. Dupré accepted the need for Philastre to carry out a full translation of the Vietnamese code. In a dispatch to Paris in 1873, Dupré supported Philastre's position and noted the need to delay. He then asked a more fundamental question: Was change desirable in any case?

Such as it is, with its imperfections, the Annamite legislation, based on the Chinese legal system, is far from being a barbarous work open to criticism; it is the translation into legal precepts of the principles of renowned philosophers; it is founded on principles of undoubted equity.[57]

Here, essentially, matters rested for the next six years. Philastre's immense translation of the Vietnamese code became available in 1876 and was distributed to the inspectors of native affairs with the admonition that it "must henceforth be the only [code] used in matters submitted to the native tribunals."[58]

During the 1870's various decisions placed the rendering of justice in the hands of a particular member of the administrative hierarchy within any one administrative region. Although it was argued that these decisions represented a partial separation of powers and would allow an inspector to become a specialist in matters connected with justice, the fact remained that justice, in the seventies, was rendered by those with little training to prepare them for their task and the difficulties of using an alien legal system.[59]

Concentration on such developments, dear to the hearts of legalistic French historians, gives a false picture of developments in Cochinchina. Recurrent armed opposition to the French administration remained an important feature of the colonial relationship through much of the seventies. Because of this, summary justice was common. The extreme instances cited by Le Myre de Vilers shortly after his arrival in 1879 may not have been the norm. There is, nevertheless, abundant evidence of the execution of "rebels" without due process and contrary to the regulations operating in Cochinchina.[60] In less grave matters, Philastre's translation of the code did not abolish the problems associated with Aubaret's less complete translation. Rather than specifying a range of penalties for classes of crimes, as do most western penal codes, the Vietnamese code sought to stipulate a particular punishment for each and every conceivable infringement of the law. Lacking even an index, the Vietnamese code was anathema to such minds as Le Myre de Vilers'. It must have proved extremely difficult to use for the majority of the French administrators.

Thus, well before 1879 and the arrival of Cochinchina's first civil governor, many steps had been taken towards eliminating any semblance of a Vietnamese system of justice. The "native tribunals" envisaged in the 1864 decree had never come to pass, and even an attempt to associate Vietnamese assessors with the rendering of civil justice, introduced in 1877, was eliminated the following year when it was decided that persons qualified to take part in the judicial process did not exist. Efforts to use the Vietnamese code had met with many difficulties, and by the late seventies its use was, at best, irregular. The struggle waged by Philastre, Luro, and a limited number of other Frenchmen had been unequal from the start. To succeed in conserving the bulk of Vietnamese law, it would have been necessary to have better auxiliaries than Ba-Tuong, whose knowledge of the Vietnamese code was "approximate." In addition, the unsettled conditions that prevailed and the long time that elapsed before any of the administrators discovered, through Philastre's translation, what the code actually was, aided the efforts of those who wished, from the earliest time in the French occupation, to eliminate the use of Vietnamese law altogether. The corpus of Vietnamese penal law was interred forever shortly after the transition to civil rule in 1879, but the system was moribund for a decade before.

While problems of justice and administration were discussed in Saigon, relatively little concern was paid to the effect of the French presence on the rural communes. In the countryside, the French occupation of Cochinchina encouraged expanded rice cultivation. The administration urged greater cultivation of rice in the hope of finding a dependable export staple. The really spectacular expansion of areas under cultivation came in the final decade of the nineteenth century and the first decade of the twentieth, but the increases in the first few years were still dramatic. The area under rice cultivation doubled between 1865 and 1867, while there was an increase of almost a third in the area cultivated between 1870 and 1878.[61] The migration traditional in Vietnamese history had not ceased in Cochinchina because of an alien government presence, and Vietnamese settlers continued to move into new areas to take up agricultural land. Writing in 1892, but describing a development that was in progress during the sixties and seventies, Monsignor Colombert noted the move towards the west: "There, they say, is the country of the future; agriculture is developing at an extraordinary rate, and the population without property moves towards the west *en masse*." [62] Already a limited number of Vietnamese were becoming substantial landowners. Some of the most notable of these, such as Le-Phat-Dat, were Christians. Few questions were asked when *collaborateurs* claimed that land was theirs. The persistent oral tradition that many land fortunes were made from such doubtful titles seems likely.

The French administration pronounced itself anxious to avoid interference in the daily affairs of the peasantry, and in particular in the management of the commune. Its activities in such matters as land surveys and tax raising, however, made it impossible to avoid involvement. The complicated issue of taxation under the French administration still awaits serious study, but all commentators agree that the substitution of French for Vietnamese rule brought an increase in the tax burden of the rural population.[63] Under the rule of the admirals the basic characteristics of the Vietnamese taxation system were maintained. Personal tax was only levied on the *inscrits,* or registered members of the commune, and the existing Vietnamese survey records were taken as the basis for taxes on

various agricultural products. The French administration was more
costly than the Vietnamese and so required higher tax contributions. Some of this cost was met by the establishment of an opium
farm, despite the severe reservations of many French administrators.[64]

All taxation operations required the cooperation of the cantonal
chiefs and the councils of notables within the commune. The *tong*,
or canton chiefs, were in an indeterminate position. Chosen, in theory, by the councils of several communes, their tenure of office had
to be confirmed by the local French administrator. They and their
deputies, the *pho-tong*, bore the responsibility for transmitting the
orders of the administration to the communes. Their duties as intermediaries were not easy, and before the end of the century comments suggest that appointments of able *tong* were often difficult.[65] It was within the commune itself, however, that the demands of the French administration weighed heaviest.

The first ideas that the French administrators gained of the
Vietnamese commune came from Aubaret's observations in his
preface to the *Gia-Dinh Thong-Chi*. There he made the common
error regarding the *thon-truong* as having honors and responsibilities comparable to those of a French *maire*.[66] As the result of this
assumption, the mayor became the unpaid agent of the administration, assuming a multiplicity of tasks on behalf of the central authority in Saigon. By the 1880's he was responsible for notifying
the commune of new government regulations, for the general security of the commune, and for reporting infractions of the law.
While in taxation matters he was associated with other members of
the council of notables of the commune, the mayor bore important
responsibilities in this field too.[67] One of the best informed observers in Cochinchina could write, in a report published in 1880:
"The change that has been brought to the Annamite institutions,
either through formal decision of the government or through indirect influence of our ideas, makes it difficult to trace a really exact
picture of the communal administration as it exists today." [68]

The mayor had gained greater importance than had ever been

the case under the traditional system. At the same time, he was frequently caught in the middle in clashes between the interests of
the administration and the commune.

French involvement in the affairs of the commune, either
through the mayor or on occasion through the direct intervention
of the local French officials, meant that the commune was less isolated, that its theoretical autonomy was considerably affected. The
French administration, constantly seeking to ensure the maximum
control over all aspects of the Vietnamese population's life, proclaimed an unending series of regulations that reached down to
the commune level. The introduction of a registry system—the
French *état-civil*—was regarded as essential and became the responsibility of the communal authorities. The various educational
programs required the cooperation of the commune. As the
notables' responsibilities mounted, so did their inclination to serve
decrease. In brief, during the first two decades of the colonial
presence, French involvement in the commune, by omission and
commission, had already begun to bring substantial change to the
council of notables and the commune as a whole.

The administration's indifference to the changes that it brought
to the commune sprang directly from a conviction that the
notables were untrustworthy and rapacious. This was the view of
Governor Ohier, who, rather in contrast to the other early governors, showed a strong inclination to extend French control over the
commune during his interim direction of the colony in 1868 and
1869. His efforts to ascertain the extent to which village notables
misappropriated village funds and exploited those whom they administered has already been the subject of detailed study.[69] Prominent figures, both French and Vietnamese, were convened by
Ohier to consider the problem, and a series of questionnaires were
placed before village assemblies "elected" for the purpose and
composed of individuals who were neither mayors nor cantonal
chiefs. The results of this enterprise were meager, and more interest attaches to the lengthy report submitted to the governor by
Tran-Ba-Loc, for that provides an insight into the thinking of a

Vietnamese closely associated with the French administration and upon whom that administration frequently relied for advice.[70]

Loc's picture of his fellow countrymen was a bleak one. He depicted the notables as embezzlers of commune funds, usurers, smokers of opium, and nepotists. When *corvées* were organized, the relatives of the notables never took part. Money was collected under duress for religious ceremonies within the commune and then appropriated for the notables' own use. Government decisions that would benefit the whole population of the commune were suppressed. Loc recommended the most stringent controls over the notables. Payments made by members of the commune were to be recorded in a register. Religious observations should be on a voluntary basis, and participation in *corvées* should be more equitable. In all Loc's recommendations there was the assumption that malfeasance was the rule rather than the exception, and that strict administrative control would suffice to eliminate this. It is impossible to determine how accurate Loc's picture of unrelieved deception and dishonesty really was, nor can the extent to which his assessments were influenced by his own alienation from the bulk of the rural population be accurately estimated.

As for Ohier's survey of conditions in the communes, little in fact was done and many undoubted abuses continued for some time. What is clear is that criticisms of the commune notables formulated by those Vietnamese most closely linked to and trusted by the administration reinforced the readiness of French officials to believe that the communes were ripe for change. The transformation of the mayor of the commune from a servant of the commune into an executive agent of the French administration disturbed an administrator such as Luro but not his superiors, who believed in the need to conform to French standards. As the communes were increasingly subject to regulation by the government in Saigon, the duties of the commune officials were affected, and the status of the notables declined.

Change in the communes was not as dramatic as the developments in justice and general administration. In the absence of any feasible alternative, French officials administered a population previously under the control of Vietnamese mandarins. Long paces had been taken toward the final elimination of the traditional system of justice, and the ultimate goal of substituting the French penal code for the Vietnamese code was within reach at the end of the seventies. By that time Cochinchina faced the prospect of great change. The French administration had introduced changes and pursued ends that accorded with its belief in modern civilization. Meaningful opposition to these policies was gone, and the Vietnamese in Cochinchina on whom the French relied for advice were vocal partisans of the changes that they saw taking place.

4

Education and *Quoc-Ngu*—The Development of a New Order

The final substitution of the French penal code for the Vietnamese legal system was inevitable; the native society was unable to pose alternatives to the slow but relentless elimination of Vietnamese methods. An even more dramatic change was involved in the educational and linguistic developments that took place in the same period, but there was a difference. While the introduction of *quoc-ngu* on a wide scale throughout Cochinchina also represented a break with the past, here the Vietnamese played a vital role with the French and did not merely acquiesce because there was no alternative. In education the part played by the Vietnamese was less striking, yet here again there is a sense of positive contribution, if only by a limited number of Vietnamese. Cochinchinese society could not provide administrators or experts in Vietnamese justice, but it could and did provide a limited number of outstanding individuals without whom the passionate French desire to inculcate the essentials of their educational system and social philosophy could not have made any worthwhile progress.

The French administrators believed that *quoc-ngu* provided them with a strong weapon in the battle to eliminate the Chinese characters that were the traditional vehicle for written records in Viet-Nam. Chinese characters, written exactly as in China but pronounced in a Vietnamese fashion, were used for official business and for literary works. In *chu-nom*, another writing system used widely in Viet-Nam, Chinese characters were again the basis, but here the characters rendered the Vietnamese language. Combinations of characters were used to give both the sense and the sound of a particular Vietnamese word. Neither of these systems had appealed to the early Christian missionaries, who instead devised a transcription that rendered Vietnamese in the Roman alphabet. The great missionary Alexander of Rhodes is credited with codifying and systematizing the transcription, the work of his fellow missionaries. The phonetics of the *quoc-ngu* transcription were based on Portuguese, which was, in the seventeenth century, the trading language of Europeans in Viet-Nam. Alexander of Rhodes' great contributions were the tone marks and diacritics to indicate vowel pronunciation, essential for understanding the Vietnamese language.[1]

Missionary efforts kept the use of *quoc-ngu* alive, but before the arrival of the French the use of the transcription had not penetrated the non-Christian element of the population. Its chief use was in catechisms and in the short accounts of the lives of the saints circulated by the missions. The decision by the French administration in Cochinchina to use the *quoc-ngu* transcription rather than to rely on Chinese characters was essentially practical. The mission-trained Vietnamese interpreters upon whom the French had to rely at the outset were trained in *quoc-ngu* rather than in the use of characters. Moreover, Frenchmen recognized that the existence of a romanized transcription opened the way to learning Vietnamese without having to master ideograms. The scholarly importance of learning characters was acknowledged, but the practical necessity was discounted.

Beyond the practical considerations were the philosophic implications. The majority of the early French administrators deeply distrusted the Confucian ethic implicit in teaching through characters. Both administrators and missionaries in Cochinchina, during the sixties and seventies, believed that wholesale conversion of the Vietnamese population was a real possibility. Such a development, which was held to provide an assurance of loyalty to France, would be aided by the use of *quoc-ngu*. Any continued use of characters, on the other hand, was seen as likely to inhibit the progress of modern ideas and to encourage residual loyalties to the court at Hue. Because of the French insistence on the dangers of preserving traditional forms of education and the use of Chinese characters, Cochinchina was in the forefront of a radical change that eventually spread throughout the whole of Viet-Nam. Belief in *quoc-ngu* as an alternative to characters and an essential first step to the even more desirable use of French was generally unchallenged amongst Frenchmen in Cochinchina. There were exceptions, but Luro's voice, for all his prestige, rang out of tune with the general chorus of approval for the use of *quoc-ngu* and French in the colony's educational institutions.[2]

Of all the developments in the educational and linguistic fields, the establishment and maintenance of a government newspaper in *quoc-ngu* was perhaps the most notable. This was the *Gia-Dinh Bao* (The Journal of Gia-Dinh). The hopes held for this newspaper and the character of its political and social propaganda represent the quintessence of French efforts to carry out a civilizing mission. The newspaper was closely linked with efforts for the expansion of education, and the Vietnamese members of its staff were the most important contributors to the body of *quoc-ngu* writings published during the nineteenth century. Admiral de La Grandière, with his enthusiasm for education in the romanized transcription of Vietnamese, saw the value of publishing a *quoc-ngu* newspaper. He conceived it as having an educational as well as a purely informational value. This was in 1864.[3] The first issue of *Gia-Dinh Bao* appeared on 15 April 1865 during the interim governorship of Admiral Roze. In a dispatch describing this event, Roze clearly stated the aims of the new monthly journal. It was: "destined to diffuse among our native population the news which is worthy of their interest, to initiate them into a knowledge of the new processes for the improvement of agriculture and progress in rural industry."[4] "News which is worthy of interest" denoted both material that presented the French administration in the best light and articles that might be described in a nineteenth-century fashion as "useful knowledge": articles designed to improve agricultural production or to inform readers on the world outside Viet-Nam. Four years after the foundation of the newspaper, Admiral Ohier was proposing to place inserts [within the standard newspaper] which will recount the life of the great men of France, give anecdotes taken from picturesque magazines or from children's journals, so as to give the natives an appreciation of our character in its most noble expressions, and to interest them and satisfy the passion which they have for reading.[5]

In its first years of publication, *Gia-Dinh Bao* was a monthly newspaper. It later published twice monthly and finally, by the end of the century, on a weekly basis. In its organization the newspaper followed the model set by the French language *Courrier de Saigon.* There were two sections, the first presenting official items, the second unofficial material of more general interest. In the earliest issues, in fact, this division was less than clear-cut. An article in the official section often presented slanted news at some length. Later, as the bureaucracy of the colony grew and the number of decisions and decrees published each week multiplied, the division between strictly official announcements and articles became clearer.

The fourth issue of the first year of publication is an excellent illustration of the newspaper in its early years. At the beginning of the newspaper are meteorological notes and market prices. Some information, such as that concerning the formation of a council on agriculture and trade, had little if any political significance and is presented without propaganda veneer. But a restrained overlay becomes apparent in other announcements. The departure of a French official from the colony is reported:

Mr. Boresse, the *quan-bo* of Gia-Dinh, has just returned to Europe. . . . Because he was ill he has left behind many Vietnamese whom he loved and looked after for the last six years. Everyone in the *huyen* of Binh-Long and Binh-Duong will be able to remember how very kind and just he was, so that when they see him return here in good health they will be very happy. This is the reason why Philastre is being appointed *quan-bo.* When he was in Dinh-Tuong and Bien-Hoa he had a fine reputation in both these provinces, so people will admire him.[6]

Apolitical news items could be presented without embroidery, but the departure of a senior official in the Native Affairs Service posed the necessity, in the minds of the French officials of the period, to emphasize to the ruled the high character of the rulers. When it comes to discussion of the court at Hue, the propagandist tendencies of the newspaper are bolder:

A series of deceitful and traitorous acts having prevented peace be-tween the two countries, the King of Annam has understood the power of the French and weighed the pros and cons and seen that there is no longer any reason to be distrustful or difficult. The king has sent men to study the French language; he has dispatched officials to buy steam boats; and he has ordered craftsmen to study machines. It is said that the court wishes to welcome learned persons from France so that they can teach trades to the population. It is said, too, that the court has decided to obtain all information which will permit them to maintain relations with France. It definitely does not distrust the idea of working together any more. The Hue government knows that the French have no intention of putting aside the authority of Annam or of sacking the country. Because Annam was recalcitrant, it would not agree to make peace. But now the time to establish peace has come.[7]

In a quite literal sense, it may have been that such articles repre-sented preaching to the converted, since the bulk of those able to read *quoc-ngu* were Catholics who already distrusted the Hue court. But the newspaper was also intended as a teaching aid in schools. The intent of the article is clear. That this particular article was signed by Paulus Huynh-Tinh-Cua, one of the most prominent of the Vietnamese Catholics in the French service, emphasizes the absolute separation of the first generation of Vietnamese Catholics living under French rule from their traditional government.

Heavy stress was laid on the value of cooperating with the French administration. The newspaper made a special point of re-cording rewards given to Vietnamese who had been closely associ-ated with the establishment of the new colonial administration in Cochinchina. The first item in the issue for August 1865 records the rewards given canton chiefs "who had for so long worked for the good of the country, who had been worthy of trust, and who had displayed loyalty of more than the usual sort." These men received certificates attesting to their loyalty and were promised a continu-ing monthly financial reward from the government.[8]

By the 1870's, the tendency for the newspaper to become more and more heavily administrative is apparent. But the items of useful knowledge continue, for example, the "Continuation of an Account of Feathers and Feather Farms in the Region of Kien-Giang," [9] and a long series of articles on the history of Viet-Nam.[10] Reference to the Hue court is seldom made without stressing French virtue and Vietnamese perfidy. Those Vietnamese who resisted French power in the south were denounced in an article on the conclusion of a peace treaty between France and Viet-Nam in 1874:

> France and Annam have concluded a peace treaty binding them to live as peaceful neighbors. The Government of Annam hands over the six provinces of Cochinchina to the French government. For its part, the French government consents to aid the Annamese government so that its provinces and cities may exist in peace.
>
> Thus, the soldiers who urge and plot rebellion, who hasten to sacrifice villages and to oppress the people, no longer have any reason whatever for rebellion, cruelty, or agitation among the people.[11]

Promulgation of decisions and decrees on legal and taxation matters occurred beside heavily political accounts of current events, articles of useful knowledge, and even advertisements for forthcoming horse races.

No matter what was being announced or described, the important point was that it was being done in Vietnamese written in *quoc-ngu*. The number of books in *quoc-ngu* at this stage of Cochinchina's history remained very small. *Gia-Dinh Bao* cannot have provided easy or interesting reading matter for the schools in which it was used to teach *quoc-ngu,* but it was a symbol of the way in which the romanized transcription could be used. As such, it played a vital role in effecting the complete elimination of Chinese characters.

Frenchmen played an important part in organizing and editing *Gia-Dinh Bao.* Its first editor was Potteaux, an interpreter for the French administration for many years. But among the personnel associated with the newspaper the most interesting were the two notable Vietnamese linguists, Pétrus Ky and Paulus Cua. A Catholic like Ky, Cua joined the French administration in 1861 and was closely associated with it until his death in 1907. He compiled a major Vietnamese dictionary, published in Saigon in 1895 and 1896, and his writings ranged from translations of traditional Vietnamese stories from Chinese characters into *quoc-ngu,* to articles and pamphlets on scientific subjects and the compilation of court judgments.[12] Little of Cua's personality emerges from the records of his life. He was able and industrious, but in contrast to Pétrus Ky, about whom so much is known and whose character is so clearly delineated in his private correspondence, Cua remains an ill-defined if scholarly figure. His contribution to the development of a *quoc-ngu* literature is undoubted. The fact that *Gia-Dinh Bao* was able to function as it did owed much to his energies. But the deeper motives for his wholehearted cooperation with the French and his view of Franco-Vietnamese relations remain obscure. His Catholicism may provide the best answer.[13]

It is not surprising that French historians of the colonial period have found Pétrus Truong-Vinh-Ky such an admirable figure. He was a man of great linguistic capacities and at the same time a fervent believer in the role that France proclaimed for herself in Viet-Nam.[14] Born in 1837, the son of a military mandarin, Truong-Vinh-Ky was educated by Catholic priests, both Vietnamese and French. His father's official position seems to have protected his immediate family during the early years of Ky's life, but he died when Ky was nine, and the family suffered for their faith during the period of persecutions. Study of Chinese characters, Ky's first educational experience, was followed by study of *quoc-ngu,* first in Cochinchina and then in the Catholic mission of Pinhalu in Cambodia, near the court at Oudong. A natural capacity for languages was stimulated at the missionary training center maintained by the French Missions Etrangères order on the island of Penang. He remained there for six years between 1852 and 1858. It was on Penang that Ky gained his first acquaintance with the French language and achieved the mastery of it that permitted him to be one of the first interpreters, during the early years of the French presence.

Pétrus Ky returned to Cochinchina in 1859; he decided not to enter the priesthood but continued working as a teacher in Catholic missions. It was through his missionary associations that he was recommended to members of the French forces in the Saigon region, and in 1860 began his employment by and devotion to the French administration. During the four decades of this association, his duties and his responsibilities were manifold. He acted initially as an interpreter and accompanied the Vietnamese mission to Europe, in 1863, when the court of Hue sought to revise the 1862 peace treaty with France. He taught in the Collège des Interprètes and later at the Collège des Stagiaires. He was for a time editor of *Gia-Dinh Bao*. To him the French administration turned for advice on matters of administration.[15] In the seventies and eighties he moved outside a purely advisory function in political affairs, first making a detailed report on the political situation in northern Viet-Nam and later acting in close collaboration with Paul Bert as an agent of the French government within the Hue court. Throughout his life he was a prolific author. He was the first Vietnamese to prepare a history of Viet-Nam in French. The range of his works included linguistics, history, geography, natural history, and philosophy. His life still awaits a biography free from the prejudices of both French and Vietnamese views of the colonial period.[16]

From Ky's substantial correspondence one may gain a real sense of the man and of his relationship with the French in Cochinchina. Letters in his personal dossier in the Saigon archives show him as a man of independent spirit who, loyal though he was to the French administration, bridled at any suspected insult to himself or his family. Writing a letter of resignation in 1868 following some real or imagined slight he proclaimed:

. . . I have understood only too well the general tone of it [a letter to which Ky is replying from the Director of the Interior, Vial] to hesitate a single moment over the conduct which I must take.

Only my resignation can give me peace of mind. . . .

Returning to private life, my heart is always with France, my feeble services belong to her.[17]

The crisis, if such it really was, passed quickly. During the next ten years Ky had one of the most productive periods of his life. He published his *Cours d'histoire annamite,*[18] taught in the Collège des Stagiaires, and prepared numerous grammars, vocabularies, and texts for the slowly developing school system. A visit to Tonkin in 1876 produced a short travel book and a political report in which Ky wrote with great assurance about the relationship that France might have with those sections of Viet-Nam which retained their independence. The political report also projects the image of a man whose heart and soul were linked to French interests and French success:

I have no doubt that the influence of the French government [in Tonkin] can without difficulty become altogether preponderant and be of great weight in bringing the adoption of reforms that are of imperious necessity—political reforms—economic reforms—reforms of administrative policy and for the administration of financial matters, in legislation, etc., etc.

I have the firm conviction that the Government of Hue is powerless to carry out this great work and that France alone is capable of raising up this decaying nation.[19]

In another section of the same report, Ky showed that his Catholic background was no barrier to critical comment on his coreligionists. There was extreme hostility, he observed, between the Vietnamese scholarly class and the Christians of Tonkin, who suffered frequent persecution, but "the truth is that the Catholics have ceded nothing to their opponents, ninety-nine times [out of a hundred] in their reprisals." The account of his discussions with the Vietnamese mandarins in Tonkin reflects a similar air of detachment. The tone is that of a schoolmaster lecturing a none-too-bright pupil.

In the eyes of many in the French administration, Ky had indeed become French both in his mode of expression and in his outlook. When Luro completed his *Bulletin individuel de note* in 1875, he referred to Ky as "completely French"; later he called him "the most Frenchified Annamite we have." [20] Nowhere is the accuracy of this comment more clearly affirmed than in a long letter that Ky wrote to a correspondent in France concerning the future publication of books in *quoc-ngu:*

This form of writing, thanks to the active concern of the government of the colony, has assumed an imposing character of public utility. The administration would certainly be anxious to increase the number of works [published in *quoc-ngu*] to spread their use so as to encourage the wider use of this form of writing, which is called to play the greatest role in the work of progress and the development of abilities . . . thanks to this writing, our poor disinherited country will be able to enter into the community of peoples and the great issues which the West has brought before the world; the sciences whose unexpected revelations strike the spirit and confound the intelligence will no longer be unfathomable mysteries to us, and these old errors, prejudices, these absurd beliefs will disappear, giving way to true knowledge, to the high and serious inspiration of a wise philosophy. But for that one must have books, books, and still more books.[21]

The tone of Ky's letter, with its disavowal of the past, was to become familiar in Vietnamese writing during the first few decades of the twentieth century. In many ways Ky foreshadowed the political outlook of Pham-Quynh, an important supporter of French political positions during the 1920's and 1930's. Both Ky and Pham-Quynh present the image of Viet-Nam as a disinherited country, one with a political and intellectual history that had left it ill-prepared for the challenges of the modern world. The suggestion at least is present that Viet-Nam, in accepting the culture of China, had handicapped not only its political but also its intellectual development.[22] Truong-Vinh-Ky sincerely believed what he wrote, and his life provides a striking example of the total commitment of those Vietnamese who, divorced by religion and inclination from the traditional order, marched in the advance guard of those who argued for Franco-Vietnamese cooperation.

While Truong-Vinh-Ky and Huynh-Tinh-Cua labored to provide the nucleus of a *quoc-ngu* literature, the colonial administration slowly developed the institutions in which the transcription could be taught. In this task the role of Catholic missionaries was of great importance. Their mission schools in the provinces provided Vietnamese students with only a rudimentary education, but in Saigon the church-administered Ecole française de Monseigneur d'Adran was the only educational institution during the sixties that could train young Vietnamese to become more than simple interpreters. The Collège d'Adran, as the school was more commonly known, was founded in 1861 with the purpose of "inculcating morality and assimilating the Annamite younger generation." Not until after 1864, however, did it produce a significant number of qualified students who could assume jobs in the French administration.[23]

Outside Saigon the extension of French-sponsored education followed a decision promulgated on 16 July 1864. This provided that an "interpreter" would take charge of classes of young Vietnamese in each of the most important centers of the colony to teach pupils to write their language in "European characters." Subsequent informed comment on these schools showed them to have enjoyed only the most limited success. Admiral La Grandière, an enthusiast in matters of education as in everything else, could see nothing but progress. In September 1864 he reported:

> The progress made by these pupils, of whom the majority had, at the time of my arrival, only *twenty to twenty five days* of schooling; the ease with which they show that they can learn our syllables and pronounce them, have caused real surprise. . . .
>
> If, as I have every reason to hope, this movement towards our schools continues, we will have in less than a year at least a thousand young Annamites knowing how to read and write their language in Latin characters; we will thus strike a deadly blow to mandarinism, and we will finally rid ourselves of the scholars who are always inclined to troublemaking.[24]

The governor's comments at the end of the year were no less enthusiastic. By then twenty schools had been opened, and he claimed that three hundred pupils had learnt to read. These comments were made at a time when there were no *quoc-ngu* textbooks, not even the *Gia-Dinh Bao*, and when interpreters, whose incompetence was so often criticized, were filling the role of teachers.[25]

The search for an accurate picture of developments must overcome the obstacles of distorting enthusiasm and doubtful statistics.

Admiral de La Grandière's scheme for the development of schools in the provinces that would teach in *quoc-ngu* and a limited amount of French was presented in the reports of the late sixties and early seventies as an important success. In La Grandière's absence from Cochinchina, during 1865, Admiral Roze expressed his pleasure at the progress being made. He spoke of pupils who were able to read and write their language in *quoc-ngu* and to read and write French words. The latter, he admitted as an afterthought, they did not understand.[26] In the same year Roze expatiated on the readiness of Vietnamese parents to send their children to schools teaching in *quoc-ngu*.[27]

The hopes of the administration, indeed, went beyond the education of children alone. The benefits in both practical and moral terms of teaching in *quoc-ngu*, and so breaking with the character-ridden past, were also judged important to adults. Adults were encouraged to attend evening schools teaching in *quoc-ngu*.[28] By March 1869, Admiral Ohier reported that there were 104 schools in the colony, attended by 3,200 pupils. Six of these schools, essentially those in Saigon, taught in French as well as *quoc-ngu*.[29] Later in the same year the numbers attending schools organized by the French administration were reported as 4,481 pupils in 120 schools. In addition, there were 530 pupils in six schools maintained by teaching brothers of the Christian Doctrine.[30] As years passed, the reported school attendance in Cochinchina mounted. In 1870 those learning *quoc-ngu* in the provinces were said to number more than five thousand.[31]

The enthusiastic accounts of ever-growing numbers of Vietnamese children crowding the schools to learn *quoc-ngu* had, however, little reality. Admiral Dupré deflated the swollen estimates in a long dispatch written in February 1873:

I regret to say that in this important matter of public education, we are still searching and groping for our way. The results obtained up to now are far from satisfactory. Since the occupation we have seen the numerous schools of all kinds that existed disappear, and everything still has to be created. One wished to profit from substituting for the Chinese characters used by the Annamites, European characters which the missionaries have used for a long time. . . . One then ceased to teach through characters in our new schools and taught children to read and write by means of our alphabet. But the reform was premature; there was nothing to teach the pupils after reading and writing. There was a lack of books and of teachers too. . . . All our efforts ended in bringing together three to four thousand children whose parents were indemnified by the village for the sacrifice that they made in sending them.[32]

One can only explain the disparity between Dupré's comments and the earlier affirmations of success in terms of the way in which hope and enthusiasm distorted the outlook of French officials. In order to piece together an account of what actually occurred, it is necessary to rely on the comments of those who were critical of educational developments and on those occasional reports which, in discussing education, appear to have placed objectivity before an overwhelming conviction of France's mission. La Grandière's intention had been to establish schools in all major communes. Little real thought seems to have been given initially to recruiting pupils for these schools. On a number of occasions, the French administration found itself competing with the teaching endeavors of the Catholic Church.

Such was the case in the "Affaire de l'Ecole centrale de Mytho" of 1872, a clash between an inspector of native affairs in My-Tho and a priest, Father Lize. The priest resented the inspector's recruiting children for the government school from among the children of his parishoners and ordered them to "obey God rather than men." The impact of such a clash of personalities in a small French community may be imagined. There were exchanges between the administration and the bishop in whose diocese the incident took place, and a full report was prepared for the governor's consideration. This report throws an interesting light on the way in which attendance at government schools was ensured:

First the villages received the order to provide pupils; one from each small or medium-sized village, two from the large villages, three from those few with exceptionally large populations.

Since the administration had not undertaken to meet the cost of their maintenance, an additional tax of 7 francs 50 centimes was decided upon to meet this. The value of this procedure seems open to question, but this has not been the matter for complaint [by the priests]. The Brothers do not complain against the measure; they seek their share of the children with a satisfactory subvention.

Fundamentally, this is nothing new. The schools in the interior of the country have never had pupils on a voluntary basis in any large number. They are, for the most part, recruited and paid for by the villages in the same way as militia men, and at even greater cost.[33]

Luro, in his *Cours d'administration,* makes the same point. The *quoc-ngu* school had no real attraction for the villagers of Cochinchina in this early period. The requirement that children should attend these new schools was circumvented by sending the poorest children in a commune and paying a special subsidy to their parents.[34]

The quality of the teachers in the early schools was poor. With the exception of the *Gia-Dinh Bao,* there were almost no teaching materials, and teaching was by rote. As Luro aptly observed, the pupils might be compared with a parrot that was able to write.[35] In contrast to traditional teaching, the instruction in these government schools was without any moral character. This concerned such observers as Luro and Philastre, and it was a major factor in the reluctance of Vietnamese in the provinces to send their children to the government schools. It did not concern those members of the French administration who saw the need to eliminate the influence of Confucian thought. The Vietnamese within the villages showed their attachment to the traditional system by sending those children who had attended a government school during the day to spend part of the evening learning characters from the teachers who continued to live in the communes.[36]

These unsuccessful efforts were, nevertheless, only one aspect of the French educational effort in Cochinchina. In 1874 the obvious faults of the system led to a general reorganization of educational efforts. Before this, however, there were two other developments in the educational field of particular interest: the maintenance of schools in Saigon that taught Vietnamese children both *quoc-ngu* and French, and, most interesting of all, the efforts to develop an elite through the dispatch of young Vietnamese for prolonged periods of training in France. In Saigon the Collège d'Adran continued to be the only important institution providing Vietnamese trained to assume auxiliary positions within the administration up to 1871. There were other *collèges* maintained by Catholic teaching brothers in provincial centers, and in 1868 an Institution Municipal was founded in Saigon particularly for French children. In 1871, however, in an effort to train more young Vietnamese who could teach and act as clerks and interpreters, the decision was taken to found the Ecole Normale of Saigon.[37] The net result of all these efforts was far from satisfactory to the French administration. The director of the Ecole Normale might write, "Never before has the emulation been so great; never have the pupils understood so well the importance of education . . . ,"[38] but the administrators knew that their programs continued to meet difficulties because of the problems of recruiting really competent Vietnamese.

Moreover, the hope that Vietnamese who had studied in France would provide the necessary auxiliaries was not realized. This remarkable exercise in colonial education began within less than ten years of the French arrival in Viet-Nam. In 1865, Admiral Roze arranged for three young Vietnamese to travel to France so that they could gain an impression of the wonders of the country from which their rulers came. These "intelligent" young men, identified only as Tom, Gui, and Cao, were seventeen, sixteen, and fifteen years of age.[39] Their reactions are not recorded in the archives. They were the precursors of the students who, from 1866 onwards, went to two Catholic teaching establishments in France, the Institution Sainte Marie in La Seyne, and the Pensionnat des Frères des Ecoles Chrétiennes in Marseille.[40] It would be interesting to know more of the selection process by which these children and young men were selected for what must have been to them an epic voyage. There are references to the choice being made from among the children of "influential families."[41] This meant the children of those Vietnamese, often Catholic, who had cooperated with the new administration and often held positions within it. Such was the case with Tran-Ba-Loc's younger brother, Tran-Ba-Huu, who attended the Marist Brothers' school at La Seyne, as did Loc's maternal cousin.[42]

The number of Vietnamese studying in France rose from fourteen in 1866 to ninety in 1870.[43] The ages of the young Vietnamese sent abroad varied considerably, ranging, according to one document, from eleven to twenty.[44] In the Catholic institutions they were first taught French for at least a year, and then the rudiments of a primary education.[45] Such a voyage to France, and the subsequent involvement in the strict discipline of a Catholic school, must have had an extraordinary impact on the young Vietnamese. There is one limited reference to the unhappiness that many of them surely felt. A provincial newspaper stated in an article written in January 1868 that three of the students were held against their wish to return home. Investigations by the minister of the colonies suggested that it was possible that one child was, indeed, held against his will. But it was decided not to make an issue of this, since it was considered there would be more "profit for the newspaper than for religion and authority" in any investigation that might take place.[46]

By 1871 the French administration in Cochinchina was expressing considerable doubts about the utility of the program. "One had thought," Admiral Dupré wrote, "that after a stay of two or three years in the metropole, these young people would have gained sufficient learning to enable them to be usefully employed in the different public services of the colony." [47] But this had not been the case. At the time Dupré wrote, forty-two students had returned from France, and of these only eight or ten were able to render more or less useful services. Dupré's conclusions did not surprise the head of the Marist Brothers' school at La Seyne. He noted that at least one year of the two or three the young Vietnamese spent in France was required to learn French. The scheme of sending young Vietnamese to France for study in Catholic schools continued in a much reduced form until the end of the seventies. In succeeding decades there was increased emphasis on lay education for those Vietnamese who studied outside their country.

In Cochinchina itself the Catholic Church continued to play an important part in educational matters. The Collège d'Adran in Saigon, and smaller *collèges* outside the capital, were staffed by teaching brothers. So was the Institut Taberd, founded in 1874 expressly for the children of mixed alliances between Frenchmen and Vietnamese women. Orphanages directed by the Sisters of Saint Paul of Chartres were always listed as part of the educational structure of the colony. It is probably more correct to see these as essentially charitable rather than educational institutions. There were also the Catholic schools in France to which Vietnamese were sent. Throughout the colony Catholic missions linked evangelism with limited educational efforts. This, as has already been shown, could lead to clashes between civil and religious interests. An assessment of the importance of this missionary educational endeavor is as difficult as consideration of the French administration's educational program. Enthusiasm colors the missionary reports in the same way as it does the reports of the civil administrators. In just the same way, too, there are occasional brief revelations deploring the lack of progress and casting severe doubt on the accounts that have gone before. The statistics provided in the *Lettres communes* of the Missions Etrangères for the mid-1870's show between three and four thousand Vietnamese attending mission schools.[48] Judging mainly by later discussions on the curriculum of these mission schools, it appears that the emphasis was on religious instruction through the medium of *quoc-ngu*.[49]

General dissatisfaction with the educational system established by Admiral de La Grandière led to the reforms of 1874. As the French administration expanded, the need for competent Vietnamese members of the administration became more pressing. A larger administration meant that there were more Frenchmen who did not speak Vietnamese, and a greater number of Vietnamese clerks, interpreters, and telegraphists was required. The existing program of public education did not meet these needs. Reporting to the Private Council, the director of the interior noted that the system had resulted in the villages sending the children of their poorest members to the schools, that the teachers in the schools giving instruction in *quoc-ngu* were generally of very poor quality, and that the

Ecole Normale in Saigon was in need of reform.[50] This blanket condemnation led to considerable change. In a decision of 17 November 1874, the existing *quoc-ngu* schools were suppressed. To take their place it was proposed to establish one "primary school" in each administrative division of the colony, with state-supported pupils. In place of the previously haphazard attendance procedures, children would now be expected to attend for three years. The primary schools were to be staffed by both Frenchmen and Vietnamese teachers, whose qualifications would be controlled by the state. Courses at the new primary schools were to last three years and would be in *quoc-ngu* and French, and to a very limited extent in Chinese characters. Standard subjects such as arithmetic, geometry, and "notions" of history and geography were the essentials of instruction. Because of the demands for new staff, especially the need for French teachers, the new primary schools were to be introduced, initially, only in six major centers: Saigon, Cholon, My-Tho, Vinh-Long, Ben-Tre, and Soc-Trang.[51]

The best pupils from these schools would go on for further study to the Collège Indigène, which was now to replace the Ecole Normale. This secondary institution took the name of a former French minister of the colonies, Chasseloup-Laubat, and it is under this name that it is usually described in contemporary accounts. Here again the course was to last three years. One hundred Vietnamese children each year were to enter, their costs to be met by the French administration. The introductory lessons stipulated as a part of the curriculum in the primary schools became a "reasoned study of the French language" in the secondary school.[52]

Two years later, Philastre described the situation of the schools that he encountered in the course of a long administrative tour:

The majority of the schools established in the various Annamite markets have been closed and have been replaced by *collèges* set up in the administrative centers. The population considers this an economy and a benefit; instead of renting three or four children from their parents so that they may be "furnished" to the school in the neighboring village, each village now needs only to rent one or two children and to "furnish" them to the college of the Inspection. Some villages do not even provide any children at all.

In my view, not only on the basis of my observation over a number of years but also as the result of the advice which I have had from the administrators and directors of the schools, if we do not openly force the villages to provide a certain number of pupils, we take advantage, at least, of our former mistakes and the majority of villages still believe that they are obliged to provide pupils as in the past. "If anyone told them they were not obliged to do so, there would be no more pupils.". . .

Moreover, if this is so, if there are only a few Annamite employees who, to *give proof of their zeal,* send their children to school, if the mass of the population only sees the schools with defiance, this comes from the antipathy evoked as the result of the coercive measures that were formerly used for state schools and against the native teachers of the free [traditional] Annamite schools. The situation is related to religious prejudices and, finally, *above all because the children learnt absolutely nothing in our schools.*

They learn nothing because there are no teachers. The only fields of study known to the Annamites are those of Chinese philosophy and morality, and these were given very much more limited treatment in our schools than in those of the traditional teachers.

It is only with difficulty that one can find, today, in the whole of the colony, both Frenchmen and Annamites, enough personnel to teach in and organize a single central school from which serious Annamite teachers will later graduate. All the more reason that it is impossible to provide for the needs of twelve or fifteen schools.[53]

Allowance must always be made for the convictions that dominated Philastre's and Luro's criticisms of the situation in Cochinchina. Yet the slow progress of later years and the difficulties that others described provide substantial confirmation of their estimates. The bulk of the administration was either ready to accept the necessity of slow progress and meager results or believed that these were temporary problems that would soon disappear. Certainly, Philastre's colleagues did not share his concern at the disappearance of instruction in Chinese philosophy.

Sustained by these attitudes and aided in their programs by such Vietnamese as Pétrus Ky and Paulus Cua, the French officials worked throughout the seventies to achieve the substitution of *quoc-ngu* for characters. Their ultimate goal was an educational system with instruction in the French language and the introduction of modern learning, as the French understood it. Despite the failures and difficulties, it was decided, in 1878, to enforce the use of *quoc-ngu* as the sole language, other than French, permitted in all official documents.[54] A similar decision had been taken in 1869, but it had remained a dead letter.[55] The 1878 decision was expected to bring increased attendance in the schools teaching *quoc-ngu*, since there would now be a further reason to learn the transcription.[56] The goal of complete substitution of romanized writing for characters had been accepted by the rulers; it now became only a matter of time before the ruled accepted it also.

Countering the change were the private schools teaching characters in the villages. These small schools remained a part of Vietnamese village life until the end of the century, but the *raison d'être* for their existence became less and less clear. There were no longer any triennial examinations in Cochinchina, and the ruling administration had no place for those trained in characters. By the end of the seventies the number of teachers who could instruct in characters was declining. The French administration's alternative, the schools teaching in *quoc-ngu* and French, still did not function satisfactorily, but they provided the framework for continuing efforts to inculcate French values and western learning. Change was slow and progress difficult. It was, nevertheless, taking place. Within less than a generation from the end of the seventies total substitution of *quoc-ngu* for characters had been achieved. This provides another yardstick by which to judge the developments up to 1879, which so often seem to smack of self-delusion and attempts to achieve the impossible.

5

Old Ideals in
a New Framework

The régime of the admirals had lasted twenty years. The ideals that permeated the thoughts and actions of the administrators during this period of naval control did not, in any sense, disappear with the change to a civilian governor in 1879. There was a change of pace, both in Cochinchina itself and in the home ministry, with the efforts to accelerate progress toward an institutional framework within the colony which more nearly approximated metropolitan models. But these institutional changes and innovations had easily recognizable antecedents in the preceding years. At times, the progression from past models was clear, a linear development in which new decisions taken under civil rule built immediately upon the developments of the preceding decades. The final substitution of the French penal code for the Vietnamese code falls within this category. On other occasions, the development of a totally new institution, such as an elected Colonial Council with Vietnamese participation, was the logical application of principles that had already been applied or discussed in relation to earlier institutions. The hope and belief that the Vietnamese population could be remade in the French image transcended the identity of the governor.[1]

Disagreement between Admiral Lafont (1877–1879) and the minister of the colonies over economic policies in Cochinchina was the immediate reason for the end of naval rule. Important changes in France in attitudes towards colonies in general was the underlying consideration.[2] In Le Myre de Vilers (1879–1883) the French government had chosen a firm believer in the "assimilationist" policies that now had strong support in the metropole. For him, the failure to ensure a strict separation of judicial and executive powers, the reliance on an alien legal system, and a general state of affairs in which language difficulties made it almost impossible to talk to Vietnamese were equally repugnant. His personal views were similar to the long and detailed instructions that he received from the minister, Jaurégiberry, at the time of his appointment. The essence of these lay in the opening paragraphs. Twenty years of naval rule had left the way open to change, he was told, and "The necessity for progressive assimilation thus takes precedence in all your thoughts and must inspire all your acts." [3]

Le Myre de Vilers was instructed to establish a Colonial Council with some Vietnamese membership, since their exclusion from the new body would have been incompatible with the general policy of assimilation. The new governor was encouraged to improve educational opportunities for Vietnamese and also to extend the arrangements that had permitted young Vietnamese to study in France. Commenting on these instructions many years later, Le Myre de Vilers argued that they stressed assimilation to an excessive degree and that, following his protests, the minister agreed that for a time existing Vietnamese institutions should be permitted to remain in existence. [4] The record of his governorship, however, shows little evidence of Fabian restraint. Whatever his early reservations, he initiated considerable change. Le Myre de Vilers' final word in the long debate over criminal justice, in 1881, reflected his over-all policy.

The problems of the judicial system in Cochinchina preoccupied the new governor. The need for change and for the acceptance of standards approximating those of France are themes that occur constantly in his dispatches. Shortly after he arrived in Cochinchina he set up a committee to consider the whole question of justice. He had been struck by the "insufficiencies" of the system and wished to make a thorough review of the question. [5] No Vietnamese sat on the committee, which was composed of members of the legal service and administrators of native affairs. The report adopted by the committee argued for the clear separation of powers and, thus, for the elimination of the existing system in which a member of the Native Affairs Service heard legal cases in the countryside. Justice, the report stated, should be rendered by a specially trained group of magistrates, qualified both in law and the Vietnamese language.[6]

The majority of the committee did not recommend changing the practice of judging by the Vietnamese code in penal matters. Reflecting some of the preoccupations that had dominated earlier discussions of law, the majority report tried to find parallels between its recommendations and Vietnamese practice. In place of the "native tribunals" operating within each of the colony's eighteen administrative divisions, it sought a more limited number of tribunals with jurisdiction over both Vietnamese and French. The president of such a court should be similar to the *tong-doc,* it was suggested. The proposed new tribunal of appeal in Saigon was regarded as the equivalent of the group of mandarins in Hue who traditionally reviewed sentences handed down by provincial mandarins. One member of the committee, Silvestre, an administrator of native affairs and an able student of Vietnamese custom, presented a separate report which stressed the need for gradual change in legal matters. A private lawyer, Blanscubé, dissented from the majority view by calling for the adoption of the French penal code in the colony.[7]

In the face of this divided counsel, Le Myre de Vilers expressed some reservations about the course he should follow. He questioned the wisdom of reducing the number of tribunals available to the Vietnamese population, as the majority of the committee had suggested, and he noted the need to treat Blanscubé's proposal with extreme prudence. But with this call for prudence, he reported that he had asked Silvestre and a member of the colony's legal staff to make a comparison of the French and Vietnamese penal codes. Moreover, his own estimation of the Vietnamese code left little doubt that he believed it inadequate: "[it] cannot be considered as the basis of justice in a country; it does not even have a table of contents. Our native judges, who are more or less without experience, judge on the basis of equity. They really cannot be content to use such a text." [8] So long as the code continued in use, it would have to be organized into a more rational form, and the articles that prescribed barbarous punishments would have to be eliminated. Even better, France in Cochinchina should follow the traditional practice of conquerors and apply its own law. This was a right that the "conquering people cannot avoid exercising." [9] It seemed, in short, that the principle was clear, but he had still not made up his mind about the timing of change.

In October 1879, Le Myre de Vilers put aside all hesitation and made his beliefs known to the minister of the colonies. He was convinced that the time had come to institute the French penal code. The continuing use of the Vietnamese code was

contrary to the basic principles of law and could [only] have been preserved if we possessed a code, a text of some sort, of the legislation which our administrators, judges of limited experience, are called upon to apply. But the Chinese code printed at our cost in characters is a closed book to our agents, and the translation by Philastre, which testifies to the extensive linguistic knowledge of its author, is no more than a compilation without order or method.

In these circumstances, it is necessary either to gather together the old texts, to classify them, reorganize them, and establish a new code, or to promulgate the French penal code, adapting it to the customs of our Asian subjects.[10]

The latter course, in his view, was the only one worth following. The governor felt that such a development would be welcomed by the Vietnamese population since they would have an organized code more lenient than their traditional legal system.

Four months afterwards, in March 1880, a decree promulgated Le Myre de Vilers' recommendations. The French penal code, with slight modifications, was applied to the population of Cochinchina.[11] The twenty-year struggle between those who sought to defend the traditional system and those who believed that duty demanded the use of the French penal code had been resolved. It had been of no avail for Luro and Philastre, and later for Silvestre, to argue in favor of tradition and the rights of the conquered people. They had not been able to point to Vietnamese within Cochinchina who were capable of assuming the role of judges, knowledgeable in their country's laws. From 1880 onwards the record of legal developments in Cochinchina is of changes in administrative policy rather than in principle. It is true that the institution of French civil law was never fully achieved, even in the twentieth century, but there is much evidence to show that less and less attention was paid to traditional Vietnamese practices by a magistrature, that, increasingly drawn from the French colonial service as a whole, knew little of the special conditions and customs of Viet-Nam.

The colonial records provide few clues to the reaction of the Vietnamese population to this fundamental change. Ironically, it is the French administration's staunch supporter, Tran-Ba-Loc, who indicates the difficulties of Vietnamese appearing before tribunals directed by European administrators. Le Myre de Vilers had asked Loc to comment on the administration of justice in Cochinchina. His reply, dated 17 December 1879, could not have influenced the governor's decision of late October, unless he had made earlier verbal comments. After expressing Loc's familiar reservations about the honesty of those village notables who arbitrated minor disputes within the commune, it passed on to the wider issues of justice. Loc called for the establishment, as a matter of urgency, of an appeals tribunal in Saigon. The clear implication was that judgments at a lower level were often made without a full knowledge of the facts. The presence of French judges, Loc noted, created various problems:

It frequently happens that individuals are disturbed when they are before the judges, and fear makes their words confused. . . . It often happens that people act as if they were gagged in the presence of their judge, and this explains the ease with which they [the French] are tricked.

It is because of these various considerations that the judge must act towards the accused as a parent questioning children in his home.[12]

The difficulties implied in Loc's account only increased as there was greater emphasis on French law administered by men with scant knowledge of Cochinchina.[13]

The application of French penal law in 1880 still left unresolved the vexing question of a separation of powers. Le Myre de Vilers dealt with this problem at length in a general report of 14 July 1880.[14] He criticized the officials of the Native Affairs Service. In theory, he noted, they were men of wide talents and considerable linguistic ability. In fact, they were only agents of the colony's executive and were totally ignorant of the rules and principles of the services that they administered. They rendered justice without knowledge of either French or Vietnamese law. Their impartiality in legal matters was severely undermined by the fact that a majority lived with Vietnamese concubines. In these circumstances, a true separation of powers was essential. The governor's arguments were persuasive, and by a decree of 25 May 1881 the French administrator working in the field was stripped of his judicial responsibilities.[15]

Le Myre de Vilers' judgments on the administrators may have been too harsh, but it is hard to cite any outstanding men to refute him. From the 1880's onwards, the French civil servants whose duties brought them into contact with the Vietnamese population are much less clearly delineated. There was a substantial increase in the number of officials as more and more posts within the administration, even at a lower level, were filled by Frenchmen. No figures such as Luro and Philastre emerge from the records. With the colony settled and the outer posts linked to Saigon by telegraph, the role of the central authority became paramount. Possibly most important for the Vietnamese population, still clinging to ideals from the past, the French administrator of the late nineteenth century could in no sense be compared with the scholar-mandarin of Vietnamese tradition.

During the next twenty years, many more changes were made in the judicial organization of Cochinchina. All, however, took place in the new framework, which assumed a separation of powers. The chief debate among the French officials in the colony was the size of each judicial officer's region. Under the system that had existed before the separation of powers, a form of justice was available in each administrative division. By 1881 this meant that each of the twenty-two *arrondissements* into which Cochinchina was divided for administrative purposes had its own tribunal. The decree of May 1881 provided only six tribunals for the interior of the colony, a dramatic reduction in the number of courts. So sudden was this reduction that, contrary to the whole spirit of the new law, recourse had to be made to the administrators once again. Limited judicial powers were restored to the administrators by decisions circulated in May 1882 and January 1883. Describing this development in 1895, an observer noted, with understatement, that such decisions ran counter to the 1881 decree and created tensions between the magistrates and the administrators.[16]

The new decisions were unwelcome to the Vietnamese. Although the rendering of justice by an officer of the Native Affairs Service may have been less than satisfactory, the presence of these officials throughout the colony provided a reasonable guarantee for Vietnamese of justice in civil actions and prompt decisions in criminal matters. Under the new organization delays in the administration of justice were inevitable; six tribunals could not handle the same number of cases as twenty-two.[17] Some Vietnamese in rural areas tried to settle their civil disputes either through the arbitration of a canton chief, a *tong*, or through one of the Vietnamese auxiliary officials in the French administration. This situation was most unsatisfactory to the colonial government, which had severe reservations about the honesty and capacity of its non-French employees.[18]

From 1885 onwards a number of measures were introduced to counter the complaints of both French and Vietnamese that justice had become less accessible and more expensive. One French provincial administrator provided a vivid picture of the confusion that now existed in the mind of a Vietnamese who wished to have a dispute settled legally. The Vietnamese no longer knew whom to contact. A complainant found he was required to deal with a *greffier* (the clerk of the court) or the *greffier's* interpreter. It was then necessary to pay for the tax stamp placed upon the written complaint. Every step was marked by slowness and delay. The magistrates rarely understood Vietnamese. The decree of 1881, which introduced the separation of powers, had provided also for recruitment to the Cochinchina Judicial Service from the French colonial magistrature as a whole. It was true that under Article 38 of the decree those holding judicial positions were supposed to have a knowledge of Vietnamese. But this was a provision honored in the breach. "With one exception, apart from three former administrators, no magistrate conforms to the provisions of Article 38." [19]

Such protests could not stem the tide. The only sure way to have met the charge of slower and more difficult application of justice would have been to revert, in some degree, to the old system, under which administrative and judicial powers were merged and recognized as complementary in Cochinchina's special situation. In place of this unacceptable alternative, the debate, with little Vietnamese participation, ranged over a variety of administrative solutions. The critics, both official and unofficial, of the existing system saw the appointment of a number of justices of the peace with extended powers as one way to meet the situation. These officials, lower in rank than magistrates but full-time government employees, in contrast to justices of the peace in British and American practice, would, it was argued, be more readily recruited and could hear cases throughout the colony. In theory, the critics had partly gained their point when, in 1886, a decree appointed seven justices of the peace and left six tribunals operating in the colony.[20] This provision was not implemented, and the critics argued for an even greater number of justices of the peace. The administrators of native affairs, according to the director of the interior, believed that there should be a justice of the peace in each *arrondissement*. In November 1887 a new decree replaced that of the year before, which had still not been put into operation. It reduced the number of tribunals in the colony, but it too was never implemented. A decree of June 1888 creating two tribunals and six justices of the peace had a brief life before a further decree, in June 1889, introduced some permanency into judicial arrangements. This decree provided for a tribunal in fourteen of the seventeen *arrondissements* into which Cochinchina was then divided. One tribunal was abolished in 1892, and the number was further reduced to ten in 1895.

These details have an interest beyond the sterile record of hesitation and change. With such uncertainty in the organization of justice, the Vietnamese population was at a severe disadvantage. For a brief period, under the decree of 1889, the ratio of those rendering justice to the Vietnamese population had been improved, but by 1895 the ratio had reverted to a point much the same as that of 1881.[21] At no time did the Vietnamese population, or its representatives, play an important part in the developments. The voices of the Vietnamese members of the Colonial Council were occasionally raised, seeking improvements. In this issue, as in discussion of education, the councillors do not seem to have been unaware of the concerns of their constituents. Decisions, however, took little account of their views. In concluding his long and highly informative report on developments up to 1895, Baudin, the colony's *procureur général,* summed up the general situation in Cochinchina. Contrary to the conditions laid down in decrees, many judicial officers did not speak Vietnamese. A lack of judicial officers who spoke the local language may not have been important in countries where the colonized peoples spoke French, but this was not so in Cochinchina; moreover, many civil cases continued to be decided on the basis of customary law:

> Here then is why, in the name of France and the authority of French justice, I ask that recruitment should take place in such a manner that we cease to give an able and intelligent people the lamentable spectacle of our ignorance! I would desire that the Annamites, who only respect the scholar, he who has developed his intelligence, need no longer ask themselves why although our interpreters speak French, although we insist that even our office messengers speak our language, they see that in general our magistrates do not know the language of the country.[22]

The legal evolution that took place in the eighties and nineties stopped short of full application of French law. As Baudin noted, many civil cases were decided, in theory, on the basis of customary law. The fact that the magistrature was without expertise in either

Vietnamese law or the Vietnamese language opened the way to suggestions that the French civil code be used. This did not happen, despite various efforts to modify the entire French civil code for use in Cochinchina. A committee, largely Vietnamese in composition, was established to consider the question in 1880.[23] It was not until 1883, however, that any important decisions were taken in this sphere. Although a draft code of civil law, drawing on Vietnamese custom, the Vietnamese code, and the French civil code, had been prepared, it was decided not to use it since such a change was judged too radical.

Instead, a decree of 3 October 1883 applied a limited number of articles from the French civil code concerning nationality to the population of Cochinchina, at the same time setting out a précis of the Vietnamese provisions on such basic legal questions as marriage, divorce, and paternity. These attempted, with some success, to follow established Vietnamese practice.[24] The précis was the product of a collaboration between the vice president of the court of appeal in Saigon, Lasserre, and a group of Vietnamese including Tran-Ba-Loc, Pétrus Ky, and Paulus Cua.[25]

Lasserre's proposals for a total change in the civil legislation of the colony were published a year later, in 1884. His comments on the problems of law in Cochinchina show the French legal mind at odds with the Vietnamese system and reflect a widespread attitude among officials in the legal branch of the administration:

The Annamite legislator, in fact, instead of posing general principles and drawing deductions from them as required, foresees the various possible hypothetical situations and regulates these in a manner which is almost exclusive. As a result, there are important gaps which embarrass the magistrate who must apply the law. It is unnecessary to insist on the inconvenience of such a system, which leaves the person receiving justice dependent on the discretion of the judge.[26]

As an enlightened Frenchman, Lasserre could not accept those aspects of the Vietnamese legal tradition that ran counter to civilized practice. Under Vietnamese law, sterility of the wife was grounds for divorce. Not only would the acceptance of such a provision lead to "wounding" discussions liable to damage public morality, but the allegation of sterility was, in any case, difficult to prove.[27] Lasserre's interest in the problems of civil law was considerable, and in the same year, 1884, he published a collection of civil law judgments in Cochinchina. The collection shows that when Vietnamese custom or law had a direct relevance to the matter before the courts, some efforts were made to follow it; if, on the other hand, there was no clear Vietnamese precedent, resort was quickly made to French practice and common sense.[28]

The decisions taken in Le Myre de Vilers' governorship completed the virtual exclusion of Vietnamese from participation in the administration of justice. Developments in later years built on the pattern that he laid down. His actions reflected his own strong beliefs in the necessity to introduce French methods. Nevertheless, by 1880 the situation in Cochinchina demanded action. The lack of either Vietnamese or French officials who could readily use the Vietnamese code left the field open to the innovators. Their actions, stressing French practice and placing Cochinchina within the ambit of the colonial legal service as a whole, ensured great change for the Vietnamese population. The perceptive lieutenant governor of Cochinchina, Rodier, speaking in 1905, listed the failings of the judicial officials among the factors that had disaffected the Vietnamese rural population. His familiar and justified criticism that the Frenchmen who administered justice in Cochinchina were generally unable to communicate with those who passed before their tribunals brought indignant protests from the magistrature and reprimand from the governor general of Indochina and the home ministry.[29] What mattered was not the discussion of problems but the preservation of prestige.

In the same way that French legal standards were regarded as appropriate for the colony, the establishment of a Colonial Council including Vietnamese members was a necessity in Cochinchina's progression toward the ultimate goal of assimilation. The instructions issued to Le Myre de Vilers observed that "a representative system limited to nationals or naturalized persons only, by excluding the natives from all participation in the business of government, would not reflect sufficiently the goal of assimilation which we have in view. . . ."[30] A mixed system was thus desirable, with a limited number of Vietnamese members of the Council elected on a restricted franchise. The debates in the Colonial Council between 1880 and about 1906 provide a picture of Vietnamese members who were, on the whole, fervent supporters of the *status quo* and of French cultural values. Their speeches catalogue the limited concerns of the Cochinchinese elite who had firmly linked their future with the French. The debates also provide revealing insights into the attitudes of French members of the colonial society. The gratuitous insults leveled at the most faithful supporters of the French explain some of the motivations behind the new, modernist nationalist movements that began to appear in the first two decades of the twentieth century.

The first civil governor of Cochinchina acted quickly upon his instructions to institute a Colonial Council, whose chief responsibility was control of the colony's budget. A decree of 8 February 1880, which laid down the rules governing the Council's constitution, was promulgated in Cochinchina on 5 May. Article 16 of this decree provided that the native members of the Council should be elected from six constituencies within the colony through an electoral system based on the existing communes. Each commune's council of notables sent a delegate to take part in the election of a representative.[31] The decree reflected confidence in the effectiveness of French educational efforts by stipulating that by 1886 the Vietnamese members of the Council had to be able to speak French. This provision was modified several times and still could not be applied strictly in the early years of the twentieth century. The fact that Vietnamese members continued to require interpreters remained a source of friction between the native councillors, as they were called, and the French membership.

The composition of the Council was set at six elected French members, six elected Vietnamese members, two members designated by the governor from his Private Council, and two members designated by the Saigon Chamber of Commerce. Le Myre de Vilers had considered the possibility of recommending equality of membership for French and Vietnamese but rejected the idea. Although noting that Vietnamese could be expected to obey "servilely" for a long time, he saw a necessity for ensuring the position of the French.[32] During the first decade of the Council's existence, the Vietnamese voters occasionally sent French representatives to the Council instead of their own compatriots.[33] Whether pressures were exerted to achieve this, or whether it reflected a readiness among those Vietnamese who had achieved positions of some local power or personal wealth to associate their destinies with the French, cannot be easily judged. There may have been French interference with the elective process. Discussion of French control of the *arrondissement* councils, which functioned from 1882, showed the manner in which French administrators asserted their will.[34]

In the early years, the Vietnamese members played an extremely reserved role, fully justifying Le Myre de Vilers' faith in their "servility." Much of the discussion took place without their comprehending what was being said. Excusing himself for presenting a proposal to the Council in writing, one member noted that he had done so because of "the difficulty which I experience in understanding all which is said and having to give my opinions or arrive at my opinions." [35] According to official observers, the situation had not greatly changed eight years later. The secretary general of the French administration in Cochinchina, reporting to Governor General Richaud (1888–1889) in 1888, argued that the presence of Vietnamese members in the Council was useless. The native councillors could not participate in discussion of issues brought before the Council and should be permitted a consultative vote only. Richaud agreed with this estimation, informing Paris that "the experience of these past years has demonstrated definitively that the Annamite councillors are incapable of playing a useful part in the discussions of the council." [36] The sharp change that Richaud advocated did not gain favor, and Vietnamese participation, with voting rights, continued.

The Vietnamese members normally voted as a bloc, and when a matter excited their interest, they demonstrated strong solidarity.

Such was the case during a special session convened in 1881 to consider the colony's opium and alcohol farms, when the four Vietnamese members expressed strong criticism of the existing system, which left the sale of opium in the hands of corrupt Chinese tax farmers. More important, the Vietnamese members deplored the spread of opium among the Vietnamese population as a social evil, which had been condemned in traditional Vietnamese practice.[37] Unity of purpose on such matters was ineffectual against the weighted composition of the Council, however. In this instance, moreover, the French majority was convinced of the necessity of maintaining the lucrative revenue from the sale of opium.

Over the years the Vietnamese membership of the Colonial Council displayed a consistent interest in two particular matters: education and the associated question of *quoc-ngu*, and the problems of cantonal and communal administration. The Vietnamese writers who applied to the Council for financial assistance in the publication of works written in *quoc-ngu* could always depend on a sympathetic reception from their countrymen.[38] Since some of the more prominent Vietnamese members of the Colonial Council were Catholics, this devotion to *quoc-ngu* was not surprising.[39] The association of other Vietnamese members with the colonial administration familiarized them with the romanized transcription. This was demonstrated in what is probably the first election pamphlet in *quoc-ngu,* prepared by a successful candidate, Tran-Tu-Luong, in the election of 1886:

I served the government for more than twenty-two years and reached the rank of *phu,* first class, and then I asked to retire. I am well acquainted with all matters, whatever is important to my countrymen. And I know how to speak and write French and Chinese. Now I wish to become a member of the Colonial Council so that I can do my best to protect and help Annamites in all matters which concern them. I have known and understood all this work during these many years and am capable in it.[40]

The Vietnamese members supported all the French administration's efforts to develop a program of public education in Cochinchina and praised the ultimate goal of widespread education in

French in terms little different from those of their European coun-
terparts on the Council. As for traditional education, they regarded
the use of Chinese characters as "dangerous" and "impolitic." [41]
The close links that some of the Vietnamese councillors had with
the Catholic Church led to their seeking special financial support
for the efforts of the missionaries. Tran-Ba-Tho, Loc's son, spoke of
the missionaries as the "first pioneers of Annamite civilization, who
have acted to raise up our people and teach them the French
language." [42]

The Vietnamese members frequently directed the attention of
the Council to the difficulties experienced by the villages in attract-
ing able men to serve on the councils of notables and to fill the
posts of canton chief and deputy canton chief. There was a complaint in 1893 that members of these councils were often called
upon to carry out government duties without receiving any exemption from government taxes or *corvées*. The Vietnamese councillors' request that such exemptions should be made was rejected.[43]

Four years later, the low wages paid by the colonial administration to the canton chiefs was a matter for complaint. Councillor
Tran-Ba-Tho observed that recruitment of qualified notables was
becoming more and more difficult, and that the demands made on
canton chiefs, almost always former village notables, discouraged
men of ability from assuming these posts.[44] In the same year Tho
pointed to the fact that village notables often had to travel considerable distances to testify in legal cases without any reimbursement
for their expenses.[45] The concern of the Vietnamese councillors for
the deteriorating situation in the communes suggests an awareness
of the problems faced by the rural population far beyond what
might have been expected from the *collaborateur* element. It
emphasizes the significant decay present in the communes' institutions at a time when the French administration was indifferent to
the problem.

Vietnamese members of the Colonial Council enjoyed certain
perquisites. Some were elected to the Council already substantial
landowners. This was true of Tran-Ba-Tho and Le-Phat-Dat. It is

probably correct to assume that other councillors were also men of some substance before their election, since they were the choice of the notables, traditionally the more prosperous members of the rural population. Even if this was so, membership on the Council led to the further acquisition of land through free concessions. The Council was responsible for approving land concessions to both Frenchmen and Vietnamese, and the names of Vietnamese councillors figure quite prominently among those who received grants.[46] Under a policy that favored giving educational opportunities to those who supported the French, it is not surprising that the children of Vietnamese members of the Council should have had little difficulty in gaining scholarships.[47]

If they enjoyed these marks of official favor, the Vietnamese councillors had also to endure considerable criticism from the elected French members, who on occasion acted with flagrant racial arrogance. In the early years, such behavior drew little response from the Vietnamese, who presumably only partly understood the comments levelled against them. Speaking in 1882, Councillor Vienot, an elected French member, decried the fact that the Vietnamese sitting in the Colonial Council could not participate in debates because of their inability to speak French. Vietnamese members, he proclaimed, should be chosen from those who had gained French nationality and could speak French. The tone of his remarks is well illustrated in the closing sentences of his speech: "We are in a conquered land where we only have a right to remain while keeping ourselves the masters of the population." [48] To this attack the Vietnamese members did respond, by letter. But the response was mild and did little more than explain that the Vietnamese members endeavored to keep abreast of events within the Council through the interpreters provided. Since they did not speak French, the Vietnamese councillors could not enjoy the benefit of naturalization.[49]

The difficulty of the Vietnamese members of the Council in following the debates in French remained a point of criticism over the years and was the basis of a particularly sharp exchange in 1903. On that occasion Councillor Paris, who had little sympathy for the Vietnamese, rehearsed the history of official decisions that had required that Vietnamese councillors should, after a certain delay, be required to speak in French and follow the proceedings of the Council in that language. It was the original intention that no translation would be allowed after 1886, but this had been extended to 1892. Now, in 1903, although the Vietnamese members of the Council had some competence in French, interpreters still translated the debates for them. An explanation was required. It was partly provided by the president of the Council, Cuniac, who noted that interpretation was necessary to ensure that the Vietnamese members did not miss the nuances of the matters under discussion. At this point Paris seemed vindicated when one of the Vietnamese present required an interpreter to learn what was under discussion. But final honors in the exchange seem to have gone to Councillor Diep, who ended the discussion by observing that interpretation was required since the Vietnamese councillors sometimes had difficulty in following long conversations in French. The problem, he noted, was a common one for French administrators trying to follow long conversations in Vietnamese.[50]

Tensions that had been apparent, but to some extent muted, in earlier years, were more obvious in the twentieth century. In 1905, as the result of bloc voting by the Vietnamese members of the Council and a split vote among the French members, Councillor Tran-Ba-Diep was elected vice president of the Colonial Council, an unprecedented event. Within four days he announced his resignation, "for reasons of personal convenience." Speaking on Tran-Ba-Diep's behalf, another Vietnamese councillor, Diep-Van-Cuong, denied that his compatriot had succumbed to pressure from the French members of the council.[51] In fact, he had. A French member had signified his intention to resign, and contemporary commentary leaves no doubt that Tran-Ba-Diep's decision was a gesture of reconciliation.[52]

The Vietnamese representatives in the Colonial Council in the early twentieth century accepted their inferior position, and while they protested against accusations levelled against them, the tone of their protests was one of regret rather than anger. They could still believe that French tutelage offered the Vietnamese of Cochin-china the best path to the rewards of education and the civilization of the West. The *contretemps* of 1905 was succeeded the next year by a fresh attack on the Vietnamese councillors. For a short period, the Vietnamese councillors were in the majority on the floor of the Council; and a French member deplored this. It was essential, he argued, that henceforth the Vietnamese representatives within the Council should be naturalized French citizens to ensure that the Vietnamese who represented their countrymen would be loyal to France.[53]

The response of the Vietnamese members, a few weeks after-wards, referred to how these words had "profoundly affected" them. They affirmed their loyalty to France. Tran-Ba-Diep spoke of the policy of association, a happy innovation "leading to the fu-sion of French and Annamite interests which will involve, of neces-sity, a communion of ideas between two peoples; and the solidarity which binds them will bring forth sympathetic feelings, necessary to the development of the country and to its defense."[54] This was the voice of Toynbee's "Herodians." Their commitment to France's role in Cochinchina was real. The most wounding slight that they could sustain was a questioning of their loyalty. In a special way, they showed that the civilizing mission had achieved partial success.

The call in the Colonial Council for Vietnamese members who were naturalized French citizens reflected the fact that French citi-zenship had been open to the Vietnamese population of Cochin-china since 1881. By any standards, this decision remains a remark-able one. But its unusual character—only twenty years after Cochinchina became a French colony—should not hide the fact that, while naturalization confirmed French policies of assimila-tion, it reflected other, more utilitarian motivations. Moreover, the number of Vietnamese who benefited from naturalization was ex-tremely limited in the period before the First World War.

When he proposed to the minister of the colonies that Vietnam-ese should be permitted to become French citizens, Le Myre de Vilers pointed to the increasing reliance that the French administration would have to place on its Vietnamese subjects. Since this was so, it seemed desirable that employees, particularly those who played a part in the colony's legal apparatus, should become French citizens. It would be dangerous to permit unworthy men to gain the benefit of this honor. All applicants, therefore, would be required to show their fitness by demonstrating that they could speak French and that they had "rallied to our domination":

I do not hide from myself the fact that the requests [for naturalization] will be rare at the beginning, but their number will increase little by little, given the character of the Annamite, which has defiance as its most particular characteristic. Once reassured, when they have recognized the advantages and the security that naturalization gives them, I am almost certain that they will hasten to claim it. We will have in this measure a powerful encouragement for the diffusion and teaching of French.[55]

The metropolitan authorities shared Le Myre de Vilers' views, and a decree providing for the naturalization of Vietnamese was promulgated in 1881. Applicants for this honor normally had to demonstrate their capacity in French, but this provision was waived in the case of Vietnamese who had been decorated with the Legion of Honor or the Military Medal and Medal of Honor.[56]

The number of Vietnamese who could qualify for French citizenship was small, and Le Myre de Vilers' prediction that the rate of application would be slow seemed correct. Familiar names appear among the earliest applicants. Do-Huu-Phuong, the reliable auxiliary based in Cholon, was one of the first to apply in 1881.[57] Tran-Ba-Tho entered his application in 1883.[58] On the basis of fragmentary records, however, it seems that a substantial proportion of the early applications came from less important figures, particularly from members of the local military forces recruited by the French. Records that note simply that application had been made on behalf of "native sharpshooters" provide little indication of the reasons that prompted their application or the extent to which success in their requests affected their position within Vietnamese society.[59] Comment in a newspaper that represented the interests of nonofficial French residents in Cochinchina questioned the whole concept of granting citizenship to Vietnamese. In a leading article, the *Indépendant de Saigon* of 28 October 1882 argued that the result of the decree on naturalization had been to give French citizenship to those least respected by their fellow countrymen: soldiers and those who worked within the French administration. One prominent supporter of the French position in Cochinchina, Pétrus Ky, did not believe that naturalization was necessary to demonstrate loyalty to France. His comments were invoked, in 1906, when the Vietnamese councillors were under attack for not having sought naturalization: "Remain Annamites since we are born Annamites; I do not see any utility in being naturalized." [60]

Even if a Vietnamese wished to avail himself of the provisions of the naturalization decree, a rigid bureaucracy stood in his way. The early correspondence on naturalization shows the unbending insistence of French officials that Vietnamese should adopt a "family name." The fact that the family name, in Vietnamese practice, precedes the given name caused considerable discussion.[61] Through the years up to 1905, the number of Vietnamese receiving French citizenship each year was very limited. In any one year, for instance, there might be no more than three applications.[62] The bulk of the applicants left no permanent mark on the history of Cochinchina. They were clerks in the administration, nursing orderlies in the military hospitals, telegraphists in the postal services. It seems an open question whether, in a number of these cases, the decision to seek citizenship was a personal one made by the applicant. In the letters of support that accompanied the applications and testified to the capacity of the Vietnamese in the French language one may sense some urging on the part of the sponsors.[63]

The 1906 census of Cochinchina showed 254 naturalized French citizens in the colony.[64] This figure includes all *naturalisés*. A number of Chinese made successful applications, as did the nationals of other European countries living in Saigon.

Discussion in the Colonial Council provides some interesting comments on the type of Vietnamese who applied for naturalization and indicates clearly that the Vietnamese members of the

Council did not regard the holding of French citizenship as an essential test of loyalty. Speaking on this issue in 1906, Councillor Phong denied the assertion of a French member, Dr. Flandrin, that the Vietnamese with citizenship formed the elite of the population. Phong also rejected Flandrin's suggestion that the Vietnamese membership of the Council should be drawn from the *naturalisés:*

To choose six persons from among 120 or 130 naturalized citizens to represent two million inhabitants is impossible and inadmissible, for the naturalized citizens are not at all the elite of the Annamite population as the doctor thinks. It is, indeed, quite to the contrary.[65]

Phong went on to note that when naturalization opportunities were first offered, many respectable Vietnamese families still feared persecution from the French. These did not seek naturalization, or send their children to French schools. Others, such as Pétrus Ky, did not see the value of naturalization. The bulk of those who sought and obtained naturalization in the early years had served in the armed forces or were the "rare pupils who were at school in France and in the *lycées* of Algeria." Later, many found their applications rejected for minor technical reasons. Given all these circumstances, it is not surprising that the number of Vietnamese who either had or sought French nationality was limited.

The issue of naturalization was not a major one in the period covered by this study. It could, and did, raise heated discussion, but to a considerable degree this was an example of Frenchmen seizing a readily available stick to beat the Vietnamese dog. Other issues were used for the same purpose. If criticism was to be made, the critic never had much difficulty in finding a basis for condemnation. Naturalization provides evidence of the consistency of French colonial theorizing in Cochinchina. It was a "proper" accompaniment to the other innovations that came with the change to civil rule. The inauguration of the French penal code and the participation of Vietnamese in the deliberative business of the colony implied the right, if only on a limited basis, of Vietnamese to become truly French. Among those who accepted the opportunity to become naturalized, some achieved an extraordinary meta-morphosis. But in the years under discussion it was not the test of allegiance to the French administration among the colonial elite of Cochinchina.

The institutional changes recounted were French implantations. They are of interest for their effect on Vietnamese society and, par-ticularly in the case of the Colonial Council, for the extent to which they reflect Vietnamese reactions to the changing situation. The final substitution of the French penal code during Le Myre de Vilers' governorship was of profound importance in contributing to the abolition of the remnants of the old Vietnamese administrative pattern. In contrast to the other changes in the last two decades of the nineteenth century, these developments seem strangely lacking in positive Vietnamese participation. This participation was found in the encouragement of *quoc-ngu* and the advancement of public education. It was present in the life of the small and closely knit group of Vietnamese whom the French regarded as the elite of Cochinchina, and who held much the same estimation themselves. Moreover, in the slow decline of the traditionally stable Vietnam-ese commune, French actions were, at least, directly matched by Vietnamese reactions. Finally, Vietnamese participation was the essence of the slow growth of modern nationalism which stirred in the early years of the twentieth century. Consideration of these themes forms the basis of the next three chapters.

6

The Old Colony—The Heyday of Collaboration

> There are many nice cafes,
> Officials on leave go to the de la Paix.
> One meets the mandarin Do-Huu-Phuong,
> And Bonnet is seated there chatting.
> You will often see Monsieur Blanchy there,
> While Morin, too, finds a reason to come.
>
> .   .   .   .   .
>
> One wanders about and meets old friends,
> For people on leave go there to relax.[1]

The Vietnamese rhymes of this poem are lost in translation, but the sense of old Cochinchina hands gathering at the famous Paris restaurant survives. Most were French, but the author of the poem, Truong-Minh-Ky, found no problem in associating Phuong with them. Presumably Truong-Minh-Ky also joined those he describes in reminiscing about the warmth and pleasures of Cochinchina in contrast to the cold grey skies of Paris. The scene illustrates important aspects of Cochinchina's history in the late nineteenth century. It was becoming fashionable to refer to the region as the old colony,[2] in contrast to the new French possessions in Tonkin and Annam. At the same time, the phrase suggested the colony's stability, reflected in a colonial society with a real degree of association and friendship between a small but important group of Frenchmen and Vietnamese. They may not have met together in cafes in Saigon, as they did in Paris, but there is considerable evidence of harmonious social contacts between French and those Vietnamese who had long identified their interests with France.[3]

By the turn of the century France had controlled Cochinchina

for forty years. As the oldest component part of the French Indochinese Union, its separate identity was clearly established. Indeed, with the governor general of Indochina living for part of the
year in Hanoi, Paul Doumer felt that the lieutenant governor of
Cochinchina, and the Cochinchinese administration as a whole,
had altogether too much freedom. Programs to inculcate the use of
French and *quoc-ngu* had ensured that Chinese characters would
no longer form an important part of Vietnamese life. Great economic changes were in view, which, during the twentieth century,
opened vast areas of Cochinchina to agricultural development and
brought the social evil of absentee landlordism. The decay of the
traditional administrative structure of the commune was another
index of change. After decades of acknowledging that their presence was altering this basic administrative unit, the French administrators were finally forced to involve themselves in a full-scale
effort to give some permanency to institutions within the commune.

The age of the colony permitted the euphoric meetings that Paul
Doumer records between Tran-Ba-Loc and himself, but it also
bred the new nationalist spirit, which looked beyond mere blind
resistence to the development of movements that linked theory and
principle with action. Surface stability was an apparent feature of
Cochinchina for long periods of France's rule in the twentieth century, but the last two decades of the nineteenth century seem particularly serene. In part this was the calm after the storms of the
conquest period. In part it was the special quality of a colony in
which the excesses of a rigid colonial society still did not exist.
Nowhere was this more apparent than in the relations between
members of the French administration and that group of Vietnamese who had been the earliest to join their fates with those of the
invaders. This period was, in many ways, the heyday of collaboration.

Many of the insights that illuminate the special position of the
Vietnamese who were closely associated with the French in
Cochinchina come from isolated vignettes rather than lengthy his-
torical episodes. Much is revealed by a brief letter from Tran-Ba-
Loc to the director of the interior, written in 1887, in which Loc

recommended a minor French employee working in Cai-Be for promotion.[4] Whether this recommendation helped the employee is not revealed in the archives. It is, however, clear that Loc believed that his role in the colonial society of Cochinchina included recommending the advancement of French employees of the colonial administration. Indeed, he had been approached time and again by the administration to give his opinion on matters ranging from law to taxation, from education to the administration of the commune.

The same sudden insight emerges from an account of the funeral of Le-Phat-Dat, considered the wealthiest Vietnamese of his day. The ceremony was attended by senior members of the French administration as well as by a crowd of Vietnamese, which included the president of the Association of Former Students of the Institut Taberd and the Collège d'Adran, former Colonial Councillor Duom.[5] The close links between the Catholic Church and the Vietnamese elite in colonial society are emphasized here. Both Dat and Duom were Catholics, and both had been members of the Colonial Council. Frenchmen attended Dat's funeral because he had been one of those Vietnamese with whom the French had found it possible to establish a relationship. He had testified to his Catholicism through gifts to Catholic institutions and to his belief in the value of close links with France by gaining French citizenship. At the time of his death in 1900, three of his eight children had already gained naturalization.

A further illustration of the close contacts between the members of this colonial elite occurs in an introductory section that precedes the poem *Chu Quac Thai Hoi* (The International Exposition), part of which was quoted at the beginning of this chapter. Seven of Truong-Minh-Ky's compatriots wrote short poems of praise for his longer poetic account of a journey to France. There are familiar names among those who contributed: Pétrus Ky, Paulus Cua, and Tran-Ba-Tho.[6] But, significantly, praise for Truong-Minh-Ky's poetry came too from members of the French community. Landes was one of those who read and praised his accounts of visits to France in 1880 and 1889.[7]

The elite was not large. It fulfilled those definitions of an elite group that insist on the awareness by the members of the group of their own special position. The Vietnamese who were prominent in the colonial society by the turn of the century were largely Catholic. New figures may be discerned in the first decade of the twentieth century who appear to represent a departure from the norms of the early *collaborateurs*. Conscious of their own position, the elite intermarried, ensured that their children would benefit from association with the French, and maintained their own links with senior members of the French administration. Truong-Vinh-Ky, Tran-Ba-Loc, and Do-Huu-Phuong, more than any other Vietnamese of their period, moved with ease and confidence through a life that was half Vietnamese and half French. A review of their lives in the eighties and nineties distills much of the essence of a relationship between the French and the Vietnamese in Cochinchina which, if it always assumed French control, was not viewed by this elite as involving subjugation.

Pétrus Ky's most important appointment came in the eighties. He had accomplished his mission to Tonkin in 1876 with credit. His life in Saigon was devoted to teaching, the preparation of manuscripts for publication, and his correspondence with some of the most prominent scholars in France. The great lexicographer Littré was among Ky's correspondents. The appointment of Paul Bert as French resident general in Annam and Tonkin brought Ky a role in France's efforts in Viet-Nam greater than any he had undertaken before. On Bert's urging, Ky became an observer within the *Co-Mat,* the secret council of the court of Hue. This was in 1886, following the French *coup de force* of July 1885, which had led to the retreat from Hue of the young king, Ham-Nghi, and many of the senior court mandarins. In Ham-Nghi's place, the French had placed their own nominee, Dong-Khanh. Confusion and fear within the court left the way open for substantial French interference, as Bert readily recognized.

There are gaps in the history of Ky's short but important association with the Vietnamese court. Sufficient information is available to show that Bert believed that Ky could achieve great things for France.[8] Bert had come to Viet-Nam after a distinguished career, first as a biologist and then as a parliamentarian. He believed he could further French interests by gaining the sympathy of the Vietnamese court, and in particular of the young king, Dong-Khanh. Bert's aims coincided with Ky's desire to visit Hue to consult materials in the royal archives. During an initial visit, beginning in April 1886, Ky provided Bert with information on the political atmosphere of the Hue court. Subsequently, beginning in June of the same year, Ky undertook to ensure that those who determined the policy of the court were men sympathetic to France. Bert also intended that Ky should teach French to the young king.

Ky's efforts did not last long. In September 1886 he returned to Saigon suffering from the ill health that persisted until the end of his life.[9] Paul Bert's sudden death in November 1886 removed the sponsor who had appointed Ky to a position that, in the eyes of some French officials, was too important for a Vietnamese teacher of languages.[10] Ky had not achieved any great success in the task that he had been set. In view of the short time available, this is hardly surprising. The remarkable aspect of the whole affair is Bert's selection of Ky for a role of such importance. Bert's letters to Ky and to the administration in Cochinchina show his high opinion of the scholarly Vietnamese: "Since his arrival in Hue, Monsieur T. V. K. has gained an authority within the court which enables him to render great services to the French cause." [11] The warmth of Ky's letters to Bert shows that he appreciated the honor of the appointment. The sniping of a few critics in Cochinchina mattered little when he had been closely linked with one of the best-known Frenchmen of the age.

The final years of Ky's life passed with virtually no involvement in public affairs. He continued to work on translations of Vietnamese literature from Chinese characters into *quoc-ngu,* but ill health restricted his output. Members of his large family entered the French administration and at the time of Ky's death, in 1898, one son was a *huyen* and another worked within the government secretariat. His youngest son, Tong, became secretary to the governor's private council in later years.[12] Ky's long association with the French did not bring him great wealth. Seven years after

III. Do-Huu-Phuong in the early 1880's. His obituary, prepared in 1915, noted that "From an early date he assimilated our tastes and customs" (from C. Lemire, *L'Indo-Chine*, Paris, 1884).

his death, the Colonial Council agreed to pay a special pension to his widow in view of the long service that her late husband had given to the administration.[13] Ky gave the best description of the task that he had set for himself and which, by his own standards, he partly achieved. Describing his writings, in 1882, he noted: "I have never deviated from the principal and direct goal that I proposed to myself. . . . This goal is the transformation and the assimilation of the Annamite people." [14]

Despite his association with political affairs in 1876 and 1886, Ky will be best remembered for his contribution to literature and the advancement of *quoc-ngu*. His true *métier* was that of the scholar. Tran-Ba-Loc provides the direct contrast. He was an activist, best known in his own lifetime for the zeal with which he pursued the enemies of French colonial expansion. The limited written records that Loc left emphasize his authoritarian character. This character certainly emerges in the long report that he prepared in 1869, and it is evident, too, in the comments on Vietnamese society in his letter to Le Myre de Vilers in 1879. Loc believed that the government should instruct the population in virtue and morality. He was not worried about the Christian element of the population, but he was disturbed that the others, left without moral instruction through Chinese characters, might be lacking in moral rectitude.[15]

Loc's last great feat of arms took place outside his native Cochinchina. In suppressing a section of the Scholars' Revolt, in 1886, he achieved his most notable military success. Faced with disorder in central Viet-Nam, the French unleashed Loc at the head of a small army raised in Cochinchina against those who resisted French attempts to control the court of Hue. Even his admirer and biographer, Dürrwell, notes that Loc exercised fierce and merciless repressions. Dürrwell excuses such punitive measures with the observation that violence must be met with violence.[16] It was for his success in this operation that Loc received the honorary title of *tong-doc* of Thuan-Khanh, the region that he pacified.

For the rest of Loc's life his chief preoccupations were with the region about My-Tho. He helped develop the great drainage system that opened up much of the Plain of Reeds to agricultural production. His own landholdings increased; Governor General Paul Doumer described Loc as one of the richest Vietnamese in Cochin-china in the closing years of his life.[17] Doumer pressed honors upon Loc. He accorded him a place within the Superior Council of Indochina, a body concerned with issues affecting all territories under French control in the region, and made him a member of the suite that accompanied Doumer when he made an official visit to Bangkok in 1899. There is every reason to accept Doumer's as-sertion that Loc reacted with gratitude and pleasure to these marks of favor. The governor general's account of his final visit to Loc's home, when Loc was close to death, is couched in melodramatic terms, but it expresses the warmth of feeling that could exist be-tween members of the French and Vietnamese communities in Cochinchina at this time.[18] Tran-Ba-Loc, just as was the case with Pétrus Ky, summarized his own devotion to French rule in Cochinchina, years before he died: "If I have served France to this day, it has been so as to be able to cover the object of my affections with the shadow of my influence." [19]

Loc had only one son, Tran-Ba-Tho, a member, for a period, of the Colonial Council. As Loc's son, it is not surprising that Tho should have received some education in France and worked for the administration.[20] In discussions within the Colonial Council, Tho showed a forceful personality, which may account for Doumer's later observation that Tho had not always been regarded in a kindly fashion by the French community. As heir to his father's wealth, Tho devoted his energies to managing the properties ac-cumulated during Loc's lifetime. In confirmation of the cohesion of this small elite community, one of Tho's daughters married Truong-Vinh-Ky's youngest son, Truong-Vinh-Tong.[21]

Pétrus Ky was familiar to scholars in both Cochinchina and France; Loc bent his sword to France's will. Both felt honored to serve a new administration that, in their view, had brought a new and better life to Cochinchina. Yet neither achieved the breadth of fame in his own lifetime which attached to Do-Huu-Phuong, the *phu* of Cholon. Part of this renown stemmed from Phuong's urbane character. His hospitality was a byword among those who visited Saigon; one traveller, writing in the nineties, observed:

When one visits Cholen [*sic*], one must not miss a visit to the rich and well-known Phu of the city. . . . The Phu received us in a marvellous fashion. He is an Annamite of some fifty years of age . . . he always wears European clothes and he has not hesitated to give his sons a French education. . . . His home is a curious mixture of Europe and Asia.[22]

Phuong's reputation had in no sense diminished in 1912 when another French writer, in describing the attractions of Cochinchina, stressed the pleasures of Phuong's table.[23]

Do-Huu-Phuong eagerly adopted French habits of behavior, but he went further. He visited France no less than four times.[24] Truong-Minh-Ky's picture of Phuong enjoying the pleasures of the Café de la Paix is not the only account of his taste for this fashionable rendezvous. His affection for the cafe was well enough known to be noted also by Paul Doumer.[25] His first visit to France was in 1878. He went again in 1884, 1889, and 1894. When the opportunity to adopt French citizenship was opened to the Vietnamese population of Cochinchina, Phuong was among the first to apply for and benefit from this distinction. In the final two decades of the nineteenth century he was more concerned with the maintenance of good order in Cholon than with the manhunts and repressions that marked his early years of employment with the French. After his retirement in 1899, he spent much of his time in charitable work, his particular interest being to establish a school for girls in Saigon.

The French administration rewarded Phuong's devotion with marks of honor. He was made a *chevalier* of the Legion of Honor as early as 1873 and promoted to officer within the order in 1884, commander in 1891. After his retirement he became a member of the Superior Council of Indochina, an honor he shared with Loc. No personal honor, however, was probably as important as his sons' success in the French armed forces. Phuong's trips to France were, in part, to observe his sons' progress as they studied in France. At the time of his death in 1915, one of his sons was a lieutenant colonel in the French army and another was a lieutenant in the French air force. Two other sons were serving in the French administration in Cochinchina.[26]

Phuong's genuine affection for the Frenchmen with whom he worked and the apparent ease with which he and his male children moved in French circles stand out in the record of his life. His daughters, by contrast, were brought up in a more traditional fashion, but they still mixed with the French community in Saigon.[27] Given Phuong's urbanity and devotion to France, it is not surprising to find that he was elected a vice president of the Society for Indochinese Studies when that body was constituted in 1883.[28] If there are hints that Pétrus Ky at times excited the resentment of members of the official community, no such shadow ever seems to have hung over Phuong's dealings with his colonial masters. Only in an enigmatic poem written in 1897 is there any hint that Phuong felt some Vietnamese questioned his role.[29] This is one of the rare instances in which Phuong's personality is revealed through his own writing. Otherwise, his urbanity and success seem matched by the blandness and lack of particularity in his character. Perhaps this was the secret of his happy relations with the French in Cochinchina. Once his decision to adhere to the colonial administration was made, he had no second thoughts. He served his new masters as a soldier, as an administrator, and possibly even as a procurer. In return they honored him and advanced his sons.

Phuong, Loc, and Ky all made their decision to work with the French administration at the beginning of the colonial period. So did other important Vietnamese figures whose activities or personalities are not as clearly documented. Huynh-Tinh-Cua worked for the diffusion of *quoc-ngu* from the sixties into the nineties. By comparison with Ky, we know little of him. Trusty Vietnamese fighters on the French behalf such as Ca and Tan left little record behind them. By the eighties, however, there were Vietnamese in Cochinchina who had grown up in a colony under French control and then entered the French service, some clearly associated with the elite group. The background of these men was more diversified than that of the early *collaborateurs*, who so frequently combined mission training and Catholicism with their employment in the new administration.

Truong-Minh-Ky (no relative of Truong-Vinh-Ky) was the

great-nephew of the Vietnamese general who had ruled over Cambodia in the 1830's, Truong-Minh-Giang. Although he was educated in Catholic institutions, Truong-Minh-Ky never became a convert. His writings in *quoc-ngu,* nevertheless, betray a strong Christian influence. Among his longer works was a dramatic piece, "Joseph." [30] In the nineteenth century, Truong-Minh-Ky probably ranks third, after Pétrus Ky and Paulus Cua, as an author of works to spread the use of *quoc-ngu.* His long narrative poems describing the two visits that he made to France reveal him absorbing the new sights with delight. All the famous tourist attractions were enumerated: the Etoile, Chartres, the Place Vendôme, even the Bourse:

> The Bourse is where men meet to trade
> They deal in goods and money here.
> Shares of money and loans too
> Some men sell and others buy.
> When they meet they bring goods in this way.
> They fix a price, the goods change hands another day.[31]

Le-Van-Phat was another Vietnamese whose notable ancestry did not prevent close association with the French. His grandfather had been a mandarin at the court of Hue and held office at the time the French attacked Viet-Nam.[32] Phat's contributions to the *Bulletin de la Société des Etudes Indochinoises* were marked by his concern to make more of Vietnamese life comprehensible to the French. As a member of the Society, and of the Alliance Française, he was sufficiently confident of his position within the colonial elite to observe that the bulk of Frenchmen in Cochinchina still knew little of the country in which they lived:

The few native women who have a knowledge of French and the good fortune to contract an alliance with Frenchmen are generally Catholics or former pensioners from convents. Knowing nothing of what goes on in the homes of their non-Catholic fellows, how can they usefully inform their European husbands or lovers? [33]

The Society for Indochinese Studies was a gathering place for those Frenchmen with a deep interest in Cochinchina and for Viet-

namese whose wealth or senior position among the Vietnamese
employed by the French administration brought them into frequent contact with the European element of colonial society. Of
the 260 ordinary members of the society in 1908, thirty-three were
Vietnamese. These included former Colonial Council members,
Tran-Ba-Tho among them, senior Vietnamese officials, and teachers.[34] Pétrus Ky and Paulus Cua belonged to the society in their
lifetimes.

One of the Vietnamese members recorded on the 1908 membership list of the society was Bui-Quang-Chieu, who later founded
the Constitutionalist Party in Cochinchina. He was the product of
a traditionalist background, but the fact that his forebears had held
mandarinal posts and fought against the French in the conquest
period did not prevent his seeking and winning scholarships provided by the French administration. He studied first in Algeria and
then in France, where he graduated as an agricultural engineer in
1897.[35] Born in 1872, Chieu and others whose families initially opposed the French assumption of power in Cochinchina accepted
French education as the one real alternative open to them and became respected members of the educated Vietnamese community.

For each person on whom some comment may be made, there is
another about whom there is only the barest information. Some in
this latter category were renowned in their own day for the easy
relations that they enjoyed with the French. Le-Phat-Dat was one
of these: the richest man in Cochinchina, it was said, and an associate of the French, but little more is known of him. The records of
the Colonial Council during the time he was a member give no
sense of his personality. The obituary notice of another Vietnamese
of great wealth, Huynh-Cong-Mieng, leaves many unanswered
questions. The son of the Vietnamese general Huynh-Cong-Tau, he
died in 1899, leaving a large fortune and the reputation for close
contacts with the French community.[36]

The identifiable figures in this era of general good feeling between the small Vietnamese elite and the French community in
Cochinchina were *collaborateurs* in the technical and not the opprobrious sense of the word. They worked with and contributed to

the French administration. To suggest that they were other than convinced of the value of France's presence in Cochinchina is to distort the facts. Dürrwell's admiration for Loc and Doumer's for the same man; Ky's friendship with Paul Bert; Landes' following the *quoc-ngu* publications of Truong-Minh-Ky with real interest; all these were mutually acceptable relationships. By the standards of a later period, these relationships may have been marked by inequality, but it seems false to attribute a perception of this to the Vietnamese of the late nineteenth century. Indeed, how much inequality was there when one of Do-Huu-Phuong's sons was a colonel in the French army and married to a Frenchwoman? Self-interest certainly played a part in some of these relationships. This, however, is scarcely a motive confined to colonial situations.

Most of the early *collaborateurs* died before the end of the first decade of the twentieth century. In some cases their descendants gained wealth and status by remaining firm supporters of the French position in Cochinchina. In general, however, those who had linked their lives with the French administration as its employees were not the Vietnamese who rose to financial prominence. Tran-Ba-Loc, Do-Huu-Phuong, and Le-Phat-Dat were exceptions. Their land interests assured their families financial prosperity in subsequent years. But this was not the case for either Truong-Vinh-Ky or Truong-Minh-Ky. The men of wealth during the twentieth century in Cochinchina were the descendants, in the main, of figures who were historically anonymous in the nineteenth century. They took advantage of liberal land concessions, bought up concessions unused by French speculators, and became wealthy absentee landlords. For these men, in contrast to the *collaborateurs* described in this chapter, the achievement of wealth was all important. The *collaborateurs* of the first fifty years of the French presence in Cochinchina may be unattractive figures for those whose attitudes have been shaped by modern Vietnamese nationalism. But it is only just to recognize their sincere belief in the value of French colonialism and the value of their loyalty to it.

7

The Old Colony—
The Countryside

Rapid increase in the settlement of untilled lands in Cochinchina was one of the two principal themes in the history of the rural areas during the last two decades of the nineteenth century. The other was the decay of the commune's administrative structure. These themes represent the rural equivalent of the changes that marked the development of the "old colony" in and about Saigon. Just as thirty years of French rule had provided the setting in which the *collaborateur* element flourished, the same lapse of time led to major change outside the capital. Change in the rural regions may be less well documented, but it was no less fundamental.

In considering the expansion of land settlement, the background of land grant recipients is generally unknown. The Vietnamese members of the Colonial Council were prominent among those receiving land concessions, but they were only a fraction of the overall total. To a great extent, the history of expanded land use in Cochinchina, from the 1880's to the early years of the twentieth century, must be recounted in statistics rather than personalities. These statistics provide a picture of sudden and dramatic increase in land exploitation. The growth of individual fortunes was accompanied by the slow but important evolution of a rural proletariat. Various factors accounted for this latter development, and the opportunities for more prosperous individuals to gain large-scale holdings must be counted one of them.

The majority of those who acquired large land concessions were Frenchmen. French colonial philosophy held that true colonization required the permanent settlement of Frenchmen in part of "Overseas France." There was land speculation and the acquisition of land by corporate groups, but many individuals hoped to emulate the French *colons* in northern Africa. Moreover, the regulations dealing with land grants favored Frenchmen.[1] This did not, however, prevent Vietnamese acquiring land, sometimes in substantial parcels,[2] and although Frenchmen played a particularly important part in the massive drainage required to bring the water-sodden delta into production, Vietnamese were also active in this endeavor.[3]

The statistics for land concessions, rice exports, and areas under rice production provide indices of the great changes in Cochinchina. In 1880, two hundred hectares of land were granted by free concession. From 1890 onwards, the annual figures for land concessions never dropped below 10,000 and at times exceeded 30,000 hectares. In 1904, more than 100,000 hectares were alienated in free concessions.[4] Many of these concessions were not exploited,[5] and this gave an opportunity to wealthy Vietnamese to increase their holdings beyond what they could acquire by grants. Nevertheless, despite some failure to exploit concessions, the growth in rice exports from Cochinchina and of land actually under rice production was very large. In 1881, just over four million piculs of rice were exported, and the area under rice cultivation was calculated to be little more than 600,000 hectares. By 1894, nine million piculs were exported and more than a million hectares cultivated.[6] Much rice land was not part of the concession area; nevertheless, the concession system was a major spur towards increased production.

In promoting land development in Cochinchina, the French followed a traditional Vietnamese policy for the south but on a vastly different scale. As a frontier land, the south of Viet-Nam had received an influx of Vietnamese colonists, who slowly but effectively dispossessed the Cambodian population of sole use of the land. The Catholic Church in Cochinchina noted the continuing appeal of the western lands as an obstacle to conversion.[7] Some of those who turned towards the promise of land in the west were undoubtedly part of the rural proletariat, which had been noted by some

French observers as early as the eighties. The existence of such a group had certainly been reported to Paris by the colonial administration as early as 1881. The home authorities saw it as "an inevitable consequence of the development of civilization." [8] One reason for the increase of this migratory rural proletariat was the French decisions that altered the structure and character of the Vietnamese commune.

The respect of Luro and Philastre for Vietnamese tradition colored their estimations of the past with a romantic aura. Faced with evidence of change and the obvious failure of many French policies to pose viable alternatives to Vietnamese practice, they idealized what used to be. The traditional administration of the commune, explained in detail in Luro's great administrative course, was in his eyes "old," "good," and "suited the people." "What interest," Luro asked, "is there for us to change it?" [9] The collective aspect of the commune appealed to a number of French observers. They approved the commune's corporate responsibility for tax obligations, with its own assessments of the amounts to be paid by the registered members of the commune and provision for the survival of the nonregistered members. Luro's views to the contrary, the lot of the poorer members of the commune was often far from satisfactory. The Vietnamese population's constant southward movement over the centuries reveals a dispossessed substratum of society that could not benefit in existing communes.

The collective commune, with only the registered members paying tax, was the traditional Vietnamese arrangement. Initially, the French administration was content to leave the system largely intact. The commune remained responsible for the supply of tax revenues and for the division of the population into registered and nonregistered members. Changes of detail had, nevertheless, brought significant alteration by 1880. The difficult position of the mayor has already been outlined. Le Myre de Vilers' close scrutiny of the commune's structure revealed that French tax demands weighed increasingly on the landless class at a time when the landowners were becoming more prosperous. Tran-Ba-Loc's critical view of the village notables may have been given too much weight,[10] but there seems reason to accept the governor's general estimation that the former notables of the commune, having abandoned their positions to the poorer members of the commune, now devoted themselves to furthering their personal fortunes.[11]

To ensure greater equity in the raising of taxes, Le Myre de Vilers instituted on 15 November 1880 a regulation that classified all male members of the population between eighteen and sixty years as registered citizens and at the same time substantially lowered the rate of personal tax. To secure the colony's revenue in the wake of this measure, an effort was made to arrive at a more accurate assessment of landholdings. It was widely recognized that the declarations made each year by the communes, upon which land taxes were based, greatly underestimated the amount of land under cultivation.[12]

The changes in taxation procedure instituted by Le Myre de Vilers, and subsequent changes by other administrations, were a complete departure from Vietnamese practice. For the French colonial administration, the responsibility of the individual was a fundamental part of modern government. The collective instinct of the Vietnamese communes and their members may have had a basis in Vietnamese history, but it had none in the French system. Taxation of the Vietnamese population of Cochinchina was a chronic problem that persisted well beyond the period treated in this study. It fostered resentment both of the system and of the officials responsible for administering it. French efforts to raise tax revenue at the expense of traditional methods was one of the underlying grievances of the rural population that led to sporadic outbreaks of rural violence.[13]

Though he changed the taxation structure of the colony, Le Myre de Vilers doubted the desirability of altering the existing administration of the commune, although he was convinced that the notables were corrupt.[14] Ironically his new taxation measures further diminished the attraction of serving on the council of notables for the class of Vietnamese that had formerly furnished its members. Luro had warned his students at the Collège des Stagiaires to avoid changing the administration of the commune, but change was well under way at the time he made this admonition. When Landes, one of the most scholarly of the second generation of French administrators in Cochinchina, wrote on the commune in 1880, he observed that the changes that had already taken place as the result of French interference were so substantial that an exact account of the existing administration of the commune was extremely difficult. Old names and forms still survived, but they had been greatly altered in fact.[15]

Landes' comments show a degree of pessimism. This was not the mood of the French administration when it reviewed the situation of the communes in 1887. A report prepared by the Director of the Interior and endorsed by Governor Filippini noted important changes in the commune but considered that these had affected neither "its strength nor its vitality." [16] Later developments showed the hollowness of this judgment. The optimistic tone of the long report is made more curious by the fact that it details the elements of government interference that led to ever-increasing difficulties in recruiting notables. The mayor, because of his duties to the commune and to the French administration, had to be approved both by his fellow notables and by the local French administrator. His duties were legion. He was responsible for promulgating and executing government decisions and had the responsibility for general order and for supervising the local police. Along with the *huong-than,* the *huong-hao,* and the *thu-bo,* three other notables, he had to authenticate all documents drawn up by individuals living within the commune. A decision of 28 December 1882 left the mayor in charge of administering matters connected with the government opium and alcohol monopolies. In association with other notables, but particularly with the *huong-than* and *huong-hao,* the mayor had become a full-time agent of the French administration, exempt from taxation because of his duties, but unpaid and constantly subject to a conflict of interests between his responsibilities to the commune and to the French. A frequent grievance of later years was the time the mayor had to spend travelling between his commune and the local French administrator's office.

The 1887 report candidly admitted the considerable gaps in

French knowledge of the commune's organization. It noted that there was no complete uniformity from one commune to another in the tasks assigned to notables bearing the same title. In general, for instance, the notable known as the *huong-ca* acted on behalf of the commune in disputes with the central administration. But this was not always the case. The communal budget, the source of its funds, and its administration were known to the French in only the broadest terms. The important related question of venality among the notables caused some disagreement. It was customary, the 1887 report observed, to assume that the village notables were corrupt and furthering their personal fortunes at the expense of their fellow villagers. This, it may be observed, was the picture consistently put to the administration by Tran-Ba-Loc. Governor Filippini and his Director of the Interior had little doubt that this was so. They rightly observed, however, that if the opportunities for personal enrichment were so great, it should have been much easier than it was to find men to fill the positions. Indeed, despite the confident assertion of the report that the commune had lost none of its vigor, concern was expressed that continuing difficulty in recruiting notables could face the colony with added expense. The beauty of the communal system, in French eyes, was that it provided a means of administering the rural regions at a minimum cost to the colony. The collapse of the traditional communal administration could only lead to higher costs.

In the view of this long report, seven years of civil rule had introduced many desirable reforms in the Vietnamese commune. Filippini approved the change from collective taxing to a procedure based on individual contributions, the improved methods of land assessment, and the extension of French justice. Just as important, the use of *quoc-ngu* had "passed into the mores" of the people. The excessive optimism of this final observation was qualified by the report's own admission that there was a certain inconvenience in the use of *quoc-ngu*, since the bulk of the adult population did not read the romanized transcription of their language; it was still necessary to circulate government decisions and announcements in Chinese characters as well as *quoc-ngu*.

Filippini's report strongly favored retaining the communal system of administration because of the financial savings to the French authorities. Although there was abundant evidence that the old system of administration in the communes was breaking down, the French in Cochinchina, for financial reasons, showed a marked reluctance to halt this decline. Combined with this consideration was a specifically French prejudice against paying communal officials, since this was not a practice in France.

There was no shortage of warnings of the decline taking place. The Vietnamese councillors were particularly concerned about the developments that they reported to the Colonial Council. In 1893 three of these councillors presented a letter to the Council in which they noted that, while the mayor of the commune received exemption from personal tax and *corvées* because of his government duties, this was not true for the *huong-hao* and *huong-than*. Sent to the Council in January and referred to the administration for consideration, the letter was still unanswered in December of 1893. The Vietnamese councillors once again sought some relief for these notables. The reaction of the colonial officials was negative. The exemption that the Vietnamese councillors sought was unacceptable since it would create a class of privileged persons in the countryside.[17]

There is evidence that some members of the official community were aware of the situation of the village notables, even if they were unprepared to act to help them. When the lieutenant governor of Cochinchina, Ducos, reported to the governor general of Indochina in December of 1895, his comments were blunt. He noted that the position occupied by the mayors, *huong-hao*, and *huong-than* of the villages was "scarcely enviable." Their responsibilities to the government burdened the chiefs and deputy chiefs of the cantons with travel costs, loss of time, and the possibility of fines if they failed to attend the various court cases in which they played some official part. The result was a lack of candidates to fill these positions.[18]

Two years later, in 1897, Tran-Ba-Tho requested the administration to take account of this situation. He referred to the frequent necessity for village notables to attend court cases in order to testify in matters that had developed in their region. No provision existed for the payment of the expenses of these notables, who found themselves out of pocket because of their positions. The administration was unwilling to consider Tho's request. Councils of notables, the lieutenant governor noted, had their own sources of funds, and these should be used to meet the expenses of notables who had to travel to court cases. Moreover, it was the administration's understanding that procedures did exist for the reimbursement of expenses, and the notables should be aware of this. Tho's concluding remarks had a bitter tone: "In France, men are civilized; they know their rights. It is not the same in Cochinchina." [19]

In spite of the warnings over a long period and the recognition that important changes were taking place within the communes of Cochinchina, there was still an element of surprise in early twentieth-century observations that it had become extremely difficult to recruit notables. In a report prepared for the meeting of the Superior Council of Indochina in 1902, the lieutenant governor of Cochinchina noted:

The recruitment of notables becomes, unfortunately, more and more difficult in some provinces; the prosperous and honorable families show a certain repugnance for these perilous functions, which thus too often fall into the hands of those who are unskilled, and even, sometimes, dishonest.[20]

The following year, in his opening address to the Colonial Council in Cochinchina, Lieutenant Governor Rodier presented a bleak picture of communal administration. The rural administrators, he reported, were alarmed by the increasing difficulty of filling positions on the councils of notables. Those who could be pushed into occupying the important posts of mayor, *huong-hao,* and *huong-than* served only under protest and refused to occupy the post for longer than one year. For them it was a year of servitude. To save the commune as an institution, Rodier urged increasing the prestige of the notables and permitting them certain limited disciplinary powers.

There was now sufficient general concern in the colony to bring the appointment of a special commission to consider the position of the notables within the commune. It began its work in August 1903 and was composed of two Colonial Council members, one Vietnamese and one French, an administrator, and two magistrates.[21] The commission had considerable difficulty in obtaining satisfactory information concerning the normal hierarchy of a council of notables; there was variation from village to village and as a result of the changes that had come over the period of the French presence in Cochinchina. Aided by elderly Vietnamese informants, the commission finally drew up a list of notables and their hierarchic order and assigned to one of them the duty of acting as a "chairman" of the council. Although the commission accepted that the communes in the Ba-Ria region had best preserved the traditional form, probably because it was one of the oldest settled parts of the south, it did not follow the practice that existed there of assigning the "chairmanship" to the *huong-chu* but allotted it instead to the *huong-ca*.[22] The commission condoned further change by recommending that a government employee responsible for registering births, deaths, and marriages should be considered a major notable with the right to be present at meetings of the council.[23]

The commission had no ready solution for the problem of recruiting able men to the position of notable within the council. It did, however, observe that, if possible, men of property should be recruited since the government could control them by the threat of confiscation.[24] Basing itself on what it believed were traditional practices, the commission laid down specific duties for each notable.[25] This decision, which ignored the opinion of early commentators on the commune, who stressed the flexibility of responsibilities, reflected the French desire for administrative convenience.

The major unresolved question was how to increase the fallen prestige of the communal council. Some Vietnamese had argued in favor of permitting notables to carry out punishment for minor offenses with a cane. Corporal punishment was rejected by the French members of the commission as contrary to the proper standards of a modern society. Instead they argued for the right of the notables to imprison for periods up to twenty-four hours members of the commune who had committed minor transgressions.[26]

The commission's conclusions were embodied in a decision of 27 August 1904. Lieutenant Governor Rodier recognized that this was a stopgap measure, and he spoke in 1905 of continuing difficulty in recruiting notables.[27] The commune was still burdened with massive responsibilities by the alien government that controlled Cochinchina. There was little attraction for a property-owning Vietnamese to involve himself in the administration of a commune, when this might lay him open to prosecution by the French administration for failing to meet his responsibilities. Members of the propertied class who would traditionally have filled places on the council of notables now devoted themselves to expanding their land interests. The outward form of a council of notables survived into later decades of the twentieth century, but the decay was sharply evident by the turn of the century. French efforts to keep the councils in existence, chiefly for financial reasons, were not matched by an understanding and awareness of the changes that other French decisions were bringing. The autonomy of the commune was constantly eroded by French decisions that linked activities within the commune to the central administration in a direct fashion and as the insistence on individual reponsibility destroyed traditional reliance on collective obligation.

There is little evidence that the village notables sought positions on the communal councils in order eventually to gain posts on the *arrondissement* councils established by Governor Le Myre de Vilers. The first civil governor of Cochinchina decided to establish these councils as a further reflection of French belief in representative institutions and to aid in public works decisions within each administrative division. The membership of these *arrondissement* councils, or provincial councils as they came to be called, was made up of chiefs and deputy chiefs of cantons, presided over by the local French administrator.[28] From the start, in 1882, these councils were the creatures of French will. The *procès-verbaux* of meetings show that Vietnamese members did not hesitate to express their opinion on such matters as where a new bridge should be built or a road constructed, but the administrator's opinion prevailed. This point was given strong emphasis by Vietnamese members of the Colonial Council at a later date. Complaining about excessive demands by administrators for *corvées,* five Vietnamese councillors noted in 1890 that "the administrators always triumph through the vote of the majority, over which, for the greater part of the time, they impose their will." [29]

The chiefs and deputy chiefs of cantons were traditionally drawn from the councils of notables. The communes within a canton would, through their councils of notables, designate a canton chief, *tong,* and a deputy canton chief, *pho-tong.* Even more than the mayors, the *tong* had become agents of the French administration. But, in contrast to the mayors, these officials were paid for their duties. By the turn of the century, the old system of selecting canton chiefs and their deputies had largely disappeared. On some occasions they were designated directly by the French administrator. On other occasions they were chosen by "consultative election." A slate of candidates selected by an administrator would be presented to the notables for subsequent decision. In contrast to the older practice of respected notables assuming cantonal duties, it was reported that newly rich but uneducated Vietnamese now sought to gain nomination for these posts. Believing that advantage might follow upon their association with the French, these men now sought to gain support by buying it from those who would be in a position to help them.[30]

The changing character of the *tong* and of his duties was a further reflection of the disorientation of the countryside. As the colony grew "old" and the prospects for prosperity seemed greater, France's presence in Cochinchina brought change, at a forced rate to the rural population. The presence of overwhelmingly superior French force and the lack of leaders who could rally the rural population discouraged risings against French rule. These did take place from time to time, but never on a scale that threatened French control over Cochinchina. Troubles in the countryside were frequently connected with the activities of secret societies. French observers in the Cochinchinese administration attributed subversive tendencies to the *dao-lanh* sect in particular.[31]

French accounts of the discovery of a secret society seldom detail the motives for its formation or its true aims. It was not uncommon for a French administrator to describe a secret society with Vietnamese membership as "similar" to the Heaven and Earth Society.[32] At times the allegation was made that the direct purpose of a secret society was to overthrow French rule. The blending of eccentric religious belief and a vaguely anti-French posture cannot really be considered as reflecting a nationalist movement. Secret societies were the response of a rural population cut adrift from its basic traditional system of organization. The mandarins had gone, the administration of the commune was changing, and as the rural proletariat increased in size, the situation was ripe for those who claimed special insight and promised an alternative to the disturbed conditions of the present. The grandiose titles that members of secret groups awarded themselves emphasize not the potential of their power but the hopelessness of any action that they launched against the French.[33] This was not the new wave of nationalism. That came as much as a response to events outside Viet-Nam as to developments within and was promoted by men of some education, not by rural mystics.

Disorientation in the rural areas was the result of a complex intermingling of factors. As much through lack of understanding as through intent, the alien presence eroded the administrative structure of the commune and speeded the formation of a rural proletariat. For the most part, Vietnamese traditional practice and French goals had little if anything in common. The one common sphere of Vietnamese and French interests was the expansion of settlement and agriculture. But what had once left some place for the smallholder now became excessively concerned with the development of large productive holdings that would speed agricultural exports. Here Vietnamese played their part. The understandable search of those Vietnamese who acquired large-scale landholdings for increased personal wealth provided no answer for the fate of the dispossessed and the impoverished. The worst was still to come, but the change in the countryside by the early twentieth century was full of foreboding for the future.

8

Education and *Quoc-Ngu*— A Qualified Triumph

By the first decade of the twentieth century, the persistent efforts of the French administration in Cochinchina to establish an effective educational program had, at last, brought some success. Pétrus Ky had seen *quoc-ngu* as the certain way to emancipate his country from the shackles of the past. In the early twentieth century many shared his view and saw Cochinchina's destiny linked with France. The emancipation that others experienced brought them to seek a very different goal. The logic of colonial interaction in Cochinchina ensured that the first champions of modern nationalist thought should come particularly from the small group of Vietnamese who could use *quoc-ngu* and French. The impact of modern education had a dramatic effect on Viet-Nam in the 1920's and 1930's. Both then and before, the search for change in Cochinchina was led, in large part, by men who had experienced French-directed education. This educational system, increasingly in the years after 1879, stressed quality over quantity.

That this tendency existed did not mean that all hope for the mass transformation of the Vietnamese population into French-speaking subjects had vanished. Nor were the exaggerated estimates totally eliminated. It was evident that past failures had brought a degree of scepticism to members of the administration; claims of success were more frequently countered by assessments based on harsh reality. There was a much greater reliance on French teachers in Cochinchina once the period of civil rule began, and Vietnamese students sent to educational institutions in France and Algeria, though fewer in number, stayed longer and had more success in their studies than those sent under the ill-fated programs of the earlier period.

There were many changes of detail in the organization of the educational system in Cochinchina between 1879 and 1905. Some essential aspects, however, remained the same over the whole of this period. The administration recognized the impossibility of furnishing capable students for more advanced schools in Saigon without a thorough elementary education. Building on the reorganization of 1874, the authorities tried to channel students through two levels of education before they undertook courses in Saigon. The level of education in Saigon was given various descriptions. It was sometimes called secondary, but in character it was advanced primary education. Ideally, a young Vietnamese would reach the Collège Chasseloup-Laubat after passing through a cantonal school and then a school at the *arrondissement* level in which courses in both *quoc-ngu* and French were under the over-all supervision of a French teacher. Once he had reached Saigon, a student received a considerable portion of his instruction in French.[1]

Alongside the administration's schools were the less carefully supervised village schools. The cantonal schools fell in between. The funds for their upkeep were provided not by the central authorities but by the budget of the *arrondissement*. There was supposed to be a degree of surveillance of the courses taught in these schools, but commentary on them makes it clear that this seldom operated in any regular fashion. The teaching in village schools was through *quoc-ngu* and Chinese characters. French repugnance towards characters had not vanished, but the government recognized the need for translators, in view of the continuing use of characters by older members of the population. More and more, however, as the use of characters declined and the number of scholars available to teach them dwindled, these remnants of traditional learning faded away.

During the eighties, the disinclination of the Vietnamese population in the countryside to send their children to schools teaching in *quoc-ngu* persisted. Although the director of education claimed in

1882 that it was no longer necessary to require parents to send their children,[2] other commentators challenged his assertion. The chairman of a committee set up in 1884 to consider reorganizing education in the colony had quite a different view:

In general, the Annamite still does not understand the importance of education; the educated and prosperous Annamite does not see what utility it can have for the *dan* [people] destined to work for the whole of their lives in the fields; and the substitution of Latin characters for Chinese is far from being universally accepted.[3]

Moreover, the level of teaching, particularly in cantonal schools, remained very low. When Governor Filippini reported this in 1887, he attributed it to the failure of the colonial administration to make a determined attempt to spread the use of French. Despite the various efforts, "it must be recognized that education has made scarcely any progress." [4]

Governor General Richaud's comments, the following year, were no more optimistic, but they did give greater detail on the reasons for continuing slow progress. His observations also touched upon one of the fundamental failings of the French program of education in Cochinchina. There was no doubt in Richaud's mind that "education such as we give to the native does not relate to any of his needs." [5]

We take children from their villages at the age of eight to ten years; we send them to our cantonal schools, from which they emerge after having learned to spell out painfully a few lines of *Gia-Dinh Bao*.

The education of these children rarely goes further.

They do not gain any notion of morality, nor of that special education so esteemed by Annamites.

The majority return to their villages after a year or two lost in this manner and give their families, through their airs of self-sufficiency and the ignorance which they manifest, a sad picture of our system of public instruction. Also, we often see happen what Luro noted fifteen years ago: parents send their children back to the schools teaching in characters after they leave our French schools.[6]

Richaud's recognition that French-sponsored education did not meet the needs of the Vietnamese population was a basic explanation of the administration's problems. Yet, even at the time he made this observation, many factors were at work to qualify his assessment. French education provided a way into the colonial administration. Indeed, with few exceptions, there were no places open to Vietnamese who did not use *quoc-ngu* at least. Unless a Vietnamese family was sufficiently prosperous to dismiss questions of employment, passage through the public education system provided the most certain road to a job and income for those who wanted more than a life spent in agricultural labor. Teaching that stressed morality could still be admired, but practical considerations posed stronger demands. The statistics provided on education in the colony are generally highly unsatisfactory, but there seems no reason to question the rapid decline in the number of schools teaching in Chinese characters towards the end of the century.[7]

Sufficient time had passed since the colony's foundation for the children of a growing number of Vietnamese employees of the French administration to require education. Many parents were willing to commit their children to an education in schools that had no links with the past of characters and Confucian ideals. The French authorities provided scholarships for Vietnamese pupils in the more advanced institutions of Saigon, and these scholarships were sought, successfully, by parents who worked for the administration.[8]

The Vietnamese who studied abroad also helped to erode resistance to new forms of education. Like the pupils who studied in the colony's schools at the government's expense, they were generally the children of Vietnamese employees of the French administration.[9] The limited number of Vietnamese from Cochinchina who attended the Ecole Coloniale in Paris appear to have been an exception to this rule.[10] The protestations of loyalty from six Vietnamese students at a *lycée* in Algiers may not reflect mature consideration of relations between Vietnamese of Cochinchina and France. But when these young Vietnamese wrote of their desire to know "French soil, its riches" and stated that this had been their "dream ever since we began to spell out French seated on the primary school benches,"[11] they most certainly had made an important break with the past.

Richaud's criticism of the communal and cantonal schools had much point to it. His statement that the teachers in these lower schools were often drawn from the ranks of "boys" and "cooks" who had learned a few words of French in domestic service had validity. Nevertheless, the combination of French determination to inculcate a new system of education and the slow disappearance of traditional teachers of characters, in a situation that offered neither place nor official honor to their efforts, had its effect. The fact that Bui-Quang-Chieu graduated as a fully qualified agricultural engineer before the end of the century testified to this. So did the entrance of one of Do-Huu-Phuong's sons into St. Cyr. Despite some misgivings about the social consequences of a Vietnamese being entitled to be called Doctor, the Colonial Council provided funds to permit a Vietnamese to study medicine in France in 1901.[12] The number of Vietnamese who had completed their education in Algiers and France and in the secondary institutions of the colony by the first decade of the twentieth century was not large. It was, however, a significant demonstration that, with all its defects, the new system provided an alternative to the traditional system.

There were, in addition, some new departures. Continued dissatisfaction with the quality of the Vietnamese teaching in cantonal schools led to the founding of a teachers' training college. The institution was approved in 1895 and apparently began functioning immediately, since it was referred to as being in its second year of existence in 1897.[13] In the closing years of the nineteenth century, the first trade schools to train Vietnamese skilled craftsmen also were established under government control.[14] There was diversification of the more advanced educational program offered to Vietnamese students in Saigon. A limited number of naturalized Vietnamese received a fully French education at the Collège Chasseloup-Laubat. Others were part of the "Franco-Annamite" system in an annex of the Collège Chasseloup-Laubat, and at the Ecole Normale and the Collège at My-Tho. By 1904 there were more than six hundred Vietnamese attending government schools above the level of the *arrondissement* or, as they were now called, provincial schools. More than four hundred Vietnamese attended schools maintained by the municipalities of Saigon and Cholon.

There were 4,000 Vietnamese pupils in provincial schools, more than 12,000 in cantonal schools, and about 9,500 pupils in schools maintained by the Catholic Church and the Vietnamese communes.[15]

The immediate qualification should be made that the numbers recorded as attending a particular institution usually represented the maximum attendance. Particularly for the provincial and cantonal schools, there are suggestions that attendance was irregular and resulted in very ineffective teaching. The poor training of teachers has been frequently cited in this study. One Vietnamese member of the Colonial Council believed in 1906 that the government should appoint an inspector to watch over the activities of the cantonal schools. He stated, and his claims were not denied by the director of education who was present, that French administrators frequently used cantonal school teachers to carry out administrative tasks. Left to themselves, the cantonal schoolteachers often did not open their schools. If there was an inspection by an official from the central administration, the teachers made special arrangements to ensure that all the seats in the school were filled for the day.[16]

Dissimulation of this sort could scarcely be practiced in the Saigon schools, and they continued to teach an important number of Vietnamese each year, a notable success in the French effort to extend modern education throughout Cochinchina. It is not the absolute numbers that are important in assessing this educational effort in Cochinchina, although by comparison with other colonial situations they are remarkable, but rather the educational impact that the French administration achieved within such a short period. A working if imperfect substitute had been provided for the traditional system. It disseminated a new writing system, so that what had once been the sole preserve of the small Catholic enclaves became quite genuinely the national writing of Viet-Nam; and it instilled a limited, but surprisingly widespread knowledge of French.[17] The French educational program did not provide an immediate substitute for the Confucian moral system. This worried many thoughtful Vietnamese, who found themselves looking both to the future and to the past. In later years the freedom of social thought in the West, which became known through translations and French publications, was contrasted bitterly with the restrictions of Western colonial rule.

The role of the Catholic Church in the development of education in Cochinchina seldom brought objective comment in the late nineteenth century. As a result, historical analysis must pick its way through the charges and countercharges levelled and rebutted by the two sides in the argument. Up to the introduction of civil rule, the Catholic teaching brothers in Cochinchina had made an important contribution by staffing the Collège d'Adran. In 1880, however, the Colonial Council withdrew the government subvention that had been provided for the school up to that date, to the intense annoyance of the ecclesiastical authorities.[18] In 1883 the clerical teachers withdrew from the college. From this date, the most important efforts of the Church in the educational field were in the rural areas, in small missions. Some of the bitterest debates that arose over the Catholic Church's endeavors revolved about the extent to which the teaching in mission stations was in French. All parties to the controversy admitted that the bulk of the teaching was in *quoc-ngu*. The anticlerical critics argued that French was the proper vehicle for instruction. The Church replied that the loyalist Vietnamese were those who did not speak French.[19] The anticlerical French critics further alleged that the level of instruction, even in *quoc-ngu*, was poor and that the Church provided not education, but a limited instruction in prayers and the catechism.[20] Vietnamese members of the Colonial Council who had enjoyed a French education denounced the allegation of disloyalty, while those who were members of the Church defended mission education.[21] The best assessment must discount the excesses on both sides. It seems probable that the Church's statistics were inflated, in much the same way that the government inflated its figures. If instruction was limited, this was also true of the government schools. Yet even the most sceptical must acknowledge that Catholic efforts in the countryside helped in the diffusion of *quoc-ngu*. Cochinchina was a relatively arid field for the missionaries to till, and again and again the Catholic Church blamed this failure on the continued nomadic character of the Vietnamese in the South. At times there was tension between Catholic and non-Catholic Vietnamese villagers.[22] Despite these problems and the limited progress of the Church's campaign for conversions, missionary commitment to the extension of *quoc-ngu* did not waver.

In its decision of 1878 the French administration had decreed that after 1882 *quoc-ngu* was to be the only acceptable official form of writing in the colony, apart from French.[23] In the succeeding two decades, there was ample evidence that this decision was not fully enforced and that the use of characters persisted, even if in a diminishing fashion. But the strong commitment to *quoc-ngu* finally brought its own triumph. There was an ever-greater use of the new writing medium. There was also a running debate over the years about the merits of educating Vietnamese in French, rather than the transcription. Another much discussed question, at times linked to the first, was the extent to which education should teach morals. The continuing anxiety of the *collaborateur* element that there should be a moral content to education testified to the strength of Confucian thought in Vietnamese life, and the capacity of education in *quoc-ngu* to infuse moral virtues was frequently discussed.

The literary triumvirate of Pétrus Ky, Paulus Cua, and Truong-Minh-Ky contributed the bulk of new writings in *quoc-ngu,* but in the development of the transcription the contribution of Frenchmen was considerable: they alone took part in the sharp discussion of the changes that might be introduced into the transcription of Vietnamese.

The issue touched on the much more important question of whether or not *quoc-ngu* was to be the standard writing form throughout Viet-Nam. Scholars, administrators, and missionaries argued over the appropriate way in which to render the romanization of Vietnamese, but with little practical effect. Aymonier, the scholarly student of Cambodian history and epigraphy, fought hard for a new transcription that would take more account of

French pronunciation than did the existing system, which had taken its phonetic values from Portuguese.[24] The great missionary scholar Father Léopold Cadière shared some of Aymonier's views and was at the International Congress of Far Eastern Studies in 1902 when that body called on the Ecole Française d'Extrême-Orient to devise a more "rational" transcription of Vietnamese.[25] Nothing in fact happened. Whatever the faults of the standard transcription, it had become the established form.

The real battle, again with Frenchmen as the chief participants, was fought over the old issue of whether or not to work for a total substitution of French for Vietnamese in Cochinchina. Here again Aymonier was one of the chief figures in the controversy. There were, from time to time, expressions of discontent, from Vietnamese, about the use of *quoc-ngu* in Cochinchina. A notable instance of this was a petition in the *Saigonnais* for 10 December 1885. This petition, signed by a number of Vietnamese, argued that the Colonial Council should suppress what they described as *"quoc-ngu chinois,"* since it contained a mass of Chinese words unknown to the ordinary Vietnamese.[26] Landes, who devoted much of his time in Viet-Nam to translating Vietnamese folk stories into French and who compiled one of the greatest collections of material in *quoc-ngu,* believed that the petition had little real support and recorded his assessment that Chinese words had, irrevocably, become part of the Vietnamese language.[27]

This was not Aymonier's view. The 1885 petition was part of the salvo of criticisms that he directed against *quoc-ngu.* It was a dialect, a *patois,* a confusing mixture of Vietnamese and Chinese words. It posed the risk, Aymonier warned, in a criticism not altogether consistent with his previous argument, of exciting the nationalist feelings of the population. The very words *quoc-ngu* (national language) might incite the assertion of independence from the French. France's goal, he maintained, was to reform the Vietnamese race and to open their minds to the benefits of European civilization. To achieve this goal, the surest way was to teach French and to spread the use of that language wherever possible.[28] His outspoken comments were met by equally convinced advocates of the other point of view. The head of the Collège Chasseloup-Laubat in Saigon argued vigorously in favor of the continued use of *quoc-ngu* as a "tool" of incontestable value, which could eventually lead to greater use of French. Already, he noted, Vietnamese students in his college customarily mixed French words with *quoc-ngu* when writing letters.[29]

These exchanges emphasize the important role of Frenchmen in the continuing evolution of *quoc-ngu* before the end of the nineteenth century. This was demonstrated further by the part Frenchmen played in the publication of *quoc-ngu* newspapers. By the end of the nineteenth century, however, a number of Vietnamese had begun to comment on this issue, until then an essentially French preserve. Their comments reflected their concern for the moral content of education.

Even the Catholic *collaborateur* Loc had expressed reservations about the lack of moral content in an educational system taught through *quoc-ngu*. He was not concerned for his fellow Catholics; they had a faith to replace the precepts of Confucian philosophy. But with the removal of teaching in characters, there was a need, he argued in 1879, to provide the "pagans" with a literature in *quoc-ngu* to inculcate the five virtues of humanity, justice, urbanity, prudence, and fidelity.[30] To some extent this was what Pétrus Ky and his associates attempted to do. There was a strong moral tone to their pamphlets. But around the turn of the century there was evidence that members of the Vietnamese colonial elite in Cochinchina were dissatisfied by the insufficient moral content of existing publications. Loc's son, Tho, deplored the inadequacy of the official publication *Gia-Dinh Bao,* observing, fairly accurately, that it no longer contained more than official announcements and advertisements for patent medicines. It "no longer taught anything to the Annamites." [31]

In 1908, shortly before his death, Tho published a long study in which he attempted to draw together many of the traditional stories that had been used to teach Confucian virtues but which were not available in *quoc-ngu.*[32] In a preface to this work, he argued that the lack of respect shown by the Vietnamese who spoke French resulted from their isolation from teaching in characters, with its moral overlay. In a full turn of the wheel, the son of Tran-Ba-Loc now argued for a return to some teaching in characters to prevent children losing touch completely with their country's past and its customs. Echoing his father's observations, he accepted that it was possible to teach Confucian morality through *quoc-ngu*, but he noted a lack of books with which to do so.[33]

Not all of Tho's generation shared his outlook. Councillor Diep-Van-Cuong, speaking in the Colonial Council in 1906, saw no reason why it should not be possible to teach the precepts of Confucian philosophy through French, "the instrument of civilization." [34] Le-Van-Phat, despite his earlier insistence on the need for Frenchmen to learn something of the domestic life of the country that they ruled, saw little value in teaching traditional moral values in schools. Was the moral value and the moral content of French thought any less valuable? he asked. "Then why do we not learn this morality, this new talisman that has worked to bring so many miracles in France, in order to assimilate ourselves completely to them in thought and deed." [35]

While these debates between advocates of French and of *quoc-ngu*, of Eastern and Western philosophical principles, took place, the corpus of printed material in *quoc-ngu* gradually grew larger. The books, or, more accurately, pamphlets, of Pétrus Ky, Paulus Cua, and Truong-Minh-Ky were published in a steady stream. The bulk of these publications were compilations of traditional stories and short moral texts. The more distinctive were such items as Pétrus Ky's account of his visit to Tonkin and Truong-Minh-Ky's poems about his visits to France. Possibly because he commenced writing some years after the arrival of the French, Truong-Minh-Ky essayed more ambitious themes, such as a verse play about Joseph in *quoc-ngu* and the translation of works from French. When we remember that these three men played an important part in routine administrative activities, their output is remarkable. Yet the greatest amount of material in *quoc-ngu* continued to be published in newspaper form, and here both public and private French support were of the highest importance.

Gia-Dinh Bao had commenced publication in 1865. It was not until 1897 that another *quoc-ngu* newspaper was established that published in Cochinchina for any sustained period. The character of *Gia-Dinh Bao* changed as the years went by. The wide-ranging coverage of its early period slowly dwindled to purely official tabulations of administration decisions and announcements, with only an occasional short poem to leaven the monotony. Tran-Ba-Tho's comment was a fair one: there was no longer anything to interest a Vietnamese in the newspaper, apart from an announcement directly affecting an individual. The French administration defended the character of the newspaper without apology. When Tho made his remarks, he asked that the official newspaper should include accounts of the meetings of the Colonial Council in its pages. Failing this, he suggested that a subvention should be given to the newspaper *Nam Ky* (The Southern Region), which began publication in 1897. In reply, the lieutenant governor observed:

This [official] newspaper passes under the control of higher authority, and everything that it publishes is of a considered nature; the Annamites do not discuss it. The *Gia-Dinh Bao* is an official newspaper, while *Nam Ky* may publish what it wishes, without, however, stirring up political matters that could lead our natives astray and compromise the security that we have spent twenty years achieving in this country. . . . Monsieur Tho is too intelligent not to understand that in the villages, if we attempt to keep the natives informed of our discussions in the Colonial Council we will not attain our goal. The *dan* [people] understand nothing, and they mislead themselves for the greater part of the time.[36]

The owner and editor of *Nam Ky* was a Frenchman named Schreiner, who had a varied career as a publicist in Viet-Nam. Schreiner did not intend that the newspaper should provide the Vietnamese who could read it with any information on "political matters that could . . . lead our natives astray." His views on education were set out in an article that he contributed to the Bulletin of the Society of Indochinese Studies in 1908. In his opinion, Vietnamese should be the vehicle of instruction for the native population of Cochinchina, and it should be used to propagate French thought and Western knowledge.[37]

Nam Ky carried out its owner's recommendations. Much in the fashion of *Gia-Dinh Bao* in its early days, the new newspaper published articles of "useful knowledge," usually prepared by Schreiner himself. The themes were treated in a simple fashion:

Last time I wrote about European geography. I said that next time I would tell my friends clearly about government, trade, and so forth in Western countries.

Normally, when many men, women, and children associate with each other and live together they must have one person whom they designate to act for the group. When one is by oneself, then one is in charge of one's own activities. But when a person, with his wife and children, lives with many others, then he cannot act as he wishes any more.[38]

This article goes on to treat such issues as constitutional monarchy, unitary republics, and federations. It must have been a relief after such articles, and others treating diseases and the lives of Catherine of Russia and the Count of Assas, for the reader to encounter a serialized version of the story of Ali Baba and the Forty Thieves.[39]

Articles of a more political nature appeared in the first really important unofficial *quoc-ngu* newspaper, *Nong-Co Min Dam* (The Tribune of the Old Agricultural People), which began publication in 1901. As with *Nam Ky*, there was a French interest in the publication. A Frenchman named Canavaggio was the owner, but the direction of the newspaper was in Vietnamese hands. By 1907 a Vietnamese named Gilbert Chieu was editor of the newspaper. A year later, when he was editor of another newspaper, *Luc Tinh Tan Van* (News of the Six Provinces), Chieu was arrested for complicity in the partly royalist and partly modernist nationalist movement that sought to place Prince Cuong-De on the throne of a rejuvenated Viet-Nam.[40] Following 1905 there were clear signs of political ferment. The degrading defeat of the Russian forces at the hands of the Japanese in the Russo-Japanese War had a profound effect on educated Vietnamese. Chieu, a former employee of the French administration and a naturalized French citizen, was one of those who responded to the new climate of opinion. His articles in *Nong-Co Min Dam* constantly exhorted the Vietnamese population of Cochinchina to act in a unified fashion in order to improve their economic position. Efforts by Vietnamese to gain economic independence, particularly from the Chinese minority, were given special prominence.[41] Articles solicited financial contributions for the various commercial enterprises that Chieu set up in Saigon and in some provincial centers, which were later denounced by the French administration as forums of sedition.[42]

Chieu's use of the press and his efforts to link political action with the development of economic strength among the Vietnamese inhabitants of Cochinchina were marks of a new spirit of modern nationalism. In terms of immediate results, they were a failure. Indeed, the French response to a series of nationalist incidents and manifestations in the years after 1905 was to adopt ever more repressive policies. So far as the development of *quoc-ngu* is concerned, however, the appearance of newspapers that made directly political appeals to the readers may be taken as a true sign of the transcription's coming of age. All was prepared now for what one Vietnamese student of her country's journalism has called the "flowering period." [43] The road had been long and arduous, and large segments of the population probably were still untouched by the use of *quoc-ngu* in the first decade of the twentieth century. Nevertheless, the political use of the language in its romanized transcription suggests a sudden growth, which might not have been expected on the basis of comments made in the nineties.

During the last two decades of the nineteenth century, the criticism levelled at the education system often carried the explicit comment, and always the implied concern, that poor teaching was hindering the spread of *quoc-ngu*. This was certainly true. Moreover, even if younger members of the population were gaining some rudimentary knowledge of the new way of writing their language, a large proportion of the Vietnamese of Cochinchina had not been exposed to the use of *quoc-ngu*. As late as 1901, three Vietnamese members of the Colonial Council prepared a motion noting the very small number of Vietnamese in the countryside who were able to read the transcription. The translation of decisions in *quoc-ngu* and the publication of *Gia-Dinh Bao*, they noted, were admirable measures, but they were insufficient to provide the population with information on government decisions. Instead, these Vietnamese councillors called for all decisions to be read aloud in the villages after the population had been assembled by beating a gong.[44]

Gilbert Chieu's call for the development of economic strength, his denunciations of Chinese control of business, and the circulation of these views in *quoc-ngu* were a far cry from this. In 1907 the number of Vietnamese who could use the transcription was still small, but it was growing rapidly. The long years of preparation had finally borne fruit. But as in so many other aspects of the history of Cochinchina, the fruit was different from what had been expected when the seeds were planted. There was much truth in the assessment of a critical French observer who surveyed the swiftly changing colony in 1905 and deplored what he saw:

> All that is our work, and the chief cause of it, is our obsession for proselytizing, our mania for assimilation.
> Traditional Annamite society, so well organized to satisfy the needs of the people, has in the final analysis been destroyed by us.[45]

The persistent French adherence to assimilative goals in educational policy enabled the colonial administration to overcome obstacles that might otherwise have baffled their efforts. The conviction that a substantial number of Vietnamese should speak French was never lost. The belief that a romanized transcription of Vietnamese was practically desirable and an effective weapon to counter Confucian thought brought the ultimate triumph of *quoc-ngu*. Most contemporary French observers believed their policies were a success. Difficulties were noted, but dismissed as momentary or trivial. The exclusion of moral content from the new education was a casualty of "progress." It was this situation to which the anonymous observer was reacting when he deplored the general destruction of Vietnamese society. Yet it would be wrong to ignore the partial triumph of French educational aims and to end on a completely negative note. The "mania for assimilation" brought new knowledge to Viet-Nam, and its diffusion through the widening use of the romanized transcription played a vital part in the formation of modern Viet-Nam. The events of the twentieth century, though largely unrecorded in this study, form the essential epilogue to the changes wrought in the first fifty years of colonial interaction.

Part III

CAMBODIA

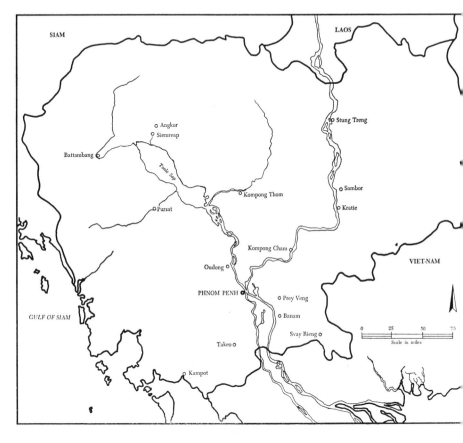

Map 3. Cambodia, showing principal centers in the nineteenth century (Cambodⁱ
national borders are those existing in 1967).

9

Cambodia before the Storm (1863–1883)

When French power was established in Cochinchina, it brought an end to the southern and western expansion of a state that, whatever its weaknesses, appeared certain to play a vigorous role in the Indochinese region. Cambodia, however, in contrast to Viet-Nam, was by the 1860's the final vestige of a formerly great empire, a prize fought over by Siam and Viet-Nam as those two nations moved toward a final confrontation in the rich lower reaches of the Mekong. France in Cambodia played a role not incomprehensible to the Cambodian court. King Ang Duong may have looked to France for aid against his more powerful neighbors. His son Norodom, the chief figure in Cambodian history for most of the second half of the nineteenth century, had received an early experience of the vulnerability of his country if no protector came to its aid. But if the French position could be understood, at least in part, by Norodom, this did not alter the fact that French power was alien to Cambodia in a way that ensured a series of conflicts between the "protectors" and the "protected" king. As France sought to achieve greater and greater control over the conduct of government in Cambodia and to institute reforms in a system regarded as antiquated and uncivilized, there were increasingly frequent clashes between protagonists with irreconcilable views of the state. That the major clash, in 1884, came as late as it did was due to the restrained role that the French first assumed in Cambodia.

French interest in Cambodia was subsidiary to her more immediate involvement in Cochinchina. Contacts in the fifties, missionary accounts, and preliminary soundings in the early sixties gave the impression of a decaying kingdom, rent by internal rivalries—

not a promising field for colonial endeavor. But Cambodia had obvious geographic importance: the country bestrode the great
Mekong River, seen by Frenchmen in the first days of their presence in Cambodia as a route to the riches of China. And its borders
marched with Siam. The wish to restrict Siam's expansion, and
what were believed to be British interests working through Siam,
dominated much of French thinking on Asia throughout the nineteenth century. Control of Cambodia's foreign relations, and protection of France's position in Cochinchina through this control,
became the first aim of French policy in the kingdom and the
raison d'être of the Protectorate Treaty that the French concluded
with Norodom in 1863.

Even in the restricted aims of France's first years of sustained
contact, one may perceive the seeds of later conflict. In part, the
slowly developing tension between Norodom and the French was
the result of the basic difficulties inherent in any forced relationship between the strong and the weak. The king's action was circumscribed by the French, and this led to angry confrontations. In
part also, major French policy decisions, particularly those relating
to the cession of territory to Siam, touched upon one of the most
delicate issues in Cambodian politics, the still further reduction of
an already territorially impoverished kingdom. Finally, almost from
the beginning of its involvement in Cambodia's affairs, France
sought to ensure that it could replace Norodom, if necessary, with
another prince more pliable to French demands. Frenchmen did
not create the family feuds that plagued the Cambodian royal
house, but they introduced an entirely new element into these
perennial disputes.

Norodom dominates the Cambodian stage, but his character is
extraordinarily difficult to delineate, as are the motivations that
guided many of his actions. One former French official in Cambodia, Collard, has suggested that it is proper to consider Norodom's life in three parts, divided by the dates 1877 and 1884.[1] The
earlier date marks the first major departure from the terms of the
Protectorate Treaty of 1863 and the beginning of French attempts
to institute basic administrative reforms to limit Norodom's power.

The second date marks the year in which Norodom faced a French effort to transform his kingdom into a pale copy of Cochinchina. Up till 1877, Collard sees Norodom as a ruler untroubled by the cares of office and ready to live in friendship with the French. The middle seventies, in Collard's view, introduced a new element of seriousness into Norodom's character as he reacted to the internal threats to his throne and accepted French advice on the need for reform. But the vigor with which France attempted to institute major changes in 1884 alienated Norodom from the protecting power and embittered the final days of his life.

This summary of Collard is, perhaps, a simplification of a simplification. It is important, nevertheless, because the picture that Collard presents is the one traditionally offered by French writers, and departures from it have tended to be no less two dimensional.[2] Norodom was thirty when he was crowned king of Cambodia. He had lived much of his life in Bangkok, and all agree that his residence in the Siamese court had left a profound mark upon him. The young Cambodian prince had been sponsored by Mongkut when he first entered a Buddhist monastery.[3] His taste for Siamese music, for the Siamese language, and for Siamese women persisted throughout his life. It remained a constant irritant to the French representative in Phnom Penh, since both Siam and the British interests in that country were viewed with the greatest suspicion. There can be no doubt that Siam, and the ruler of Siam in particular, were exemplars to Norodom. He once indicated the extent of his resentment of French control over Cambodia's foreign policy with the remark that the King of Siam had "a court of consuls; here there is only one representative." [4]

This concern with Siam is one of the many continuities of Norodom's life that transcends any periodization such as Collard's. Norodom's great wish to restore Cambodia's prestige by regaining control over border regions that had passed to the French in Cochinchina and to Siam in the west was another.[5] A further constant was his distrust of his half brother Sisowath, whose early disaffection from Norodom made him a tool of the French. The long tradition of internecine conflict and the lack of close family ties be-

tween half brothers who often spent little of their childhood together explain the readiness with which sons of the same father
quarrelled over the throne. Norodom spoke accurately when he
complained that Sisowath had "two faces," one for the French and
one for Cambodia.[6]

These continuities must be kept firmly in mind when considering
the changing nature of Norodom's association with the French.
The year 1884 was crucial in Norodom's life and in Cambodian history. For this reason, and notwithstanding the steady deterioration
in his relations with the French over the years preceding the 1884
convention, it seems an appropriate point of division. Until 1884
there were still opportunities for dialogue between the Cambodian
ruler and the French who "protected" his kingdom. But Norodom
probably never forgave the French for the forced signature they
exacted from him in 1884. More and more concerned with his own
comfort and the well-being of his household in subsequent years,
he nevertheless struggled against the constant increase of French
power. It was a fight he could not win, and he died, in 1904, spir-
itually exhausted by this unequal battle and physically worn out by
years of ill health and indulgence.

Accounts of Norodom throughout his life testify to his intelligence and to his lively interest in the world outside Cambodia.
Henri Mouhot's description of his meeting with Norodom, at
Oudong in 1859 when King Ang Duong was still alive, gives the
impression of a lively personality conversing easily and confidently.[7] Later in Norodom's life it was possible for a Frenchman
who deplored the way in which the king passed his days to nevertheless remark:

We will be wrong to believe (with the great majority of French pub-
licists) that Norodom is a king in the African style, easy to amuse and
distracted from his hereditary rights with necklaces of glass beads and
music boxes. Norodom was born and raised in the Court of Siam, where
he gained a great sense of Asian politics and a very high appreciation of
the nobility of his race. One may say, without deceiving oneself, that he
is the first Cambodian of his kingdom, if he is not the only one.[8]

There is no lack of contradictory assertions, but the motivations of those Frenchmen who made them are suspect, at the very least. Norodom displeased Le Myre de Vilers, who was repelled by the financial profligacy that he saw in the Cambodian court.[9] Governor Thomson, failing to understand why Norodom resisted his efforts to gain greater French control over Cambodian revenue, instituted the fatal 1884 convention.[10] And there is a patronizing air to many of Doudart de Lagrée's comments on the Cambodian "kinglet." [11]

The bulk of these criticisms came from men unprepared to see in Norodom's rejection of French demands one of the few ways open to the king to show his displeasure with French control. There was a tendency, instead, to condemn Norodom as lacking in either intelligence or vision. The argument that he had the inclinations of an absolute oriental ruler is much easier to sustain. Norodom was frequently unable to assert his will over large sections of his kingdom. He came to the throne with one half brother in revolt and another contemplating dissidence. At various times throughout his reign, pretenders to the throne troubled the kingdom with revolts and uprisings, which he was unable to suppress without French help. In the closing years of his life French control became such that he was no longer able to take any real part in the direction of the country. But within the court, his will was law. This fact is well illustrated in his insistence, late in the seventies, that the court should accompany him on a pilgrimage to Phnom Chisor, an Angkorian site to the south of Phnom Penh, which has continued to be a religious center to the present day. This site had the reputation of bringing ill luck to officials who visited it, and there was considerable reluctance to obey Norodom's order. The king would brook no refusal from his officials, however, and led them to the top of the hill on which the shrine is set.[12]

At Phnom Chisor, and elsewhere, he tolerated no challenge to his authority. There are suggestions that his father, Ang Duong, had once thrashed Norodom for daring to associate with the king's female household. There is no doubt that he treated his own male

IV. The Phnom Penh market in the late 1860's (from F. Garnier, *Voyage d'exploration en Indo-Chine*, Paris, 1885).

children with equal rigor, beating them if they transgressed the strict regulations surrounding the life of the Cambodian court and sentencing them to confinement in chains for months on end for more serious breaches of the rules.[13] Punishment for crimes of *lèse-majesté* committed by a Cambodian outside the royal family was more terrible, and infidelity by a member of his female establishment brought death.[14] While his power was still relatively unrestricted by the French protectorate, Norodom's control over his senior officials was strict, and there are accounts of his beating ministers who displeased him.[15]

Norodom was a man of strong appetites. He would on occasion drink deeply of the sherry and French brandy for which he had early acquired a taste. He smoked opium. It is difficult to be precise about the extent to which this latter indulgence was part of his early life. Aymonier, writing in 1874, referred to both Norodom

and Sisowath as heavy users of opium, but there is no way of
knowing by what standards he judged them.[16] The use that
Norodom made of the drug in later life was almost certainly connected with his ill health, for gout and finally cancer left him few
periods free of pain. His taste for dancing was legendary. Norodom
admired the traditional court dances and used them as a backdrop
to banquets that were limited in length only by the endurance of
the guests. He had grown up in the Siamese court, and he ensured
that some members of his royal ballet should be Siamese. His
musical tastes embraced melodies performed by the traditional
Cambodian orchestra of strings, xylophones, gongs, reed instru-
ments, and drums, but he also had a Filipino band to provide
variety.[17]

No doubt the court of the Cambodian king at times appeared
tawdry and lacking in regal dignity to the French. They deplored
what Le Myre de Vilers once called the joining of Asiatic luxury
to all "the refinements of European comfort." [18] They were repelled
by the influence of women over the conduct of the kingdom's
affairs, seeing in the traditional intriguing of the palace women an
unacceptable interference with progress towards more modern
government.[19] What shocked the French was, however, the norm
in the Cambodian court. When other members of the royal family
often could not be trusted, and when officials, particularly if they
were given senior provincial appointments, frequently intrigued
against the central power, the king found a certain security in
the female household that surrounded him. Indeed, in the later
years of his life there is strong evidence that Norodom increasingly
relied on his women even in financial affairs.[20]

The opportunities for political intrigue within the court suggest a
fluid, introspective court society. The instability of an individual's
position within the royal family, depending on whether or not he
was favored with the ruler's approbation, was reinforced by the
rule prohibiting a princess from marrying below her station. This
rule often led to princes marrying their half sisters, as well as to
unmarried princesses contracting liaisons with commoners in the
same way that neglected women of the king's own household

sometimes turned to one of his many sons.[21] It is impossible to know how closely court life in the earlier centuries had paralleled this shifting, at times female-dominated world of intrigue. By Norodom's reign, however, the limitations on Cambodia's external relations and the kingdom's reduced territory appear to have encouraged such a situation.

If the Cambodian court lacked dignity in the eyes of a Frenchman, it is unlikely that this was the case for the Cambodian population. Indeed, it is through the eyes of one of the more perceptive French observers in Cambodia that we may glimpse some of the fantasy and majesty that surrounded Norodom and his court when the king went forth among his people:

> To meet in one's travels the Asian monarch and the Cambodian court returning from an excursion in oriental style, with disorder adding to its curious character, is really good fortune.
>
> Two hundred elephants, rolling the ancient seats, gilded or black, which they support, carry the king and the princes under roofs of scarlet bamboo screening and pass like a parade, filled with women of the harem and with dancers half naked beneath their scarves. They disappear with the horsemen, the carriages, and those on foot, in a cloud of dust, leaving the impression of an unforgettable enchanted picture.[22]

The king's person was so sacred that when he once fell from his carriage in Phnom Penh, no Cambodian dared touch him for fear of defiling the royal presence. It was left to a passing European to aid Norodom.[23] In a maturer judgment, Aymonier summarized the place of the king within Cambodian society:

> The attachment of the Cambodians to their hereditary chiefs is as profound as it is sincere. The nation has long been accustomed to the idea of not separating its own existence from that of the royal house. The monarch is the living incarnation, the august and supreme personification of nationality.[24]

Norodom, then, was no "African king" to be amused by glass beads, but a ruler who, even if his domains did not match those of his ancestors, was conscious of his great heritage and jealous of his prerogatives. Like his father, his resources limited his power and

left him at the mercy of stronger states. Briefly, in 1863, the influence of Siam was sufficient to bring him into confrontation with
France, but in the years that followed he never openly flouted
France's position. At least twice, he tried to do so secretly, but
without success. The Protectorate Treaty was established on 11
August 1863.[25] It required Norodom to hand over to France the
conduct of his country's foreign relations and prohibited the king
from receiving any foreign consuls within his kingdom without
French authorization. In return, France pledged herself to give
"protection" to Cambodia, recognized the sovereignty of the king,
and undertook to assist in maintaining internal order as well as in
protecting the country against external attack. Other clauses protected the rights of Catholic missionaries and of Frenchmen resident in Cambodia. To oversee France's rights in Cambodia, a
French representative was to be appointed to the Cambodian
court at Oudong.

The signature of the 1863 treaty was chiefly the result of French
pressure. How much it accorded with Norodom's concern to attain
some independence from Siam is difficult to decide. French
sources, written shortly after the event, do not attempt to disguise
Norodom's hesitancy to sign the treaty, which Admiral de La
Grandière urged upon him, since the king feared that it would dis-
please Siam.[26] Quite apart from his long residence in Bangkok,
Norodom owed his seat on the Cambodian throne to Siamese support in 1862. These considerations could not be ignored, particularly as there were representatives of the Siamese king at Oudong
to remind him of his debt to Siam. Moreover, it was far from clear
in 1863 that France was securely established in Cochinchina. The
Hue court still hoped to buy the French off and to resume control
over the provinces that France had occupied; as the French
maneuvered at Phnom Penh, Vietnamese mandarins were still absent in France. The Siamese made sure that Norodom appreciated
the possibility that Vietnamese might once again be in a position to
attack Cambodia, should it be left unprotected by Siam.

At the same time, the French desire to establish a protectorate
over Cambodia offered Norodom a chance to be rid of the control

V. King Norodom as a young man in 1859 before he gained the throne (from *Le Tour du Monde*, 1863, in which Mouhot's accounts of his travels first appeared).

of Siam. In an interesting comment on the establishment of the protectorate, the knowledgeable Moura observed that Norodom deeply resented the tribute that Siam extracted annually from Cambodia's ruler. It was not that the size of the tribute or its value was particularly large; it was the act of tribute that excited Norodom's displeasure. According to Moura, France's agreement to provide protection without payment was one of the factors that led Norodom to accept the urgings of Admiral de La Grandière and to sign the 1863 treaty.[27]

Norodom's will quickly wavered after the treaty was signed. The 1863 treaty had to be sent to France for ratification, and this was slow in coming. Although the French maintained a representative close to Oudong, Siamese influence at the court gradually gained the upper hand. In December 1863, just three months after the conclusion of the Franco-Cambodian treaty, Norodom secretly signed a new treaty with Siam that completely undermined the provisions of the French-imposed agreement. In this new treaty, concluded and ratified without French knowledge, the king of Cambodia was referred to as nothing more important than a "governor," nothing more than a senior official within the Siamese administrative hierarchy. What is more, under this new secret convention, Norodom was forced to renounce his claims over the provinces of Battambang and Siemreap.[28] The enormity of such a sacrifice can be appreciated when it is placed against the recurrent and vigorous demands that he later made of the French that these two provinces be restored to Cambodian sovereignty.

The convention was kept secret and was, in fact, overtaken by events. French knowledge of its existence came only after France's predominance over Cambodia had been clearly established. This was achieved at Norodom's coronation.[29] The ceremony, in June 1864, came after the French had demonstrated that they were prepared to fight for their position in Cambodia.

In late 1863 and early 1864, Norodom was not only under pressure from Siamese representatives at Oudong, but was also waiting anxiously for the day when he would be crowned ruler of the kingdom. The most important items of the Cambodian royal regalia, the crown and the sacred sword, were retained in Bangkok. Without these the ceremony could not take place. As time passed, Norodom despaired of the Siamese ever sending the insignia and resolved to travel to Bangkok so that the coronation could take place there. This would have provided the Siamese with further powerful arguments that Cambodia was nothing more than a fief of Siam.

On 2 February 1864 the French representative at Oudong, Doudart de Lagrée, notified the Cambodian court that the Franco-Cambodian treaty had been ratified. But the treaty itself was still not to hand. Norodom, reacting to continued pressure from Siam, decided to travel to Bangkok to be crowned and notified Lagrée of his intention. The French representative warned him against such a step, stating that such a decision would have unpleasant consequences. Despite this warning, Norodom persisted in his plan, and on 3 March he set off for the seaport of Kampot down the road built by his father, Ang Duong. Lagrée acted swiftly. He led a detachment of French sailors to the court, occupied the principal buildings, and hoisted the French tricolor. The arrival of three gunboats from Saigon and the discharge of salutes, heard by Norodom as he proceeded slowly south, convinced the king that flouting the French would be unwise. He returned to Oudong, accepting, for the moment, the paramountcy of the French. When he was crowned, on 3 June 1864, it was in a joint ceremony with the representatives of France and Siam each playing a part. His reign name was provided by the king of Siam, while the French representative at the ceremony handed Norodom the crown. It was, for Norodom, the culmination of four years of waiting and hoping. He was, the reports of the ceremony note, ecstatic.[30]

Norodom's throne would have been extremely precarious without French support. One half brother, Si Votha, made no secret of his intention to contest the throne, and Sisowath was likely to adopt the same attitude if the Siamese king allowed him to leave Bangkok. Votha's long history of opposition to Norodom, which led to a life of discomfort in the most isolated regions of the kingdom, suggests some deep personal antagonism between the two princes.[31] By contrast, Sisowath emerges from the records as an opportunist who, although he ardently coveted the throne, was yet prepared to win it by more subtle means than outright revolt. For the moment, however, it was not princely rebels who threatened Norodom but rebels who claimed to be princes. The first of these was Assoa, who claimed descent from Ang Em, the brother of King Ang Chan (1806–1834) and King Ang Duong.[32]

This claim had no truth. Assoa was a former slave. In the unsettled conditions of Cambodia, however, his claim was accepted by a credulous peasantry for some time, until he was delivered into French hands in October 1866 by Vietnamese mandarins of the western provinces of Cochinchina. A much more serious threat came from Poucombo, an adventurer with striking charismatic powers who claimed to be a grandson of King Ang Chan. He was, in fact, a member of a small minority group, the Kuoy, now almost completely assimilated into the Cambodian population. Once again, what was important for a disoriented peasantry was not the veracity of his claims but the fact that Poucombo made them. Backed by Vietnamese vagabonds, and possibly by mandarins who hoped to embarrass the French, Poucombo rallied a large part of the Cambodian population in the east of the kingdom in Ba Phnom Province and about Tay-Ninh in Cochinchina to his cause. During 1865 and 1866 he had considerable success, sacking villages that resisted him and eluding French efforts to capture him. His followers may have numbered as many as ten thousand, and for a period he appeared to threaten the court at Oudong. Not until December 1867 was he finally captured and put to death by his own countrymen.[33]

These events offered some reassurance to Norodom that there was value in alliance with France. Moreover, even in regions free from revolt, immediately after Norodom's coronation there was disaffection and resistance to demonstration of authority by the central power.[34] Yet, if French power worked to save Norodom from the rebels, he cannot have reacted with pleasure to the trust that the Saigon-based authorities now put in his half brother Sisowath. According to Doudart de Lagrée, when Norodom learnt that

Sisowath was in Saigon he was terrified.[35] Prince Sisowath had entered into negotiations with Admiral de La Grandière in January
1865 with the aim of returning to Cambodia. The admiral did not
accede to this request, but he allowed the prince to come to Saigon. The possibility of playing off Sisowath and his kingly half
brother was well to the fore in French minds. The acting governor
of Cochinchina, Admiral Roze (1865), believed that Sisowath was
more intelligent than Norodom and "more acceptable to the Cambodians than the king."[36] Although Lagrée was unconvinced of
Sisowath's intelligence, he did agree with Roze's estimation that
Sisowath was a more popular figure than Norodom.[37]

By 1867 the first serious discussion about the possibility and desirability of removing Norodom from the throne of Cambodia was
taking place. The minister of the colonies asked Admiral de La
Grandière to consider the matter, since it did not seem proper that
France should be giving its support to a king who had secretly
conspired to contract a treaty with Siam.[38] La Grandière saw no
immediate utility in removing Norodom since, in his estimation,
Sisowath did not possess "more aptitude, energy, or intelligence"
than Norodom.[39] Nevertheless, in June 1867 the admiral reported
that he had "required" Norodom to appoint Sisowath as "commander" of the eastern provinces of Cambodia where Poucombo's
efforts had been most successful. This forced reconciliation gave
Sisowath an opportunity to demonstrate his adherence to the
French, and he took an active part in the drives against Poucombo's supporters.[40]

One year later, La Grandière prevailed on Norodom to appoint
Sisowath as *obbareach*, a position that would almost certainly
assure him the throne if the king died suddenly.[41] To the support
of an independent position for Norodom's half brother, the French
added a further galling blow. Without consultation, the French
government concluded an agreement with Siam under which, in
exchange for Siam's giving up any claims over Cambodia, France
ceded the western provinces of Battambang and Siemreap to Siam,
thus giving formal recognition to the *de facto* control that Bangkok
had exercised over the regions since the end of the eighteenth cen-

tury.[42] The Franco-Siamese convention was negotiated during 1865 and signed in 1867. Norodom expressed his resentment at the actions of the French government. In a written protest, he noted that he reserved his rights, and those of his heirs, over the ceded provinces.[43]

The first four years of the French protectorate had thus left no doubt as to where power over the ultimate direction of affairs in Cambodia lay. The main compensation for Norodom, and a very important one, was his occupancy of the throne. Even the direction of the kingdom's internal affairs, in theory his alone, became the subject of increasingly close French scrutiny with the appointment, in 1868, of Jean Moura as the French representative. For the next eleven years Moura's life was spent almost entirely in Cambodia, advising, persuading, and at times browbeating Norodom. As his massive monographic study of Cambodia shows, he was a man of high ability. If there is some evidence for his impatience with Norodom, and what Moura saw as the king's vices, there is also evidence that Norodom was prepared to work with and through Moura when it appeared to be in his interest. Such an occasion occurred in 1869.

The important province of Kompong Svai, to the north of Phnom Penh, had a long history of factious resistance to the Cambodian throne. Following the retirement from the province of its former governor, Norodom had sought to bring some order by dividing the province into three smaller units. The first two new governors whom he sent to take up their posts were chased away by the inhabitants. A third was killed. Because of this history of violence, other officials were unwilling to accept posts within Kompong Svai and refused the positions that Norodom offered them. Finally, one official accepted, on condition that Moura accompany him when he went to take up his appointment.

Moura was aware of the province's history of trouble. Through an informant he learned of the suggestion that he should accompany the new governor. At first, however, no direct approach was made to Moura. One of Norodom's officials introduced the subject of Kompong Svai into discussion with Moura and made veiled allusions to the possibility that the Frenchman should lend his prestige to the new governor. The French representative rejected this oblique approach, telling the Cambodian official that Norodom must ask him directly. He would then make his decision on the basis of how the question was put and the actual conditions in the province. In the maneuvering for prestige and influence, Moura won this round. Norodom summoned him and asked him to go to Kompong Svai. Moura, after a deliberate delay, agreed to go. By his own report the visit was a considerable success; Moura exhorted the population, which gathered to see him, to respect and honor the new governor.[44]

While the appeal to Moura for aid in the administration of Kompong Svai reflected Norodom's ambiguous position under the Protectorate Treaty, in other spheres of government he acted as a traditional Cambodian ruler, without regard to the French presence. His decision in 1870 to call together a body of officials to revise Cambodia's laws so as "to enlighten his kingdom, in order to govern it well and to assure its security by his power" was the effort of a king far from cowed by the French.[45] That the commission achieved little accords with the undoubted decline in Norodom's freedom of action and his subsequent increasing introspection as France took an ever more active role in Cambodia.

Not all was tension and political maneuvering at the Cambodian court, however. The king's taste for pleasure has already been noted, and the association with Europeans gave Norodom access to new products of Western technology and other symbols of Western civilization which intrigued and amused him. In 1865, through the French merchant and adventurer Caraman, he ordered water pumps, a telegraph machine, a camera, an electric motor, and portraits of the French royal family.[46] The French authorities provided Norodom with a steam-driven yacht, and after the capital of Cambodia was transferred downstream from Oudong to Phnom Penh in 1866, the French government shipped to Cambodia for Norodom's use the Victorian-baroque villa that the Empress Eugénie had used when she was present at the opening of the Suez Canal. It was, for a period, his favorite palace.[47]

Moreover, while the life of the court went on almost entirely apart from the small resident European community, there was a section of Phnom Penh society where East and West did mingle. Sometimes this mingling had official overtones. Writing in 1885, the protectorate's medical officer noted the way in which, during the earlier period, the doctor attached to the protectorate staff treated the royal family and established quite close relations with members of it.[48] Norodom is reported to have played billiards with members of the official French community during the sixties and early seventies. Less credible is the suggestion that while playing he took advice from French officials on reforms that should be instituted in his kingdom.[49]

Norodom's court was cosmopolitan. Siamese occupied important positions within the court and, as late as 1889, the palace cavalry was composed of Siamese.[50] His father had had close associations with some of the Chinese who worked in and about the Siamese court. A number of these men accompanied Ang Duong back to Cambodia and continued to be associated with his son. Also linked with Norodom, in a relationship difficult to analyze, was a motley group of Europeans who blended occasional business relationships with a curious *camaraderie*. Caraman, one of the earliest French settlers in Cambodia, lived for decades in partial amity with Norodom, now supplying him with European luxuries, now in dispute with the king over the nonfulfilment of a contract.[51] Le Faucheur, another early settler, was involved in the early commerce of Phnom Penh and at the same time an associate, of sorts, of Norodom.[52] There were others: the widow Marrot and her son, to whom Norodom was said to owe large sums of money; Ternisien, a creole from Guadeloupe who had once been a magistrate in Cochinchina; and Blanscubé, the French spokesman in the Colonial Council of Cochinchina for the Indians resident in that colony.[53] These and other European expatriates, such as German businessmen in Phnom Penh, were associates, if not friends, of Norodom.[54]

Of the principal Cambodian figures at court in this period it is difficult to say very much. In the early years of the protectorate,

Norodom, his half brothers, and to a lesser extent the queen mother, still living in a world of rigid traditionalism at the former capital of Oudong, stand out as the main participants in events. Possibly the French observers reporting on these early years had not yet gained sufficient sense of the inner workings of the court to provide any detailed account of its lesser figures. Not until the final decades of the nineteenth century is it possible to write in detail about leading Cambodian officials.

One exception to this general observation was the *kralahom*, the minister of the navy, who is revealed as a supporter of the French presence in Cambodia through a record of conversation prepared by Moura in 1875. This Cambodian official felt that the protectorate meant peace in the land, but his views were not, he noted, always shared by others:

Since Cambodia is under the protection of France it is peaceful within and sheltered from foreign invasions. . . . Formerly, there was always war. . . . Today the officials have homes built of masonry which they never dared have before; thoughtful men are setting themselves up in a more comfortable fashion; the chief monks are rushing to erect suitable pagodas. . . . But the people do not have enough of your advice and counsel in matters connected with administration and finance. You have the whole people for you . . . you also have some honest and intelligent officials who know your intentions, but you cannot hide from yourself the fact that you are an obstacle for the majority of the officials, who most certainly wish that you would close your eyes to their conduct and would only appear to shoot down the people when, by chance, they cry out against the injustices and spoilations to which they are subjected today.[55]

From the early seventies onward, French concern for change and reform led to more frequent confrontations with Norodom. A counterpoint to this theme was the developing discussion of who should succeed Norodom, either at his death or in the event of a forced abdication. In 1870, Sisowath was installed, as La Grandière had earlier proposed, as *obbareach*.[56] The country was at peace and Moura rarely interfered in the affairs of the kingdom so as "not to excite the susceptibilities" of the king.[57] By 1874, however, French preoccupation with effecting reforms in Cambodia had triumphed over the earlier reluctance to interfere. Two principal motivations lay behind this developing policy. The practical result of the existing Cambodian administration, in French eyes, was actual and threatened rebellion. The French considered heavy taxes the cause for recurrent uprisings in the provinces,[58] and they blamed Norodom. The turbulent history of the fifty years before the arrival of the French had left much of Cambodia ravaged and desolated, and had weakened the control of the court over the outlying regions, so further encouraging rebellion. The French administration, particularly after the Poucombo revolt, knew that any real challenge to Norodom would have to be put down by French forces. This alone was sufficient to lead them to consider urging reform. More general considerations of the French civilizing role came into play when they observed the continuing institution of slavery and urged its abolition.

The problem of how to institute reform remained. Norodom showed no inclination to alter the administration that he had inherited. But the Frenchmen who puzzled over the issue noted that the situation could be expected to change when he no longer occupied the throne. During 1872, Admiral Dupré had given advice that should Norodom die, Sisowath was to succeed only after he had accepted French advice to establish a civil list and surrendered control over the finances of the kingdom into French hands.[59] In 1874 came the first of the many crises in Norodom's health which were to bring hope, and then disappointment, to the French administration. Although it was not clear whether or not Norodom was really close to death, the possibility was sufficient to evoke a lively correspondence between the French representatives in Cambodia and Cochinchina and the home ministry.

The initial reaction, which Moura supported, was that, despite the grave faults of the situation, nothing should be done in the king's lifetime. The governor of Cochinchina, Krantz, noted that once Norodom was dead, and Sisowath on the throne, it would be different; Sisowath, though "just as prodigal and just as given to vice," did not have "a taste for absolute power." [60] Certainly

Moura had given his superior a gloomy picture of the administration of the kingdom. Norodom, Moura asserted, was isolated from his people and even from his own ministers, relying on palace women for advice.[61]

Norodom was not to die yet, however, and Krantz's successor as governor of Cochinchina, Admiral Duperré, was inclined to be tolerant of the manner in which Norodom governed his country. Whether through calculation or a passing phase of resignation, Norodom presented himself to Duperré as ready to cooperate with Moura on all issues.[62] Moreover, Duperré observed, if Norodom was at times uncooperative, he had substantial grievances to level again the French in relation to the frontiers of his kingdom. Apart from the disputed provinces of Battambang and Siemreap, the French had never held to their engagement to rectify the frontier situation near Chau-Doc and Ha-Tien, where large numbers of Cambodians lived, previously under Vietnamese, and now under French, control.[63] Finally, it seemed unlikely that Norodom's reign could last much longer in view of the state of his health.[64]

In the meantime it was possible to intrigue for the future. On Duperré's orders, Moura engaged Sisowath in a long and confidential discussion of the events likely to occur on the king's death. A full record of the conversation has been preserved, transcribed by Moura immediately after the interview in the form of a dialogue.[65] It leaves no doubt about Sisowath's attitudes and his readiness to work with the French to achieve the Cambodian throne. The interview opened with Moura stating Duperré's concern to establish good administration in Cambodia. Another concern of the admiral was the state of the king's health, and Moura had been asked to report on who would be the most worthy candidate for the throne when "an unfortunate event might occur." To this blunt, if slightly veiled, opening gambit, Sisowath replied: "I cannot commit myself before the right moment comes, but if the Admiral really wishés to support my rights to the throne, I promise to act according to his wishes."

But Moura eloquently disclaimed any wish to have commitments from the king's half brother. He himself was not in a position to make any commitment from the French side. Reacting to Siso-wath's reply, he pointed out that the *obbareach*'s succession was not absolutely assured. Norodom might press to have one of his sons succeed him, and according to the rules of succession, it was more normal for a son to succeed his father than a half brother his half brother. The choice would depend on the great officials of the kingdom—and the French. The record goes on:

The second king: I know this, and I know most importantly that it is you [the French] who will propose who will be king.

The representative: I am convinced of this, too, and so much the better for the kingdom! But I do not think that the French government would ever give its protection to a prince who did not recognize in advance the necessity to make changes in the treaty [of 1863] and in the administration of the country, which I am going to outline to you. . . .

The reforms that Moura outlined had already been discussed in correspondence with Paris: control of the kingdom's finances, the establishment of a council of government of which the French representative would be a member, the institution of a civil list. As the demands were listed, Sisowath's responses brought him further and further into the French web. Some of his closing comments, and those of Moura, complete the picture of French intrigue and Sisowath's overpowering desire to gain the throne:

The second king: Indeed, I can say to you, from this moment, I find these propositions too reasonable and the changes that you speak of too necessary not to accept them if I am ever king.

. . . . .

The second king: The system that you have just succinctly outlined, if it is put into action in Cambodia, will transform the country in four or five years. Cambodians are very easy to administer, and if one places them under such a wise and equitable system, they will be grateful and there will be unending peace in a country which has only known revolutions.

The representative: Remain, therefore, with these good attitudes, and then count on us. I will not speak to you again about these matters, which must stay just between us. . . . I recommend you to find a way to gain again the popularity which you have previously enjoyed in

Cambodia and Cochinchina and above all to merit the esteem and the affection of the French authorities.

The vigor of Sisowath's response to, Moura's propositions encouraged Admiral Duperré to suggest that a secret convention should be prepared for Sisowath to sign, indicating his approval of the reforms required by the French. Doubts about the wisdom of such an action among officials in Paris prevented this.[66]

There was a brief period of calm until, one year later, a new rising against Norodom's authority broke out in the country. Si Votha had returned to Cambodia. Begging the pardon of the king of Siam for his unauthorized departure, Votha left Bangkok, swiftly passed through Battambang, and travelled onward to the higher regions of the Mekong. He had little difficulty in quickly raising a large band of supporters and began to harry the officials loyal to his half brother Norodom.[67] He besieged the provincial capital at Kompong Thom and ranged through the turbulent province of Kompong Svai. Forces dispatched under Norodom's order failed to apprehend him.

The situation gave the French authorities a particularly attractive bargaining position. The reforms that they had long wished to implement, but had postponed rather than face a confrontation with Norodom, could be demanded against a promise to aid the king in resisting his half brother. Duperré, analyzing the reports that reached him in Saigon, argued that the real cause of the revolt was the great dissatisfaction that Norodom's policies had aroused in the country. In the circumstances, Duperré saw "no urgency to support King Norodom, who has remained deaf to our advice for so long." Help would be granted if he accepted the reforms recommended to him.[68]

The apparent ease with which those who challenged Norodom's authority were able to recruit supporters demands some explanation. Frenchmen such as Admiral Duperré—and even those closer to the events, such as Moura and Aymonier—insisted on the limited popularity of Norodom. Yet, in the uprising of 1885–1886 it was Norodom's prestige that ultimately brought resistance to French forces to an end. Votha was able to embarrass the king and gain recruits so quickly in large part through his personal qualities, which inspired loyalty to the end of his life. Moreover, fifty years of internal strife and foreign war had destroyed the network of internal administration. The king's temporal power did not stretch far beyond his capital. This left the control of provincial regions in the hands of the governors, who added their own exactions to the taxation demands of the central authority. This situation, together with the generally unsettled state of the country, probably goes far to explain Norodom's difficulty in meeting Votha's challenge. When he travelled in the countryside, the king's semidivine status brought respect approaching worship,[69] but when he was confined to Phnom Penh, challenges emerged in the outer areas.

As 1876 drew to a close, Admiral Duperré acted on his thoughts and demanded reforms from Norodom. He wrote to the king requiring changes, but to no immediate effect.[70] Votha remained in revolt, now striking at an outpost of Norodom's government, now slipping back to his sanctuary among the Stiengs, one of the tribal groups on the fringes of Cambodian society. The French were inclined to do nothing. Duperré remained convinced that Norodom's life was ending and that when a new monarch gained the throne it would be on French terms. For the moment it was desirable to leave the Cambodian king "in the grip of the rebellion that he has provoked."[71]

During the latter part of 1876, Moura had been on leave from Cambodia, his place having been taken by Philastre. In December he returned. His knowledge of the court and of Norodom led to the reopening of negotiations for change, and these were brought to what appeared to be a successful conclusion in January 1877. On 15 January Norodom proclaimed a series of reforms, and in return the French now bent their efforts to defeating Votha.[72] The French authorities did not achieve all the desired reform, but Norodom accepted several important changes. He agreed to abolish the special position accorded the *obbareach* and the queen mother on the death of the incumbents. The title of *abjoreach*, previously accorded to a king who had abdicated, was eliminated, and the powers of officials serving other members of the royal family other than the king were ended. In order to improve the process of government, the French insisted that matters of state should be discussed in a council composed of the five principal Cambodian ministers, sitting apart from the king. Decisions would then be placed before him for approval. No new tax could be instituted without this council's approval. Slavery was to be eliminated by degrees; to begin with, no person was henceforth to be enslaved for life, and the possibility of purchasing freedom was to be open to all debt slaves.[73]

Even more significant than the proclaimed reforms was a secret convention concluded between Norodom and Duperré. This provided that the French representative in Phnom Penh could, "when he expressed the wish," sit as a member of the council of ministers with a "consultative voice." His presence was obligatory when such matters as finance, the legal system, foreign trade, and internal disturbance were discussed.[74] This agreement was not quite as far-reaching as the provisions regulating the British residential system in Malaya, but it clearly foreshadowed an arrangement in which "advice" had to be accepted.

French-led troops suppressed Si Votha's rebellion but failed to capture the prince. He was sighted during an engagement in February 1877 but escaped, mounted on an elephant.[75] Calm returned to the countryside, and the French awaited indications that changes had been effected in the administration of the kingdom. The new governor of Cochinchina, Admiral Lafont, noted that Norodom had received him courteously and vowed his attachment to France, but doubt remained that any real progress towards change was being achieved.[76] There was good basis for this doubt. Not only was Norodom unready to take action to effect the changes that the French desired; he had begun to look for ways to counterbalance the overwhelming French influence over Cambodia. The result was the mysterious Spanish treaty affair, which caused concern to the French for more than four years.

Diplomatically, the issue was without result. The affair commands attention for the indication that it gives of Norodom's continuing efforts to elude or counter control of his kingdom. As with the secret treaty Norodom concluded with Siam in December 1863, news of the king's negotiations did not reach the French until after a treaty had been concluded. The preserved documents leave many unanswered questions and testify to the embarrassment it caused. The government of Spain disavowed the treaty, leaving the impression that the maneuvering had been on the personal initiative of the Spanish consul in Saigon. At some point in 1877, Norodom had entered into secret contacts with this consul. Writing in the early 1880's, French observers believed that an interpreter working for Norodom (a Spanish national) may have provided the link between the king and the consul.[77] It was also thought possible that Spanish businessmen resident in Phnom Penh played some part in the affair.

Without a text of the treaty to consult, it is difficult to give any precise account of its terms. In Paul Collard's view it would have involved nothing less than Cambodia entering into direct relations with Spain, quite without regard for French rights. This may be an overstated interpretation, since any contact that Norodom developed would have infringed France's position. The impressionistic accounts of the intrigue suggest that Norodom wished, at least, to reach some commercial agreement with Spain and, if possible, to gain the right to have a Spanish consul accredited to his court. In this, Norodom misjudged the French. Only a few months before negotiations began, the French had been ready to see him threatened by rebellion when he failed to cooperate with them. Yet, as Le Myre de Vilers remarked in 1881, Norodom's decision to seek relations with another European power was in the true Cambodian tradition of attempting to balance one power against another. Previously Cambodia had sought to play Siam against Viet-Nam. With Spanish encouragement, it may have seemed just as reasonable to attempt to play France against Spain.

By the time Le Myre de Vilers' instructions were prepared in Paris in 1879, as he prepared to take up his post as governor of Cochinchina, the French government was aware in broad terms of Norodom's essay at independence. The governor was instructed to make perfectly clear to Norodom that agreements with powers other than France would not be tolerated. Le Myre de Vilers faithfully followed his brief. Convinced in 1879 that secret negotiations were still in progress, he forbade the king to receive a visit from a special Spanish diplomatic mission then travelling in the Far East. This led to the exquisite irony, fully appreciated by the French and deeply resented by Norodom, that gifts from the Spaniards had to be passed on to the king by the French representative, Aymonier. It was a bitter moment for Norodom. There are suggestions in the correspondence for 1880 and 1881 that Norodom may still have looked for a way to develop a link with Spain, but watched over by the French, there was little he could do.

Resentment of Norodom's intrigues played a large part in the hardening of French attitudes clearly apparent in the early eighties. Thus, well before the climactic events of 1885, the French authorities and the Cambodian king consistently found themselves in opposition. The changes in personnel on the French side were important. Moura had left Cambodia in 1879, never to return, and he was succeeded by men without his long experience with the court and Norodom. Now at the head of the colony of Cochinchina, and so in charge of France's relations with Cambodia, was Le Myre de Vilers, a man preoccupied with order and a firm supporter of France's civilizing mission. As he surveyed the "prodigality" of Norodom's court, a clash became inevitable.

Reports from Cochinchina that stressed the parlous state of Cambodia and recorded Norodom's refusal to honor the agreements of 1877 had their effect in Paris. It was more than French pride could accept. Norodom had entered secretly into relations with Spain, and may have attempted to do so again. Contrary to his undertakings, he had allotted the rights of the country's opium farm without consulting the French representative, noting by way of apology that he was drunk at the time.[78] Such conduct was sufficient, at some stage during 1880, for Le Myre de Vilers to consider proposing to Paris that Sisowath should be placed on the throne forthwith and Norodom exiled to Tahiti or Reunion Island.[79] The minister of the colonies shared Le Myre de Vilers' concern, and late in 1881 the governor received instructions calling for a stronger line with Norodom.[80]

The next year, Le Myre de Vilers acted to impose France's will. To counter Norodom's failure to control the kingdom's finances, the governor forced the king's agreement to meeting the cost of the protectorate. He warned Norodom that failure to agree would lead to a French decision to end the 1863 Protectorate Treaty. Against such a threat Norodom had no defense, except to register his discontent with Paris. This he did in a letter addressed to the president. He accused Le Myre de Vilers of requiring him to make concessions under threat and without justification. The governor's actions impaired his traditional rights, for not only had he insisted that Cambodia meet the cost of the protectorate, but he had also eliminated the king's rights to taxes from Vietnamese living in Cambodia and on markets and ferries, traditional sources of income.[81]

It was a brave protest, but to no avail. Le Myre de Vilers was acting with the support of his home government against a state that, short of a direct act of arms against the French, had no real way to withstand any demands. The French were aware of the divisions within the royal family and ready to exploit them to their own advantage. There was little sympathy among official Frenchmen for the "fantasies" of the Cambodian king. Moreover, the governor of Cochinchina had a talent for describing the Cambodian court in terms that made it repugnant to minds wrapped in European prejudices and values. In a long report, which he prepared towards the end of his posting, Le Myre de Vilers observed that until 1877 there had been virtually no check on Norodom's actions. The agreements negotiated in that year had not been executed. At the same time, the country sustained the evils of oriental rule in its worst forms:

Hunting after and sale of human beings is still carried on among the Phnongs [a generic and pejorative Cambodian word for hill peoples] and the Stiengs;
The officials, who are unpaid, continue their exactions and live by pillage;
The venality of the magistrates has not diminished;
Instances of brigandage multiply;
Public services exist only in name;

The roads and bridges, through lack of maintenance, have become impassable;

By contrast, the expenses of the court increase each year; the king, through vanity, has allowed himself to join the refinements of European comfort to the luxury of Asia;

Filipino bands and Cambodian orchestras;

Carriages of all sorts and two hundred and fifty elephants, driven and looked after by numerous slaves;

A flotilla of steam-driven vessels and innumerable boats of all sorts;

A Filipino bodyguard and a Cambodian bodyguard, infantry, cavalry, artillery, bodyguards, pages, etc. . . . in the European style;

. . . European servants, Chinese, Annamites, Filipinos, Cambodians, Phnongs, etc., etc.;

Immoderate acquisition of diamonds and jewels;

Finally, and to crown everything, a harem, made up of four hundred women, which becomes larger each year through the recruitment of young girls carried on in Siam through the intermediary of an Indian, Ibrahim, who is an English subject.[82]

It may be asked whether when Governor Thomson succeeded Le Myre de Vilers he read beyond this catalogue of failings to the qualification to the denunciation. It would be unwise, Le Myre de Vilers added, to strip all power from Norodom. If the king believed that the honor of his position was truly threatened, he might very well withdraw into the interior of the country. The population would rally to him, for "the Cambodian is profoundly attached to the monarchic form." [83]

Le Myre de Vilers saw a better way to attack the problem, and his recommendation points to one of the significant accompaniments of the first twenty years of French rule in Cambodia. It was in France's interest, he noted, to give even greater encouragement to the immigration of Vietnamese into Cambodia. The continual seepage of Vietnamese into the regions about Ha-Tien and Chau-Doc had transformed those areas into Vietnamese territory. The same could happen throughout Cambodia.[84] No precise figures exist for the Vietnamese immigration into Cambodia that took place in the nineteenth century, following the establishment of the protectorate. There had been earlier settlements during the grim days of the thirties and forties, when a Vietnamese general ruled in Phnom Penh, and certain commercial endeavors had already become Vietnamese monopolies before the French arrival. The biggest fishing enterprises on the Great Lake, for instance, were in Vietnamese hands.[85] The Catholic missionaries noted the spread of Vietnamese settlement along the Mekong as far north as Chhlong.[86]

Nothing would be simpler, Le Myre de Vilers argued, than to profit from this immigration into Cambodia. Indeed, it was in France's fundamental interest to do so. He believed that within fifty years the Vietnamese would constitute the most important element of Cambodia's population. When that situation had been achieved, Cambodia, and the Cambodians, would no longer present a problem:

We will lose our time in trying to galvanize this race that a fatal law seems to have condemned to disappear. In intervening in its administration, we would create innumerable difficulties without obtaining any result, for we would have to resolve most grave social issues.[87]

Faced with the resistance of Norodom and his court to the French, Le Myre de Vilers, whose whole career in Indochina showed action and vigor, chose not to attempt early change. He did negotiate some conventions with Norodom, such as the guarantee that Frenchmen involved in legal disputes with Cambodians would have a hearing before a mixed Franco-Cambodian tribunal, but his interference in internal affairs did not go as far as enforcing the 1877 agreements.[88] He displayed no great concern to institute educational reforms. There was a small French-directed school in Phnom Penh by the early eighties, but it catered chiefly for Chinese and Vietnamese children. As its director observed, there was such a marked antipathy between Cambodians and the children of other nationalities that very few Cambodians attended.[89]

Although his allusion to the threat of a national revolt if Norodom was removed was a brief one, Le Myre de Vilers apparently considered this sufficiently likely for him to hold his hand. French power in Cambodia was enough to meet local challenges to

Norodom's authority, and in moments of stress it could be used to coerce the king into accepting French advice. But it was still not sufficient in the early 1880's, at least in Le Myre de Vilers' judgment, for France to risk the dangers of a full-scale revolt. Moreover, from 1880 onwards, France was increasingly engaged in efforts to assert its position in Tonkin. This aroused domestic political controversy and strained the resources of the colonial civil service. So long as the outcome of events in the north of Viet-Nam was uncertain, it must have appeared inadvisable to take risks in Phnom Penh.

Yet it would be wrong to underestimate the effect of Cambodian resistance to change in forcing Le Myre de Vilers to postpone action. The kingdom was a pale shadow of its glorious past, and the ruler at times seemed little more powerful than the governors of his most important provinces—but he was the king. Attended by more than three hundred pages, his word was law within the palace and for the Cambodian population of Phnom Penh. When a horseman came to the palace wall, he dismounted and walked until he had passed the royal sanctuary, making obeisance to the physical symbols of royalty.[90] The importance of royalty was such that only a member of the royal family or a person who claimed to be could mount an effective rebellion against the king. The weakness of the king and the generally disordered state of the kingdom had led to a more than usual number of these challenges in the first twenty years of Norodom's reign.

French involvement in Cambodia had begun reluctantly and been directed initially to strategic and commercial interests. Once established, however, the protectorate slowly encompassed a greater sphere of activity as the French sought to impose their will on Norodom. Recognizing the existing tensions within the royal family, the French turned these to their own advantage. Stubborn resistance and intrigue were the only weapons left to Norodom. Faced with dire French threats, he would feign agreement. This he did in 1877, turning to Spain with the hope of countering the pressure of French officials. He resented his position deeply. The exalted state of Asian kingship had eluded him for nearly four years at the start of his reign while he waited for conditions to permit a coronation. When he was crowned, he was ecstatic. He protested that the reforms urged upon him would undermine his traditional rights. The new technology of the West intrigued him, but he had no time for new standards of behavior. He was intelligent, but he did not perceive that his obstinacy could one day lead to a total disregard for his feelings and interests. In contrast, Sisowath sensed the power and resources of the European newcomers and placed his fate in their hands.

When the major clash between Norodom and the French came, it revealed miscalculation on both sides. The restraints on Norodom's power had not eliminated his capacity to rally support. But this was not understood by a governor of Cochinchina who placed the implementation of a rational administration above all else. In resisting to the point where he risked deposition, and later giving his approval, at very least tacitly, to the anti-French rising in 1885, Norodom revealed a faith in the capacity of traditional institutions to reverse events. His judgment was partially vindicated in the years immediately after the rising took place, but that vindication only lent bitter urgency to the later efforts of French officials to assert their will in the tragic closing years of the king's life.

10

Years of Revolt (1884–1886)

The first twenty years of contact between Norodom and the French established a pattern of interaction. French officials would suggest changes in the nature of the country's administration, which were normally met by Norodom's refusal to agree on either the necessity or the desirability of change; acting from their position of strength, the French authorities then brought power to bear on the king to force his agreement. But there was a final step in the evolution of this pattern of French dictation and Cambodian acceptance. In general, Norodom's agreement to follow French advice was not implemented. This was notably the case with the 1877 proclamations, which set up a more rational form of government, with a special role for the French representative, and abolished slavery throughout the kingdom. The possibility that enforcement might lead to a major revolt against French control persuaded Le Myre de Vilers to abstain from precipitate action. His successor, however, took a different position.

When Governor Charles Thomson became the second civil governor in Cochinchina in 1883, and hence the French official with ultimate authority over Cambodia, French interests in the Indochinese region were expanding. By inclination, Thomson was ready to ensure that within his own sphere of responsibility France had supreme power. Unlike his predecessors, he was not ready to see an agreement forced from Norodom and then not honored. He failed to realize that Norodom was in no mood for compromise either. French sources show that Norodom was watching events in Tonkin closely and was encouraged by them to make some moves to resist further French demands for change.[1] Despite the agreements negotiated by Le Myre de Vilers, Norodom held out against French demands that he and his government should meet the cost of the protectorate over Cambodia. Prolonged discussion during July 1883 finally brought an agreement, in September, that from the beginning of 1884 the French administration in Cochinchina should take over the collection of taxes on opium and alcohol sold in Cambodia. This arrangement would meet the cost of the protectorate. It was the French understanding that Norodom was also ready to approve the installation of police posts throughout Cambodia, to provide a greater degree of security, and would provide Governor Thomson with the draft of a new "constitution" implementing previously agreed reforms.[2]

While Thomson badgered Norodom, he was in contact with Sisowath. On French urging, the king's half brother willingly signed a "very confidential" convention approving the program of reforms demanded by the governor.[3] Sisowath was in Thomson's eyes "this prince, who is absolutely devoted to our policy, [who] has long ago adopted our general views leading to the modification of the protectorate." [4] Only three months later, the *obbareach* apparently felt the need to give further proof of his support of French policy. At the beginning of 1884 he sent a telegram from Phnom Penh to Governor Thomson in Saigon, reiterating his devotion to France.[5] The knowledge of this ready support was an important factor in the events that culminated in Norodom's forced signature of the convention of 17 June 1884. The presumption was that if Norodom did resist French pressure, then Sisowath would mount the throne as a French puppet.

During the first months of 1884, the king appeared to accept the French presence in his kingdon with reasonably good grace. An impressive ceremony took place in March 1884 to mark the inauguration of the "mixed tribunal," the body with French and Cambodian membership that would have jurisdiction over contraventions of the new taxation system negotiated in September 1883. Thomson, however, wanted more. He next proposed that France should assume direct control of Cambodia's customs service. This was Norodom's sticking point and the immediate origin of the tense negotiations in June. The clash was the end product of basic differences in outlook between the French and Norodom. The issue was less important than the underlying questions of principle. More than any preceding event, Norodom saw Thomson's demand in April 1884 that control of the customs service be ceded to France as eroding his personal position within the kingdom. He refused, setting forth his reasons in a letter summarizing the history of his relations with France:

> In the beginning I concluded a treaty of alliance and friendship with the French government and the high French officials; I was directed to observe this treaty faithfully.
>
> Now the Cambodian government sees that this new affair [the customs convention] is going to diminish the prestige of Cambodian authority.
>
> . . . . .
>
> The Cambodian government and the Cambodian people are not accustomed to giving up their ancient ways in order to adopt new ones. It will be thought that the king has lost all authority over his subjects.[6]

Concern that French control of customs would destroy his prestige within the kingdom marked Norodom's approach to the negotiations in June 1884. As Thomson pressed the king to accept the latest diminution of his power, Norodom reiterated his position. He stated that his officials were unanimous in advising him not to sign "a convention that would violate the ancient customs and destroy the royal prestige." [7] In interviews with Thomson on 5 and 7 June, Norodom insisted that he was ready to act in accordance with the terms of the 1863 treaty, but he wanted no further departures from the provisions of that document. Thomson also made his position clear. If Norodom refused to make the changes that the governor sought, the French government would be obliged to show Norodom that its protection applied "less to the person of the king than to the Kingdom of Cambodia." [8] The implication was clear, but in his new mood of firm obstinacy Norodom did not weaken.

In the face of this refusal to negotiate, Thomson felt France's

and his own personal honor engaged. After the inconclusive exchanges of 5 and 7 June, Thomson again endeavored to see
Norodom. The king refused to see him, stating that he was unwell.
This Thomson did not believe. As a precaution against public disorders, he summoned troop reinforcements and three gunboats
from Saigon on 13 June.[9] Acting on his own initiative, the governor decided that since Norodom persisted in his refusal to accept
the proposed customs convention, he would now impose a much
more stringent convention that would revolutionize the administration of the kingdom. Moreover, Thomson was ready to do what
had so often been discussed before: remove Norodom from the
throne. By 16 June there was an atmosphere of high excitement
among the Frenchmen in Phnom Penh and a state of apprehension
in the royal court. The new French troops had arrived from down-
river. At one o'clock in the morning on 17 June, Thomson completed dictating a dispatch summarizing the developments that
had already taken place and noted that in five hours he would pro-
ceed to the palace and demand satisfaction from Norodom. If this
was not given, he intended to dethrone Norodom and set Sisowath
in his place. If by any chance Sisowath failed to behave in the way
which Thomson expected, the governor noted that he would arrange for a council of officials to rule the country until the question of succession to the throne was resolved.[10]

The events that took place when Thomson proceeded to the palace have become one of the best known *tableaux* in nineteenth-
century Cambodian history. Thomson took a detachment of troops
with him, which remained under arms throughout the tense interview with Norodom. The gunboats stood by in clear view just off
the palace. The exchanges between Norodom and Thomson have
become the basis of legends that, though certainly rendering the
spirit of the confrontation, are not confirmed by documentary
sources written at the time. The best-known version of the scene,
repeated in modern Cambodian reconstructions, is provided by
Collard. He was not an eyewitness, but his service in Cambodia
began shortly after, in 1885, and he heard of the events from the
participants.[11] Reveillère, writing under his pseudonym Paul

Branda, also described the events of 17 June after talking with the participants. But, again, there is no documentary confirmation of the dramatic words that he attributes to Thomson and Norodom.[12] According to Collard's "authorized" version, Thomson penetrated to the king's chamber in a brusque display of *lèse-majesté*, wakening the king with the noise of his entry. He then read aloud to Norodom the text of a new, far-reaching convention that transformed Cambodia from a protectorate into something very close to a colony. Hearing the terms of the new convention, the king's secretary and interpreter, Col de Monteiro, is said to have cried, "Sire, this is not a convention that is proposed to your majesty, this is an abdication." De Monteiro was hurried from the room under guard. Norodom, left alone, had no choice but to sign. Thomson commented, "Gentlemen, here is a page of history." [13]

Branda's account provides dramatic dialogue to supplement the picture presented by Collard. He quotes Thomson as telling Norodom, after the king's initial refusal to sign, that if he did not do so, he would be confined aboard one of the gunboats lying off the palace. "What will you do with me aboard the *Alouette?*" Norodom is supposed to have asked. "That is my secret," was Thomson's reported reply.[14]

Although the official accounts of the events in the early morning of 17 June 1884 lack the verbal drama of later reconstructions, there is still a sense of excitement to the scene that they describe. Accompanied by a detachment of troops, Thomson marched to see Norodom, determined to impose a new convention. Norodom insisted that his earlier refusal to see the governor had been the result of genuine ill health. Faced with Thomson's show of force, he now indicated his willingness to sign the controversial customs agreement. But Thomson now wanted to exact the much higher price of complete administrative reorganization in recompense for the affront Norodom had given him. He told the king that he must either sign the new convention or abdicate. Faced with this choice, Norodom signed. At some stage during this encounter Col de Monteiro was accused of falsely translating some of the exchanges between the king and the governor. It was for this act, rather than the ringing declaration that Collard quotes, that he was removed under guard.[15]

As Thomson talked with Norodom, Sisowath waited in the wings. Before Norodom had to face the governor, Sisowath had already told Thomson that he was at the disposal of the French authorities. During the night of 17 June, after the convention had been concluded, he spoke with Thomson, congratulating him on the developments of the day and again indicating his readiness to serve the French cause. Thomson's estimation that it would only be with the greatest difficulty that Norodom would be able to bring himself to pardon Sisowath is not surprising.[16]

The cost to Norodom of the convention that Thomson extorted was high indeed. Under the terms of the first article of the convention, the king was obliged to "accept all the administrative, judicial, financial, and commercial reforms which, in the future, the Government of the Republic will judge it useful to introduce in order to facilitate the accomplishment of its Protectorate." Instead of a protectorate, directed by a representative in Phnom Penh with scant interest in affairs outside the capital, Thomson now proposed appointing French residents to provincial regions to control the administration of Cambodian officials. The number of provinces was to be drastically reduced, and the duties of the Cambodian officials within those provinces were to be "assimilated" to those of officials within the *arrondissements* of Cochinchina. Since there was no institution within Cambodia approximating the Vietnamese commune, Thomson proposed that a similar institution should be created, complete with a "mayor" and a council of notables, to ease the administrative task of the French. The business of the kingdom was left in the hands of the council of ministers, but its action was to be clearly subordinate to the resident general, who would have in addition the right to private audiences with the king. French residents in provincial centers were to exercise a strict control over the administration of justice. In order to assist in the economic development of Cambodia, the right to real property would be established. And slavery, long the bane of liberal critics of the Cambodian state, was to be definitively abolished.[17]

Norodom's acquiescence to Thomson's threats and the early response of the court officials to the proposed changes under the convention appeared to justify those who predicted that the *coup de force* would provoke no reaction because the Cambodian people would be sympathetic to the changes that the French wished to introduce.[18] Thomson's long elaboration of the detailed administrative innovations that would follow upon the convention did not provide the slightest suggestion of concern about untoward reactions to his humiliation of Norodom. For the moment, this estimation seemed justified by Norodom's confining himself to a written protest, addressed to the president of the French Republic. In this letter, Norodom denounced the new convention and the manner in which it was forced upon him. His illness, which had prevented his seeing Thomson and led to the governor's wrath, had been genuine, not feigned. He protested further against Col de Monteiro's removal from the discussions of 17 June; this had prevented his secretary from speaking to him at a difficult moment in the interview.[19] The authorities in France showed no inclination to take account of Norodom's protest, and Thomson worked diligently to implement the reforms listed in the convention.[20]

The new calendar year began with apparent calm, but before the end of January a large part of Cambodia was in a state of armed resistance to the French, and all thought of achieving real reform in the administration of the kingdom had to be subordinated to the immediate task of maintaining the French position in the country. The very fact of the revolt against French authority has long been minimized by French writers. An official military history of the French army in Indochina, written with more regard to glorification of French arms than to historical accuracy, observes that following the outbreak of the revolt in January 1885, "after numerous columns and reconnaissances . . . [there was] calm in the country at the end of 1885." [21] In fact, as French sources well show, it was not until France had concentrated some four thousand troops in Cambodia and gained the assistance of the king and his forces that a shaky calm was achieved, at the end of 1886. In the interim, bands of Cambodians in revolt against the French had roamed, almost at will, throughout Cambodia. There were fears at one stage that Phnom Penh itself might fall to the insurgents. In the classic tradition of the guerrilla, the Cambodian bands attacked only when advantage was on their side and were sustained by a strong belief in the virtue of their cause.

If there has been neglect of the history of the rising, there remains confusion about its origins. An account of the principal developments during 1885 and 1886 provides some basis for a more detailed examination of the origins and aims of the affair. On 8 January 1885 an isolated French military outpost at Sambor, just above the modern town of Kratie, was attacked by partisans of Prince Si Votha. This attack, which Thomson immediately interpreted as the result of Norodom's secret machinations, acted as a signal for uprisings in various parts of the country.[22] Thomson's original notification of the attack on Sambor was made on 10 January. By 12 January he reported general disorder over most of Cambodia, with banditry added to resistance to French authority. Even by this early date the French were considering whether leading members of the royal family might not be involved. Sisowath alone seems to have been above suspicion, as he denounced to the French an emissary from his half brother Votha who had sought to make contact with him and Norodom.[23]

Events during the revolt took place in four main geographical regions. Forces loyal to Votha had substantial control of large sections of Cambodia to the northeast of Phnom Penh. The state of the country in this region was well summarized in a report prepared by the French resident at Kompong Cham in January 1886:

We cannot deceive ourselves; with the exception of a few points on the river where our supporters still hold on, with difficulty, the insurrection is master of the whole region. Throughout, bands move about the country, taxing the population, recruiting men, burning the houses of our partisans, and attempting to take their women and children so that they can be removed to the interior as a way to force others to make their submission.

. . . . .

To give an exact idea of the situation, in terms of the attitude of the population, everyone works against an effort to make an evaluation of the state of the countryside. The Cambodian population is entirely won over to the rebellion.[24]

Despite the presence of the Cambodian minister of the navy, the *kralahom,* to aid the French, the situation in September 1886 seemed little improved and the threat from Votha's supporters just as great.[25]

Votha's strength in the northeastern region of the country was probably connected with the links he had established earlier with hill peoples of that region living on the edge of lowland Khmer society. There is evidence of minority groups playing a role in dynastic disputes throughout Cambodian history. During the fifteenth century a major revolt led by Prince Dharmaraja depended on the support of the Kuoy minority.[26] In a rather different fashion, the heroic and magical role of a member of the Pear minority, living in the west of the kingdom, who sacrificed himself to save the kingdom, is enshrined in a Cambodian legend linked with the Pursat area.[27]

In the east of Cambodia, around the modern centers of Svay Rieng and Prey Veng, the impetus for revolt was less closely associated with any one figure. This region had been one of the principal reservoirs of recruits for Poucombo's bands. Now, in 1885, there was a renewed readiness to resist the French-supported authority in Phnom Penh. One Cambodian source estimates nine thousand insurgents in the region.[28] Disorders spilled across the borders between Cambodia and Cochinchina, and villagers of Cambodian descent living near Tay-Ninh joined forces with bands from the Ba Phnom region inside Cambodia. Thomson's suggestion that the unrest in eastern Cambodia and in the area south of the capital was linked with Cambodian resentment of Vietnamese infiltration, which had tacit French support, is of particular interest.[29]

Other direct evidence shows that fear of future French control of life at the village level was one of the inspirations for the insurgents in the region about Takeo.[30] Here, too, it seems possible that concern for further Vietnamese appropriation of land was linked with the fear that the constitution of a real property system would take the control of land out of Cambodian hands.[31] In the south and southwest, in contrast to the east, there were identifiable leaders of the insurgents. For the most part, they were men of the traditional ruling class, governors and less important provincial officials. In a country where regional unrest often was associated with figures who claimed magical powers, it is no surprise to find that one leader of the rising in the Kampot region gained followers through his claim to invulnerability.[32] The seaport of Kampot was one of the chief focuses of insurgent activity in the southern and southwestern regions of the kingdom. For more than a year, the French garrison in Kampot was held in check by the insurgents, who were able to muster up to a thousand besiegers.[33] In the rest of the region there was the same pattern of pillage and arson against French positions and the homes of those who did not join the rising.

The provinces to the northwest of Phnom Penh constituted the fourth distinct region. Here again the insurgents were led by men from the governing class. No region seems to have suffered more than the plains about Pursat. This area was the traditional marching ground for Siamese armies when they came to invade Cambodia, and it had been devastated during the years of war in the 1830's and 1840's. With the onset of the 1885–1886 rising, devastation was once again common in the area, and it has been estimated that over forty thousand inhabitants emigrated from the region to Siamese-controlled Battambang in order to escape clashes between the insurgents and the French-led forces.[34] The capital of Phnom Penh, and the nearby former capital at Oudong, might be described as constituting one further region during the revolt. Phnom Penh was the center of French resistance to the insurgency and the point from which mobile columns spread out to undertake pacification efforts in the countryside. Nevertheless, despite the concentration of French power in Phnom Penh, the authority of the protectorate did not extend far outside the city limits, and in May 1885 the capital came under attack from the insurgents.[35]

Although the motivations behind the rising varied, and despite the regional cast to events, there was a substantial degree of military unity to the way in which the rising unfolded. Individuals and institutions associated with the protectorate were attacked. The distilleries operated by Chinese who sold their spirits to the protectorate or were the agents of the French alcohol monopoly were burnt and the lives of the Chinese threatened.[36] The Catholic missions, clearly linked with the French administration's position in the country, also suffered.[37] Increased French forces found it difficult to make any impression on the insurgent bands. The Frenchmen started from a position of disadvantage. As Lieutenant Dufour points out, they were almost completely without detailed information on the country in which they were expected to fight. By contrast, the Cambodian insurgents took advantage of their close knowledge of the country to lay effective ambushes, particularly along the rivers about Kompong Chhnang and Pursat.[38]

The insurgents avoided direct contact with superior forces, preferring to fire upon the French from a distance and then to retreat. By the time the French, advancing in double time through the tropical heat, reached the point from which the shot had come, nothing was to be found.[39] In the villages, the French found only old men, women, and children, for the ablebodied males were either with the insurgents or had fled when the French forces came into view. Yet, it was precisely the isolated villages that the French were unable to protect from the insurgents if their population showed any inclination to resist demands for recruits and material aids.[40] In the frustrating circumstances of guerrilla war, the French forces at times responded harshly and with little thought for the political implications of their rigor. The French resident general in Cambodia wrote:

The day the French troops invaded Cambodia, after the unhappy events of Sambor and Banam, they considered themselves to be in a conquered country and the inhabitants had to suffer all the calamities of a state of war; thefts from private homes and from pagodas, assassinations, rapes. . . . Such behavior had inevitably to bring the greatest part of the population to oppose us and engendered hatreds which it will be difficult to eliminate.[41]

There were instances of individual French commanders taking the law into their own hands and executing insurgents without regard to any legal process.[42] This was opposed by the civil authorities, but they supported execution of rebels provided the legal formalities were observed.[43]

By the middle of 1886 it was clear that purely military action could not solve the French dilemma in Cambodia. As Governor Filippini wrote:

The two provinces of Banam and Kratie, the only ones that were more or less peaceful, in the sense that civil authority was recognized and respected, were nevertheless troubled by incursions of pillagers and by the attempts at revolt of several bands. The province of Kompong Thom was almost entirely in the hands of Si Votha's bands. Kompong Chhnang and Kompong Cham were completely troubled, and although the situation was a little better in Pursat, this last province was no less troubled by constant rebel incursions; in Kampot we could scarcely maintain our posts for the troops and the customs service; finally, in Phnom Penh, only a few kilometers from the capital, the rebels made frequent appearances, stealing elephants and forcing the population to pay taxes to them.[44]

In an earlier description of the same period, Filippini had stated that French influence barely extended beyond a few kilometers around military posts anywhere in Cambodia.[45]

Not the least of the difficulties that the French faced was the high rate of disease among the troops that they committed against the Cambodian insurgents. Sudden death from disease was a normal part of life for Europeans in the tropics during the nineteenth century, but the scale on which disease affected the troops in Cambodia was extraordinary. None of the columns sent against the insurgents seems to have been exempt. In one notable instance, 75 of a detachment of 120 men had to be hospitalized on their return from an operation. The chief French doctor described the situation following the beginning of the monsoon rains:

The onset of the rains has reawakened malarial infections, and intestinal disorders have assumed a gravity which, up till now, I have never seen before. Finally, to these internal diseases, some recent military incidents have added to the wounded; twenty-one entered [hospital] the same day after the first attack on the fort at Pursat.[46]

The untenable nature of the situation forced the French to make new departures in their thinking. Most importantly, the part which could be played by the king was belatedly recognized, as was the extent to which the 1884 convention and subsequent developments had wounded the susceptibilities of large numbers of Cambodians. For the first time, an effort was made to reap some benefit from Norodom's prestige. This was in direct contrast to earlier lines of thought, when no effort was spared to inculpate Norodom in the organization of the rising and nothing was done to assuage his grievances.

The most detailed investigation of Norodom's possible involvement was made by Klobukowski, Thomson's *chef du cabinet*. In a manuscript report of more than two hundred pages he attempted to find an explanation for resistance to the French.[47] The broad bent of his conclusions was that Norodom was "legally the responsible originator of this agitation." Klobukowski's explanation of the way in which the revolt was plotted, however, was less simple. It warrants repetition, not because it is sufficiently supported by other evidence to be uncritically accepted, but because it may reflect some of the developments in the Cambodian court after Thomson's humiliation of Norodom in 1884. According to Klobukowski, Norodom had been forced into revolt by the various court figures who believed that their position was threatened. These included a Frenchwoman, the widow Marrot, and her son; a creole, Ternisien, who had once been a magistrate in Cochinchina; the old *colon*, Caraman; the deputy for Cochinchina in the French Parliament, Blanscubé; and the latter's secretary, Chabrier. On the Cambodian side, Klobukowski denounced the king's secretary, Col de Monteiro, a brother of Norodom, Nupparat, and a son, Duong Chacr.

Although Klobukowski's allegations must be treated with considerable reserve, his view of developments cannot be completely dismissed. There seems little doubt that Madame Marrot, to whom Norodom owed substantial amounts of money, and Caraman, who had long conducted business with the palace, were concerned about their future role once there was stricter French control over Cambodia. There is a strong possibility that their concern resulted in recommendations to Norodom to resist the convention that Thomson had imposed. Certainly Blanscubé and Madame Marrot's son played a part in forwarding Norodom's letter of protest to the president of France. It should be noted, however, that Blanscubé later disavowed Norodom and minimized the importance of the letter. As for the Cambodian figures whom Klobukowski mentions, it is far from clear whether he intended to link them with the Europeans whom he denounced. What may be said, with some assurance, is that opponents to the imposed convention were not lacking in the palace, and Prince Duong Chacr was certainly one of them.

Convinced of Norodom's weak spirit, Klobukowski pictured the king as spurred on by evil advisers, both Cambodian and European, to permit his officials to reply to the 1884 convention with armed revolt. In support of his contention, Klobukowski wrote of the letters circulated throughout Cambodia that bore the royal seal. He noted, it seems accurately, that nothing happened in the royal palace without Norodom's knowledge; it seemed impossible that he was unaware that his seal had been used in this way. For Klobukowski, only one step was open to the French; Norodom should be deposed and Sisowath placed on the throne. Although he lacked proof, Klobukowski felt sure that Norodom was in secret contact with Votha. It was unthinkable that such a person should remain on the throne, particularly since the French would need to strengthen the king's prestige in order to make the concessions required under the 1884 convention more acceptable.

The greatest difficulty attends any attempt to separate fact from speculation, and prejudice from objective reporting, when dealing with the Klobukowski version of events. He had a biased view of Norodom and close contacts with Sisowath.[48] These facts must be given full weight when considering his account of the situation. His desire to provide a total explanation, even when he was unable to cite any clear fact to back up his account of a particular development, is perhaps the most notable and most damaging characteristic of his summation. Thus, he would cite the undoubted fact of Duong Chacr's association with the rising and then link that prince with other participants without regard for the possibility that the rising afforded an opportunity for all discontented groups to register their protest against the changes which Thomson's convention portended.[49]

If one rejects Klobukowski's account of the rising as unsatisfactory, there remains a mass of disconnected evidence from which to build a more convincing description of the affair. All French commentators writing at the time of the revolt concurred in attributing a large measure of blame to Norodom. A surprisingly large number acknowledged that the terms of the 1884 convention were so wounding to Norodom's pride that some attempt to strike back should have been expected.[50] It is impossible to provide final proof, one way or the other. Letters seized from insurgents bore the royal seal.[51] Prince Si Votha endeavored to make contact with his half brother—and may have succeeded in doing so. The evidence of Votha's adopted son is particularly persuasive in this matter; when captured in 1885, he stated that some agreement did exist between Votha and Norodom.[52]

Yet Norodom consistently denied involvement with the insurgents. It may be argued that this was the only course open to him, especially since his fear of being deposed probably equalled his distrust of the French. In response to the French allegations, Norodom did not prevaricate as he had done, for instance, in the Spanish treaty affair some four years earlier. In a letter written in August 1885, Norodom energetically denied any personal association with the insurgents. He refused to admit any connection with letters bearing his seal, and he assured the governor of Cochinchina of his loyalty to France and of his reliance on the protection of the French government both for his own person and for his people. Short of taking to the field with the insurgents, there was little else that Norodom could do but deny the charges levelled against him. If his association with at least some aspects of the rising cannot be proved in any legalistic manner, the burden of probability nevertheless suggests his tacit approval, if nothing more, of this last real attempt to counter French power. Some older members of the Cambodian royal family still conserve the tradition that Norodom was indeed the inspiration behind the revolt.

There is no doubt concerning Si Votha's involvement. For the inhabitants of the northeastern region of Cambodia, Votha was a king, and he maintained his own small, if often impoverished, court. When Aymonier passed up the Mekong towards Laos in 1883, he found that Votha even maintained his own customs service, which levied small duties on those passing along sections of the river.[53] The letters that the French captured during the rising suggest that Votha tried to extend his influence beyond the region to which he had retreated after the events of 1876 and 1877. Letters from Votha to leaders of the revolt in the south and west of the kingdom urged resistance to the French and called on them to aid the king in his opposition to French control. Votha argued that the aim of French policy was to destroy Cambodia's ancient traditions and to punish and humiliate the members of the royal family who defended Cambodia's rights.[54]

Weighed against Votha's lifetime distrust of Norodom, the call for unity in his letters of 1885 must be judged as opportunistic.[55] It is difficult to believe that his long career of dissidence, both before and after the 1885–1886 period, was suddenly transformed for those two years. Votha would have recognized the appeal of apparent unity within the royal family when seeking to encourage resistance in areas where his own personal prestige was low. There is evidence that he had some success.[56] There was no reason for Votha to love the French, who had aided Norodom against him, but there was reason to support all who opposed the French once the rising had begun. If, indeed, Norodom had planned or agreed to an armed rising, there was every reason for Votha, who still had friends at court, to attempt to join his own permanent protest to the revolt, just as the French alleged he did. To deal with one fur-

ther possibility, there seems no reason to interpret the events of
1885 as an attempt by Votha to inculpate Norodom in a rising of
which the king had no knowledge.

Discontented members of the royal family were associated in
greater or lesser degree with the insurgency. Some joined the insurgents in the field; others formed a core of resistance to change
within the court.[57] Norodom's mother, living in Oudong, in isolation from the main court at Phnom Penh, was believed to be a secret supporter of the rising. This French estimation was based on
the queen mother's staunch support of the king's traditional prerogatives. Her court was alleged to harbor many supporters of the
insurgency. It certainly was a world, separate from Phnom Penh,
in which the standards of traditional Cambodian court life prevailed without any challenge from the West. The French authorities felt it highly desirable that she should join her efforts to those
that Norodom finally made to dissuade Cambodians from any further opposition to the French forces.[58]

Possibly the most interesting aspect of the revolt is the readiness
of the Cambodian officials to rise against the French. Norodom's
role is the chief focus for interest, and the reasons behind his resentment of the French are easy to find. The antagonism of other
members of the royal family towards the French is also readily
understood. But for the provincial officials, who played such an important part in raising resistance, a separate explanation is necessary. It is striking in how many cases these men emerge, from their
own letters and from reports on their activities prepared by the
French, as defenders of traditional values.

In the region to the east of Phnom Penh, the insurgent chiefs
had fomented revolt by arguing that the French would interfere
with the peasants' precious control over their land, by encouraging
Vietnamese immigration. Insurgents near Takeo responded to the
suggestion that in the future the French would levy taxes, instead
of Cambodian officials. Even if this call to revolt reflected the self-
interested fears of the officials that they would lose their traditional
incomes, it brought a response from the population. Both implicitly
and explicitly, the leaders of the insurgents rejected what they saw

as a complete change in the usages of the country and a threat to its traditions. French control over the king was repugnant, as was the diminution of the authority of the governors and the lesser provincial officials. The insurgents about Kampot told the French they fought because the king ordered them to do so; they believed and obeyed.[59] Among the most important evidence for the traditionalist character of the revolt is Norodom's proclamation of August 1886. By this point the king was convinced that there was no path open to him but cooperation with the French. Yet his proclamation was surprisingly unrepentant. It noted, "For two years the officials and the people have shown their discontent and have revolted, saying that great changes have been made in our government." [60] Now, Norodom told his people, he and his officials had decided to ask the French for a large measure of control over the affairs of the kingdom, and this had been granted.

If Norodom believed that the French intended to give him wide control over administration of the country, he was to be sorely disappointed in the years that followed. But for the moment the French were prepared to make some concessions in order to end the running sore of insurgency, which they could not otherwise heal. That Norodom's prestige contributed greatly to the ending of the rising is further proof of its traditionalist character. It also is a fact that should be placed against the more usual picture of the king exercising little control outside the immediate confines of his capital. In this instance, his presence in the countryside aided greatly in the conclusion of peace.

Governor Thomson returned to France in the middle of 1885, and when a new governor of Cochinchina, Filippini, was appointed, he was under instructions from Paris to end the rising as quickly as possible. Governor Filippini began negotiations with Norodom in 1886. He recognized both the necessity for some immediate concessions and the extent to which Norodom's honor had been engaged in the unfortunate days of June 1884.[61] On his first visit to Phnom Penh, in July 1886, at a time when the rising still held sway over most of the country, he offered concessions to Norodom in exchange for an effort by the king to bring the insurgency to an end.

Filippini's account of the meeting shows the extent to which it involved real bargaining. Norodom argued that he should have full power to pardon and punish those who took part in the rising. He asked that the French limit the number of residents to be installed in provincial regions and that they continue to leave provincial administration to Cambodian officials. He wished to maintain the right to name governors of provinces, and as a final right he asked that no land should be alienated without his consent. To all these requests, Filippini replied that Norodom must recognize that the 1884 convention had to be respected, but that he was prepared to go some distance to meet Norodom's desires. The king could continue to name governors, for instance, provided they were loyal to him and to France. On land matters, however, the governor would only agree that this question be left, for the moment, unresolved. He ended his first interview with Norodom with the warning that the French government, in exchange for the consideration which it was giving Norodom's wishes, expected to see an end to the rising by 1 January 1887. Norodom would have to ensure this.[62]

This first interview took place on 22 July. The following day the king and the governor met again, with Norodom adopting an even stronger demeanor. He sought to regain control of the state's customs services and indicated that it might not be possible to end the rising on the exact date that the governor had stipulated. Filippini again urged Norodom to ensure that his intervention did bring a successful conclusion by the appointed time. The suggestion that he might once again be faced with the prospect of forced abdication brought swift action by Norodom. He issued his proclamation calling for the insurgents to lay down their arms and noting the concessions that the French government was making to him.[63] He promised pardon for those who responded, but punishment for those who failed to do so. Norodom kept his word and made energetic efforts to bring peace to the countryside. He travelled into regions that had been under the sway of the insurgents and urged submission to his and French authority. In the southwest alone, he spent a month calling on former insurgents to lay down their arms.[64]

Other princes of the royal family played their part in calling for an end to resistance. Princes Chantavong and Neoppharot led expeditions into the interior to gain submissions.[65] Sisowath was particularly active. He had earlier worked with the French against the insurgents, but following Norodom's proclamation, he played an even larger role. He was selected to try to bring the most persistent area of insurgency, the region where Votha exercised influence, under control. Despite French admonitions to capture Votha before returning to Phnom Penh, Sisowath was not successful.[66] He brought a shaky peace to the region, but he failed in his major aim of capturing the dissident prince. French observers were probably correct in their belief that, whatever his relationship with the French, and despite his protestations of loyalty, Sisowath was reluctant to press the hunt with too much vigor. Votha was his half brother and a member of the royal family, and as such, not to be treated as merely another insurgent.[67]

As 1886 drew to a close, the insurgency died away. A few distant areas to the northeast, where Votha still exercised control, were the one exception to the general improvement throughout the rest of the country. Provincial insurgent leaders surrendered, and minor members of the royal family returned to place themselves under the surveillance of the king in the capital. The king's highest officials seconded the efforts made by members of the royal family to bring the insurgency to a close. Although the French authorities in theory had greater control over Cambodia than ever before, they had found it essential to exercise that power with restraint and to make due allowance for the sensitivities of the king. As 1887 advanced, with the exception of very occasional sporadic disorders, the country was at peace. Late in 1887 or early in 1888 even Votha's contribution to perennial unrest ceased as the prince retreated to the upriver fastnesses along the Cambodian-Laotian border. The last real Cambodian challenge to French authority had ended.

This period of revolt is important for a variety of reasons. It has initial interest as an historical episode that has not achieved the recognition that it deserves. The accounts provided by Collard and

Leclère are impressionistic at best, and at worst they tend to disguise the difficulties faced by the French in maintaining their authority. It is probably true that at no time was it likely that French troops could be forced to withdraw from their fortified strongpoints. On the other hand, retaining control of those positions was, for nearly eighteen months, all that four thousand troops could do with any certainty. At the very least, the rising threatened the whole character of France's relationship with Cambodia. The deposition of Norodom was discussed, as was the possibility that France should directly annex Cambodia and make it an outright colony in the style of Cochinchina. With other demands on French troops in Tonkin, Cambodia represented a considerable military embarrassment that the colonial authorities could ill afford. The final decision to work for peace through the king's prestige and to accept modifications of the 1884 convention reflects the incapacity of the French to achieve their aims in Cambodia through purely military means. They tried, and they failed.

The recourse to Norodom testifies to the continuing prestige of the king. Earlier in his reign there had been strong evidence of his failure to exercise real power outside the capital. The events of the revolt thus pose the question of whether by 1885 he had achieved some more positive position in relation to the outer areas of his kingdom. There seems little reason to give strong endorsement to this view. Although the king had not been able to control his provincial governors in earlier years, this did not mean that he was without prestige. There were few, indeed, apart from the similarly royal Si Votha, who would maintain their opposition to the throne in the face of the king's presence. Moreover, the way in which insurgent leaders rallied support by suggesting that the French had threatened the king and the royal family is particularly suggestive of the continuing appeal of the monarchy. That the king did bring peace to Cambodia, once he threw his weight behind French efforts, is equally strong testimony to the appeal of his person, if not of his power.

The events of this time of crisis provide one of the first important insights into a major theme in later Cambodian-French relations.

By 1884, the outlines of the great paradox of Cambodian history under the French protectorate may be discerned. This paradox is found in the continuing diminution of Cambodian power and the growing importance of the monarch as a symbol of national unity, unchallenged, as he had so often been in the past, by other members of the royal family. The paradox is further complicated by the fact that the king's temporal power, even during Ang Duong's lifetime, was severely restricted. It is probably more correct, therefore, to speak of the diminution of the king's theoretical power and the increase in his symbolic importance. When Norodom joined forces with the French there were none who could effectively oppose him. Votha's efforts in 1885–1886 were his last; he ceased to be of real importance thereafter. Not only was the combination of Norodom's prestige and French arms beyond defeat; the king, even by 1884, had added steadily to the symbols of his office. What Le Myre de Vilers reviled as a combination of oriental luxury and European comfort probably represented the most important demonstration of kingly power assembled in the Cambodian court for centuries.

The rising was important for Sisowath. Although he failed to capture Si Votha, he had further demonstrated his devotion to the French cause. This did not prevent French criticism of his capacities, but the pendulum swing from enthusiastic endorsement of the prince to denunciation of his weakness had occurred before. What was significant was his unhesitating loyalty to French aims. The period of the rising was also of considerable importance for the development of relations between the French authorities and those of the Cambodian elite who worked with them in the later period, when royal control over direction of the kingdom had been reduced to a minimum. Examination of the personal dossiers of Cambodian officials who held senior posts at the turn of the century and after reveals the extent to which cooperation with the French during the revolt enhanced a man's chances for promotion and French support.[68]

The over-all traditionalist character of the rising has been stressed. More difficult is an assessment of the rising's nationalist content. It is interesting to record the French acknowledgment of a "national hostility" to their position in Cambodia.[69] But it is more difficult to interpret just what this assessment meant. Because of the ethnic unity of Cambodia and the common language and religion, the country had certain potentialities for national unity. Nevertheless, national borders had little meaning for the ordinary Cambodian, who, if it seemed desirable, would cross to live under alien sovereignty for a wide variety of reasons. Forty thousand Cambodians did this during the period of the rising. To look for modern nationalism in the events of 1885–1886 is to seek an element yet unborn in Cambodia.

There is no evidence to suggest that the rising reflected any feeling that the French had interfered with Buddhism. Fear that increased Vietnamese immigration might lead to such interference, however, was of some importance. What undoubtedly was present was a general rejection of the French and of French control among a large number of traditional leaders, both royal and nonroyal. In a country where traditions and established custom had high prestige, the French were seen as destroying the values of the past and threatening the most elevated tradition of all, the Cambodian monarchy.

The rising profoundly affected the Cambodian population and countryside. In the years following the end of the revolt there was frequent reference to the exodus of some forty thousand Cambodians from the Pursat region into Battambang Province. One observer concluded that the Siamese government took advantage of the unrest in Cambodia to make conditions in Battambang more than usually attractive so as to promote this migration.[70] In some regions of the kingdom there was severe damage to existing ricelands. Irrigation systems were destroyed and land went out of production. Stocks of rice were burnt or scattered. This led to areas of famine within Cambodia, and it seems reasonable to accept Leclère's estimate that some ten thousand people died during the revolt, mostly as the result of famine.[71] The statistics of deaths among the armed forces are not revealed in available documentary sources. There were, however, heavy losses through disease.

Politically, the revolt temporarily preserved a measure of the king's power and frustrated the French wish to impose a strict control over the administration of the kingdom. Instead of the eight residents whom Thomson had wished to introduce under the 1884 convention, the French agreed to install only four. Despite the intention of the French authorities that the French resident general in Phnom Penh should control the activities of the council of ministers, the events of 1885–1886 had made them reluctant to move too fast in this direction, and full control did not come until 1897. The issue of slavery also lay dormant until that year, since it was found that this institution, viewed in such different terms by the French and Cambodians, was one to which the population was deeply attached. Slaves, chiefly debt bondsmen, provided an important source of wealth to the more prosperous members of the population and represented one of the few ways poor families could meet their financial obligations in times of difficulty. The royal establishment relied heavily on slaves for the maintenance of palace services, and hereditary slaves played a major part in the exploitation of cardamom in the mountains west of Pursat. Some recognition of the importance accorded slavery led the French to allow the institution to continue, even into the twentieth century.[72]

The halt in the development of French control was to prove only temporary. It was a respite dictated by necessity, and French officials did not hesitate to depart from their policy of moderation once they felt they had sufficient strength. If anything, the events of the rising reinforced French intentions to take the first opportunity to gain all real power in Cambodia. Governor Thomson had been mistaken in thinking that Norodom and his officials would not react to major changes imposed *en bloc*. The revolt that broke out in January 1885 revealed a whole spectrum of grievances against the French presence in Cambodia which could be linked with calls for the preservation of the country's national traditions. But if the period represented a partial triumph for Norodom, it was also his last triumph. In succeeding years, more skillful French officials adopted a policy of introducing reforms on a piecemeal basis that the rapidly ageing king found himself powerless to resist. This was particularly so as important senior officials began to rest their hopes of advancement and financial gain more with the French than with their monarch. Reinforcement of the king's symbolic status was important in the twentieth century. It must, however, have been of little consolation for Norodom to receive rich gifts from the French as he saw control over temporal matters slipping further from his grasp. It is not certain that Norodom uttered the words that Paul Branda attributed to him, in 1885, but there is no doubt that they expressed the king's sentiments. Forced finally to ratify the 1884 convention, Norodom is supposed to have said, "Your protection is the cremation of the monarchy." [73]

I I

The Eclipse of Norodom

The restoration of calm after the 1885–1886 rising left Norodom in a position of temporary strength. There was little immediate French inclination to force the king to the wall once more. The reports sent home to Paris expressed reservations on the degree of security achieved and about Norodom's intentions, but the policy followed immediately after 1886 aimed at preserving calm through a policy of reconciliation with the king. When the French resident general reported on the first quarter of 1888, he pictured the four main geographical regions into which the country had divided itself during the rising as largely untroubled by opposition to French control. Si Votha, lurking on the northeastern boundaries of the kingdom, was a nuisance but nothing more.[1]

Absence of major incidents meant there was calm in Cambodia; it did not mean there was stability. Indeed, there were basic factors at work that ensured that the closing years of Norodom's life would be marked by disputes and disagreements with the French. At the same time, the king's declining health led to increased maneuvering within the royal family to circumvent the apparent French desire to place the *obbareach,* Sisowath, on the throne when his half brother died. This maneuvering was traditional in the Cambodian court, and the kingdom's declining power seems to have been a spur to dynastic quarrels. The conflict between Norodom and the French was a new element in Cambodian history. Norodom, with little more than the conviction of his own rightness, attempted to block greater and greater French interference in his control of affairs.

French recognition of the dangers of pressing the king too far, and some understanding of Norodom's motives, did not prevent severe criticism of the king's actions. In the post-rising period

Norodom became very much concerned with securing the future well-being of his family and sufficient current funds to live in what he judged to be appropriate regal splendor. French control of two-thirds of his former revenue, resulting from the assumption of tax collection duties by the French, left Norodom very dependent on the protecting power.[2] To meet the expenses of his household, both for the present and for the future, the king relied heavily on the gifts of men who sought appointment to high official posts.

Cambodia's long history of warfare and internal rebellion had severely damaged whatever established procedures had existed for the administration of provincial areas. King Ang Duong's vigor and prestige appear to have provided a tenuous basis for control from the center, but there is no reason to suppose that even during his lifetime provincial governors were under much royal restraint. When Norodom assumed the throne, control became even less certain. The problem of administering the troubled region of Kompong Svai has already been described. By the eighties, provincial administration was very weak. Siamese incursions into Cambodian territory south of Angkor had been reported to the capital by local officials. From 1875, however, there had been no instructions from the court to these officials, who had to be content "to note the progress of the Siamese." [3] If there was not defiance of royal authority, there was a general lack of contact between the center and the provinces.

No set system existed for selecting provincial officials. Some service in the court was a normal requirement, and usually an official began his career as a page. These pages were almost always the sons of families that had long been associated with the monarchy. This background, or the performance of some personal service for the ruler, could lead to nomination as governor of a province, but there was no certainty and no fixed system of promotion. Such an arrangement, under ideal circumstances, could have had advantages. It offered the possibility of quick promotion for a man of talent. In a weak kingdom, however, the system encouraged abuse. Norodom's increasing alarm over the loss of his wealth made financial gifts for the king the essential qualification for appointment.

The earliest French observers of Cambodia seem agreed that it was traditional practice for the king to consult with his ministers on the appointment of provincial officials.[4] By the late 1880's, Norodom no longer did this. Ignoring the great court officials, he named and revoked governors by himself. Before he would provide a provincial official with the *tratang,* or diploma of office, Norodom expected a substantial gift of money or jewels. An official could suddenly be replaced by a wealthier contender for his post. The over-all result was a lack of continuity in the provinces and, consequently, poor administration. Once appointed, moreover, the governors sought to recoup the financial outlay that had gained them the position—at the expense of the inhabitants of the province. Governors were ill equipped to deal with resistance to central authority if it should arise. In the face of any real threat, they fled back to the capital. By the end of the eighties, the French resident general, Champeaux, reported that it was a common saying in Cambodia that only the governor had no authority in his own province.[5]

The situation was offensive to French standards of administration, but the fear of a further armed resistance made them hesitate before acting to bring change. More than ever before, they counted upon Norodom's early death and the succession of Sisowath, a prince who, they believed, would lend himself to all their plans.[6] Following the end of the Cambodian rising, there was increased consideration of the role of Vietnamese immigration into Cambodia. The possibility that these alien newcomers could supplant the Cambodians in their own land was present in the thoughts of many French officials. Such a "peaceful conquest" was seen as providing a surer means of achieving true French control in Cambodia than any further resort to armed force.[7] In the meantime, French officials were content to negotiate minor agreements with the king, such as one providing for the sale of land within the Phnom Penh city limits.[8]

While the French counted on Sisowath's future loyal cooperation once he was on the throne, his succession was not readily accepted either by Norodom or by his sons. In 1888 the French resident general in Phnom Penh reported his belief that Norodom had still not clarified his own mind on the succession. If he showed favor to any one son, it appeared to be towards Prince Duong Chacr, who had been active against the French in the rising of 1885–1886.[9] Two years later, a new French representative in Cambodia, Verné-ville, regarded Duong Chacr as a "dark cloud on the horizon." [10] Duong Chacr's talents and intelligence were the source of Verné-ville's concern. The prince's mother, Khun Sancheat Bopha, had earlier been a member of Ang Duong's female household and was, again according to Vernéville, a supporter of Siamese interests in the court with considerable influence over Norodom. Apparently in response to Vernéville's urgings, Norodom abandoned his support of Duong Chacr and placed the prince in chains.[11]

Alienated from his father, the prince fled to Bangkok, from where he addressed a letter of complaint to Le Myre de Vilers, the former governor of Cochinchina.[12] Next he travelled to France to further press his case, alleging mistreatment both by his father and by Resident Superior de Vernéville. At the same time he argued that a financial subvention, promised to him by the French govern-ment, had not been paid. Within a few months of his arrival in Paris, in June 1893, Duong Chacr was an embarrassment to the French government. His father was persuaded to authorize the prince's exile, and in August 1893, Duong Chacr was arrested after a violent scene in the Left Bank area of Paris. He was interned in Algeria, remaining there until his death in 1897 despite his pleas for exile in a climate similar to that of his own land.[13] The vigor with which the French countered Duong Chacr's possible threat to an orderly succession clearly indicates their anxiety to replace the intransigent old monarch with a willing puppet. Today, in modern Cambodia, Duong Chacr's name is largely forgotten.

Even before Duong Chacr's internment, another threat to stabil-ity had passed from the scene. After a lifetime of dissidence, Prince Si Votha died in December 1891. After the failure of his efforts in 1885 and 1886, his followers became fewer, dwindling to a few close companions by the time death finally came. In the closing years of Votha's life, he entered into hesitant and inconclusive negotiations with the French. Tired of long years of retreat in the forests of northeastern Cambodia and of living among the less civilized hill tribe people, Si Votha offered his submission to the French. At all costs, he emphasized, he wished to avoid either submitting to Norodom or having to rely on his half brother's word.[14] Although discussions took place sporadically during 1891, the old rebel never submitted to the French. Almost totally abandoned by his followers and quite without resources, he died on the last day of 1891. His long life of dissidence had never brought him within certain reach of toppling Norodom from the throne. Backed by the French, the king had always been able to resist his half brother, whatever the latter's popular appeal and gifts of oratory.[15]

Age, death, and exile all operated to make the years between 1890 and 1895 ones of relative calm. Norodom turned sixty in 1894. Recurrent ill health and personal indulgences had sapped his vigor. Duong Chacr was in exile, Si Votha dead. Norodom's mother, a staunch supporter of traditional forms and probably an important supporter of the rising, died in 1895. Her own small court of officials was broken up and integrated with the main court at Phnom Penh.[16] Norodom was still free to select and dismiss officials as he pleased, but the protectorate continued its efforts to gain control over the finances of the kingdom. From 1892 the French administration assumed responsibility for collecting all taxes within the kingdom, doing away with an earlier division of duties which had left some direct taxes in the king's hands.[17] The protectorate, in return, guaranteed the king's civil list, without exercising any real control over the way in which he disposed of the funds ceded to him. For the moment the question of slavery was allowed to die. The right of the French resident superior (his title had been changed from resident general in 1889) to sit with the Cambodian council of ministers had not been enforced. But in the provinces, there were ten French residents by 1894 in contrast to four in 1888.[18] From both the Cambodian and French points of view, the situation was far from perfect, but it had the virtue of a minimum of conflict.

That calm did not mean stability became abundantly clear in

VI. Prince Yukanthor as portrayed in one of the many cartoons which appeared during his visit to France. The caption for the cartoon reads "Prince Yukanthor has only come to France to learn baccarat, destined to replace the gambling game of thirty-six beasts" (from J. Hess, *L'Affaire Iukanthor*, Paris, 1900).

1897. The seeds of difficulty had always been present, and they only required the right combination of circumstances to spring forth in renewed and bitter confrontation between Norodom and the French. The occasion was provided when Norodom fell ill in 1897. During the previous year, Resident Superior de Vernéville had devoted increasing attention to the perennial problem of Norodom's successor. To the uncertain nature of the king's health was added the fear that Norodom might force the succession issue by abdicating in favor of his own selection for the throne. In July

1896, Vernéville underlined the dangers of such a development, for it was certain that whomever Norodom should select, it would be a prince hostile to France.[19] The resident superior's fears, in this regard, were a contributory factor in the maneuvers that he undertook in January 1897. Arguing that it was necessary to act because of the deterioration of Norodom's physical and mental health, Vernéville persuaded the council of ministers to agree to carry out business without consulting the king.[20]

Norodom was ill during January 1897, but it is questionable whether his illness was as grave as Vernéville reported. In telegraphic correspondence with acting Governor General Fourès in Hanoi, Vernéville described Norodom as close to death. In his turn, Fourès instructed Vernéville to take all steps to ensure that Sisowath assumed the throne when Norodom died, but only after the *obbareach* had signed agreements further reducing the power of the king in Cambodia. Paris, in response to Fourès' urgent telegrams, approved all the measures he proposed.[21] The king did not die, however, and when Governor General Paul Doumer paid a courtesy call on the Cambodian ruler in February 1897 he reported that, contrary to his expectations, the king appeared in reasonably good health and displayed complete mental lucidity.[22] It is through Doumer's dispatches that a clearer picture of what took place during January 1897 emerges.

Writing in November 1897, Doumer described the events in January as a *coup d'état.*[23] This is an overblown description, but it emphasizes the conspiratorial aspect of events. Vernéville did not act alone. It was necessary for a number of senior Cambodian officials to acquiesce in his plan to strip Norodom of most of his remaining control over affairs in the kingdom. Doumer believed that Prime Minister Um was an active participant in events as well as Sisowath.[24] Prince Yukanthor's particularly strong dunuenciation of Um three years later appears to support Doumer's view.[25] The governor general also noted Norodom's extreme reserve towards his former confidant, Col de Monteiro, after 1897 because of his belief that Monteiro had been a willing ally of the resident superior.[26] What Vernéville did was simple. He proclaimed that

Norodom was too ill to act on his own behalf and that in these circumstances full powers would be exercised by the council of ministers and the resident superior. In one stroke the king's power was reduced to the point where his authority scarcely extended beyond the palace.[27]

The year 1897 is thus an extremely important one in the history of relations between the Cambodian court and the French. Not only did the resident superior succeed in gaining executive power and in instituting a series of administrative reforms. From this year there is also, for the first time, a detailed record of the discussions between the chief French official in Cambodia and the Cambodian ministers. In carrying out his *"coup d'état,"* Vernéville placed himself firmly in position as chairman of the meetings of the council of ministers. At the same time, the proceedings of these council meetings were recorded to provide one of the most interesting contemporary records of the exercise of French power in Cambodia.[28] It is noteworthy that in some of the earliest sessions recorded in these minutes, the Cambodian ministers still showed themselves concerned about offending the king. When judicial reforms were discussed in a session held on 30 June 1897, the prime minister asked the resident superior not to expect ministers to act on an issue without the king's approval. He begged the new resident superior, Ducos, to understand the "difficult position in which we find ourselves." [29] Hesitancy dissipated when it became apparent that the French held the upper hand.

The French position was strengthened by the important Royal Ordinance of 11 July 1897. Prince Yukanthor later asserted that Norodom only agreed to sign this measure because Governor General Doumer threatened to dethrone him. The degree of coercion used on this occasion is not revealed in the archival sources. What is clear is that the July ordinance regularized the position that Vernéville had assumed at the beginning of the year. Some of the provisions of the ordinance, such as the abolition of slavery and the institution of a system of real property, were not fully enacted until after Norodom's death in 1904. Nevertheless, the fundamental provision of the ordinance did take effect. Under Article 2, no decision of the king had legal standing unless it was "countersigned and rendered executorial by the Resident Superior." [30] With the council of ministers under the chairmanship of the resident superior, and sitting apart from the king, the ruler's control over official appointments was effectively curtailed.

The minutes of the council of ministers' meetings make very clear the extent to which the council's chief order of business was the appointment and dismissal of officials. Since this part of official life had provided Norodom both financial gain and control over personnel, his resentment at Vernéville's usurpation of power is understandable. There was a general pattern to the selection of officials. After a vacancy had been made known, several names were put forward. Usually these nominations were presented by the minister within whose general jurisdiction, or apanage, the vacant office fell. At first, there was little French inclination to make nominations. Control was exercised by the resident superior's veto of those candidates whom he considered unsuitable. But once the first two or three years had passed, there was an increasing tendency for French officials to provide alternate nominees for vacant positions. In March 1900, for instance, the French commissioner of police nominated a candidate for the vacant governorship of the province of Barai; [31] but the French usually limited their nominations to less important officials, at least during Norodom's lifetime.

More typical of the deliberations of the council of ministers was the discussion over the appointment of an assistant to the *kralahom,* the minister of the navy, in April 1898. On this occasion there were two candidates: Mey, at this time secretary to the council; and Ouk, secretary to the protectorate's superior tribunal. Both were the sons of *balats,* the provincial officials ranking after governors, and were related to senior members of the Cambodian administration. In this instance, the fact that Ouk had been active in fighting against Votha in 1877 and later against the insurgents in the Pursat region in 1885 seems to have influenced the council in his favor. [32]

In almost every case, the influence of the French resident superior was preponderant. During the first year that the council of ministers met under his chairmanship the Cambodian ministers occasionally expressed some fear of acting directly against the probable wishes of Norodom. More often, however, they did not. When, in September 1897, the resident superior urged the council to approve a reduction in the costs of administration in the Cambodian judicial services, Prime Minister Um said, "Since it concerns balancing the budget, we can only conform to the views of the Resident Superior, who is our chief and to whom we owe devotion and obedience." [33] Yet, initially fear of the king remained, and when, in October 1897, there was discussion about the slaves attached to the royal household, the ministers hesitated to act against Norodom's wishes. They emphasized that abolishing the royal slaves would undermine the king's prestige. Not even the resident superior's mocking comment, "How scared the ministers are," could bring them to raise the issue with Norodom.[34] From 1898 onwards, however, there is little evidence to suggest that the council of ministers feared to act with the resident superior against the king.

The ministers' consistent support for the French position inevitably resulted in clashes between Norodom and his chief ministers. These began in 1898 and 1899 as Norodom tried to maintain his control over official appointments. On 6 April 1898 the council of ministers, at the request of the resident superior, approved a measure providing that the council had the right to appoint and dismiss all Cambodian officials who earned a salary of less than sixteen piastres a month, without any reference to the king. This decision was presented to Norodom for his approval twice, and on each occasion he refused, arguing that it further diminished his power. When Resident Superior Ducos brought the king's refusal before the council, all ministers concurred in maintaining their decision.[35]

This stance by the Cambodian ministers provided Ducos with a *point d'appui* in his relations with Norodom. Writing to the king in November 1898 he observed that Norodom's refusal to approve the official appointments made by the council of ministers was "injurious" to the conduct of the kingdom's business: "I had the honor to inform the Governor General of this state of affairs. The Governor General has given me instructions to pass beyond your approval and to interpret your silence as equivalent to that approval in cases where I have not received a reply in twenty days." [36] This did not mean, Ducos wrote, that Norodom's wishes would not be taken into consideration. If he objected to an appointment, the council would be glad to take his objections into consideration, but if the council continued to approve its original choice, the king's approval "would have to be given." The resident superior read this letter to the assembled ministers before sending it to the palace. The minutes record the ministers as observing, "We approve this letter, which has been written in the interest of the affairs of government." [37]

The letter was a blunt challenge to Norodom, and when, shortly after, the council of ministers made a number of appointments with which he did not agree, he made a strong response. Very much at the behest of the resident superior, the council of ministers in December 1898 elevated the secretary of the council, Thiounn, to the new rank of secretary general with membership of the council.[38] This was a fateful appointment, for Thiounn continued to serve in important positions for more than thirty years and earned the bitter enmity of the Cambodian royal family. Norodom opposed the promotion, but he was overruled.[39] When Prince Yukanthor made his sweeping denunciation in 1900 of the French role in Cambodia, Thiounn's name figured prominently among those Cambodians whom he denounced as straw men for the French. In contrast to most of the prominent Cambodians of the period, he was not from an official family. His official experience had been entirely in the service of the French, for whom he had become an interpreter in 1883.[40]

The embattled Cambodian king next refused to accept the council of ministers' decision to appoint his former confidant, Col de Monteiro, as minister of the navy, a position he had filled on an acting basis since 1895. In his refusal, Norodom appealed to the traditions of the state, arguing that Col de Monteiro did not possess the customary qualifications that had always been expected of the chief ministers of the Cambodian court:

In order to be a minister, a great official, a man is moved by these three virtues; *Puthamon,* that is, to be the possessor of knowledge and wise intelligence; *Sayamon,* the necessity to know the intentions of the stars and of *Phendey* (the earth, the kingdom); that is to say, it is necessary to know the spirit and the affairs of the capital and the outside world; it is to say, one must know the importance or the gravity of issues and the concerns of the people and seek to develop the interests of the kingdom; *Reach Montrey,* one must know the laws and know the articles by heart in a precise manner. One must have these three virtues to be an official of the royal court.[41]

Monteiro, Norodom stated, had served the court for many years, but he did not have the necessary knowledge for the post to which the council of ministers wished to appoint him. The minutes record that Monteiro was "visibly irritated" and replied, "Who are the officials who are endowed with these three virtues! I studied astronomy in Singapore, and in English." [42]

Few officials, indeed, possessed virtues of the sort that Norodom outlined in his letter. Pushed to the wall and unable to assert his will, Norodom clung to his traditional view of the state. His letter is of great interest as a record of the ideal that could still be held of a qualified official, but Norodom must have known that it would have no effect in the existing situation. The council prevailed once again, and Col de Monteiro was instated as *kralahom.* This rebuff to Norodom was followed by others in the same year. The minister of the palace, the *veang,* Poc, was appointed minister of justice, *youmreach,* over Norodom's strong objections; and two officials who appear still to have enjoyed a measure of the king's favor were dismissed from office. One was Minister of Justice Ouk, the other a senior Cambodian judge, Nguon.[43] Even when Norodom wrote to the resident superior in unfamiliarly humble and plaintive tones there was no result. That he could bring himself to adopt such a tone must be taken as a measure of his desperation:

His Majesty loves the French Government very much and has always conformed to its desires in everything which it has asked of him, without opposition. It asked him for all the country's taxes; it asked him for control over the Chinese and the Annamites, who have always been under royal authority, so that they could submit to French tribunals; also in the administration of the kingdom His Majesty has given his consent, and this, indeed, was a major matter. It is desirable that the French Government also love His Majesty, who asked to have the Khmer Kingdom placed under French protection. It was not that the French Government conquered it, as was the case with Saigon and Cochinchina.

. . . . .

From the point of view of Cambodian law, the master of the kingdom must have authority over the Cambodians, the inhabitants. If, being king, His Majesty does not have authority at all over the officials and public servants, and the people, how can he continue to exist? [44]

The rebuffs and disappointments of the early months of 1899 provide part of the explanation of the Yukanthor affair. The events surrounding Prince Yukanthor's visit to the French capital in 1900 are treasured in modern Cambodia as one of the last instances of royal resistance to French authority. Unfortunately, the one substantial printed account of the affair must be treated with care, and not all of the unanswered questions that emerge from this work are resolved by archival sources. The printed account is Jean Hess' *L'Affaire Iukanthor*.[45] The author was a journalist, and the book cannot be read without the suspicion that, whatever the inequities in relations between Cambodia and France, Hess supported the Cambodian position to make the story more newsworthy for the Parisian reader. Hess visited Phnom Penh in 1899 and wrote one of the few entirely enthusiastic accounts of Norodom ever prepared by a French observer. It was published in *Le Figaro* for 13 July 1899.

In his later full-length *exposé*, Hess dealt with some of the developments in the council of ministers that had caused such distress to Norodom. His quoted sources cannot be checked for accuracy, but it should be noted that his account of Norodom's attitude toward the minister Poc is consistent with the record of proceedings in the council of ministers. Norodom's justification of his resistance to Poc's elevation to the post of minister of justice, according to Hess, was that Poc was dishonest and deserved a place in jail rather than control of justice.[46] Hess' account may be accurate, but it is by no means evident that Poc was more corrupt than his fellow senior officials.

It is probable, as French sources maintain, that Hess played an important part in persuading Norodom to make a further protest against the actions of the French protectorate.[47] Prince Yukanthor, a favored son of the king, travelled to France and confronted the French government with a catalogue of Norodom's complaints. Hess travelled with the prince to Paris, where they arrived some time during August 1900. There is considerable evidence to suggest that Yukanthor's visit was approved by Norodom, although the king later denied this when challenged by the French to denounce Yukanthor. But at least one member of the royal family opposed the visit. Another of Norodom's sons, Prince Mayura, condemned Yukanthor in a letter that he wrote to the Saigon newspaper *Le Courrier Saigonnais,* on 14 November 1900. Mayura denounced Yukanthor as an enemy of France and urged that he be punished with exile. This was to be Yukanthor's fate. But it was Mayura's, too, for in 1916, suspected of working against French rule in Cambodia, Mayura was exiled to the remote northern Laotian town of Xieng Khouang.[48]

Once in Paris, in September, Yukanthor sent a long memorandum to the French prime minister and other members of the French cabinet.[49] He claimed to be the heir presumptive to the Cambodian throne, placing himself in direct opposition to the long-held French view that Sisowath would succeed Norodom. There is no conclusive evidence that Norodom had at last made his own choice of a successor. While it is possible that Yukanthor adopted this title to strengthen his position in France, this remains speculation.[50]

The memorandum was a long listing of Norodom's grievances. It rehearsed the events of the previous twenty years, recording the way in which Norodom had time and time again been forced to make concessions to the French authorities under duress. French control over Cambodia, Yukanthor asserted, was "complete and absolute, tighter than in a conquered country." [51] The prince singled out the "boy-interpreter" Thiounn and Prime Minister Um for his severest criticisms, arguing that they joined corrupt French officials in exploiting the country and discriminating against honest officials. There was only one senior Cambodian official for whom Yukanthor had any praise. This was Alexis Chhun, once a favorite of Doudart de Lagrée and by 1900 the official in charge of the royal treasury. According to Yukanthor, Sisowath employed thieves in his household, but this did not prevent the governor general "basing his policy on this ridiculous figure who is an object of mirth for all Cambodians."

Not only was this denunciation placed before the French government; Hess also arranged for the publication of an article incorporating Yukanthor's complaints in *Le Figaro*. The Ministry of the Colonies reacted swiftly. Under instructions from Paris, the resident superior confronted Norodom with evidence of his son's actions in Paris and demanded that the king summon Yukanthor to return. In these circumstances, Norodom had little choice but to agree, and a telegram was duly dispatched. At this point an element of comic opera intrudes. Still working in close association with Hess, Yukanthor eluded the French security officials who were dogging his steps, and instead of travelling to Marseilles in late September as he had agreed, he went to Brussels with the aim of continuing his campaign against French control in Cambodia.[52]

In Brussels, French security agents kept Yukanthor under surveillance, but despite Hess' efforts, public interest in France could not be rekindled. Yukanthor had little reason for continuing his stay in Europe and no inclination to return to possible punishment in Phnom Penh. He therefore travelled to Singapore, apparently arriving in late 1900. The protectorate authorities worked to ensure that Yukanthor suffered for his boldness. The council of ministers had been informed of the criticisms that the prince had made of some of its members, and the resident superior indicated clearly that punishment of some sort was expected.[53] After a series of interviews with Norodom, the resident superior persuaded the king to agree that Prince Yukanthor should either return to Cambodia, make a public apology to the officials whom he had insulted and to the *obbareach,* and beg the king's pardon, or accept as punishment permanent exile and the confiscation of all his possessions. The council of ministers unhesitatingly approved this proposal.[54] But Yukanthor feared punishment too greatly to return to Phnom Penh. He lived on in exile until he died in Bangkok in 1934.

Prince Yukanthor was not the only person to suffer as the result of his activities in Paris. The punishment meted out to Chhun, the one official for whom Yukanthor had praise, shows the power that the French authorities exercised and the unscrupulous fashion in which that power was used. It also provides a convincing explanation for the readiness of other Cambodian ministers and senior officials to cooperate with the protectorate administration, once they had become convinced that this was where power in the country lay. Alexis Louis Chhun was one of the small Catholic minority which was closely associated with the court. As a child he fascinated Doudart de Lagrée with his intense interest in things French and his good humor.[55] When still only thirteen, he had begun work as an interpreter for the French. He rose through various grades as an interpreter and by 1878 was a principal interpreter. In 1886 he was appointed to a position in the judicial service. Then, after a period of retirement, he was appointed head of the royal treasury.[56]

This proved to be a highly vulnerable post once the French decided to act against Chhun. In 1901 he was accused of misappropriating large sums from the royal treasury to his own use. In reply, Chhun argued that he had Norodom's authority to use the money in a private financial venture and produced a letter from the king to justify his claim. The resident superior at the time, Bulloche, maintained that the letter was a forgery. Taking the issue before the council of ministers, he informed them that King Norodom did not wish for a scandal and had therefore agreed to revoke Chhun's appointment.[57] Norodom's reaction to Bulloche's approach suggests the king's reluctance to fight once again the type of battle that he had lost so many times before. It is also suggestive of French pressure for Chhun's dismissal. For some time after, the protectorate authorities kept Chhun under daily surveillance.[58]

The faithful Chhun had to wait four years before his honor was vindicated. With the Yukanthor affair no longer a matter of deep concern for the French, and with the private admission of Resident Superior de Lamothe that Chhun had been the victim of "unsavory machinations against him," he was appointed supervisor of the king's civil list in 1905. Complete vindication came in Chhun's appointment as minister of justice in 1911.[59]

Chhun, and others, had suffered because of their loyalty to or association with the king. It is notable, however, that with few exceptions the senior officials who sided with the French were members of the traditional Cambodian elite. This can be illustrated by examining the background of a number of the ministers at the turn of the century. Not least among these Cambodian Herodians was Prime Minister Um, the subject of Yukanthor's denunciation. At the turn of the century, he was an old man; he had been born in Pursat Province in 1821. His career would seem to have been almost a model one for a high Cambodian official. At the age of sixteen he had entered the service of Ang Duong and accompanied the future king to Bangkok. He fought with Ang Duong and the Siamese against the Vietnamese who occupied Cambodia. When Ang Duong regained control of Cambodia, Um was appointed director of the royal pages. From then on he rose steadily in the royal service. In 1861, Norodom named him assistant to the minister of war, and in 1868 he became the actual minister. He was later minister of justice and finally was appointed *akhamohasena,* prime minister, in 1888.[60]

Here, then, was no newcomer who had gained high position after serving as an interpreter for the French. Yet he was denounced by Yukanthor and supported the transfer of power that placed control over official appointments in the hands of ministers and the resident superior. In protesting against Yukanthor's criticism, Um noted that the new procedure was offensive only to "the women of the palace, the members of the royal family, the king's entourage, the Siamese who break all the rules in order to make sure that their candidates triumph." [61]

Um's successor as prime minister, Poc, had a similarly traditionalist background. He was born in Battambang Province, the son of a high official, in 1833. His first appointment was in the royal customs service at Kampot, where an elder brother was the chief official. After a period as a Buddhist monk, he returned to government service as one of Norodom's pages. His advancement was steady. At varying intervals he fought against Votha, and he worked with the French to suppress the rising in the western regions of the kingdom in 1885. In 1889 he was appointed *kralahom,* minister of the navy, a post he held until he retired in 1895. He returned to service as minister of the palace (*veang*) in 1898 and was named minister of justice (*youmreach*) in 1899.[62] Even if the latter appointments were the result of French influence, Poc was of the traditional elite and, on the basis of earlier appointments, a natural contender for high office. Yet there was a falling out between him and the king.

Col de Monteiro differed from his colleagues by his partly European origins and his Christianity. His grandfather, it appears, had come to Cambodia early in the nineteenth century. His father, Ros de Monteiro, had accompanied Father Bouillevaux when the latter visited Angkor in 1850. Col was born in 1844 and was sent to Singapore at the age of eleven to study English. In 1858 he returned to Cambodia and entered the king's service as an interpreter. From 1861 onwards he occupied a variety of positions, but whatever title he had he seems always to have acted as Norodom's personal interpreter and secretary. He was associated with the royal treasury from 1886 to 1895, when he was appointed acting minister of the navy. Until 1899 there was nothing to suggest any coldness between him and Norodom. Indeed, the events of June 1884 might have been expected to solidify the bonds between Norodom and Col de Monteiro. That this was not the case has already been demonstrated in Norodom's refusal to assent to Monteiro's appointment as *kralahom* and the official's vexed reaction to Norodom's observations that he was not sufficiently qualified for the post.[63]

The readiness of the Cambodian elite to join their fortunes to the French can be demonstrated time and again in the careers of other senior officials, less well known than those just detailed but still holding ministerial positions.[64] Minister Thiounn was perhaps the outstanding example of the advancement of a "new man," a protégé of the French who was without either the family or the official background to justify his advancement in terms of traditional Cambodia. Thiounn was of mixed ancestry, probably the son of a Vietnamese-Cambodian alliance. His father had held an honorary post in the court of the queen mother but had not been a career official. In 1883, aged nineteen, Thiounn had entered the service of the French protectorate as an interpreter and rose in that position until he was appointed assistant secretary to the council of ministers in 1892.[65] He was an energetic opportunist, concerned with his own advantage and able to apply a considerable degree of ability to achieve his ends. As an invaluable auxiliary, the French authorities described him as a man on whose "fidelity and tact" they could rely. His appointment as minister of the palace, in 1902, was seen as a "real progress for our influence." [66]

The decision of such a man as Thiounn to side with the French needs little explanation. He was not a man with deep roots in the royal service. After working with the French for a considerable period, he probably had made a shrewd estimate of the extent of their power. One encounters difficulties, however, in trying to explain the wide-scale defection from the royal cause of such figures as Um, Poc, and Col de Monteiro. It is tempting to suggest that there was monetary advantage for those officials who abandoned the interests of their monarch, but without evidence, this must merely be a supposition. Certainly, cooperation with the French probably did give some material benefits, but more is needed to explain their actions. A partial answer may lie in a combination of two important factors in the Cambodian situation by the end of the nineteenth century: the age and poor health of the king, and the clear superiority of French power.

There had always been those who were ready to cooperate with the French. In 1877, Moura lamented the passing of the minister of the navy, a firm adherent to French views. But through the eighties, as the period of the rising shows, there remained a strong core of senior officials who supported the king. In duty to their king they cooperated with Norodom when he agreed to throw his personal influence behind the efforts to quell the rising. As the nineties progressed, however, it became clear that the king was less and less able to resist French pressure. While some reservations must be held about the reports of Norodom's great concern to ensure above all else the material well-being of his own household, to the extent that this was true it represented a departure from the behavior expected of a king. The king was entitled to wealth, but his rule had to be profitable for his senior officials as well.

Officials closely associated with the court were fully aware of the poor state of the king's health. They knew, too, of the French determination to see Sisowath succeed. Such a situation put their loyalty to the test. Their futures held little promise if they combined resistance to the French with alienation from the next king. Moreover, by the middle of the nineties, the possibility of armed resistance to the French was much more remote than it had been in 1885. French influence extended more widely throughout the country. By 1895 the system of French residencies was firmly established, with detachments of troops stationed at strategic points. By contrast with the middle eighties, also, France was not as involved in military operations in other sections of Indochina. The immediate realities of French power and the French presence must be given full weight. When combined with an aged and choleric ruler, whose every effort to assert his vestigial authority was blocked by the French, it is not hard to understand the decision that the officials took.

There was a further factor involved in the officials' decision to work with the French. It cannot be described with great precision, but it was clearly present in nineteenth-century Cambodia. For Cambodian officials, the survival of government was important. It may have been distasteful for officials to see limitations placed on Norodom's power, but there was never any suggestion that these officials wished to stop playing a part in the government of Cambodia because the French now held supreme power. Cambodian officials had similarly cooperated with Siamese officials in earlier periods.

Finally, the officials were responding to the general atmosphere of change evident in Cambodia by the turn of the century. Although Doumer was to describe Cambodia as the private hunting preserve of the French resident superior and to imply that virtually no changes had been made, the country had inevitably responded to nearly forty years of French presence. Some importance must be accorded the slow penetration of new blood into the country's administration. By 1900 a number of Cambodians held posts within the traditional civil service who had not risen through its ranks in the normal way. These men had worked as interpreters for the French or, in some cases, had attended the Ecole Coloniale in Paris. With the notable exception of Thiounn, they do not seem to have gained positions of real power by the end of the century. Nevertheless, some had become governors of less important provinces.[67]

There were other changes. The slow but steady immigration of Vietnamese into Cambodia continued throughout the second half of the nineteenth century. By 1908 a French census revealed some sixty thousand Vietnamese in Cambodia.[68] This is a significant figure when it is remembered that the total Cambodian population was less than one million and that Vietnamese settlement was concentrated in the southeast of the kingdom and the riverine regions. Long before the end of the nineteenth century, the French were relying on Vietnamese to fill minor clerical positions within their administration in Cambodia. If the French no longer spoke of "Vietnamizing" Cambodia, as Champeaux had in 1889, they nevertheless did not look with disfavor on the seepage of Vietnamese into Cambodia.

Nor did they express concern about the immigration of Chinese. There was some concern with Chinese secret societies, but these did not represent a major problem. The Chinese were welcomed because of the Cambodians' disinclination to engage in commerce. By 1908 there were nearly sixty thousand Chinese in Cambodia.[69] In Phnom Penh, small-scale commerce was largely in Chinese hands; but the Chinese also spread into the countryside. Their presence in small rural towns, combined with the improved communications system developed by the French, revolutionized the character of settlements away from Phnom Penh. Where before the Cambodian countryside had had few sizable settlements, the Chinese contributed to establishing regional commercial centers. A report on the small town of Kampong Kanthuot, twenty-four kilometers from Phnom Penh, written in 1903, provides a picture of the change that the presence of Chinese brought. Previously it had been a small Cambodian settlement on the Prek Thnot River. Now it was joined with Phnom Penh by road. Chinese had flocked in and "comprised by [themselves] almost all the population of Kampong Kanthuot, carrying on all sorts of trades. Three tailors scarcely suffice for the customers; the old houses on stilts . . . begin to disappear." And the Cambodian population showed no hesitation in selling rice lands to the newcomers so that they could build their houses.[70]

It is difficult to believe that these changes in the countryside had much import for the Phnom Penh-based elite. As good Cambodians, they would resent the influx of Vietnamese, but their real concern was to remain afloat in the uncertain waters of court and capital politics. There is no evidence to show, for instance, that the members of the council of ministers opposed the French-sponsored decision to engage in a major revision of the kingdom's laws, despite the fact that this was a matter usually left to the monarch's initiative.[71] To an even greater extent, real control was exercised by the French, and neither the consultation with the ministers nor the establishment of residential councils from which the residents could draw local advice represented any departure from this state of affairs.[72]

Yet Norodom, even shorn of most of his personal power, could still use his prestige to impede the changes demanded by the French. Although the major royal ordinance of 1897 had spoken confidently of the elimination of slavery, this was not entirely accomplished until after Norodom's death.[73] Full French control over the king's civil list, the establishment of standards for the re-

cruitment of senior Cambodian officials, and even the revision of
the Cambodian penal code did not come until after the old king
died.[74] Moreover, in the court itself, the king still held sway, restrained only by the French presence from inflicting traditional
punishment on those who strayed from the strict standards of behavior governing members of the royal family.[75]

Although the French protectorate had circumscribed the king's
power, there was still concern over the succession. The fact that
Yukanthor had taken Cambodia's case to France, and the interest
which it had aroused there, brought a fresh assessment of the position of the Cambodian monarchy. Some Frenchmen still thought
of eliminating the monarchy in favor of outright annexation and
government of the country as a colony. This position was rejected
by the minister of the colonies. What was important was the assurance that Norodom's death would not lead to unforeseen difficulties.[76] The French had little to fear from Sisowath. He had
spent three decades waiting in the hope of succeeding his half
brother. Less wealthy than the king, he was reduced in 1901 to
pleading for an advance against his normal pension in order to
meet unexpected expenses. He asked for four thousand piastres
and was granted two thousand five hundred.[77]

In 1902, Norodom was stricken by cancer, and by February 1904
it was clear that his death was near. The French braced themselves
to ensure that there should be no mistake. In his "very confidential"
instructions to the governor general of Indochina, the minister of
the colonies called for urgent steps to assure Sisowath's succession
after Norodom's death. The chief French official in Indochina was
instructed to send another gunboat and another company of infantry to Phnom Penh.[78]

Norodom approached the end true to his traditional view of life.
He insisted on celebrating his birthday according to custom during
the second half of January 1904, despite considerable pain.[79] He
next occupied himself with the composition of a will. In this document he made one concession to modernity by providing funds for
a school for princes and princesses, but in general it was traditional
in tone. Part of his fortune was to go toward the construction of

rest houses along the roads running to Phnom Penh from Kampot and Oudong. One article of the will was a final pronouncement opposing princesses marrying outside the royal family. Continuing a practice common in Angkorian times, he directed that a Buddha statue be cast in gold, with his demensions.[80]

King Norodom died at five o'clock in the afternoon of 25 April 1904. The council of ministers and the heads of the two Buddhist sects were called together immediately to form a council to select a new king. The French resident superior presided over the meeting, and Sisowath was chosen as the new ruler of Cambodia. The hypocrisy of high places was acted out as the French minister of the colonies sent a message to Sisowath that spoke of the "real emotion" felt by the French as they learned of Norodom's death. The late king had been, the message affirmed, a person who had "not ceased to give proof of his loyalty" to France.[81] Sisowath's first message to the minister of the colonies was more to the point; he thanked the president of the French Republic for ratifying his appointment as king.[82]

Norodom's death ended an era. He had not always been able to prevent changes in his kingdom; nevertheless, unlike his half brother and successor, he tried. His adherence to traditional behavior and values was demonstrated time and again in confrontations with the French, but because of the basic weakness of his bargaining position, when he collided with the protectorate authorities he was forced to accede to their demands. The resistance that followed the signature of the June 1884 convention, with which Norodom was almost certainly involved, represented the one real attempt to match force with force. This shook the foundations of the protectorate and brought a short triumph for Norodom. In later years, increased French power and the readiness of senior Cambodian officials to join their fortunes with the French undermined Norodom's position.

As for his surviving half brother, it would be easy to dismiss Sisowath as a man interested solely in personal power. Such an estimation would not be correct. Attainment of the throne was his overriding concern, but there was more to his character. He was a devout supporter of the Thommayut sect; his zealous efforts to advance the sect's progress in Cambodia led to disturbance in the countryside. In 1899 he encouraged a monk, previously a member of the Mohanikay sect and now an adherent of the Thommayut, to arrange for a change in religious allegiance among all the monks in the pagoda where the "convert" was chief monk. This led to conflict between the villagers who supported one or other of the sects. Sisowath's motives in this affair, however, seem to have been entirely religious. He urged the change in order that "religion might be raised up." [83]

Sisowath, once on the throne, was a pliant tool of the French authorities, and new departures marked the first years of his reign. After decades of hesitating to push Norodom too far, the French authorities seized the occasion of Sisowath's accession to introduce a long list of changes in the administration of the kingdom. Sisowath accepted French control over his civil list. Within three weeks of Norodom's death, he signed a convention setting the civil list for his reign. For the first time a French official was appointed to regulate the finances of the palace.[84] Projects that had lain fallow despite their token acceptance during Norodom's reign were reactivated. These included the revision of the Cambodian penal code and the establishment of an examination for entrance to the senior posts of the Cambodian administration.[85] Instead of the traditional system, under which each Cambodian minister was responsible for all general government business in his own apanage, the French introduced a reform giving each of the ministers a fixed set of responsibilities for the whole kingdom.

For the first time, some real progress was made towards establishing a workable system of education, however modest. It is true that Norodom had made reference to a school for princes and princesses in his will—perhaps at French urging—but achievements in the field of education up till his death had been minimal. He displayed no interest in assisting the development of French-sponsored education. It is an open question whether Sisowath was personally any better disposed to the institution of modern education, but he did recognize this was a goal with French support and provided the protectorate with space for new schools within buildings that he had occupied before he became king. In 1905 the protectorate authorities reported that there were seven hundred and fifty pupils attending schools in Phnom Penh and that twenty-nine were princes and twenty-five princesses. In the countryside, four hundred pupils attended schools supervised by the protectorate. The exact number of Cambodians in these schools is not specified. It is unlikely that it represented one half of the total.[86]

On French initiative also, a mutual education society was established in 1905 to encourage study of the French language. In the speeches made at the founding of this society, the familiar voice of the colonized enthusiast for French civilization may be heard. In the words of the secretary general of the council of ministers, Keth: "Formerly, we could be afraid of still being distant from the time of a rational diffusion of practical education, appropriate to the new needs of our country which would improve the social state of the Cambodians . . . . Our fears have disappeared in the presence of that which you [the French] have done for us since your arrival." [87]

Education, however, was just a surface affair until Norodom's death. There had been no preoccupation in Cambodia, as there had been in Cochinchina, with introducing a romanized transcription of the language. Missionary efforts were restricted almost entirely to the Vietnamese community, as the Cambodian Buddhists proved uninterested in the appeals of the Christian religion. The descendants of earlier Spanish and Portuguese associates of the Cambodian court comprised the most numerous group of Cambodians who adhered to the Catholic faith.

The real changes during Norodom's reign concerned the disposition of power. French officials sought to limit the initiatives of the king and to influence the traditional court rivalries in ways advantageous to the protectorate. In turn, these changes had considerable effect on the attitudes adopted by senior court officials, who now found themselves forced to choose between their traditional master and a new and stronger authority.

Yet, in stressing this issue of power, one should not forget the distinction made earlier between power and prestige. Outside the circle of senior court officials, it is far from certain that the diminution of Norodom's power was recognized. The members of the council of ministers knew that the resident superior held ultimate power in Cambodia, but the same was probably not true for provincial officials, even though their appointments were made by the council of ministers. Norodom regulated the life of the court with a firm hand until he died. In that closed society, which had suffered so many vicissitudes in the preceding centuries, the position of the king could not be described as diminished. Indeed, seldom before had the king's majesty been affirmed in such a rich material manner. Governor General Doumer found the royal palace at Phnom Penh offensive to his aesthetic tastes, but there is no doubt that it was grander and more imposing for Cambodians than the earlier court at Oudong. French gifts of carriages and steamboats, added to his elephants and cavalry, bolstered Norodom's prestige.

Possibly some of the best indications of the way in which the king's prestige had not only survived almost fifty years of French rule, but increased, are the accounts of Norodom's cremation. In 1863, Norodom had supervised the cremation of his father's body. King Ang Duong had died three years before, but in the years that followed Cambodia was racked by fratricidal conflict that prevented the cremation ceremony. There is no suggestion that the ceremony, when it did take place, attracted great notice outside the court at Oudong.[88] It was very different in Norodom's case. When the ceremony took place in January 1906, Phnom Penh was swollen by an enormous influx of Cambodians from the provincial regions of the country. The description of these events, provided by Collard and others, stresses the intense appeal of the ceremony for the population at large.[89] The ceremonies took place with a splendor and an *éclat* that was only possible in a country at peace, whose court was provided with adequate funds. Seventeen hundred Buddhist monks recited prayers for the repose of Norodom's soul, and French military honors were added to the traditional rites of the ceremony.

If one can perceive what the king was to the mass of his countrymen, it is much more difficult to infer what he was to himself. The years between his father's death in 1860 and his coronation in 1864 had been ones of extreme uncertainty. For almost four years Norodom had never been sure when he would be crowned and whether the Bangkok court would provide him with the essential royal regalia. The report that at his coronation he was ecstatic gives a vivid sense of the importance of this occasion to Norodom. Joy in his kingship must have evaporated by the closing years of his life. Two of his sons, princes to whom he had once shown favor, had been exiled by the French. His half brother, Sisowath, whom he had decried years before for his two-faced attitude, still waited to succeed to the throne. The king's power over his ministers had been subverted by the French, and old companions were his enemies in the council of ministers. He had been forced to accept the nomination of an upstart, Thiounn, as minister of the palace, just as he had been forced to accede to the exile of his sons and the dismissal of the one official whom Prince Yukanthor had described as honest and loyal to the throne.

Norodom's was a tragic life. His adherence to the past, his affection for old models of the state and of royal behavior, left him ill equipped to meet the challenge of a French presence in Cambodia. The fundamental element of tragedy, inevitability, was assured by his failure to perceive the ultimate collision that would follow upon his repeated opposition to change. There is no sense that he saw any positive values in the French reforms. The strength of the institutions that he sought to defend was later demonstrated in their survival and importance long after the king's death, but this provided no compensation during the closing years of Norodom's life, as he faced the bitter reality of the eclipse of his personal power.

Part IV

CONCLUSION

12

Rule and Response

In Cambodia, King Norodom's death brought the end of an era. In terms of the changing world about him and the power that the French protectorate was able to exert against his state, he had lived too long. He represented a world that could never return, and he clung to the trappings of that world until his death. There was no sudden sweeping away of the Cambodian court after his death, no dismantling of the framework of devotion to a semidivine ruler. But there was a strict limiting of the king's power. One cannot imagine Sisowath, king after decades of waiting, indulging personal caprices in the fashion of his predecessor.

In Cambodia, interaction had revolved around the relationship between Norodom and the French. In Cochinchina, the impact of the French presence was much wider. Not only the elite were affected; fundamental changes such as the transcription of the Vietnamese language and the total substitution of a French-directed administrative system for the traditional bureaucracy reached down to the people.

Nevertheless, despite their complexity, it is possible to discern a general pattern in several important changes that occurred shortly after 1900. Of great importance was the new character of Vietnamese nationalism from about 1905 onwards. During the nineteenth century Vietnamese resistance to the French presence in Viet-Nam was traditionalist. To the extent that appeals were made to the theory of a unified Viet-Nam, or to the Vietnamese emperor as a unifying symbol, there was a nationalist element present, but there was little of the philosophical aspect associated with modern nationalism. Indeed, much of the resistance to the French, both in Cochinchina and in other regions of Viet-Nam, was the desperate endeavor of men driven to arms by great changes beyond their understanding. The response of the rural population to "illuminated" monks who promised new, utopian worlds involved resistance to the French, but this was scarcely nationalism.[1]

Japan's victory over Russia in the Russo-Japanese War provided a beacon to Vietnamese, as it did to other emerging nationalist groups throughout Asia. The rights of the Asian in contrast to the position enjoyed by the European became a significant theme in subsequent nationalist thought. At the same time there was an increasing awareness of other revolutionary groups outside Viet-Nam and study of various foreign revolutionary writers. After the early years of the twentieth century, a new and more sophisticated nationalism was apparent in Viet-Nam.

The reaction of those who opposed the French had as its antithesis the growth of a clearly defined group that not only accepted the presence of the French but saw in that presence the best hope for Viet-Nam. Both of these groups, in the years to come, used *quoc-ngu* to disseminate their beliefs. The increased use of the transcription in the twentieth century is yet another reason for seeing the first decade as a terminal point, or more correctly a dividing line, in modern Vietnamese history. So, too, is the evidence of substantial decay in the traditional system of administration within the *xa,* the Vietnamese commune.

Since the continuing traditions of Cambodia and Cochinchina played a major part in determining the course of their colonial histories, it is rewarding to consider the two regions together as well as singly and to see how French aims, which had some underlying similarities in both regions, were altered by the societies in which attempts were made to achieve them.

In Cochinchina, the introduction of a French presence brought alien involvement in the most detailed aspects of daily life. By the middle of the nineteenth century, the frontier character of this vast and sparsely settled region was beginning to alter. The great underlying theme of Vietnamese history—migration towards the open frontier—was still present. Increasingly, however, the migration was controlled by the state. As new settlements were established, state representatives exercised bureaucratic control. In the precolonial national society scholarship was the key to advancement within the civil service, and the six southern provinces of the Vietnamese empire were integrated into the state examination system. Slowly, men of the south were gaining places of some importance in the mandarinate and, with those places, an investment in the established order.

French intrusion cut Cochinchina off from its traditional source of Vietnamese guidance. What might have taken place if the mandarins had not fled from the conquered region remains a matter for historical speculation. The departure of the mandarins cut away, in a single stroke, one of most important institutions binding the villages to the center of power at Hue. As southerners entered the mandarinate, they would have become part of the over-all program to establish the same style of administration, and the same standards within that administration, over the whole of Viet-Nam. The tension between each Vietnamese commune and the central government is a powerful theme in Vietnamese history. It cannot be stressed too strongly, however, that the mandarin provided the buffer to ease that tension. Whatever the popular jokes about the dishonest mandarin, there was deep pride in a Vietnamese village that could boast that one of its members had passed the state exams and become a member of the mandarinate.

Without the mandarins, the possibilities open to the French were much greater. The attempts of successive French governors in Cochinchina to institute a satisfactory system of administration in the provinces were based on the assumption that Frenchmen would hold all positions of real power. Even the early attempt to copy Vietnamese models was unable to fill the vacant administrative ranks entirely with Vietnamese. As the incompetence of many of the early collaborating Vietnamese became apparent, it was more and more necessary to rely on Frenchmen.

Because of the generally unsatisfactory character of those Vietnamese who chose to cooperate with the French, the colonial intruders came to rely heavily on those Vietnamese who, through either greater competence or energy, stood above their fellows. In the early years, *collaborateurs* were found among the sections of the population without mandarinal connections. As a result, the French presence in Cochinchina led to the advancement of individuals who might not otherwise have played any significant public role under the traditional system. It was often on their wisdom that the French relied in seeking to obtain information about the past, and because of French support, these "new men" rose to positions of power denied them in the past.

These departures from the traditions of the state make the concern shown by the *collaborateurs* over "morality," a fundamental theme of a Confucian-oriented society, of great interest. Among those who worked for the French, few acknowledged any real value in the ideals of the past. Their perception was extremely concrete. By contrast with a present in which their interests were bound to French power, the past was viewed as a time of difficulties and oppression.

For Tran-Ba-Loc, the past was symbolized by the persecution of the Catholic minority, of which he and his family were members. The present, with the French in Cochinchina, was a time when the Catholic Church was backed by the state, and he, as an employee and friend of the French, could now in his turn pursue and crush the opponents of the state. Yet Loc was concerned that there should be provision for the morality of the "pagans" who did not enjoy the benefits of Catholic conversion. He called for moral doctrines to be provided in the books made available to the bulk of the population. He was apparently unconscious of the contradictions implicit in his recommendations and his view of the evil nature of pre-French Cochinchina, which had relied on Confucianism for its moral values.

The most sophisticated renunciation of the past came from Pétrus Ky. With a background of learning that made him aware of the material differences between France and Viet-Nam, he saw in France the guide to new knowledge that could transform his country. In the goals that he pursued, however, Pétrus Ky revealed a deep concern for the moral advancement of his country. The fervor with which he embraced the new ideas of Western learning reflected his search for a guide to conduct.

The same preoccupation with an ill-defined but deeply important framework of morality was revealed in the speeches of the Vietnamese members of the Colonial Council. Staunch supporters of the French, to whom they owed their position and, increasingly, their opportunities to acquire wealth, these councillors were nevertheless disturbed by the failure of the various French educational programs to pay sufficient attention to inculcating morality.

The survival of a concern for morality as an essential accompaniment to education and as an indispensable consideration in an individual's life is a notable feature of the first forty or fifty years of Cochinchina's history under the French. The succeeding years of the twentieth century, however, suggest that French colonial domination had brought sufficient change to make Confucian standards of morality, and even the residue of their influence, an inadequate answer to the challenges of the new situation in which the Vietnamese elite found themselves. It is in this epilogue that the partly destructive and partly revolutionary influence of the French presence in Cochinchina, and indeed throughout Viet-Nam, may be observed.

Continuing migration is another major theme of Vietnamese history that survives in the record of developments in Cochinchina following the arrival of the French. The missionaries blamed the nomadic tendencies of the people for their failure to find converts. So long as there was fresh, untilled land, Vietnamese peasants would move on. Testimony to the effectiveness of this perennial migration was the hope expressed by French officials in Cambodia that the seepage of immigrants into that country would lead to the eventual "Vietnamization" of the kingdom. The decay of the Vietnamese commune in Cochinchina, eroded by a variety of French administrative decisions, probably strengthened the Vietnamese urge to move onwards.

The persistence of themes that predate the French presence is a salutary reminder of the vital role the precolonial nature of a region played in determining the extent and nature of change in a colonial situation. But the fact that it was the French who colonized Indochina had significance also. The extent to which colonial theory was part of the personal baggage of Frenchmen who served in Viet-Nam and Cambodia has been stressed frequently in this study. The "civilizing mission" and the belief that it was possible to transform Vietnamese into Frenchmen were not merely convenient rationalizations of deeper, more venal urges. French glory and the education of the Vietnamese; opportunities for naturalization and the establishment of profitable commercial enterprises; these were not separate goals in Cochinchina. It was never felt that French glory was incompatible with the transformation of an individual Vietnamese into some approximation of a Frenchman. The opportunity for Vietnamese to adopt French nationality and the remarkable extent to which a limited number of Vietnamese did adopt a French way of life, even in this early period of colonial interaction, were practical demonstrations of French belief in their own theories.

In other important spheres French theory worked remarkable changes quite early in the period of French control. Part of the reason for the French belief in their own cultural superiority lay in the contrast between European knowledge and the scientific poverty of traditional Vietnamese learning. With the exception of men like Luro and Philastre, there was a general inclination to dismiss all traditional learning, based as it was on the Chinese classics, as unproductive pedantry. The nineteenth century, it should be remembered, was a period of exciting scientific discovery, and the early French administrators in Viet-Nam respected the value of scientific inquiry. The absence of such a stream of inquiry in the traditional education that they saw in Viet-Nam reinforced their belief in the superiority of the West.

Such attitudes underlay the successful campaign to eliminate traditional education and the concurrent program to eliminate the use of Chinese characters. When early officials condemned Chinese characters as incompatible with modern knowledge, they were not coining fine phrases but expressing strongly held convictions. These beliefs, and the more mundane consideration that it was easier to learn to read *quoc-ngu* than to study Chinese characters, lay behind the determination that *quoc-ngu* should become the accepted form of writing in Viet-Nam. That determination succeeded, so that today the study of characters in Viet-Nam is the business of a limited number of scholars, while the universal use of *quoc-ngu* justifies its literal meaning: national language.

It is difficult for one whose education has been entirely in an alphabetical system of writing to plumb the real impact of education through ideographs. The linking of basic education with the teaching of moral virtues was a powerful combination in Viet-Nam. French commentators who denied that this was so pointed to the less than perfect standards of honesty among the mandarins. In making this judgment, however, they made a common mistake. There is a difference between a fact and an ideal. The facts of Vietnamese official probity in the precolonial period will remain a matter for discussion, but no matter what the true state of affairs, the ideal of the honest official remained, and those who attained this ideal were honored by both official and nonofficial members of the Vietnamese population.

Insistence on *quoc-ngu* and an educational system based on French models brought slow but important change. In pursuing their policy, the French officials had one great advantage. Their policies were not popular, and the amount of material available for instruction in *quoc-ngu* was limited and often without intrinsic interest, but their educational opponents did not possess the necessary resources to continue the battle to preserve the traditional forms of education. One by one, the village schoolteachers who composed the main bulwark of resistance died or became too old to teach. As these repositories of knowledge disappeared, there was no one to take their place. At the same time, the longer the French stayed in Cochinchina, the more Vietnamese there were who had a vested interest in mastering the new transcription. Promotion, participation in the colonial society, and intellectual satisfaction all became associated with a capacity in *quoc-ngu*. Once linked with the expression of political thought and the development of an active *quoc-ngu* press, there was no hope that the generality of the population would persevere with the education of the past and its use of characters.

In the countryside the French presence in Cochinchina played a major part in the decay of the communal institutions. As much through inadvertence and misunderstanding as through wilful intent, the French search for parallels between the Vietnamese village administration and the administration of their own towns led to disruption and decay. The power of the council of notables was sapped and with it the sense of corporate responsibility that had been an essential for the proper working of the commune. The growth of a class of large-scale landowners among the Vietnamese population, devoted to personal enrichment and without responsibilities to the less prosperous, was an additional rural theme. Its origins may be found in part in the land concessions policy promoted by the French. As the twentieth century progressed, the land-based bourgeoisie became an important element in Vietnamese society in Cochinchina. Seeing their interests closely identified with continuing French political control, they had little sympathy with nationalism and supported the *status quo*.

The withdrawal of the mandarins and their replacement by French officials led to the eventual substitution of the French penal code for the Vietnamese code. While Vietnamese procedures were still followed in civil cases, the number of French magistrates competent to apply Vietnamese legal practice was strictly limited. The availability of details on the development of a new legal system under the French makes the steps leading to the elimination of traditional procedures something of a model for the difficulties generally present in relations between the colonizers and the colonized. Without Vietnamese able to interpret their own code, it was of no avail for Frenchmen to plead the desirability of leaving unchanged such an essential part of the country's social framework. The change was made, and, if we are to believe the best-informed French commentators, justice became less accessible, less certain, and more costly.

The effects of interaction between the French newcomers and the Vietnamese of Cochinchina were pervasive. It is difficult to find any part of the indigenous society that was not affected by this interaction to some degree. In the past it has largely been left to the chronicler of military conquest and the reporter with a viewpoint closely attuned to the history of the French in Cochinchina to describe events up to the turn of the century and just beyond. The impression of limited French activity apart from military endeavor provided by these accounts is a false one. In the field of education, for instance, it is certainly true, as one modern French writer has observed, that only limited progress was made in the extension of modern education until the twentieth century.[2] The essential qualification this study proposes is that this limited progress also involved the establishment of certain vital patterns. It was in the first forty years that the French in Cochinchina succeeded in substituting their view of education for the traditional Vietnamese system, and under French promotion, with essential Vietnamese assistance, the major steps were taken towards the substitution of *quoc-ngu* for the use of characters. With its multiple implications, this was a radical and even revolutionary step.

Changes in the nature of the elite within Vietnamese society, changes in the system of justice, and the effective separation of Cochinchina from the rest of Viet-Nam were all developments important in themselves as well as being precursors of later continuing change. The period from the establishment of French control until the first decade of the twentieth century has so often remained a neglected segment of Vietnamese history, overshadowed by later events. If, in Cochinchina, it was a period for the most part unmarked by sensational events, this does not mean that it is without deep interest or that, as a time which saw the first slow adjustments between French and Vietnamese, it lacks its own special excitement.

Many of the general comments made about the unwarranted neglect of the history of Cochinchina in the second half of the nineteenth century apply with even greater force to Cambodia. The long series of problems associated with modern Vietnamese history has produced a much greater literature on that country than has been the case with Cambodia. Students of Cambodian history have had to remain content with the writings of the earlier French scholar-administrators, with their own special bias, and then to traverse an historical desert before coming to the accounts of more recent times. The considerable extent to which a traditionalist approach to government has persisted to the present day makes this neglect the more unfortunate.

Paul Doumer dismissed the history of relations between the French and Cambodia with the observation that Cambodia was little more than the French resident superior's hunting reserve. This comment gives a totally false picture of the extent of France's role in Cambodia during the first forty years of the protectorate. For its own reasons, France preserved Cambodia's existence. The hesitant French involvement in the scramble for control over Cambodia achieved nothing less than this. There seems to have been no way left for King Norodom to avoid even greater Siamese control over his kingdom in the eighteen-sixties. Even with the signing of the protectorate treaty in 1863, he was sufficiently cowed by Siamese pressure to accept the humiliation of a secret agreement with Siam that sheared even more territory from Cambodia.

Once established, the French protectorate in Cambodia involved itself in internal politics in a fashion remarkably similar to the earlier involvement of Cambodia's Asian suzerains. Because of an initial reluctance to attempt changes in Cambodia of the same magnitude as those undertaken in Cochinchina, French preoccupations were essentially limited to ensuring that the throne of the kingdom was occupied by a monarch responsive to French wishes. Norodom's unwillingness to occupy the place that succeeding French authorities planned for him was quickly recognized, and the long contest of wills began. In choosing to prop up the chief alternative contender for the Cambodian throne, Prince Sisowath, the French seized on an antagonism with a mass of tradition behind it. Over and over, the Khmer state had been brought close to ruin by the rivalries of brothers and half brothers. With Sisowath tentatively selected as Norodom's successor by the early seventies, the French authorities had to bear with the fact that the king took an unconscionable time in dying.

In the years that led up to the imposed convention of June 1884, there seems to have been an underlying awareness, sometimes ex-

plicit but mostly implicit, that the ultimate step of deposing Norodom would be going too far. This awareness stemmed from a partial recognition of the importance of the king to his people as well
as from the more limited aims pursued in Cambodia. This did not
mean, however, that French power was not exerted to Norodom's
detriment on important occasions. One of the most notable was the
French refusal, in the middle seventies, to aid the king in his conflict with another half brother, Si Votha. When Norodom was
threatened by a major rebellion raised by Votha, French arms were
put to work on the king's behalf only after concessions had been
made to French wishes.

It is difficult to estimate Norodom's own view of his relationship
with France and the extent to which he felt restricted by it. It is
possible, even with the necessary reliance on French accounts, to
comprehend that his accession to the throne was a deeply religious
moment for Norodom. Not even the fact that his coronation was
supervised by both the French and the Siamese could detract from
this. For the first ten years of Norodom's reign, perhaps even for
the first fifteen, the protectorate may have been more of an annoyance than the impossible burden that it later became. Norodom's
control over his senior provincial officials was limited, but this was
nothing new. His power over officials at court remained great, and
his kingly prestige was largely undimmed for the Cambodian population of the capital.

Just as the king of Cambodia was theoretically the ultimate
source of power, so had he traditionally provided the motivating
force in his realm. The picture of Ang Duong urging the merchants
of Kampot to greater efforts is totally in accord with the "proper"
behavior of a monarch. Concern for the respect of laws handed
down from the royal court was another preoccupation of the king
who conformed to the ideals of the state. Ang Duong's interest in
sumptuary laws and the detailed hierarchy that he set forth for the
royal family may be interpreted as kingly actions that reflected a
will to rule and to regenerate the state. Norodom's decision in 1870
to revise the country's laws was in the same tradition.[3]

As French control over Cochinchina became more assured, the

governors in Cochinchina sought to extend a more certain influence over Cambodian affairs. Until 1887, French officials in Cambodia were responsible to the governor of Cochinchina. Until the early eighties this did not have a great deal of influence on the formulation of policies in Phnom Penh. Decisions made in Phnom Penh were discussed in Saigon, but there was a general acceptance of the major differences between the two regions. With the arrival of Le Myre de Vilers in 1879, however, there was a search for uniformity. Although Le Myre de Vilers was later to note that a substantial degree of risk would attend any attempt to remove Norodom from the throne, he did not hesitate during his governorship to try and institute administrative changes that would make the administration of Cambodia similar to that in operation in Cochinchina.

His successor, Thomson, was completely convinced of the need for administrative uniformity. In his difficult relations with Norodom he found the justification for implementing a program to provide Cambodia with an administration parallel to that of Cochinchina. Control over taxes, over the appointment of officials, and over the laws was to be in the hands of residents whom Thomson wished to place in the provincial regions of Cambodia. Faced with the lack of any institution in Cambodia with the equivalent status and responsibilities to the Vietnamese commune, Thomson decreed that communes should be established. A "mayor" was to be selected and a "council of notables" established.

In striving to provide Cambodia with new institutions, Thomson attacked the most sacred of them all, the king. Out of the tangled threads of the rising of 1885–1886, the fact that the June 1884 convention reduced the king to a cipher is one of the strongest explanations for the resistance to that maladroitly imposed agreement. This neglected period of Cambodian history provides the essential commentary on the continuing importance of a Cambodian personality. Although later successful limitations were placed over the ruler of Cambodia's powers, the assumption that it was possible to treat the country in the way that had achieved a degree of success in Cochinchina was firmly rejected.

After Norodom's short triumph and the temporary acceptance by the French of the need to take a slower path towards the imposition of control, the screws tightened once again. The lesson of the Cambodian rising was not forgotten. While the French waited anxiously for Norodom's death, no further efforts were made to provoke a situation in which there was a real choice between removing Norodom from the throne and permitting him to remain. The king was threatened and after 1897 completely outmaneuvered, but he was not deposed.

Moreover, as his temporal power was constrained, his symbolic position was enhanced. The principal Cambodian officials were deeply aware of the limitations that the French had placed about Norodom. They knew that he cooperated with the French to end the rising because there was little alternative open to him. This knowledge was certainly a contributory factor in the decision of so many highly placed Cambodian officials to place their fate in French hands, rather than to put their trust in Norodom. For the people, by contrast, the Cambodian ruler remained the embodiment of the kingdom, surrounded by increasingly rich manifestations of his symbolic power. With the palace, carriages, steamboats, a large court, and the pagodas under royal patronage, the king lived amid splendor. Even among the officials, royal prestige was not entirely dimmed, whatever trust they placed in the French. Their participation in Norodom's funeral ceremonies was no act of hypocrisy.

French involvement in the affairs of the royal family and the senior officials, and the resulting paradox of lessened real power and greater symbolic significance for the king, is the dominant theme in the history of Cambodia from the time of the French arrival until Norodom's death. This involvement dwarfs, but does not eliminate, French efforts to eliminate slavery and to introduce the rudiments of a Western-oriented system of education. Further, the French presence in Cambodia aided the infiltration of Vietnamese into Cambodia, even if it denied them any significant political role, and encouraged the immigration of Chinese in an effort to encourage commerce in the country.[4] Without the same urge to develop the agricultural resources of Cambodia, as was done in Cochinchina, there was less concern with the building of roads or the construction of canals. Nevertheless, by the early 1900's some basic steps had been taken towards developing an infrastructure, and the picture of rapid change in Kampong Kanthuot following improved communications with Phnom Penh was repeated elsewhere.

When due account is taken of these subsidiary issues, the preservation of the kingdom and the involvement of the French protectorate in the royal family were the matters of major importance. The extent of the involvement and the importance of the accompanying interaction of these first forty or fifty years made this a period of vital importance for subsequent events. With the elimination of the princely offices, such as that of the *obbareach,* the king was the sole center of national interest, which was to be proved forcefully during Sisowath's reign.

Given the French presence as the alien component in both Cambodia and Cochinchina and the administrative link between Saigon and Phnom Penh, it is possible to ask what meaningful comparisons may be made between the histories of the two regions as they sustained their colonial experiences. There were important differences between the administrative methods used by the French in Cambodia and Cochinchina, but at the same time there was an underlying similarity in the aims pursued. The difference of scale between French efforts in the two regions was considerable, yet elements of the "civilizing mission" were present in both.

Whatever efforts the French made to impose unity and to utilize techniques in Cambodia similar to those used in Vietnam, the personality of the country and its people survived to maintain Cambodia's distinctive character. Thomson's hopes of developing institutions similar to those in Cochinchina were never fully realized, even at a later stage of the protectorate. In Cochinchina the retreat of the mandarins left the French free to impose their administration down to the cantonal level. Even below this the control exerted over administrative affairs was considerable. In Cambodia, by contrast, the traditional administration from the king down survived as a parallel system alongside the French administration with its French officials and Vietnamese clerks.

The presence of the king in Phnom Penh contrasted dramatically with the situation in Cochinchina. Among the earliest Vietnamese resistance movements one encounters the distraught cries of such men as Truong-Dinh as they faced their abandonment by Hue. The possibility of a resistance movement led by a member of the Vietnamese royal house had some appeal for nationalists in the south of Viet-Nam in the early twentieth century, but in no sense did the population as a whole look to Hue in the way that Cambodians looked to Phnom Penh. In Cambodia the king remained on his throne, and the people were linked with him through the Cambodian authorities, who were the king's servants. In Cochinchina the mandarins had gone, and a new bureaucracy had been introduced. The Vietnamese who became the elite within this new situation did not, on the whole, have any firm links with the old order.

In considering the impact of the French colonial presence in the two regions, therefore, one is making a comparison of contrasts, and these contrasts stem as much from the traditions the French encountered as from the different policies they pursued in Cambodia and Cochinchina. It is true that French land policy in the two regions was different. In Cochinchina great efforts were made to ensure the exploitation of land, by both Vietnamese and Frenchmen. In Cambodia, on the other hand, considerable effort was made to obtain the king's agreement that land could be alienated for development, but little was done in the way of exploitation of land. It was not merely that French interest in Cambodia was less. This was so, but it must be remembered that it was the Vietnamese who played the most important role in opening up the western regions of Cochinchina. French agricultural interests followed in the footsteps of the Vietnamese migrants who pushed the frontier to the west.

Using stock nineteenth-century descriptions, French observers deplored the "laziness" of the Cambodians and praised the "energy" of the Vietnamese. These sentiments led various administrators to advocate absorption of Cambodia into the Vietnamese orbit through ever greater Vietnamese immigration. Contrary to what might be expected, on the basis of other colonial situations, where Europeans showed greater sympathy towards less developed peoples, the less sophisticated Cambodians did not provide any special appeal to the French, who frequently compared them in unfavorable terms with the Vietnamese. Possibly this attitude changed as the twentieth century progressed, but nineteenth-century French accounts of the Cambodian character are deeply charged with scorn and disdain.

There are many obvious contrasts between what was achieved in Cambodia and Cochinchina. French support of the development of *quoc-ngu* and the official insistence on its use in Cochinchina had no parallel in Cambodia. Although the French worked to eliminate barbarous punishments from the Cambodian legal system, no major changes in the Cambodian codes, as they applied to Cambodians, were instituted during Norodom's reign. The educational effort in the two regions was markedly different, though once begun, education in Cambodia stressed French values in the same fashion as had been done earlier in Cochinchina.

The contrast between the preservation of the king in Cambodia and the way in which Cochinchina was largely cut off from the monarchial center at Hue had its parallel in the different evolutions of the elites of the two regions. Although one can point to the survival of men with mandarinal links among the colonial elite of Cochinchina, the dominant impression is of a new elite, composed of those who had opted for the French early in the colonial period. By the turn of the century an important new element was apparent, drawn from the ranks of those who were wealthy or growing wealthy as the result of their landholdings. A completely different situation obtained in Cambodia. In some exceptional instances the French had helped to high office men who had not been born into families that traditionally served the court. The bulk of the senior Cambodian officials, however, were men whose families had served the king for generations. They had reached their positions after progressing through the ranks of the traditional administration.

This made their defection to the French the more noteworthy and —reflecting the impossible choices which faced them—the more tragic.

France's involvement in Cambodia saved the country from annihilation, or at best from further dismemberment. While contemporary Cambodians blame the French with some justification for establishing borders advantageous to Viet-Nam with little account of Cambodian interests,[5] there is the further consideration that without France Cambodia might not have long survived. Once preserved, the French presence slowly worked to establish a greater unity within the country than it had known for many centuries. Much of this was done without deep thought for the consequences. Nevertheless, the suppression of regional revolts, the gradual achievement of administrative unity within the country, and the provision of a network of road communications were concrete representations of a deeply cherished national belief in the existence of a single Cambodian state.

Again, the contrast with Cochinchina is sharp. The history of Viet-Nam over the centuries is marked by territorial and political division. With the success of Gia-Long and under the unifying policies pursued by Minh-Menh, major steps were taken towards the establishment of a truly unified Vietnamese state. The frontier area of Cochinchina was still being absorbed when the French arrived, but significant progress had been made. The imposition of French control, coupled with the retreat of the mandarins, emphasized the various regionalist tendencies already present in Cochinchina and provided new barriers to communication between the south and the other sections of Viet-Nam. Looking far ahead from the period that has been the concern of this study, note may be taken of the distinctly different progress of nationalist movements in the north and the center on the one hand and in the south on the other. In Cochinchina there was always a reserve of wealthy landowners who saw their interest linked with France, a phenomenon almost totally lacking in central and northern Viet-Nam.

Such insights emphasize the unsatisfactory nature of any rigid periodization of the historical continuum. Both in Cochinchina and

Cambodia the first decade of the twentieth century may be seen as an historical highpoint but not in any sense as a time when there was a sharp break between past, present, and future. Many of the developments of the twentieth century have a clear parentage in the period examined in this study. Indeed, it is through a knowledge of the history of the nineteenth century that later events may be comprehended in the fullest way. Yet there was change in the first decade of the twentieth century, and the importance of the changing situation was recognized by more perceptive French officials. It was not merely that the revolutionary ideas that came to Viet-Nam from abroad threatened French power. There was the sense also of a new character to the movements opposed to the French.[6]

A substantial number of the politically conscious in twentieth-century Viet-Nam followed the path mapped out by Pétrus Ky. It may be possible to see in their pronouncements concern for the proper place of the individual in society. More prominent, however, is the devotion to a concept of modern knowledge that would regenerate Viet-Nam. The arguments that Frenchmen used about the unproductive character of traditional Vietnamese studies were echoed by Vietnamese in the twentieth century, who lamented their country's failure to provide any appropriate answer to the West and who sought to use modern knowledge to the advantage of Viet-Nam.

This reaction was not limited to Cochinchina. In this southern region it was more often by action and example than through explicit statement that Vietnamese demonstrated their acceptance of a new set of values. Wealthy Vietnamese landholders made sure that their sons received a French education and lent their support to institutions that promoted the French language. It was a writer from the north who perhaps best summarized the mood of those who were prepared to place their faith in France. Writing in 1923, Pham-Quynh, a descendant of mandarin stock, argued: "We are an old people who need to renew ourselves, to adopt modern life. . . . We ask France to aid us. We ask it of her in exchange for our political independence, the riches of our country, and the work of our men." [7]

Pham-Quynh hoped for a liberal association between Viet-Nam and France, but he was prepared, in practice, to accept French control over all major matters. Many among the southern bourgeoisie saw political stability as coextensive with their own prosperity and worried little about decision making. Wealth for them was more important than power. But there was a firm belief among other members of this Herodian group that the France of Montesquieu and Rousseau would heed their calls for reforms where glaring inequalities were apparent. Bui-Quang-Chieu was among the most notable of this particular persuasion. A man of the south, he led the movement in the period after the end of the First World War that sought a constitution for Cochinchina.[8] His efforts were unsuccessful. The long resistance of the colonial authorities to any real grant of power to their Vietnamese subjects ate away the hopes of those who looked to a gradualist solution for increasingly flagrant social and political inequalities.

Personal aggrandizement provides a major part of the explanation for the support that the land-wealthy men of Cochinchina gave to France during the twentieth century, at a time when revolutionary groups were emerging. A more subtle explanation must be found for the allegiance of such men as Bui-Quang-Chieu, men who believed the best of France and saw the metropole as a source of knowledge and advancement for Viet-Nam. These men were in a direct line of descent from the early *collaborateurs*, above all Ky, Paulus Cua, and Truong-Minh-Ky, who believed that the virtues inherent in French civilization could transform Viet-Nam and who moved into a colonial environment that seemed to promise a more productive and equal society than that which Viet-Nam had traditionally known. The ultimate failure of France to live up to its own proclaimed standards led to the reaction of bitter opposition to French rule, even among those who had been its supporters, and to a final national acceptance that armed resistance was the only way left to real freedom.

The accomplishments of the new revolutionary nationalists were small until after the Second World War. They tended in the early years to place their hopes in dramatic gestures, which brought harsh French repression. The inclination of the various nationalist groups to fragment their efforts played into the hands of the French authorities, who grew increasingly strict in their control of all political activity. It was in a climate in which any overt political efforts were subject to the closest scrutiny that the Vietnamese Communist Party, endowed through its background and training with a greater capacity for survival, grew to play such an important part in the more recent history of Viet-Nam.

The Vietnamese active on both sides of the political fence were not numerous before the Second World War. On occasion they could appeal successfully for mass support, but the number of those who displayed a consistent concern with political matters was limited. The nineteenth-century development of Cochinchina had presaged one major reason for the subsequent involvement of the mass of the population: the opening up of large landholdings. In the nineteenth century this development was in its infancy. With the turn of the century there was a major expansion of large-scale landholding in Cochinchina, with many Vietnamese assuming the role of absentee landlords. The tenant farmers who farmed the extensive French and Vietnamese holdings were destined to become a rural proletariat, highly susceptible to calls for agrarian reform. The emergence of this proletariat was a striking denial of the apparently rich promise of Cochinchina's open frontier.[9]

For all who had political interests, *quoc-ngu* provided an important vehicle, alongside French, for the spread of ideas. Despite censorship, a *quoc-ngu* press flourished from 1910 onwards.[10] As the twentieth century progressed, this modern romanized transcription of the Vietnamese language became the natural vehicle for Vietnamese writers in all fields of literary endeavor. The battle against characters begun in the south had to overcome some entrenched resistance from supporters of traditional education in the center and the north, but it succeeded. The convictions of the early French naval administrators and the devotion of a limited number of Vietnamese *collaborateur* writers in the early days of the French presence achieved success in the national adoption of *quoc-ngu*. Whatever regrets there were over the disappearance of characters, the immediate advantages of the transcription had a great appeal. With an awareness of the increased pace of life and the demands for scientific knowledge, modernists of all persuasions advocated the use of *quoc-ngu*.[11]

One aspect of relations between France and the Vietnamese of Cochinchina during the nineteenth century and early twentieth century evident throughout this study is the reluctance of the colonial power to allot any real responsibility to Vietnamese. There is a paradox here. The opportunity that France gave its colonial subjects to become naturalized citizens was most unusual, even if the numbers who were able to avail themselves of this possibility were small. For those who did become naturalized French citizens, there could be the most complete absorption into French society. Becoming a French citizen provided the only real opportunity for a Vietnamese to gain position and power. The great majority of wealthy and educated Vietnamese were not naturalized, and in both politics and administration there was a firm line beyond which they could not pass. Modern French writers have sometimes pointed to the election of a Vietnamese Trotskyite candidate to the Saigon city council in 1933 as an example of the liberality of French government in Viet-Nam. The vital fact was that neither this municipal councillor nor any other Vietnamese could hope for real political power. Equally, within the administration only the smallest number of Vietnamese could ever hope to achieve posts of any importance.[12] The tradition of the Colonial Council, which had been formed with care to ensure that Vietnamese could always be outvoted, was maintained.

The negative aspect of French contacts with Viet-Nam leaves a strong impression that the history of Franco-Vietnamese interaction was tragic, whatever attraction French culture had for a limited number of the urban elite. Colonial control was imposed on a section of an existing state and the separation that this brought had its implications throughout the French period in Viet-Nam. Regional identity was stressed to the detriment of national unity, and the way was left open to those who, often in search of personal advantage, were prepared to accept and indeed become the spokesmen for continuing French control. The Vietnamese contribution to this tragedy lay in the failure of the society to manifest a philosophy sufficiently resilient to withstand the onslaught on its values. Here Cambodia demonstrated a surprising capacity to survive, for the king remained a symbol of national unity, and accompanying factors worked to give reality to national unity and so to lend a more positive aspect to the history of that state.

The accession of King Sisowath was followed by accelerated French activity in Cambodia. Not only were the many projects that had hung fire during Norodom's lifetime put into operation, but new developments took place under the benevolent approval of the king. A new departure was the creation of an indigenous consultative council for Cambodia. This new body was first discussed in detail in 1912 and instituted in 1913. The most active person working for this council was Resident Superior Outrey. He had already served in Cochinchina, and it was to his experience there that he looked in proposing the consultative assembly. Outrey spoke enthusiastically of the provincial councils of Cochinchina and of the link that they provided between the French administration and the people. This new step in Cambodia, he asserted, would be in tune with "the role of social educator" that France had assumed and which would finally transform the Cambodian kingdom into a modern state.[13]

This assembly had no real power and at no time provided a forum for criticism of France. Along with many of the other reforms introduced after Norodom's death, it reflected French devotion to the forms of modern administration. A consultative assembly was as much part of this as was the establishment of a proper system for the registration of births, deaths, and marriages and the reform of the legal code.[14]

Some of the traditional themes so apparent during Norodom's reign persisted. Sisowath had won the throne, a victory he owed as much to his longevity as to any particular approval of his character by the French. Once crowned, he cooperated with the French, seldom giving the slightest hint of independence. This state of affairs, as well as the long background of family feuds, kept alive the resentment that one of Norodom's sons had not succeeded his father.

In the ten years following Norodom's death there were frequent indications of the resentment felt by members of the Norodom branch of the royal family. Yukanthor remained in exile, but his half brother Mayura was linked with various clandestine efforts to assert the inequity of Sisowath's tenure. There was little the discontented princes could do. The French held a firm grip on the kingdom. From time to time letters circulated, arguing the rights of the Norodom branch. In Mayura's case, French suspicion of his involvement in these activities led to his exile. These princely intrigues by no means attracted the interest of all Norodom's sons. A number were regarded as particularly devoted assistants of the French; and there were many others in the royal family whose only concern was to lead an agreeable life, even if this sometimes led to minor scandals in Phnom Penh.[15]

French control over the Cambodian royal family left the protectorate authorities in a position remarkably similar to that occupied by Cambodia's traditional suzerains. It was to Governor General Klobukowski, a man closely associated with Thomson in 1884, that Sisowath appealed in 1909 when seeking to ensure that one of his sons, Monivong, should succeed to the throne. Acting in a manner reminiscent of various Siamese sovereigns, the French were reluctant to make any firm commitment, preferring to suggest that Monivong probably would have their approval but promising nothing.[16]

Monivong did succeed his father, eventually, in 1927. Before the end of Sisowath's long life, however, an event took place that, more than any other in the history of Cambodia up to the time of the Second World War, demonstrated the extent to which the charismatic importance of the monarchy had not only survived but been enhanced by the French protectorate. On 5 and 6 January 1916 several hundred Cambodians arrived in Phnom Penh from

Kompong Cham Province to present a petition to the king.[17] The petitioners complained about the system of *corvées* that operated in the provinces. Sisowath on the advice of the French authorities received representatives of the group, heard their complaints, and urged them to return to their homes. This they did, but once there they encouraged other Cambodians to take their grievances over *corvée* and tax matters to the king in Phnom Penh.

The number of those travelling to Phnom Penh to protest against the *corvée* system grew. On 22 January the king issued an order promising a reduction of *corvées*, but there was no immediate effect upon the signs of popular discontent with the existing situation. In fact, only two days after the order had been issued, some five thousand protesters massed near Phnom Penh. Despite appeals by both the king and the French resident superior, the numbers grew even larger. At one stage French observers estimated that more than thirty thousand Cambodians had come to Phnom Penh to register their discontent. They laid their complaints before the king and then went away. Just to see the king convinced the unhappy peasantry that their troubles would be diminished. Even a sceptical French observer had to note: "[The crowd] . . . was motivated, apparently, at least, by the sole desire to see the king and to talk with him; it was satisfied as soon as the gates of the palace were opened to it." [18]

No completely satisfactory explanation was ever found for the sudden movement of the peasantry to Phnom Penh. The best informed Frenchmen agreed that Sisowath was seen by the Cambodians as the true center of the kingdom and as the one hope for a change in their lot. The event provided an opportunity for the formulation of all manner of theories, even the suggestion of German espionage.[19] And the possibility that discontented elements at court had played a part was not discounted, for it was still seen as a "tilting ground where coteries dispute and the rivalries of the palace come into opposition." [20]

Whatever the French destroyed in Cambodia, the preservation of the monarchy left it as a major factor in the subsequent development of twentieth-century Cambodia. The institution and the

ceremonies and traditions associated with it gave guarantees to national unity that have continuing importance today.[21] In marked
contrast, no such symbol survived in Viet-Nam. Cochinchina was
cut off from the monarchy, and even in the other two regions of
Viet-Nam the application of French power over the Vietnamese
royal house was too clearly apparent for that institution to offer
real hope to a sophisticated nationalist movement.[22]

This brief review of the events following the period of the present study stresses some of the more obvious continuities in the history of Cambodia and Cochinchina in the twentieth century. It
stresses, too, the continuing separate character of the two regions
despite their common experience of French political control. Ruled
by a culturally aggressive colonizing power, Cambodians remained
Cambodians and the Vietnamese of Cochinchina remained Vietnamese. Many, both in Cambodia and Cochinchina, came to speak
French as a first language. Some were so attracted by the values
that France embodied that they became Frenchmen in law as well
as in fact. It was not, however, changes of this sort that were of
ultimate importance for the majority of the population. For them,
colonial interaction had altered the social framework within which
they lived.

In Cambodia this social framework was more settled by the first
decade of the twentieth century than had been the case for centuries. Sustained by the French, the ruler had little to fear from
traditionally disruptive rivalries within the royal family. The threat
of invasion from Siam or Viet-Nam was absent. A slow movement
toward a general modernization of the state was under way. The
modernization process, however, developed under conditions in
which the monarchy remained and the basic values of Khmer society had not been destroyed.

In Cochinchina the twentieth century was a time when the substantial changes of the nineteenth century were followed by even
more significant changes as the impact of sustained contact between France and Viet-Nam brought its reaction. Old values had
begun to seem worthless, and new, impatient men with a knowledge of the West as well as of Asia sought to benefit from the free-

dom and opportunity that France had so often promised would be theirs once they had grasped the reality of modern education. An appreciation of the history of Cochinchina in the period of this study is critical to an understanding of the search by Vietnamese in the twentieth century for a new philosophical framework to replace that which was irrevocably damaged by the colonial experience.

STATISTICAL APPENDIX
and NOTES

Statistical Appendix

Table 1. Free alienation of land in Cochinchina, 1880–1904.
(Figures are extracted from the annual *Etat de la Cochinchine française* and are rounded to the nearest hectare.)

Year	Hectares	Year	Hectares
1880	200	1893	35,648
1881	881	1894	72,639
1882	435	1895	25,066
1883	6,876	1896	13,618
1885 *	11,724	1897	12,848
1886	9,037	1898	11,199
1887	4,946	1899	32,178
1888 †	9,037	1900	24,444
1889	10,045	1901	26,161
1890 ‡	9,037	1902	24,510
1891	11,941	1903	41,294
1892	35,749	1904	113,980

* Figures for 1884 are omitted.
† The figures for this year are the same as for 1886.
‡ The figures for this year are the same as for 1886 and 1888; a statistical error may be involved.

Table 2. Export of rice from Cochinchina and the area of land under rice cultivation, 1881–1901.

(Figures are from P. Passerat de la Chapelle, "L'Industrie du décorticage du riz en Basse-Cochinchine," *BSEI*, 1901, 1st semester, 49–85. The first column of figures is of piculs of rice exported [1 picul equals 133⅓ pounds]; the second column is of hectares rounded to the nearest hectare.)

Year	Piculs	Hectares	Year	Piculs	Hectares
1881	4,129,470	615,887	1892	9,200,430	9?6,178
1882	6,160,017	686,119	1893	10,287,695	995,861
1883	8,648,243	690,67?	1894	9,061,752	1,134,467
1884	8,659,405	694,439	1895	7,051,732	Figures on
1885	7,560,386	784,036	1896	8,081,277	the area of
1886	7,982,366	753,572	1897	10,652,032	land under
1887	8,285,675	818,392	1898	10,314,137	rice culti-
1888	8,479,450	830,263	1899	13,915,101	vation are
1889	4,755,544	834,866	1900	10,212,081	not given
1890	8,713,800	854,413	1901 *	5,238,101	from 1895
1891	6,629,357	910,861			on.

* First six months only.

Table 3. Production of rice per head of population in Cochinchina, by five year periods, 1875–1910.

(Figures are extracted from Paul Bernard, *Le Problème économique indochinois* [Paris, 1934], 94.)

Year	Kilograms	Year	Kilograms
1875–1880	518	1896–1900	619
1881–1885	613	1901–1905	637
1886–1890	604	1906–1910	768
1891–1895	664		

Notes

Chapter 1: *The Setting*

1. See Jean Moura, *Le Royaume du Cambodge* (Paris, 1883), II, and Trinh-Hoai-Duc, *Gia-Dinh Thong-Chi*, trans. Gabriel Aubaret, *Histoire et description de la Basse Cochinchine* (Paris, 1863). An excellent synoptic account of the region's history is provided by D. G. E. Hall, *A History of South-East Asia* (2nd ed.; London, 1964).

2. This is a very rough estimate. After the devastations of the 1830's and 1840's, Aymonier estimated that the Cambodian element of the population numbered around one million in the 1870's. See Etienne Aymonier, *Notice sur le Cambodge* (Paris, 1875), 19–20. More than one million Cambodians lived outside the borders of the Khmer state, in Siam, and in excess of one hundred thousand were in areas of Cochinchina under Vietnamese control.

3. Etienne Aymonier, *Le Cambodge* (Paris, 1900–1903), III, 798. The most detailed survey of Cambodian Buddhism is Adhémard Leclère's *Le Buddhisme au Cambodge* (Paris, 1899). It is a massive, but less than satisfactory, account.

4. On the role of the king in Cambodia, see Solange Thierry, "La Personne sacrée du roi dans la littérature populaire Cambodgienne," *Studies in the History of Religion: The Sacral Kingship* (Leiden, 1959), IV, 219–230. See also R. Heine-Geldern, *Conceptions of State and Kingship in Southeast Asia*, Cornell Southeast Asia Program Data Paper No. 18 (Ithaca, 1956).

5. In considering the way in which Cambodian rulers of more modern times inherited the status of a *deva-raja*, or god-king, from their Angkorian predecessors, some recent research illuminates the role of the Khmer king of Angkor. See M. C. Ricklefs, "Land and Law in the Epigraphy of Tenth-Century Cambodia," *Journal of Asian Studies*, XXVI, 3 (May 1967), 419–420, which notes the protection afforded private landowners during the tenth century by the central ruler. My

own more general study, "Notes on Early Cambodian Provincial History: Isanapura and Sambhupura," *FA*, XX, 186 (Summer 1966), 433–449, failed to provide any clear indication of central government representatives in either of these two important provincial sites during the Angkorian period but revealed important links between the capital and the provinces.

6. See Moura, *Le Royaume;* Aymonier, *Le Cambodge;* and A. Leclère, *Recherches sur le droit public des Cambodgiens* (Paris, 1894). Basing himself principally upon these sources, Jean Imbert has provided a reliable summary of the institutional situation in Cambodia in the pre-French period. See *Histoire des institutions khmères,* Tome II of the *Annales* of the Faculté de Droit de Phnom Penh (Phnom Penh, 1961), 55–60.

7. On slavery in Cambodia, see Moura, *Le Royaume,* I, 329–333, and Leclère, *Recherches* . . . , 94–107.

8. There is some reason to suppose that the sympathetic treatment accorded King Ang Duong by early French writers resulted from their desire to emphasize the independent nature of Cambodia, in opposition to the persistent Siamese claims to the right of suzerainty over Cambodia. At the same time, Professor O. W. Wolters ("The Khmer King at Basan," *Asia Major,* n.s., XII, 1, 64, n. 75) wonders whether the treatment of certain episodes by the nineteenth-century Cambodian recensions of the chronicle did not seek to enhance the status of the ruling king instead of providing an accurate rendering of the historical record.

9. The summary that follows is based on the renderings of the Cambodian chronicles provided by Moura, Aymonier, and Leclère in his *Histoire du Cambodge* (Paris, 1914) and in the collection of Doudart de Lagrée's papers edited by A. B. de Villemereuil, *Explorations et missions de Doudart de Lagrée* (Paris, 1883). A useful control document to place against these accounts of the Cambodian version of events is provided in the "Abridged Chronicle" of Cambodia, which was forwarded to the French Foreign Ministry, on behalf of the King of Siam, by the Siamese consul in Paris, Gréhan, in 1864 (AOM Indochine A-oo[4] Gréhan to the Minister of the Colonies, Paris, 23 January 1864). Although a strong bias must be recognized, it nevertheless gives insights into events in Cambodia as seen from Bangkok.

10. On Ang Duong's reign, see Moura, *Le Royaume,* II, 127–136, and Leclère, *Histoire,* 438–441. For an analysis of the decree that Ang Duong issued on the hierarchy to be observed in the Cambodian court,

see P. Bitard, "Les Membres de la famille royale du Cambodge et leurs titres d'après l'ordonnance de S. M. An Duon," *BEFEO*, XLVIII, fasc. 2 (1957), 563–572.

The quotation is from A. Pavie, "Excursion dans le Cambodge et le Royaume de Siam," *Excursions et Reconnaissances*, IX (1881), 470.

11. Moura, *Le Royaume*, II, 127.

12. Leclère, *Le Buddhisme*, 403. There is no evidence to suggest that the Thommayut sect in Cambodia played a role similar to that which Dr. D. K. Wyatt perceives for it in Thailand. In that country, Dr. Wyatt sees the Thommayut sect as an important element assisting in the program of modernization (D. K. Wyatt, "The Beginnings of Modern Education in Thailand 1868–1910," Ph. D. Thesis, Cornell University, 1966, 42–43).

13. India Office Records, India Secret Proceedings, India Secret Consultations, 25 July to 28 November 1851, No. 170, Governor of Prince of Wales Island, Singapore, and Malacca to Officiating Undersecretary to the Government of India, Penang, 21 August 1851, No. 19.

14. On the prohibitions against vagabonds, see C. Briffaut, *La Cité annamite* (Paris, 1909–1912), particularly III, "Les Errants."

15. P. Boudet, "La Conquête de la Cochinchine par les Nguyen et le rôle des émigrés chinois," *BEFEO*, XLII (1942), 115–132.

16. Aubaret, trans., *Histoire*, 18.

17. For a brilliant synthesis of material relating to political relationships between the village and the central authority, see Paul Mus, *Viêt-Nam: Sociologie d'une guerre* (Paris, 1952), Chapter 2.

18. G. C. Hickey, "Problems of Social Change in Viet-Nam," *BSEI*, n.s., XXXIII, 4 (1958), 413.

19. Aubaret, trans., *Histoire*, 19.   20. *Ibid.*, 98.

21. *Ibid.*, 91.

22. This study will not consider the role of the French in the fight for the Nguyen restoration. The most detailed examination of the background to French imperialist efforts is contained in John F. Cady, *The Roots of French Imperialism in Eastern Asia* (Ithaca, 1954).

23. Le Thanh Khoi, *Le Viêt-Nam: Histoire et civilisation* (Paris, 1955), provides useful summaries of all these developments. For a comment on the Gia-Long code, see R. Deloustal, "La Justice dans l'ancien Annam: I," particularly the preface by Cl.-E. Maître, *BEFEO*, VIII (1908), 1–2, where it is emphasized that the Gia-Long code was essentially a copy of the Manchu code. By contrast, the Le code was more distinctively Vietnamese.

24. Le Thanh Khoi, *Le Viêt-Nam*, 324–328. For a discussion of the survey of Cochinchina in 1836, see A. Schreiner, *Les Institutions annamites en Basse Cochinchine avant la conquête française* (Saigon, 1900–1902), II, 299–304.

25. Some two thousand rebels were executed and buried in a common grave just outside Saigon. A missionary was among those who were taken to Hue and executed by the process *lang-tri,* the slow death. For a Catholic account of the persecution of Christians in Viet-Nam, see Tran-Minh Tiet, *Histoire des persécutions au Viet-Nam* (Paris, 1955).

26. Cady, *French Imperialism*, 32; Le Thanh Khoi, *Le Viêt-Nam*, 342.

27. E. Deschaseaux, "Note sur les anciens *don dien* annamites dans la Basse-Cochinchine," *Excursions et Reconnaissances*, XIV (1889), 133–136.

28. For a discussion of the differences between the Chinese and the Vietnamese mandarinate, see A. B. Woodside, "Some Features of the Vietnamese Bureaucracy under the Early Nguyen Dynasty," *Harvard Papers on China*, 19 (December 1965), 1–29. Thorough analysis of the *Dai Nam Thuc Luc,* a daily record of the decisions of the Vietnamese emperor, will eventually provide insights into the workings of Vietnamese bureaucracy and replace the speculative analysis upon which much current writing must rely.

29. For an account of life in the imperial city, see Michel Duc Chaigneau, *Souvenirs de Hué* (Paris, 1867). The son of J.-B. Chaigneau and a Vietnamese Christian wife, the author of this book grew up in Hue. There is no shortage of accounts and summaries of Vietnamese court life and administration: Le Thanh Khoi, *Le Viêt-Nam*, 324–325; J.-B. E. Luro, *Le Pays d'Annam* (Paris, 1878); Pierre Pasquier, *L'Annam d'autrefois* (Paris, 1907).

30. Schreiner, *Les Institutions*, I, 287–330, describes the provincial administration in detail.

31. Discussion of the Vietnamese commune is based, chiefly, on the following sources: Luro, *Cours d'administration annamite* (Saigon, 1875); A. Landes, "La Commune annamite," *Excursions et Reconnaissances*, V (1880), 213–242; Schreiner, *Les Institutions*, II; and George D . . . [ürrwell], "La Commune annamite," *BSEI*, XLIX–L (1905), 67–88.

32. Phan Huy Chu, *Lich Trieu Hien Chuong Loai Chi* (Description

of the institutions of all the dynasties) (Hanoi, 1960–1961), I, *Du Dia Chi, Nhan Vat Chi* (Geography and Biography), 140. See also Nguyen Thanh-Nha, *Tableau économique du Viet-Nam aux XVIIe et XVIIIe siècles* (Paris, n.d.), 119–122.

33. G. Rivière, "Une Lignée de loyaux serviteurs, les Nguyen Khoa," *BAVH*, II, 3 (July–September 1915), 287–304; and L. Sogny, "Les Familles illustres d'Annam, S.E. Nguyen-Huu-Do," *BAVH*, XI, 2 (April–June 1924), 169–204.

34. Pasquier, *L'Annam,* Chapter 4.

35. The civil and military mandarinate were both divided into nine grades. Those officials who had obtained the title *cu-nhan* entered at the seventh grade. M. Texier ("Le Mandarinat au Viet-Nam au XIXe siècle," *BSEI*, n.s., XXXVII, 3 [1962], 332–376) provides an exhaustive analysis of published works in European languages dealing with the mandarinate.

36. Léopold Cadière, *Croyances et pratiques religieuses des Vietnamiens* (2nd ed.; Saigon, 1958), I, Chapters 1 and 2.

37. For a general discussion of traditional education, see Tran-Van-Trai, *L'Enseignement traditionnel en An-Nam* (Paris, 1942).

38. See Schreiner, *Les Institutions*, II, Chapter 7.

39. For a Vietnamese account of Phan-Thanh-Gian's life, see Nam Xuan Tho, *Phan Thanh Gian (1796–1867)* (Saigon, 1957).

40. John White (*A Voyage to Cochin China* [London, 1824], 232) estimated the population at 180,000 in 1819.

41. Le-Van-Phat, "La Vie intime d'un Annamite de Cochinchine et ses croyances vulgaires," *BSEI*, LII (1906), 70–81.

42. Georges Taboulet, *La Geste française en Indochine* (Paris, 1955–1956) provides in Tome I documents and historical summaries that are scholarly examples of the orthodox view.

43. C.-E. Bouillevaux, *L'Annam et le Cambodge: Voyages et notes historiques* (Paris, 1874).

44. This is an estimate based on contemporary guesses and the later, more detailed, figures supplied by the Missions Etrangères. This missionary order cited a figure of thirty thousand Christians in 1867. See the order's *Lettre commune,* Paris, 25 July 1867.

45. Cady, *French Imperialism*. Of interest, since it uses archival material not available to Professor Cady, is P. Franchini, *La Genèse de l'affaire de Cochinchine* (Paris, 1952).

46. *Lettre commune,* Paris, 5 June 1861: "It is certain for anyone

who has lived for some years in Cambodia that one can never obtain much success with Cambodians, unless it is through buying the freedom of debt slaves; but that method is long and very costly."

47. The exact import of this letter is a matter of some dispute. Writers such as Leclère, who unhesitatingly approved of a French presence in Cambodia, regard the letter as indicating that Ang Duong sought a French protectorate over his country. A detailed analysis of the period by Charles Meyniard, *Le Second Empire en Indo-Chine* (*Siam, Cambodge, Annam*) (Paris, 1891), questions this position and makes a convincing case to show that Ang Duong did not wish to have any political relationship with France resembling the protectorate eventually established.

48. The text of this letter, written in 1856, is contained in the Cambodian Ministry of Information publication *Rois de Kampuchea: Ang Duong, Norodom, N. Sihanouk* (Phnom Penh, 1957), 3–5.

49. Cady, *French Imperialism*, 160–180.

50. Franchini, *La Genèse*, 81–105.

51. One of the best accounts remains that of L. Pallu de la Barrière, *Histoire de l'expédition de Cochinchine* (2nd ed.; Paris, 1888). Pallu was a participant in the expedition that he describes.

52. Concern over possible British interference is amply demonstrated in the correspondence between Paris and Saigon contained in AF Marine BB4, 825. See, as a particular instance, the Minister of the Colonies to Admiral Bonard, Paris, 18 April 1863.

53. The most detailed study of the establishment of the protectorate is provided by R. S. Thomson's "The Establishment of the French Protectorate over Cambodia," *Far Eastern Quarterly*, IV, 4 (August 1945), 313–340. It is worth noting that the decision to establish a protectorate over Cambodia came after considerable hesitation. This is stressed in archival sources, some of which were not available to Thomson at the time he published his useful study. See in particular the correspondence contained in the volume AF Marine BB4, 825 for 1863.

Chapter 2: *The Civilizing Missioners*

1. The French term *indigène* paralleled the pejorative British use of "native" during the heyday of colonialism.

2. The best survey of French historical writings on the French presence in Viet-Nam is Jean Chesneaux, "French Historiography and the Evolution of Colonial Viet-Nam," in D. G. E. Hall, ed., *Historians of South-East Asia* (London, 1961). Chesneaux stresses throughout this essay the concern of French writers with "conquest" and their neglect of economic and social matters. His own survey of Vietnamese history, *Contribution à l'histoire de la nation vietnamienne* (Paris, 1955), is marked by a strong materialist bias.

Adulation of French actions and methods reaches perhaps its highest point in H.-F. Lhomme, *Le Gouvernement des amiraux en Cochinchine (1861–1879)* (Paris, 1901), where bias, scant source material, and general preconceptions of imperial mission result in a picture of the early years of the French presence in Cochinchina which is drastically in need of qualification. But the concern with imperial glory remains. It is a dominant theme in the important collection of documents assembled by Taboulet, *La Geste*. The recent bibliographic study by Robert Auvade, *Bibliographie critique des oeuvres parues sur l'Indochine française* (Paris, 1965), is conceived as a record of the French civilizing mission, despite its listing of material critical of the French record.

3. R. F. Betts, *Assimilation and Association in French Colonial Theory 1890–1914* (New York, 1961); M. D. Lewis, "One Hundred Million Frenchmen: The 'Assimilation' Theory in French Colonial Policy," *Comparative Studies in Society and History*, IV, 2 (January 1962), 129–153.

4. *Cochinchine Française, Procès-verbaux du Conseil Colonial* (hereafter cited as *Conseil Colonial*) (ordinary session), 18 July 1903, 3; *République Française, Discours prononcé par M. Rodier, Lieutenant Gouverneur de la Cochinchine à l'ouverture de la session du Conseil Colonial le 30 juin 1905* (Saigon, 1905), 4–6.

5. Taboulet, *La Geste*, II, 522, for instance, refers to "patient and measured assimilation" in the period before 1879.

6. An interesting sociological analysis of this point is contained in Peter Worsley's *The Third World* (London, 1964), 27. Consider his comment, "The superiority of the West was never seen as merely a matter of technology. It was a total superiority. For Livingstone, Manchester and the Bible went hand in hand. . . ."

7. *Bulletin Officiel de l'Expédition de Cochinchine* (hereafter *BOCF*) 1863, pt. 5, 310–313.

8. *Ibid.*, 1862, pt. 3, 37.

9. AOM Indochine O-01 (1) Admiral Bonard to the Minister of the Colonies, Saigon, 16 August 1862, No. 478. The emphasis is in the original.

10. *BOCF*, 1863, pt. 7, 330–331; proclamation of 20 May 1863.

11. AF Colonies C1.6 Cochinchine 1819–1863, Lieutenant Ansart to Admiral de La Grandière, Saigon, 25 April 1863.

12. G. Francis (Francis Garnier), *La Cochinchine française en 1864* (Paris, 1864), 6–7.

13. *Ibid.*, 44–45. See also Garnier's pamphlet *De La Colonisation de Cochinchine* (Paris, 1865), again with the pseudonym G. Francis.

14. One of the bitterest and most unfair attacks is contained in F. Romanet du Caillaud's *Histoire de l'intervention française au Tongking de 1872 à 1874* (Paris, 1880).

15. M. H. Abel (A. B.-L. Rieunier), *Solution pratique de la question de Cochinchine* (Paris, 1864), 4.

16. *Courrier de Saigon*, 5 May 1867.   17. *Ibid.*, 5 July 1867.

18. AF Marine BB4, 769, Admiral Rigault de Genouilly to the Minister of the Navy, Tourane, 29 January 1859.

19. *Ibid.*, Admiral Rigault de Genouilly to the Minister of the Navy, Saigon, 28 February 1859.

20. *Courrier de Saigon,* 5 February 1869. There were less than 40,000 Catholics in Cochinchina in 1869.

21. *Lettre commune*, No. 21, Paris, 31 December 1889.

22. Depierre, *Situation du Christianisme en Cochinchine à la fin du XIXe siècle* (Saigon, 1898), 6.

23. Biographical material on Luro, and some account of his association with the Collège des Stagiaires, may be found in G. Taboulet, "Jean-Baptiste Eliacin Luro: Inspecteur des Affaires Indigènes en Cochinchine," *BSEI*, n.s., XV, 1 and 2 (1940), 27–112; and J. Perin, "La Vie et l'oeuvre de Luro," *BSEI*, n.s., XV, 1 and 2 (1940), 13–25.

24. Details of the entry requirements and the course offered may be found in *BOCF*, 1873, pt. 10, 297–302.

25. The *Cours d'administration annamite*, assembled in Saigon in 1875, is a compilation of Luro's lectures. A small number of copies existed in manuscript and in lithograph form, made from a handwritten original until 1905. At that time a further thirty copies were made by order of Rodier, the lieutenant governor of Cochinchina.

Only a small number of copies are now extant. The pagination used in the present study is from a copy consulted in Saigon.

26. *Cours d'administration,* 687.

27. *Ibid.,* Lesson 38 and *passim.*   28. *Ibid.,* 499.

29. On Philastre's life, see Nel, "Philastre, sa vie et son oeuvre," *BSEI,* XLIV (1902), 3–27. See also, AVN S. L. 191, which is Philastre's personal dossier.

30. AOM Indochine O-oo(5) "Mémoire sur le projet de substituer le Code pénal français au Code annamite," prepared by Philastre, Saigon, 25 April 1873.

31. AVN S. L. 4,364 "Rapport sur un voyage d'inspection fait du 11 février au 3 mars, et du 15 mars au 6 avril 1876 dans les deux provinces de Gia-Dinh et de Bien-Hoa (circonscription de Saigon)," prepared by Philastre, Saigon, 15 August 1876.

32. Director of the Interior Piquet's comment is contained in a covering letter to Philastre's report, addressed to the Governor of Cochinchina, Saigon, 9 May 1876, in the same dossier. (The disparity in dating is not explained in the papers contained in the dossier. The 15 August report may be a later copy of an earlier report.)

33. AOM Indochine O-30(1) "Observations sur le décret organique du 25 juillet 1864," prepared by Philastre, Saigon, 18 August 1868.

34. Villemereuil, ed., *Explorations,* 389–439 *passim.*

35. AVN S. L. 5,054 Moura to the Director of the Interior in Saigon, Phnom Penh, 24 December 1875.

36. AOM Indochine A-30(26) Admiral Duperré to the Minister of the Colonies, Saigon, 18 October 1876, No. 727. Duperré wrote of his hope that "we will obtain some serious modifications in the institutions of this detestable government of a type which will re-establish peace in the kingdom."

37. AOM Indochine A-30(22) "Copie d'une note sur les modifications à apporter au traité passé en 1863 entre la France et le Cambodge," prepared by Moura, without provenance and undated; "Rapport confidentiel sur le Cambodge," prepared by Aymonier, Saigon, 24 August 1874.

38. *L'Indépendant de Saigon,* 1 June 1873.

39. *Courrier de Saigon,* 5 November 1866.

40. *Ibid.,* 20 September 1867.

41. It is difficult to estimate the extent to which French power was

challenged and seriously threatened by Vietnamese resistance movements in the early years of the colonial period. Official French military histories, most importantly the *Histoire militaire de l'Indochine
des débuts à nos jours (Janvier 1922)* (Hanoi, 1922), give only
laconic references to resistance to French authority in Cochinchina.
Archival sources are more frank, but only to a degree. There is always great difficulty in arriving at the numbers involved in a particular
incident and the extent to which a particular group posed a threat
to the French.

42. See, for instance, the Ministerial Instructions to Admiral Bonard,
Paris, 26 August 1861, in AF Marine BB4, 795.

43. AOM Indochine D-11(9) contains a printed document prepared by Paulin Vial, *Note sur l'administration de la Cochinchine*
(Saigon, n.d.), which must have been prepared in 1870 and which
deals with the financial problems posed by the Franco–Prussian War.

44. Le Myre de Vilers, *Les Institutions civiles de la Cochinchine
1879–1881* (Paris, 1908), 3.

45. *Ibid.*, 6–7.

46. AOM Indochine O-00(5) Governor Le Myre de Vilers to the
Minister of the Colonies, Saigon, 20 October 1879, No. 1,110.

47. AVN Ministerial Dispatches, the Minister of the Colonies to
Governor Le Myre de Vilers, Paris, 29 January 1881, No. 35.

48. Le Myre de Vilers recommended the extension of opportunities
for naturalization to Vietnamese shortly after his arrival in 1879. AOM
Indochine D-01(4) Governor Le Myre de Vilers to the Minister of the
Colonies, Saigon, 14 July 1880, No. 691. On the aims of the Alliance
Française, see AVN Ministerial Dispatches, the Minister of the Colonies
to Governor Thomson, Paris, 15 February 1884, unnumbered.

49. AOM Indochine A-30(67) Governor Thomson to the Minister
of the Colonies, Saigon, 30 June 1884, No. 87.

50. Paul Doumer, *L'Indochine française: Souvenirs* (Paris, 1905),
33.

51. *Conseil Colonial* (ordinary session 1882), 11 December 1882,
152.

52. *Ibid.* (ordinary session 1906), 29 October 1906, 16–17.

53. Vien Khao-Co (Institute of Archeological Research), Su Ky
(10), "Mémoire—Droits d'Annam sur la vallée (rive gauche) du
Mékong."

54. *Conseil Colonial* (ordinary session 1902), 14 October 1902,

136–137. The Bishop was engaged in special pleading. It was not really an attempt to instil French virtues against which he argued, but against a policy that took funds away from missions that taught only in *quoc-ngu*.

55. As an example of the admiration that Loc excited, see G. Dürrwell, "Tran-Ba-Loc, Tong-Doc de Thuan-Khanh, Sa vie et son oeuvre, Notice biographique d'après les documents de famille," *BSEI*, XL (1900), 27–60.

56. P. Barthélemy, *En Indochine 1894–1895* (Paris, 1899), 12, gives an account of a visit to Phuong's house.

57. *British Malaya* (rev. ed.; London, 1948), 174.

58. The whole problem of the future of the communal administration came under intense scrutiny in the period from 1900 to 1905. The issue of payments to village officials was raised many times in the debates of the Colonial Council.

59. *La Langue française et l'enseignement en Indo-Chine* (Paris, 1890).

60. AOM Indochine NF 429 Governor General Beau to the Minister of the Colonies, Hanoi, 9 March 1904, No. 576.

Chapter 3: *Establishment of an Administrative and Legal Framework (1859–1879)*

1. On the mandarins' withdrawal, see Pallu de la Barrière, *Histoire*, 159. The calculations of the number who withdrew are based in part on Lucien de Grammont, *Onze Mois de sous-préfecture en Basse-Cochinchine* (La-Roche-sur-Yon, 1863), 89, and the information contained in the *Dai-Nam Nhat-Thong-Chi* (Geography of the Vietnamese Empire), in the section *Luc-Tinh* (Cochinchina), published in a *quoc-ngu* translation by the Ministry of Culture, Saigon, as issue No. 2 (1959) of *Van-Hoa Tung-Thu*.

2. Pallu de la Barrière, *Histoire;* Vial, *Les Premières Années;* and Grammont, *Onze Mois* provide useful accounts of Vietnamese resistance to the French in the early years. An able modern summary of the period is contained in Philippe Devillers' "Au Sud-Vietnam . . . il y a cent ans," *FA*, XX, 184 (Winter 1965/1966), 139–156, and XX, 185 (Spring 1966), 325–347.

The question of Hue's relationship to events in the south during the eighteen sixties is examined in Dr. Truong Buu Lam's monograph, *Patterns of Vietnamese Response to Foreign Intervention: 1859–1900,* Monograph Series No. 11, Southeast Asia Studies, Yale University (New Haven, 1967), 6–9.

3. Vial, *Les Premières Années,* I, 215–217 and 323–326.

4. As just one example, see AVN S. L. 1,659 "Administration. Tournées administratives. Rapport du Secrétaire général sur sa tournée à Soctrang, Bactrang, Cantho, Longxuyen, Sadec, Caibe et Tanan. 1870." This report refers to some Vietnamese who had opposed the French receiving titles from mandarins who had withdrawn to Hue.

5. The tone of naval enthusiasm for French control over the six provinces is best captured in Garnier's pamphlets *La Cochinchine française* and *De La Colonisation de la Cochinchine.* Rieunier's pamphlet, *Solution pratique de la question de Cochinchine,* and the anonymous pamphlet *Etude sur les voies et moyens de la politique française en Cochinchine* (Saigon, 1864) are in very similar vein. Taboulet, *La Geste,* II, 488–520, contains documents and commentary relating to this period.

6. AOM Indochine A-30(6) "Extraits d'une lettre particulière de M. le C. Amiral de La Grandière, gouverneur de la Cochinchine adressée à M. Maudrut Dupleix," 17 January 1865.

7. AF Marine BB4, 876 "Dossier à l'appui de la dépêche au Ministre en date de 27 [25?] Juin 1867, No. 543. (The actual dispatch is not contained in the volume.) "Copie d'une dépêche du Vice Amiral Gouverneur et Commandant en chef en Cochinchine à Son Excellence Phan-Tan-Giang, Vice-Grand Censeur du Royaume d'Annam à Vinh-Long," 17 June 1867.

8. AF Marine BB4, 876 "Dossier à l'appui de la dépêche au Ministre en date de 27 [25?] Juin 1867, No. 543." "Proclamation. Le Gouverneur de la Cochinchine aux habitants des six provinces," 25 June 1867. The proclamation was circulated in both French and *quoc-ngu.*

9. Information on Phan-Thanh-Gian is available from a number of sources. The most detailed collection of documentary material is contained in P. Daudin, "Biographie de Phan-Thanh-Gian, 2e ambassadeur en France en 1863 (1796–1867)," *BSEI,* n.s., XVI, 2 (1941), 11–128. See also Dao-Thai-Hanh, "Son Excellence Phan-Thanh-Gian, Ministre de l'Annam (1796–1867)," *BAVH,* II (April–June 1915), 211–224. A biography in Vietnamese is Nam Xuan Tho, *Phan Thanh Gian.*

Phan-Thanh-Gian's suicide was in true mandarinal tradition. He believed that he had failed his emperor and that the only course open to him was death. In a letter to the Emperor of Viet-Nam, dated 8 July 1867, Phan referred to the impossibility of preventing the French takeover: see Taboulet, *La Geste*, II, 518, where there is a translation of the letter to Tu-Duc extracted from the imperial archives.

10. Pallu de la Barrière, *Histoire*, 211–212.

11. AOM Indochine A-30(12) Admiral de La Grandière to the Minister of the Colonies, Saigon, 27 August 1867, No. 754. Vial, *Les Premières Années*, II, 143.

12. Vial, *Les Premières Années*, I, 323–326.

13. The text is contained in an article by Admiral Reveillère, "Patriotisme annamite," *Revue Indo-Chinoise*, 6th Year, 190 (9 June 1902), 515–517. Reveillère took part in the punitive expedition in 1862 that found the document. The full text reads:

"All the inhabitants of the province of Go-Cong make this declaration with a common accord.

"In losing the government of our king we are in the same state of desolation as a child who has lost his father and his mother.

"Your country belongs to the Western seas, ours to the seas of the East.

"Just as the horse and the buffalo differ between themselves, so do we differ by our language, our writing, and our customs. Man has been created in different races; everywhere man has the same value, but his nature is not the same.

"Gratitude attaches us to our king; we will avenge his injuries or we will die for him. If you insist on bringing fire and the sword amongst us, disorder will last for a long time. But since we act according to the laws of heaven, our cause will finally triumph.

"If you wish for peace, give back his territory to our king. We fight with this goal.

"You have taken our provinces to add riches to your empire, and to the glory of your name. Do you wish a ransom in exchange for our territory? We will pay it on condition that you will stop fighting and withdraw your troops to your possessions. We will even have gratitude for you, and your glory will be like the universe. Do you wish a concession to watch over your commercial interests? We will consent to this.

"But if you refuse, we will not cease to fight in order to obey the wish of heaven. We fear your valor, but we fear heaven more than your power. We swear to fight eternally and without respite. When we lack everything, we will take tree branches for flags and sticks to arm our soldiers. How then will you be able to live in the middle of us?

"We ask you to examine this request with care and to put an end to a state of affairs as disagreeable for your interests as it is for ours."

14. Nguyen-Dinh-Chieu was born in Gia-Dinh province in 1822. He studied at Hue, but after going blind he established a school in Saigon in which he taught the Chinese classics. He left Saigon for Ben-Tre in 1858 and devoted much of the rest of his life to writing poems in praise of those who opposed the French. Among these were "Vieng cu Phan-Thanh-Gian" (Paying Respect to Phan-Thanh-Gian) and "Van te si dan Luc tinh" (A Funeral Oration for the Scholars and People of the Six Provinces). There are biographical notes, as well as a selection of his poems, in Thai Bach, *Nguyen Dinh Chieu* (Saigon, 1957).

15. AAE Asie 29 Indochine 3 Admiral de La Grandière to the Minister of the Colonies, Saigon, 30 June 1864, No. 840.

16. G. Coulet, *Les Sociétés secrètes en terre d'Annam* (Saigon, 1926). This detailed study provides the most comprehensive account of secret society activities in Viet-Nam during the colonial period. It is chiefly concerned with secret societies in the twentieth century, but it does make some observations on the earlier period. It is clear that in a fashion similar to developments in China, uniting in secret societies has long been a characteristic of Vietnamese society.

17. AOM Indochine A-30(29) Admiral Lafont to the Minister of the Colonies, Saigon, 15 May 1878, No. 464. See also, AVN S. L. 4,606 for papers connected with the same incident, and AVN Tanan, 38, dealing with repression of opposition to the French between 1869 and 1879.

18. *Tho Nam Ky ou Lettre cochinchinoise sur les événements de la guerre franco-annamite,* translated by M. D. Chaigneau (Paris, 1876), lines 310–320 and 340–343.

19. The best available biography of Pétrus Ky is that by Jean Bouchot, *Pétrus J.-B. Truong-Vinh-Ky, 1837–1898* (2nd ed.; Saigon, 1927). Subsequent Vietnamese treatment of Ky draws heavily on Bouchot's study. See, for instance, Khong Xuan-Thu, *Truong Vinh Ky 1837–1898* (Saigon, 1958). On Cua's importance, see Dinh-Xuan-Nguyen, *Apport français dans la littérature vietnamienne (1641–1954)* (Saigon, 1961).

Some details on Cua's life are contained in A. Brébion and A. Cabaton, *Dictionnaire de bio-bibliographie générale, ancienne et moderne de l'Indochine française,* published as Tome VIII of the *Annales* of the Académie des Sciences Coloniales (Paris, 1935), 197.

20. AF Marine BB4, 788 Admiral Charner to the Minister of the Colonies, Saigon, 12 August 1861, No. 327.

21. In addition to the biography by Dürrwell, "Tran-Ba-Loc . . . ," the present study makes use of material on Loc contained in his personal dossier, AVN S. L. 311.

22. AVN S. L. 311. The quotation is from Loc's *Bulletin individuel de note* for 1877.

23. *Courrier de Saigon,* 5 December 1865, gives background on Ca's activities in the period just after the French presence was firmly established. From the French point of view, he had "recognized the power and the correctness of the administration." Ca's personal dossier provides further evidence of his continuing utility to the French administration (AVN S. L. 1,121).

24. A detailed account of Phuong's life is contained in his personal dossier, AVN S. L. 312, "Notice biographique sur M. Do-Huu-Phuong, Doc-Phu-Su, Tong-Doc honoraire." A *ba-ho* was a canton chief who had occupied his post for a considerable time and received imperial recognition. Such non-mandarinal officials were normally among the wealthiest members of their community. See Luro, *Cours d'administration,* 105–107.

25. Vial, *Les Premières Années,* I, 153.

26. *Ibid.,* 109. There is a continuing oral tradition, revealed to the writer in interviews with descendants of the Cochinchinese elite, that Catholic Vietnamese were able to capitalize upon their religion and the support that they received from the French to gain substantial land holdings at the expense of non-Catholic Vietnamese. Tradition also suggests that part of the reason for the preferment accorded Phuong was that he procured women for French officials. A contemporary allegation making the same point may be found in a letter contained in Phuong's personal dossier, AVN S. L. 312, from a group of Vietnamese, addressed to the French administration, and dated 30 June 1873. The original of the letter is in Chinese characters, and it is accompanied by a French translation.

27. The details on Tuong's life are taken from Nguyen Ba The, *Ton Tho Tuong 1825–1877* (Saigon, 1957), 5–31, *passim.* Some account

of Tuong's literary contest with Phan-Van-Tri may be found in Nguyen-Van-Han, "Une Joute littéraire et politique en 1870," *FA,* IX, 87 (August 1953), 673–677.

28. Philastre had a critical view of Tuong: see AOM Indochine O-oo(5) "Mémoire sur le projet de substituer le Code pénal français au Code annamite," prepared by Philastre, Saigon, 25 April 1873. Taboulet's article, "Jean-Baptiste Eliacin Luro, Inspecteur des Affaires indigènes en Cochinchine," however, quotes Luro as stating that Tuong was "the most remarkable man in the six provinces for his level of instruction" (pp. 93 and 94).

29. Pallu de la Barrière, *Histoire,* 158. See also AOM Indochine A-30(6) Admiral de la Grandière to the Minister of the Colonies, Saigon, 29 September 1863, No. 296.

30. AVN S. L. 4,364 "Rapport sur un voyage d'inspection fait du 11 février au 3 mars, et du 15 mars au 6 avril dans les deux provinces de Gia-Dinh et Bien-Hoa (circonscription de Saigon)," prepared by Philastre, 15 August 1876.

31. *Cours d'administration,* 94.

32. AOM Indochine O-30(1) Luro to Philastre, Can-Tho, 6 September 1868.

33. AOM Indochine I-20(3) "Cochinchine. Direction de l'Intérieur. Inspecteurs, administrateurs des Affaires indigènes, bulletins individuels et notes. 1876."

34. AOM Indochine O-30(1) Luro to Philastre, Can-Tho, 6 September 1868.

35. AOM Indochine Z-oo(8) The Apostolic Vicar of Saigon to the Director [of the Interior?], Saigon, 12 September 1872. The letter claims that of sixty inspectors working in Cochinchina, fifty-eight are living with Vietnamese concubines.

Chaigneau, *Tho Thiep Theo Tho Nam Ky, Suite de la lettre annamite, poème sur la conduite des jeunes Annamites après la guerre* (Paris, 1876), lines 67–82 and 119–125, presents a picture of prostitutes acting as intermediaries between the French and those Vietnamese who wished to conduct business with the administration. See also Luro's *Cours d'administration,* 688, where he specifically includes "women of poor morals" among those limited few who had learnt to speak French.

36. The emphasis placed on the use of French in Cochinchina will be the concern of later chapters, particularly Chapters 4 and 8.

37. Material relating to Admiral Charner's administration is found in AF Marine BB4, 788 and AF Marine BB4, 795. See, in particular, AF Marine BB4, 788 Admiral Charner to the Minister of the Colonies, Saigon, 29 April 1861, No. 245 and No. 246.

38. In particular, see AOM Indochine A-30(3) Admiral Bonard to the Minister of the Colonies, Saigon, 3 December 1861, No. 34, and AOM Indochine A-oo(2) Admiral Bonard to the Minister of the Colonies, Saigon, 27 February 1862, No. 112.

39. AOM Indochine A-20(1) Admiral Bonard to the Minister of the Colonies, Saigon, 8 January 1863, unnumbered.

40. AOM Indochine A-30(6) Admiral de La Grandière to the Minister of the Colonies, Saigon, 29 September 1863, No. 296; AOM Indochine A-20(3) Admiral de La Grandière to the Minister of the Colonies, Saigon, 31 December 1864, No. 1,121.

41. Some impression of the rigor with which opposition to the French was combatted may be gained from a dossier held in the Vietnamese archives, AVN S. L. 4,420 which lists judgments rendered at My-Tho between 1862 and 1869.

42. AOM Indochine O-oo(1), Commandant d'Ariès to Admiral Bonard, Saigon, 16 December 1861. This letter summarizes developments in the legal field up to the time the letter was written.

43. AOM Indochine O-oo(1) Admiral Bonard to the Minister of the Colonies, Saigon, 16 August 1862, No. 478.

44. AOM Indochine O-oo(1) "Note sur la justice" prepared by Governor Le Myre de Vilers in 1881. This dossier reviews the various intentions of Le Myre de Vilers' predecessors. He appears to doubt that Vietnamese judges ever acted on cases, once the French had arrived. Dossier AVN S. L. 4,420 suggests that a limited number of cases may have been heard by Vietnamese in the period until the end of 1864.

45. AOM Indochine O-oo(1) Personal Letter, Admiral de La Grandière to the Minister of the Colonies, Saigon, undated (late 1863 or early 1864). See also AOM Indochine D-11(1) "Notes sur l'administration des Annamites" prepared by La Grandière, 1864.

46. *BOCF*, 1864, pt. 9, 100–108. The decree of 25 July 1864 was promulgated in Cochinchina on 24 September 1864.

47. AOM Indochine O-30(1) "Observation sur le décret organique du 25 Juillet 1864," Saigon, 18 August 1868.

48. AOM Indochine O-30(1) Procureur impérial to Admiral Ohier,

Saigon, 5 May 1868. Arbitration by Vietnamese employees was, however, described as "very rare."

49. AOM Indochine O-oo(8) "Note sur la justice" prepared by Governor Le Myre de Vilers, 1881.

50. AVN S. L. 283 Inspector of Native Affairs, Sa-Dec, telegraphing to the Director of the Interior, 5 November 1872.

51. AOM Indochine O-30(1) Procureur impérial to Admiral Ohier, Saigon, 5 May 1868. "In fact, the Annamite penal law is no longer exclusively applied by the inspectors. . . . As for those who have the intention of judging according to the dispositions of the Annamite criminal legislation . . . they encounter, on each occasion, difficulties in its application which are very serious even for men accustomed to interpreting the law."

52. Le Myre de Vilers, *Les Institutions civiles*, 70.

53. For this exchange, see AOM Indochine O-30(1) "Observations sur le décret organique du 25 Juillet 1864" prepared by Philastre, Saigon, 18 August 1868, and Procureur impérial Parqueient [the spelling of this name is uncertain] to Philastre, Saigon, 28 August 1868.

54. AF Marine BB4, 899 Admiral Ohier to the Minister of the Colonies, 2 March 1869. Replies to questionnaires circulated by Ohier in AVN S. L. 1,720 make it clear that there was far from unanimity on Ohier's proposal.

55. AOM Indochine A-20(7) Admiral Ohier to the Minister of the Colonies, Saigon, 30 November 1868, No. 1,084.

56. AOM Indochine O-oo(5) "Mémoire sur le projet de substituer le Code pénal français au Code annamite" prepared by Philastre, Saigon, 25 April 1873. The account in the body of the text of developments connected with the proposal to substitute the French penal code for the Vietnamese code relies heavily on this document.

57. AOM Indochine O-oo(5) Admiral Dupré to the Minister of the Colonies, Saigon, 21 July 1873, No. 595. Dupré's attitude on justice contrasts strongly with his expansionist tendencies demonstrated in relation to Tonkin. It was Dupré who gave support to Garnier's *coup de force* in 1873.

58. AVN S. L. 280 Circular letter from Béliard, Director of the Interior to Administrators of Native Affairs, Saigon, 20 November 1876, No. 35. The first edition of Philastre's translation was published in Paris in 1876. A second edition was published in 1909.

59. Various decisions in the seventies consolidated earlier provisions about the recruitment, advancement, and responsibilities of the members of the Native Affairs Service. See, in particular, *BOCF*, 1873, pt. 4, 122–128, and *BOCF*, 1876, pt. 7, 174–181. In the mid-seventies the term Administrator of Native Affairs supplanted that of Inspector of Native Affairs.

60. Le Myre de Vilers, *Les Institutions civiles*, 68, quotes the following interchange between an administrator and the Governor of Cochinchina: "Governor, I have the honor to submit for your approval the judgment condemning one Tu who, captured yesterday morning, was executed yesterday evening." The governor signed "approved." This despite a clear ruling that all capital punishments had to be considered by the governor before they were carried out.

61. AOM Indochine A-30(11) "Note de l'Amiral Ohier sur la colonie française de la Cochinchine" aboard the *Guerrière*, 15 December 1867, provides the information for the years 1865 to 1867. The increase in the cultivated area between 1870 and 1878 is calculated from figures provided in the *Annuaire de la Cochinchine française* (Saigon) for 1870, 198, and *La Cochinchine française en 1878* (Paris, 1878), 263.

62. *Lettre commune*, No. 25, Paris, 31 December 1892.

63. See the detailed account of the evolution of the taxation system contained in P. Cultru, *Histoire de la Cochinchine française des origines à 1883* (Paris, 1910), 260–264. Cultru was of the opinion that there had been a substantial increase in the tax rate. See also Luro, *Cours d'administration*, 373.

64. *Cours d'administration*, 584.

65. *Conseil Colonial* (ordinary session 1902), 16 October 1902, 146.

66. Aubaret, *Histoire*, x.

67. AOM Indochine D-51(3) Governor Filippini to the Minister of the Colonies, Saigon, 2 July 1887, No. 84, enclosing "Notes sur l'organisation de la commune annamite."

68. Landes, "La Commune annamite," 221.

69. Roger Pinto, "Les Assemblées des villages convoquées par l'Amiral Ohier," *BSEI*, n.s., XIX, No. 1 (1st trimester 1944), 9–55.

70. AVN S. L. 394 "Phung-Linh Quan Lon Nguon Soai" (Report to the Governor Commander in Chief), Cai-Be, 8 June 1869, prepared by Loc. The writer is indebted to Dr. Truong Buu Lam for kind help on difficult questions of translation in this early *quoc-ngu* document.

AVN S. L. 371 contains a shorter report by Loc making many of the same recommendations.

Chapter 4: *Education and* Quoc-Ngu— *The Development of a New Order*

1. For discussion of the part played in the development of *quoc-ngu* by Alexander of Rhodes, which also includes some observations on *chu-nom,* see Maurice Durand, "Alexandre de Rhodes," *BSEI,* n.s., XXXII, 1 (1st trimester, 1957), 5–30.

2. As typical examples of the rejection of Chinese characters in favor of *quoc-ngu,* see AOM Indochine A-20(2) Admiral de La Grandière to the Minister of the Colonies, Saigon, 31 December 1863, unnumbered, enclosing a general report for 1863, and the anonymous pamphlet *Etudes sur les voies et moyens de la politique française en Indochine,* 13.

3. AOM Indochine A-30(6) Admiral de La Grandière to the Minister of the Colonies, Saigon, 29 September 1864, No. 985.

4. AOM Indochine A-30(8) Admiral Roze to the Minister of the Colonies, Saigon, 9 May 1865, No. 1,360.

Early issues of *Gia-Dinh Bao* are extremely rare. The best collection, which contains only scattered copies for some years, is held in the library of the Ecole des Langues Orientales Vivantes in Paris. The collection held in the National Library in Saigon does not begin until 1880; see Le-Ngoc-Tru, ed., *Muc-Luc Bao Chi Viet-Ngu* (Saigon, 1966).

5. AOM Indochine X-00(1) "Extrait d'une lettre adressée au Ministre par le Gouverneur p.i. de la Cochinchine," Saigon, 2 March 1869.

6. *Gia-Dinh Bao,* No. 4 (July 1865).

7. *Ibid.,* No. 5 (August 1865).   8. *Ibid.*

9. *Ibid.,* No. 11 (June 1872).

10. Entitled "Chuyen Sach Su Nuoc Annam," these articles ran in *Gia-Dinh Bao* on an irregular basis during 1874 and 1875. The literal translation of the title is The Book of Vietnamese History. The author was not identified. It seems probable that it was Pétrus Ky.

11. *Gia-Dinh Bao,* No. 9 (1 May 1874).

12. *Conseil Colonial* (ordinary session 1885), 8 January 1886, 171. A considerable number of Cua's works were listed during discussion in the Conseil Colonial.

13. It is striking, for instance, to note the lack of biographical information in the entry for Cua in Brébion and Cabaton's *Dictionnaire de bio-bibliographie*.

14. Jean Bouchot's study, *Pétrus J.-B. Truong-Vinh-Ky*, is both extremely useful and the archetype of French commentary on Ky. It draws on family documents. Some of Bouchot's judgments reflect the period when it was written. Consider, for instance, the comment that Bouchot makes about Ky's entry into the French administration: "He was in the eyes of his fellow countrymen not a great mandarin, for such a title was only acquired following a participation in an examination according to the Rites, but something different and superior, if I dare say it; he was, in a fashion, a great *foreign mandarin* and of those regions that show the superiority of their civilization in such a striking manner." The emphasis is in the original text.

15. AVN S. L. 1,699 provides an instance of this in the letter from Ky to Inspector Kergaradec, Choquan, 14 September 1869, in which Ky discusses communal administration.

16. Recent Vietnamese studies of Ky's life, such as those by Khong Xuan-Thu, *Truong Vinh Ky*, and Nguyen-Huong, "Truong-Vinh-Ky (1837–1898)," *Van-Hoa Nguyet-San*, XIV, 12 (December 1965), 1,709–1,737 make use of Bouchot's work. The present study has also drawn on public and private archives in Paris and Saigon, including Ky's personal dossier in the Vietnamese archives and family papers held in the Pétrus Ky Museum on the site of his home in the Saigon suburb of Choquan.

The range of Ky's writings may be seen from consulting various bibliographies of his works. There are bibliographies in Bouchot's study, in Henri Cordier's obituary notice on Ky in *T'oung Pao*, series II, I (1900), 262–268. The most complete listing is Ky's own *Catalogue des ouvrages publiés et édités jusqu'à ce jour par P.J.B. Truong Vinh Ky à l'usage des écoles indochinoises* (Choquan, 1892). This is in mimeographed form and was consulted among the Ky papers held in the Vien Khao-Co (Institute for Archeological Research), Saigon. It contains 141 separate listings.

17. AVN S. L. 172 Ky to Vial, Choquan, 3 October 1868, in Ky's personal dossier.

18. *Cours d'histoire annamite à l'usage des écoles de la Basse-Cochinchine* (Saigon, 1875–1877).

19. Bouchot reproduces this report in his biography of Ky, pages 34–41, without any indication of the provenance. This writer has consulted a copy of the report in Ky's own hand in his letterbook, "Correspondance 1873 et 1874" (in fact it covers the years 1873–1877), in the Pétrus Ky Museum. It is noted in the letterbook as No. 50, "Rapport à l'Amiral par l'intermédiaire de M. Regnault de Premesnil," Choquan, 28 April 1876. The political report was never published in Ky's lifetime. The published account is *Voyage au Tonkin en 1876—Chuyen di Bac-Ki nam At-hoi* (Saigon, 1881). The text is in Vietnamese.

20. AVN S. L. 172; Luro's report is dated 16 June 1875.

21. Pétrus Ky Museum, "Correspondance 1873 et 1874," No. 105, Pétrus Ky to Monsieur Perrin of the Société Philologique, Saigon, 3 September 1877.

22. For Pham-Quynh's views, see his *Quelques Conférences à Paris* (Hanoi, 1923), 116–118.

23. The quotation is from the document "Institutions fondées en Cochinchine," dated 1864 and contained in AAE Asie Tome 29 Indochine 3. See also, AOM Indochine A-20(3) Admiral de La Grandière to the Minister of the Colonies, Saigon, 31 December 1864, No. 1,121, enclosing a general report for 1864.

24. AOM Indochine A-30(6) Admiral de La Grandière to the Minister of the Colonies, Saigon, 29 September 1864, No. 985. The emphasis is in the original.

25. AOM Indochine A-20(3) Admiral de La Grandière to the Minister of the Colonies, Saigon, 31 December 1864, No. 1,121, enclosing a general report for 1864.

26. AOM Indochine A-30(8) Admiral Roze to the Minister of the Colonies, Saigon, 29 March 1865, No. 1.

27. *Ibid.*, Admiral Roze to the Minister of the Colonies, Saigon, 26 November 1865, unnumbered.

28. AM Marine BB4, 876 Admiral Ohier to the Minister of the Colonies, Saigon, 28 November 1868, No. 1,083.

29. *Ibid.*, 899 Admiral Ohier to the Minister of the Colonies, 2 March 1869, unnumbered.

30. AOM Indochine A-20(8) "Rapport pour l'exposé général de la situation de l'Empire," Saigon, 28 August 1869.

31. AOM Indochine A-20(11) Admiral Cornulier-Lucinière to the Minister of the Colonies, Saigon, 27 September 1870, No. 816.

32. AOM Indochine A-20(14) Admiral Dupré to the Minister of the Colonies, Saigon, 1 February 1873, No. 115.

33. AVN S. L. 2,727 "Affaire de l'Ecole Centrale de Mytho," 1872.

34. *Cours d'administration,* 681.   35. *Ibid.,* 682.

36. *Ibid.,* 682–683. See also Taboulet, *La Geste,* II, 592–597.

37. *BOCF,* 1871, pt. 7, 230–232.

38. AVN S. L. 2,756 "Rapport mensuel adressé à Monsieur le Directeur de l'Intérieur," prepared by Robert, Director of the Ecole Normale, Saigon, 25 April 1874.

39. AOM Indochine A-30(8) Admiral Roze to the Minister of the Colonies, Saigon, 7 April 1865, No. 1,279.

40. AOM Indochine X-11(1). This dossier contains considerable correspondence on the program.

41. AVN Ministerial Dispatch to Admiral Ohier, Paris, 7 May 1869.

42. George Dürrwell, *Ma Chère Cochinchine* (Paris, 1911), 265. See also the personal dossier of Tran-Ba-Huu, AVN S. L. 2,743.

43. AVN Ministerial Dispatch to Admiral de La Grandière, Paris, 22 November 1866; AOM Indochine A-20(11) Admiral Cornulier-Lucinière to the Minister of the Colonies, Saigon, 27 September 1870, No. 816.

44. AOM Indochine X-11(1) Director of the Institution Sainte Marie, La Seyne, to the Minister of the Colonies, 15 January 1868.

45. *Ibid.,* 24 October 1871.

46. AVN Ministerial Dispatch to Admiral Ohier, Paris, 6 June 1868. The article was printed in *La Phare de Loire,* 5 January 1868.

47. AOM Indochine X-11(1) Admiral Dupré to the Minister of the Colonies, Saigon, 11 July 1871, No. 364.

48. *Lettre commune,* No. 3, 31 December 1875; No. 8, 31 December 1877; No. 9, 31 December 1878.

49. Mission education was a source of heated discussion in the late nineties. See, for instance, *Conseil Colonial* (ordinary session 1897–1898), 26 November 1897, 108.

50. AOM Indochine D-450(4) "Conseil Privé, Extrait du registre des délibérations," 17 November 1874.

51. *Ibid.* Until primary schools were established on a universal basis, the *quoc-ngu* schools were to continue. There is no evidence to suggest that they did so for any lengthy period.

52. *Ibid.*

53. AVN S. L. 4,364 "Rapport sur un voyage d'inspection fait du 11 février au 3 mars, et du 15 mars au 6 avril 1876 dans les deux provinces de Gia-Dinh et de Bien-Hoa (circonscription de Saigon)," 15 August 1876. The emphasis is in the original, as are the quotation marks. Philastre places quotes about the word "furnish" since this was the word used by the French administration; he wishes to contrast this with the actual situation, in which coercion and "renting" were involved.

54. The decision was taken on 6 April 1878.

55. AOM Indochine X-00(1) "Extrait d'une lettre adressée au Ministre par le Gouverneur p.i. [Ohier] de la Cochinchine," Saigon, 2 March 1869; and "Extrait d'un rapport annuel du Gouverneur p.i. de la Cochinchine, Ohier, au Ministre de la Marine, sur la situation de la colonie," Saigon, 13 September 1869.

56. AOM Indochine X-00(1) "Extrait—Exposé de la situation de la Cochinchine pour 1878," undated.

Chapter 5: *Old Ideals in a New Framework*

1. Attention has already been given in Chapter 2 to the way in which French writers have based their periodization on the division that they saw between periods of "association" and "assimilation" and the contrast between military and civil rule. It is noteworthy that Vietnamese writers seem to have accepted this division, at least implicitly, in their treatment of the early colonial period. See Phan-Khoang, *Viet-Nam Phap Thuoc Su* (History of Viet-Nam under French Colonialism) (Saigon, 1961), 180–199.

2. Taboulet, *La Geste*, II, 601–602; Cultru, *Histoire*, 305–320.

3. The bulk of the instructions appear in Le Myre de Vilers' *Les Institutions civiles*, 1–12. A document that appears to be a draft of these instructions, despite a date on it of November 1878, may be found in dossier AOM Indochine A-11(3). The quotation is from page 2 of Le Myre de Vilers' book.

4. *Les Institutions civiles*, 12–13.

5. AOM Indochine O-01(7) Governor Le Myre de Vilers to the Minister of the Colonies, Saigon, 5 September 1879, No. 995.

6. *Ibid.*, enclosing "Rapport de la commission chargée d'étudier les modifications à apporter à la justice indigène," undated.

7. *Ibid.*, enclosing an untitled mémoire prepared by Silvestre, Saigon, 14 August 1879.

8. *Ibid.* By "native judges," Le Myre de Vilers meant the Frenchmen hearing cases involving Vietnamese.

9. *Ibid.*

10. AOM Indochine O-oo(5) Governor Le Myre de Vilers to the Minister of the Colonies, Saigon, 20 October 1879, No. 1, 110.

11. *BOCF*, 1880, pt. 4, 153–158. The French penal code was instituted, with the exception of a limited number of articles that it was felt were inapplicable to Cochinchina. In addition, some modifications were made. For instance, Article 13 was modified to provide that in Cochinchina execution of a person found guilty of parricide would take place publicly. An example of the suppression of an article was the elimination of Article 339 dealing with the penalties incurred by a man who kept a mistress in his home against his wife's wishes. In a country where concubinage had a legal status, such an article was clearly inapplicable.

12. AVN S. L. 394 Tran-Ba-Loc to the Governor of Cochinchina, 17 December 1879. A French translation from the *quoc-ngu* original appears in the dossier. The report was later printed in *Excursions et Reconnaissances*, II (1880), 146–154.

13. Official French comment on the change is well reflected in A. Bouinais and A. Paulus, *L'Indo-Chine française contemporaine, Cochinchine, Cambodge, Tonkin, Annam,* 2 vols. (2nd ed.; Paris, 1885), I, 27. The authors note that it was "a happy measure which substituted for the Annamite code, difficult for us to apply and often no more than a table of strokes with the cane, laws based on a deep knowledge of human nature, on high philosophic principles, and prepared by eminent jurists." Bouinais served as aide-de-camp to Le Myre de Vilers.

14. *Les Institutions civiles,* 15–36.

15. *BOCF*, 1881, 298–313.

16. AOM Indochine O-o1(23) "Rapport au Gouverneur Général" prepared by A. Baudin, Procureur Général, Saigon, 4 July 1895. This is a fundamental document for any discussion of justice in Cochinchina following the institution of civil rule. It details all important decisions and reveals Baudin to have been a man of clear judgment and a sceptical turn of mind. In contrast to so many of his colleagues, he was competent in Vietnamese.

17. This is discussed in Baudin's report. See also *Conseil Colonial* (extraordinary session 1883), 9 January 1884, and (ordinary session 1885), 7 and 8 January 1885.

18. Evidence that there was still considerable reliance on minor Vietnamese officials comes from several sources. The observation was made in the Colonial Council on several occasions during 1884 and 1885. See also the correspondence in dossier AOM Indochine O-01(16), dealing with the administration of justice in Cochinchina.

19. AOM Indochine O-01(16) "Notes sur le fonctionnement des services judiciaires actuels (1881–1887)" prepared by Chavassieux, Tay-Ninh, 8 August 1887. Commenting on the difficulties that French administrators had encountered in attempting to understand Vietnamese legal practice, Chavassieux makes a striking observation on the place of Catholics in Vietnamese society: "Our best assistants, the Catholics, had the great disadvantage of being foreigners in their own country, almost in the same way as we [are]."

20. AOM Indochine O-01(23) "Rapport au Gouverneur Général" prepared by Baudin, Saigon, 4 July 1895.

21. *Ibid.* Baudin provides the following table:

Date	Population	No. of tribunals	Ratio
1881	1,550,000	7	1 to 221,000
1886	1,765,135	13	1 to 135,779
1888	1,854,214	9	1 to 206,000
1889	1,876,689	15	1 to 125,112
1895	2,065,000	10	1 to 206,500

22. "Rapport au Gouverneur Général." One observer has noted that the magistrates recruited for service in Cochinchina not only could not speak Vietnamese but were frequently chosen from the population of older French colonies. Such "colored" officials were said to be greatly resented by the Vietnamese. See L. de Saussure, *Psychologie de la colonisation française dans ses rapports avec les sociétés indigènes,* quoted in M. Barruel, *De La Substitution progressive des tribunaux français aux tribunaux indigènes en Indo-Chine* (Confolens, 1905), 199.

23. *BOCF*, 1880, pt. 12, 660–661.

24. The full text may be found in the *Recueil général permanent des actes relatifs à l'organisation et la réglementation de l'Indochine* (Hanoi, Haiphong, 1909), 819–828.

25. Dürrwell, *Ma Chère Cochinchine*, 269.

26. *Cochinchine Française, Projet de Code civil à l'usage des Annamites, par M. Lasserre* (Saigon, 1884), 6.

27. *Ibid.*, 55.

28. *Cochinchine Française, Recueil de jurisprudence en matière indigène, années 1880–1885*, prepared by Lasserre (Saigon, 1884).

H. L. Jammes, *Souvenirs du pays d'Annam* (Paris, 1900), Chapter 14, gives an impressionistic but probably accurate account of the difficulties surrounding the rendering of justice in civil cases in Cochinchina.

29. *Conseil Colonial* (extraordinary session 1905), 30 June 1905, 5, and (ordinary session 1905), 15 September 1905, 4. The correspondence evoked by Rodier's comments may be found in dossier AOM Indochine NF 55.

30. *Les Institutions civiles*, 3.

31. *Recueil général permanent des actes relatifs à l'organisation et la réglementation de l'Indochine*, 192–196.

32. *Les Institutions civiles*, 37.

33. In the first election, in 1880, two Frenchmen represented Vietnamese constituencies. The practice of electing Frenchmen to Vietnamese seats had ended by 1888. The number of Vietnamese electors in the first election was, by constituency: Bien-Hoa, 313; Saigon, 563; Tra-Vinh, 453; Vinh-Long, 333; Chau-Doc, 203; My-Tho, 508; total, 2,373.

34. *Conseil Colonial* (ordinary session 1890–1891), 30 December 1890, 53. For further discussion of these councils, see Chapter 7.

35. *Conseil Colonial* (ordinary session 1880), 8 November 1880, 42.

36. AOM Indochine D-440(4) Governor General Richaud to the Minister of the Colonies, Saigon, 9 June 1888, No. 1,082.

37. *Conseil Colonial* (extraordinary session 1881), 8, 9, and 10 February 1881, 3–25.

38. It was normal practice for Pétrus Ky and Paulus Cua to apply to the Council for financial assistance in their publishing efforts. See, for instance, *Conseil Colonial* (ordinary session 1882), 15 November 1882, 14–15.

39. Tran-Ba-Tho and Le-Phat-Dat were two of the more prominent Catholic members.

40. AOM Indochine D-441(3) Governor Filippini to the Minister of the Colonies, Saigon, 28 October 1886, No. 3,381, forwarded a

copy of the pamphlet and noted that it and one other circulated by an unsuccessful candidate were the only ones of their sort.

41. *Conseil Colonial* (ordinary session 1906), 17 November 1906, 143.

42. *Ibid.* (ordinary session 1897–1898), 22 November 1897, 58.

43. *Ibid.* (ordinary session 1893–1894), 19 December 1893, 113.

44. *Ibid.* (ordinary session 1896–1897), 24 January 1897, 284.

45. *Ibid.* (ordinary session 1897–1898), 26 November 1897, 105 and 145.

46. *Ibid.* (ordinary session 1900), 3 August 1900, Councillor Ho-Bao-Toan received a grant of 200 hectares; (ordinary session 1904), 6 August 1904, Councillor Tran-Ba-Diep received a grant of 100 hectares.

47. See as examples *ibid.* (ordinary session 1893–1894), 21 December 1893, where scholarships were awarded to sons of two of the Vietnamese councillors, Nang and Duom, to attend the Institut Taberd, which had become essentially a school for Vietnamese; and (ordinary session 1892–1893), 12 January 1893, where the son of Councillor Cao-Van-Sanh was awarded a scholarship for study in Algeria (the boy had earlier attended the Institut Taberd on a scholarship). This is not an exhaustive listing.

48. *Ibid.* (ordinary session 1882), 11 December 1882, 151–152.

49. *Ibid.*, 16 December 1882, 200.

50. *Ibid.* (second extraordinary session 1903), 5 December 1903, 7–8.

51. *Ibid.* (ordinary session 1905), 15 September 1905, 8.

52. *Ibid.*, 19 September 1905, 9. See also *Bulletin du Comité de l'Asie Française,* 55 (October 1905), 396.

53. *Conseil Colonial* (ordinary session 1906), 29 October 1906, 16–17.

54. *Ibid.*, 20 November 1906, 215.

55. AOM Indochine D-01(4) Governor Le Myre de Vilers to the Minister of the Colonies, Saigon, 14 July 1880, No. 691. The dispatch is incorporated in Le Myre de Vilers' *Les Institutions civiles,* 15–36.

56. *BOCF,* 1881, 293.

57. AOM Indochine G-40(1) Governor Le Myre de Vilers to the Minister of the Colonies, Saigon, 23 November 1881, No. 1,279.

58. *Ibid.*, Governor Le Myre de Vilers to the Minister of the Colonies, Saigon, 5 January 1883, unnumbered.

59. *Ibid.*, Governor Le Myre de Vilers to the Minister of the Colonies, Saigon, 23 November 1881, No. 1,287, for instance, requests naturalization for nine *tirailleurs,* but the details of their application do not accompany the dispatch.

60. *Conseil Colonial* (ordinary session 1906), 20 November 1906, 214. Councillor Phong quoted Pétrus Ky.

61. AVN Ministerial Dispatches, Minister of the Colonies to Governor Le Myre de Vilers, Paris, 30 December 1881.

62. *République Française, Journal Officiel de l'Indo-Chine Française,* 1898, 216, 1,230, 1,474.

63. Information on occupations and French promotion of the idea of naturalization is gathered from lists of applicants in the *Journal Officiel* and the minutes of the governor's Private Council, in which applications were reviewed.

64. AOM Indochine G-01(6) Governor General p.i. Bonhoure to the Minister of the Colonies, Hanoi, 13 May 1908, 1,237. There were 112 men, 44 women, 54 boys, and 44 girls who had been naturalized. The total Vietnamese population of Cochinchina was 2,432,373.

65. *Conseil Colonial* (ordinary session 1906), 20 November 1906, 214.

Chapter 6: *The Old Colony—The Heyday of Collaboration*

1. Truong-Minh-Ky, *Chu Quac Thai Hoi, Exposition universelle de 1889* (Saigon, 1891); title in French and Vietnamese, text in Vietnamese. Of the French mentioned in these lines, from page 22 of the text, only Blanchy is readily identifiable. He was president of the Colonial Council in Saigon.

2. The term was used by Paul Doumer in 1898. AOM Indochine D-431(3) Governor General Doumer to the Minister of the Colonies, Saigon, 28 February 1898, No. 536. See also, P. d'Enjoy, *La Colonisation de la Cochin-Chine: Manuel de colon* (Paris, 1898), 6.

3. It may be significant that Dürrwell, in his long account of Saigon in Chapter 4 of *Ma Chère Cochinchine,* makes no mention of Vietnamese frequenting the public gathering places of polite Saigon French society. One must presume that social meetings were confined to private houses.

4. AVN S. L. 311 Loc to the Director of the Interior, Cai-Be, 15 October 1887.

5. Information in this paragraph is drawn from Dat's obituary notices. See *Nam Ky* (French ed.), 30 November 1900, and *Le Courrier Saigonnais,* 24 and 28 November 1900 and 1 December 1900. Dat was born in 1838. He joined the French administration as an interpreter and was later appointed a *huyen.* His wealth was derived chiefly from his immense landholdings.

6. *Chu Quac Thai Hoi, Exposition universelle de 1889.*

7. The account of the earlier trip made by Truong-Minh-Ky was published as *Nhu Tay Nhut Trinh, De Saigon à Paris* (Saigon, 1889); title in French and Vietnamese, text in Vietnamese.

8. This period in Ky's life is treated in some detail in Bouchot's biography, Chapter 4. Among the manuscripts preserved in the Pétrus Ky Museum is a series of letters from Ky to Bert, entitled "Six Mois de la vie politique." Bouchot has drawn on these in his account of the period.

9. On the basis of Ky's own correspondence, it does seem that he returned to Saigon in September. Khong Xuan-Thu, *Truong Vinh Ky,* x, gives the date of his return as 14 October.

10. The director of the interior for the Cochinchinese administration, Villard, opposed Ky's employment by Bert from the start. Bert's successor, Paulin Vial, firmly rejected any idea of Ky's continuing to act as a French agent in the court.

11. AVN S. L. 172 Resident General Paul Bert to the Governor of Cochinchina, Hue, 22 September 1886. The abbreviation of Ky's name is in the original.

12. The information on positions held by Ky's sons at the time of his death comes from a family circular announcing his death held in the Vien Khao-Co (Institute for Archeological Research), Saigon, Tieu Su (37), Tu sach Truong Vinh Ky. Tai-lieu gia-dinh va linh-tinh. (Biographical papers, 37, Truong Vinh Ky papers; Family and miscellaneous papers). Bouchot noted Tong's appointment in his biography of Ky.

13. *Conseil Colonial* (ordinary session 1904), 5 August 1904, 92.

14. *Ibid.* (ordinary session 1882), 15 November 1882, 14–15, when a letter from Ky was placed before the Council.

15. AVN S. L. 394 Tran-Ba-Loc to the Governor of Cochinchina, 17 December 1879.

16. *Ma Chère Cochinchine,* 278.

17. Doumer, *L'Indo-Chine française: Souvenirs* (2nd ed.; Paris, n.d.), 71–74.

18. *Ibid.*

19. AVN S. L. 311 Loc to the Director of the Interior, Cai-Be, 12 March 1880.

20. *Ibid.* This dossier, which is Loc's personal dossier, contains letters from him to the administration seeking to ensure that his son Tho received a French education.

21. Information supplied by a private source.

22. P. Barthélemy, *En Indochine, 1894–1895,* 12.

23. P. Nicolas, *Notes sur la vie française en Cochinchine* (Paris, 1912), 148.

24. AVN S. L. 312. In this, Phuong's personal dossier, there is correspondence concerning visits made by Phuong to France.

25. *L'Indo-Chine française,* 79.

26. The biographical material is chiefly from Phuong's personal dossier, AVN S. L. 312.

27. Doumer, *L'Indo-Chine française,* 2nd ed., 79.

28. *BSEI,* 1883, 1st semester, fasc.1, 51 and 52.

29. *Nam Ky* (*quoc-ngu* ed.), 18 November 1897.

30. *Conseil Colonial* (ordinary session 1885), 8 January 1886; *ibid.* (ordinary session 1887), 25 January 1887. These provide indications of Truong-Minh-Ky's work. He translated Fontaine's fables into *quoc-ngu* for the *Gia-Dinh Bao* and also made a translation of Fénélon's play about the great French ecclesiastical figure Télémaque.

31. *Nhu Tay Nhut Trinh,* 23.

32. Brébion and Cabaton, *Dictionnaire de bio-bibliographie,* 237.

33. Le-Van-Phat, "La Vie intime d'un Annamite de Cochinchine et ses croyances vulgaires," 6.

34. *BSEI,* LV (2nd semester, 1908), 101–109.

35. Information on Chieu's career comes from AOM Indochine X-02(5), *Conseil Colonial* (ordinary session 1893–1894), 31 December 1893, and private sources.

36. *Nam Ky* (*quoc-ngu* ed.), 26 January 1899.

Chapter 7: *The Old Colony—The Countryside*

1. This discrimination operated in various ways. Most importantly, the Vietnamese receiving a concession was required to pay tax on the land at an earlier date than a Frenchman. In 1900, for instance, the Vietnamese landholder paid tax after two years, the Frenchman after five. For discussion of this point, see AOM Indochine H-12(10) Inspector General of the Colonies Piquié to the Minister of the Colonies, Saigon, 8 May 1900, No. 108. AOM Indochine F-10(3) A. Grodet to the Undersecretary of State for the Colonies, Paris, 14 November 1890, gives an account of the various provisions that had regulated land concessions in Cochinchina up to that date.

2. All grants of land over twenty hectares had to be approved by the Colonial Council. Details of concessions can therefore be obtained through consulting the minutes of the Council. Grodet's letter (note 1, above) remarks on the limited number of large concessions to Vietnamese up to 1900. In subsequent years larger grants were made. See, for instance, *Conseil Colonial* (ordinary session 1904), 6 August 1904. On this day grants of 2,907, 539, and 278 hectares were made to Vietnamese.

3. On Loc's participation in the drainage of the Plain of Reeds section of Cochinchina, see Dürrwell, *Ma Chère Cochinchine,* 281–282.

4. See the Statistical Appendix.

5. *Conseil Colonial* (ordinary session 1904), 6 August 1904, 104–105.

6. See the Statistical Appendix.

7. *Lettre commune,* No. 25, Paris, 31 December 1892.

8. AVN Ministerial Dispatches. The Minister of the Colonies to Governor Le Myre de Vilers, Paris, 29 January 1881, No. 35.

9. *Cours d'administration,* 125.

10. AVN S. L. 394 Loc to the Governor of Cochinchina, 17 December 1879.

11. Le Myre de Vilers, *Les Institutions civiles,* 137–168. See also, Cultru, *Histoire,* 349–371.

12. This point is discussed in both Le Myre de Vilers' and Cultru's works cited in the preceding footnote. Over-all land surveys were not completed for many years. When partial surveys had been completed

in 1886, very large discrepancies were revealed. Thus, in the Tra-Vinh area it was found that 110,570 hectares were under cultivation but only 60,252 had been declared in production. See *Conseil Colonial* (ordinary session 1886), 27 January 1887, 135.

13. The difficulties of making an adequate study of taxation in Cochinchina, and the desirability of such a study, have already been noted. One useful source for any consideration of the taxation issue in the early twentieth century is the *Bulletin du Comité de l'Asie Française*. Although this monthly journal was published in Paris by a section of the colonial lobby, it contains a mass of useful commentary on the taxation question.

14. *Les Institutions civiles*, 146.

15. "La Commune annamite," 221.

16. AOM Indochine D-51(3) Governor Filippini to the Minister of the Colonies, Saigon, 2 July 1887, No. 84, enclosing "Notes sur l'organisation de la commune annamite." Material in the succeeding paragraphs is drawn from this report.

17. *Conseil Colonial* (ordinary session 1892–1893), 18 January 1893, 144; (ordinary session 1893–1894), 19 December 1893, 113, and 21 December 1893, 143.

18. AOM Indochine A-20(42) "Rapport mensuel au Gouverneur Général" prepared by Lieutenant Governor Ducos, Saigon, 18 January 1896.

19. *Conseil Colonial* (ordinary session 1897–1898), 26 November 1897, 105, and 1 December 1897, 145.

20. *République Française, Conseil Supérieure de l'Indochine (première commission), Situation de la Cochinchine* (ordinary session 1902), No. 4, 1.

21. P. Kresser, *La Commune annamite en Cochinchine: Le Recrutement des notables* (Paris, 1935), 31–33. Kresser, basing his study directly on the commission's report, gives a detailed account of its proceedings and conclusions.

22. Kresser, *La Commune annamite*, 34–35. Even in seeking a "chairman," the commission was probably projecting French concepts on to a Vietnamese model.

23. *La Commune annamite*, 35.   24. *Ibid.*, 36.

25. *Ibid.*, 39–44.   26. *Ibid.*, 55.

27. *Conseil Colonial* (extraordinary session 1905), 30 June 1905, 5. Rodier described the reforms as a "palliatif."

28. AOM Indochine D-51(2) Governor Le Myre de Vilers to the Minister of the Colonies, Saigon, 27 April 1882, No. 416. The decision instituting the councils dated from 12 May 1882.

29. *Conseil Colonial* (ordinary session 1890–1891), 30 December 1890, 53.

30. *Ibid.* (ordinary session 1902), 16 October 1902, 146.

31. AOM Indochine A-11(4) Instructions from Governor Le Myre de Vilers to General Trentinian, Governor p.i. of Cochinchina, Saigon, 4 March 1881, makes a typical comment on the *dao-lanh:* "As happens each year, the *Dao-lanh* . . . sow disquiet among our rural population." The *dao-lanh* sect, literally the "good religion," is not discussed by Coulet's *Les Sociétés secrètes,* the most complete account of secret societies in Viet-Nam. It appears to have been the most important of a number of sects. There were others to which occasional reference is made. In a letter of 11 November 1875 to Father Dumoulin, Pétrus Ky referred to a sect called *dai-dao,* literally "harmonious religion"; Pétrus Ky Museum "Correspondance."

32. See, for instance, AVN S. L. 2,730 "Rapports mensuels" for Cochinchina, March 1888.

33. AVN Rachgia 9 Administrator of Rach-Gia to the Lieutenant Governor of Cochinchina, Rach-Gia, 14 January 1896. This letter encloses translations of documents in Chinese characters appointing individuals to various high positions. Thus, one Nguyen-Truong-Tho was appointed as civil governor of An-Ha (An-Giang) and Ha-Tien.

See also AOM Indochine A-20(21) "Gouvernement de la Cochinchine, M. A. Filippini, Gouverneur, Rapport général de fin d'année, Situation extérieure et intérieure de la Cochinchine en Mai 1886–1887." This describes the activities of a Vietnamese named Nam-Thiep, who was active in the Chau-Doc region, where he had a reputation as a healer of all illnesses. He proclaimed himself the "Great Wind" and announced that he would drive the French from Cochinchina. A small French expedition quickly removed this "threat."

Chapter 8: *Education and* Quoc-Ngu—*A Qualified Triumph*

1. AOM Indochine X-00(1) "Renseignements fournis par le directeur de l'enseignement—Situation en 1882," Saigon, 12 April 1882.

2. *Ibid.*

3. *Cochinchine Française: Réorganisation de l'instruction publique en Cochinchine* (Saigon, 1884), 4.

4. AOM Indochine A-20(21) "Gouvernement de la Cochinchine, M. A. Filippini, Gouverneur, Rapport général de fin d'année, Situation extérieure et intérieure de la Cochinchine en Mai 1886–1887."

5. *Conseil Colonial* (ordinary session 1888), 19 November 1888, 6. See also, AOM Indochine A-30(80) Governor General Richaud to the Minister of the Colonies, Saigon, 27 August 1888, No. 33, Confidential, which reports on a tour that Richaud made through Cochinchina and includes critical comments on education.

6. *Conseil Colonial* (ordinary session 1888), 19 November 1888, 6.

7. The most complete statistics are contained in the official publication *Cochinchine Française, Etat de la Cochinchine* (Saigon, annually). Unfortunately, the statistics for schools teaching in characters are combined with figures for the number of mission schools. See, however, the comment on schools teaching in characters in the *Etat* for 1903, page 72, which notes the decline. See also, *République Française, Conseil Supérieur de l'Indochine, 1ère commission, Fonctionnement de l'enseignement publique* (ordinary session 1906).

8. Approval for the granting of government scholarships had to be given by the Colonial Council. The minutes of the Council meetings thus provide a record of each child's family background. See, simply as one example, *Conseil Colonial* (ordinary session 1893–1894), 21 December 1893, 136–141.

9. Examination of the minutes of the Colonial Council leads to this conclusion. It should be noted that the number of Vietnamese granted scholarships for study in France and Algeria was very small, seldom more than three or four each year.

10. The Ecole Coloniale was founded with the stated intention of providing education for elite groups within Indochina. The matriculation register, now held as part of the AOM Indochine archives in Paris, records that twelve Vietnamese entering from Cochinchina between 1885 and 1913 had fathers who were petty officials, farmers, and merchants.

11. AOM Indochine X-02(3), quoted in a letter from Le Myre de Vilers to the Minister of the Colonies, Paris, 8 April 1894. Le Myre de Vilers was at this time the *député* for Cochinchina in the French Parliament.

12. *République Française, Journal Officiel de l'Indo-China*, 1901,

containing the minutes of the Colonial Council (ordinary session 1901), 30 October 1901, 2,007–2,009.

13. *Conseil Colonial* (extraordinary session 1897), 7 May 1897, 48.

14. The *écoles professionelles,* or trade schools, were a favorite topic of discussion for the French members of the Colonial Council. It was not until the early 1900's, however, that any real success was achieved in attempts to found these institutions.

15. Statistics for education are unsatisfactory chiefly because of the varied fashion in which they are presented from year to year, even in the same source. The information supplied for 1904 in the *Etat de la Cochinchine* is some of the most complete available. Pages 71–74 are summarized below.

School	No. of teachers	French	Vietnamese	No. of pupils
Chasseloup-Laubat	22	12	10	112 [*]
My-Tho College	12	6	6	179
Ecole Normale	8	2	6	60
Ecole Primaire (Saigon)	8	1	7	270
Ecole Professionelle	9	3	6	60

[*] There were 141 European pupils at Chasseloup-Laubat.

In the provincial schools there were 17 French teachers, 74 Vietnamese teachers, and 5,060 Vietnamese pupils.

In the three municipal schools maintained in Saigon and Cholon there were 15 French teachers, 11 Vietnamese teachers, 192 French pupils, and 434 Vietnamese pupils.

There were 164 cantonal schools, with 311 teachers and 12,000 pupils; 76 communal schools, with 89 teachers and 2,700 pupils; and 304 "free schools," chiefly mission schools but including some schools teaching in characters maintained by the communes, with 9,458 pupils.

16. *Conseil Colonial* (ordinary session 1906), 17 November 1906, 7. These comments were made by Councillor Phong.

17. The comment made by D'Enjoy in his *La Colonisation de la Cochin-Chine* (p. 31) should perhaps be treated with some reserve, since it appears in a "Colonist's Manual." It nevertheless provides some sense of the extent to which French had spread in Cochinchina: "The colonist will not, then, feel he is an expatriate. He will be able, almost everywhere, to make himself understood in his mother tongue, provided he speaks very slowly. And he will himself understand those Annamites who speak to him when they reply in pidgin."

18. *Conseil Colonial* (ordinary session 1882), 13 December 1882, 187–188. For Catholic reaction, see *Lettre commune,* Paris, 13 December 1881.

19. Debate was particularly heated in the 1897 and 1902 sessions of the Council.

20. E. Roucoules, "Etude sur l'instruction publique en Cochinchine," *BSEI,* 1889, 2nd semester, 27.

21. *Conseil Colonial* (ordinary session 1902), 14 October 1902, 136–137.

22. The educational activities of the missions were described by Bishop Colombert, after noting that they were carried out chiefly by Vietnamese priests: "In the countryside, these priests give a careful Christian instruction, with education in Annamite, which leaves the children in a condition that suits them, without turning them into classless individuals." The bishop used the term *déclassés,* which might be alternatively translated as "rootless." (On the nomadic tendency of the Vietnamese, see, as one example, *Lettre commune* No. 41, Paris, 31 December 1904.) The dossier AVN Tanan 33 describes the tensions that could arise between Catholic and non-Catholic Vietnamese villagers.

23. AOM Indochine D-450(6) "Cochinchine Française; Conseil Privé, Extrait du registre des délibérations," 1 December 1879.

24. Aymonier, *Nos Transcriptions: Etude sur les systèmes d'écriture en caractères européens en Cochinchine française* (Saigon, 1886).

25. L. Cadière, "La Question de *quoc-ngu,*" *Revue Indo-Chinoise,* 9 (15 May 1904), 585–600; 10 (31 May 1904), 700–705; 11 (15 June 1904), 784–788; 12 (30 June 1904), 872–876; 1 (15 July 1904), 58–63.

26. A. Landes, "Notes sur le *quoc-ngu,*" *BSEI,* 1886, 1st semester, 5–22, quotes from this petition.

27. *Ibid.* See also Landes' article, "Notes sur la langue et la littérature annamite," *Excursions et Reconnaissances,* VIII (1884), 119–130.

28. Aymonier's views were expressed in a number of publications. In addition to *La Langue française en Indochine* (Paris, 1891), see *La Langue française et l'enseignement en Indochine* (Paris, 1890), "L'Enseignement en Indo-Chine" (an article in the Paris newspaper *Le Temps* for 17 October 1889), and AOM Indochine A-00(32) "Situation politique en Indochine," Vichy, 18 August 1889.

29. E. Roucoules, "Le Français, le *quoc-ngu* et l'enseignement

publique en Indochine: Réponse à M. Aymonier," *BSEI*, 1890, 1st semester, 6–10.

30. AVN S. L. 394 Loc to Governor Le Myre de Vilers, 17 December 1879.

31. *Conseil Colonial* (ordinary session 1897–1898), 2 December 1897, 152. Tho's description of the newspaper was accurate. Issues in later years did feature many advertisements for patent medicines, which described themselves as panaceas for all ills.

32. Tran-Ba-Tho, "La Piété filiale (Préceptes de la morale confucéene)," *BSEI*, LIV (1908), 1st semester, 57–156.

33. *Ibid.*, 57–59.

34. *Conseil Colonial* (ordinary session 1906), 17 November 1906, 143–144.

35. Le-Van-Phat, "Introduction des caractères chinois dans le programme de l'enseignement indigène," *BSEI*, LIV (1908), 1st semester, 189.

36. *Conseil Colonial* (ordinary session 1897–1898), 2 December 1897, 152.

37. A. Schreiner, "Conférence sur l'enseignement en Indo-Chine," *BSEI*, LIV (1908) 1st semester, 171–172.

38. *Nam Ky* (*quoc-ngu* ed.), 18 November 1897.

39. This appeared during 1898.

40. For some account of this incident, see Coulet, *Les Sociétés secrètes*, 12–13, and the *Bulletin du Comité de l'Asie Française*, 93 (December 1908).

41. See, for instance, issues for 3 and 17 December 1907. The newspaper also published a French supplement, which denounced Chinese economic dominance. The supplement of 10 December 1907 referred to Chinese businessmen as "filthy vampires."

42. *Nong-Co Min Dam*, 3 December 1907.

43. Doan-Thi-Do, *Le Journalisme au Viêt-Nam et les périodiques viêtnamiens conservés à la Bibliothèque Nationale* (Paris, 1958).

44. *Conseil Colonial* (ordinary session 1901), 2 November 1901, 130.

45. Anon., *La Politique indigène en Cochinchine* (Saigon, 1905).

Chapter 9: *Cambodia before the Storm (1863–1883)*

1. Paul Collard, *Cambodge et Cambodgiens* (Paris, 1921), Chapter 10. Unfortunately, there is no Cambodian source to place against the

many, and generally critical, French accounts of Norodom. There are suggestions, in modern Phnom Penh, that Norodom kept a personal journal, but the writer was unable to verify this suggestion. A host of legends surround the king. As Professor George Coedès remarked, these blossomed almost immediately after the king's death. "Etudes Cambodgiennes, XVI—Essai de classification des documents historiques cambodgiens conservés à la Bibliothèque de l'Ecole Française d'Extrême-Orient," *BEFEO*, XVIII (1918), fasc. 9, 15, n. 3.

2. Jean Hess, *L'Affaire Iukanthor: Les Dessous d'un protectorat* (Paris, 1900), provides a good example of undiluted and uncritical praise of Norodom.

3. Louis de Carné, *Voyage en Indo-Chine et dans l'empire chinois* (Paris, 1872), 33. It seems proper to assume that, under Mongkut's sponsorship, Norodom entered a monastery of the Thommayut sect. On the basis of what the writer regards as unimpeachable evidence from an oral source, one may also note that Norodom also spent some time as a monk in a Mohanikay monastery near Oudong.

4. Norodom made this remark in 1879, in conversation with Aymonier, who was then the French representative in Phnom Penh. See AAE Asie 48 Indochine 22 Governor Le Myre de Vilers to the Minister of the Colonies, Saigon, 13 November 1879, No. 38.

5. AAE Asie 74 Indochine 40 Trimestrial report prepared by Resident General de Champeaux, Phnom Penh, 15 January 1889. In conversation with Champeaux, Norodom stated: "I consider as belonging to Cambodia all Cambodian regions without exception." Norodom clearly meant all regions in which Cambodians lived, including Viet-Nam and Siam.

6. AOM Indochine A-30(66) Governor Thomson to the Minister of the Colonies, Saigon, 27 July 1883, No. 230.

7. "Voyages dans les Royaumes de Siam, de Cambodge, de Laos et autres parties générales de l'Indo-Chine," *Le Tour du Monde*, 1863, 275–278.

8. AAE Asie 73 Indochine 39 Trimestrial report prepared by Resident General de Champeaux, Phnom Penh, no date (second trimester 1888).

9. AAE Asie 48 Indochine 22 Governor Le Myre de Vilers to the Minister of the Colonies, Saigon, 15 April 1882, No. 30.

10. See dossier AOM Indochine A-30 (67), which contains a mass of correspondence relating to the conclusion of the 1884 convention.

11. Villemereuil, *Explorations,* 389–439, *passim.*

12. Louis Delaporte, *Voyage au Cambodge* (Paris, 1880), 26.

13. P. Branda (*pseud.* Paul Reveillère), *Ça et là: Cochinchine et Cambodge: L'Âme khmère: Ang-Kor* (Paris, 1887), 2–4, describes such a beating. In 1891, Norodom placed one of his sons, Prince Duong Chacr, in chains for defying him. See AOM Indochine A-30(96) Duong Chacr to the Minister of the Colonies, Phnom Penh, 7 May 1891.

14. In 1873 Norodom executed four women of his household and two men, apparently for infidelity. See AOM Indochine A-30(22) "Rapport confidentiel sur le Cambodge" prepared by Aymonier, 24 August 1874. In 1875, Leclère notes (*Les Codes cambodgiens* [Paris, 1898], I, 176) a palace page who had slept with one of Norodom's wives was executed along with two female servants who had acted as intermediaries in the affair. The heads of the executed persons were exposed on bamboo poles. The guilty wife was spared the indignity of execution by a firing squad and was decapitated.

In 1884, Norodom was restrained from having one of his sons dragged through Phnom Penh behind horses as a punishment for a liaison with one of the king's women. On French urging he did not kill the woman but had her whipped, while the son was confined in chains. See AOM Indochine A-30(68) Governor Thomson to the Minister of the Colonies, Saigon, 27 September 1884, No. 130.

15. E. Boulanger, *Un Hiver au Cambodge* (Tours, 1887), 128.

16. AOM Indochine A-30(22) "Rapport confidentiel sur le Cambodge" prepared by Aymonier, 24 August 1874.

17. AAE Asie 48 Indochine 22 Governor Le Myre de Vilers to the Minister of the Colonies, 15 April 1882, No. 30. Collard maintains (*Cambodge,* 129), without giving details, that Norodom even managed to arrange for several members of King Chulalongkorn's royal ballet to leave Bangkok to join his troupe. The Filipino band is described in Le Myre de Vilers' dispatch.

18. AAE Asie 48 Indochine 22 Governor Le Myre de Vilers to the Minister of the Colonies, 15 April 1882, No. 30.

19. AOM Indochine A-30(44) Le Myre de Vilers to the Minister of the Colonies, Saigon, 4 August 1880, No. 114.

20. AC F. 42 (T.99) 10,153. This dossier contains correspondence between King Sisowath and the French resident superior in Phnom Penh concerning the estate of a former member of King Norodom's

female establishment, Moneang Sum. There are gaps in the correspondence, but it seems clear that Norodom entrusted this woman with part of the Cambodian crown jewels.

21. AC "Lettres au départ échangées avec le palais" 1905–1909 Resident Superior Morel to King Sisowath, Phnom Penh, 8 August 1905, No. 55, "Au Sujet de l'attitude de certaines princesses." The letter notes in part: "The absolute ban imposed upon them, according to the ancient usages of the palace, preventing them from marrying outside the royal family, condemns the great majority to celibacy. As a result there are grave inconveniences, and disorders are frequently caused by women whom this abnormal state pushes to misconduct. The law does not allow them to satisfy their desires except by taking lovers without regard to their social class.

"Scandalous incidents occur at every moment and accounts of these are passed from mouth to mouth and become the object of banter for the people of the city."

22. Pavie, "Excursions dans le Cambodge et le Royaume de Siam," *Excursions et Reconnaissances*, X (1881), 145–146.

23. Moura, *Le Royaume*, I, 226.   24. *Le Cambodge*, I, 56.

25. The full text of the treaty is contained in Villemereuil, *Explorations*, 89–94.

26. Probably the best brief account of developments is found in Taboulet, *La Geste*, II, 630–631.

27. AVN S. L. 1,839 Moura to the Director of the Interior, Piquet, Phnom Penh, 4 May 1874, Personal. Taboulet reproduces extracts from this letter in *La Geste*, II, 662–664, after the heading "La Politique du Désinteressement." He omits some important passages, however, which contain Moura's critical comments on the way in which the French authorities in Saigon have treated Norodom's interests with regard to Cambodia's frontiers.

28. The full text of the treaty appears in Villemereuil, *Explorations*, 95–101. There is an interesting contemporaneous document that provides a commentary on the terms that Siam forced on Norodom through this treaty. Siam was represented in France by a consul. During the period of uncertainty over whether or not France would remain in Cochinchina and maintain its protectorate over Cambodia, the Siamese government was not idle and asserted its claim to control of Cambodia. As part of this campaign the consul was instructed to present the French government with a "Chronique abrégée du Cambodge." See

AOM Indochine A-oo(4) Consul Gréhan to the Minister of the Colonies, Paris, 23 January 1864, enclosing the "Chronique."

29. The treaty was revealed to the surprised French in the Singapore newspaper *Straits Times.* See AOM Indochine A-30(6) Admiral de La Grandière to the Minister of the Colonies, Saigon, 29 October 1864, No. 1,020.

30. AOM Indochine A-30(6) Admiral de La Grandière to the Minister of the Colonies, Saigon, 8 June 1864, No. 786. See also Taboulet, *La Geste,* II, 633–636.

31. Collard, *Cambodge,* 83, refers to the source of Votha's antagonism as being too delicate to be revealed. There seems some reason to accept the suggestions of the less discreet Branda, *Ça et là,* 290, that the two half brothers quarrelled over one of the members of their dead father's household.

32. Moura, *Le Royaume,* II, 152. See also AOM Indochine A-30(8).

33. Moura, *Le Royaume,* II, 159–170. Information in the archives about Poucombo is chiefly concerned with his relations with Vietnamese mandarins. See AOM Indochine A-30(12).

34. Villemereuil, *Explorations,* 103.

35. AOM Indochine A-30(8) Doudart de Lagrée to Admiral Roze, Kampot, 6 May 1865.

36. *Ibid.,* Admiral Roze to the Minister of the Colonies, Saigon, 27 May 1865, No. 1,394.

37. *Ibid.,* Doudart de Lagrée to Admiral Roze, Kampot, 6 May 1865.

38. AOM Indochine A-30(12) The Minister of the Colonies to Admiral de La Grandière, Paris, 14 March 1867, unnumbered.

39. *Ibid.,* Admiral de La Grandière to the Minister of the Colonies, Saigon, 29 April 1867, No. 376.

40. *Ibid.,* 28 June, No. 546.

41. *Ibid.,* 31 January 1868, No. 97.

42. For a brief account of the events leading to the conclusion of this treaty, see Taboulet, *La Geste,* II, 653–654, and for the protests against the treaty by Admiral de La Grandière, who was not consulted on its value, pp. 655–656.

43. AOM Indochine A-30(12) Admiral de La Grandière to the Minister of the Colonies, Saigon, 31 January 1868, No. 97, enclosing a letter from Norodom to La Grandière, undated.

44. AOM Indochine A-30(14) Moura to Governor Ohier, Phnom Penh, 25 August 1869 and 14 September 1869.

45. Leclère, *Les Codes cambodgiens,* I, 1.

46. AC L.5 (M.02) 9,836. The items listed were set out in correspondence between Caraman and Norodom.

47. Collard, *Cambodge,* 94.

48. AC S. O. 3 12,030 "Rapport sur le service de santé du Cambodge pendant le 2e semestre de 1885 présenté par le docteur Maurel," Phnom Penh, 1885.

49. Collard, *Cambodge,* 118.

50. AAE Asie 74 Indochine 40 Trimestrial report from Resident General de Champeaux, Phnom Penh, 15 January 1889.

51. AC L.5 (M.02). This, Caraman's personal dossier, provides a mass of information on his personal activities and business endeavors in Cambodia.

52. Taboulet, *La Geste,* II, 656–660.

53. AOM Indochine A-30(74) "Enquête sur les événements du Cambodge. Rapport de M. Klobukowski, chef du cabinet de M. le Gouverneur Thomson," Saigon, 23 July 1885.

54. AOM Indochine A-30(52) Le Myre de Vilers to the Minister of the Colonies, Deauville, 12 September 1881. "Germans are his friends; Frenchmen, with whom he abandons himself to debauchery, are always opponents of our Representative."

55. AOM Indochine A-30(22) "Copie d'une note relative à un entretien entre le 2e Roi du Cambodge et le Représentant du Protectorat, au sujet de certaines réformes à introduire dans notre traité et dans l'administration du pays," Phnom Penh, 13 May 1875. In *Le Royaume,* II, 183, Moura describes the *kralahom* as "the most intelligent, the most active, and the most estimable of the Cambodian ministers." His death was "a real loss for the French government, whose policy he supported."

56. AM Marine BB4, 889 Admiral Cornulier-Lucinière to the Minister of the Colonies, Saigon, 20 June 1870, unnumbered. The installation was on 28 May.

57. AOM Indochine A-30(18) Admiral Dupré to the Minister of the Colonies, Saigon, 8 December 1871, No. 691.

58. AOM Indochine A-30(22) Admiral Krantz to the Minister of the Colonies, Saigon, 30 January 1874, No. 524.

59. *Ibid.,* 3 June, No. 428, Confidential. This notes Dupré's earlier decision.

60. *Ibid.,* 25 August, No. 722.

61. *Ibid.*, "Copie d'une note sur les modifications à apporter au traité passé en 1863 entre la France et le Cambodge," an attachment to Krantz's dispatch cited in note 60.

62. AOM Indochine A-30(26) Admiral Duperré to the Minister of the Colonies, Saigon, 12 March 1875, No. 194. Norodom was quoted as replying to all of Duperré's recommendations, "I will do what Monsieur Moura judges useful."

63. AAE Asie 33 Indochine 7 Admiral Duperré to the Minister of the Colonies, Saigon, 22 October 1875, unnumbered. For a recent Cambodian account of this issue, see Sarin Chhak, *Les Frontières du Cambodge* (Paris, 1966), 125–130.

64. AOM Indochine A-30(26) Admiral Duperré to the Minister of the Colonies, Saigon, 22 October 1875, unnumbered.

65. *Ibid.*, "Copie d'une note relative à un entretien entre le 2e Roi du Cambodge et le Représentant du Protectorat, au sujet de certaines réformes à introduire dans notre traité et dans l'administration du pays," Phnom Penh, 13 May 1875. It is difficult to believe that the conversation as reproduced by Moura, with its heavily formal phrasing, is a verbatim record. Nevertheless, all available evidence contributes to affirm that Sisowath did hold the views that Moura records, and there is no reason to question the basic authenticity of the document.

66. AOM Indochine A-30(26) Admiral Duperré to the Minister of the Colonies, Saigon, 22 October 1875, unnumbered. And see also the Minister of the Colonies to Admiral Duperré, Paris, February 1876, unnumbered.

67. *Ibid.* contains Votha's letter to the King of Siam, enclosed with Minister of Foreign Affairs to the Minister of the Colonies, Versailles, 26 June 1876. Moura, *Le Royaume*, II, 174–178, gives an outline of the rising that Votha led.

68. AOM Indochine A-30(26) Admiral Duperré to the Minister of the Colonies, Saigon, 7 August 1876, No. 539.

69. AOM Indochine A-30(18) Admiral Dupré to the Minister of the Colonies, Saigon, 8 December 1871, No. 691, describes the homage rendered Norodom when he visited Siemreap in 1871.

70. AOM Indochine A-30(26) "Copie d'une lettre adressée a S.M. Norodom Roi du Cambodge, par le Contre-Amiral, Gouverneur et Commandant en Chef en Cochinchine," Saigon, 29 September 1876.

71. *Ibid.*, Admiral Duperré to the Minister of the Colonies, Saigon, 18 November 1876, No. 844.

72. *Ibid.*, 12 February 1877, No. 133. For some account of the operations against Votha, see Moura, *Le Royaume*, II, 181–184.

73. AOM Indochine A-30(26) contains the text of Norodom's proclamation as an attachment to Minister of Foreign Affairs to the Minister of the Colonies, Paris, 5 April 1877. See also Moura, *Le Royaume*, II, 179–180.

74. The convention was considered secret for only a short period. The text of the convention may be found in AOM Indochine A-30(26) Minister of Foreign Affairs to the Minister of the Colonies, Paris, 5 April 1877.

75. Service Historique de l'Armée de Terre, Section Outre-Mer, Fonds Tonkin, 80, 1872–1890, No. 5, Governor Duperré to the Minister of the Colonies, Saigon, 10 March 1877, No. 212.

76. AOM Indochine A-30(34) Admiral Lafont to the Minister of the Colonies, Saigon, November 1877, No. 1,036.

77. There is a brief and not very informative reference to this affair in Collard, *Cambodge,* 124. The present summary of events surrounding Norodom's negotiations is based on the following main documents: AAE Asie 48 Indochine 22 Governor Le Myre de Vilers to the Minister of the Colonies, Saigon, 13 November 1879, No. 38; AOM Indochine A-30(45) Governor Le Myre de Vilers to the Minister of the Colonies, Saigon, 7 June 1880, No. 100; AAE Asie 48 Indochine 22 Governor Le Myre de Vilers to the Minister of the Colonies, Saigon, 11 October 1880, No. 122; AOM Indochine A-30(52) Governor p.i. Trentinian to the Minister of the Colonies, Saigon, 31 July 1881, No. 181; Governor Le Myre de Vilers to the Minister of the Colonies, Deauville, 12 September 1881. See also, Le Myre de Vilers, *Les Institutions civiles,* 12.

78. AOM Indochine A-30(52) Governor p.i. Trentinian to the Minister of the Colonies, Saigon, 31 July 1881, No. 181.

79. *Ibid.*, Governor Le Myre de Vilers to the Minister of the Colonies, Deauville, 12 September 1881.

80. AOM Indochine A-11(5) Copy of instructions to Le Myre de Vilers from the Minister of the Colonies, Paris, 27 September 1881, Confidential.

81. AOM Indochine A-30(52) Governor Le Myre de Vilers to the Minister of the Colonies, Saigon, 19 November 1881, No. 192, enclosing an undated letter from King Norodom to the President of the French Republic.

82. AAE Asie 48 Indochine 22 Governor Le Myre de Vilers to the Minister of the Colonies, Saigon, 15 April 1882, No. 30.

83. *Ibid.*   84. *Ibid.*

85. AC O.9(U.82) 11,117. Report from Leclère to the Resident Superior of Cambodia, Phnom Penh, 14 June 1901, No. 366.

86. *Lettre commune,* No. 14, Paris, 31 December 1883.

87. AAE Asie 48 Indochine 22 Governor Le Myre de Vilers to the Minister of the Colonies, Saigon, 15 April 1882, No. 30.

88. AOM Indochine A-30(52) Governor Le Myre de Vilers to the Minister of the Colonies, Saigon, 19 November 1881, No. 192.

89. AC R. O 11,868 Report by the Director of the Phnom Penh School, Phnom Penh, 24 February 1883. There had been earlier attempts to establish schools, but these did not meet with success.

90. Moura, *Le Royaume,* I, 221–225, gives an excellent description of Norodom's court which he had so often observed. As testimony to the power Norodom exerted over his officials, there is Moura's description (Tome I, page 226) of the occasion when Norodom learned of the possibilities of Western surgery. He evinced a wish to see an operation. Noting that one of his officials had two thumbs on one hand, he ordered him to submit to an operation by the resident French surgeon. The operation took place with Norodom as an observer.

Chapter 10: *Years of Revolt (1884–1886)*

1. AOM Indochine A-30(66) Governor Thomson to the Minister of the Colonies, Saigon, 30 July 1883, No. 228.

2. AAE Asie 48 Indochine 22 Governor Thomson to the Minister of the Colonies, Saigon, 23 September 1883, No. 256, Confidential.

3. *Ibid.*

4. AOM Indochine A-30(66) Governor Thomson to the Minister of the Colonies, Saigon, 1 January 1884, No. 1.

5. *Ibid.*

6. AOM Indochine A-30(67) Translation of a letter from King Norodom to Governor Thomson, Phnom Penh, 7 June 1884.

7. *Ibid.*, Governor Thomson to the Minister of the Colonies, Phnom Penh, 16 June 1884, No. 1.

8. *Ibid.*

9. *Ibid.*, Telegraphic dispatch from Governor Thomson to the Minister of the Colonies, Phnom Penh, 13 June 1884. When the requested reinforcements arrived in Phnom Penh, the French forces at Thomson's disposal numbered 339.

10. *Ibid.*, Governor Thomson to the Minister of the Colonies, Phnom Penh, 16 June 1884, No. 1. The extent to which Thomson was acting without instructions is indicated in the text of a telegram sent from the minister of the colonies to Thomson (Paris, 17 June 1884), contained in this same dossier. The telegram cautioned against any sudden change in Cambodia.

11. Collard, *Cambodge,* 109–111. Collard's version of events is quoted by Prince Norodom Sihanouk in his short history of the Cambodian monarchy, *La Monarchie cambodgienne* (Phnom Penh, 1961).

12. Branda, *Ça et là,* 7–9.   13. Collard, *Cambodge,* 111.

14. Branda, *Ça et là,* 8.

15. This account of events on 17 June 1884 is based principally on the documents contained in dossier AOM Indochine A-30(67), and in particular on Governor Thomson to the Minister of the Colonies, Phnom Penh, 17 June 1884, No. 2, and Thomson to the Minister of the Colonies, Saigon, 30 June 1884, Nos. 87, 91, 92, and 96. In addition there are references to the events in Klobukowski's "Enquête sur les événements du Cambodge." Klobukowski accompanied Thomson to the palace, and he notes that Col de Monteiro was removed for false translation. This document is contained in AOM Indochine A-30(74).

16. AOM Indochine A-30(67) Governor Thomson to the Minister of the Colonies, Saigon, 30 June 1884, No. 91. This dispatch has an enclosure, a letter from Sisowath to Thomson in which the prince thanked the governor for his "generous attitude towards Cambodia."

17. The text of the convention is contained in L. de Reinach, *Recueil de traités conclus par la France en Extrême-Orient (1648–1902)* (Paris, 1902–1907), I, 208–210.

18. AOM Indochine NF 582 "Note relative à la convention du 17 Juin entre le Gouvernement du Cambodge et le Gouvernement de la République," Paris, 3 August 1884, prepared by Champeaux.

19. *Ibid.*, King Norodom to the President of the French Republic, Phnom Penh, 20 August 1884.

20. AOM Indochine A-30(67) Governor Thomson to the Minister of the Colonies, Saigon, 7 August 1884, No. 111. See also *Protectorat*

Français, Bulletin Officiel du Cambodge, 1884, 1, 10–49. The official position of the French government in relation to the events in Cambodia is set out in detail in a report prepared for the Chamber of Deputies by Eugène Ténot, 29 January 1885. See *République Française, Chambre des Députés (session ordinaire de 1885), Documents parlementaires, Annexes aux procès-verbaux des séances, Projets et propositions de loi—exposés des motifs et rapports,* February 1885–January 1886, 49–57.

21. *Histoire militaire de l'Indochine,* 37. Since the writer carried out research in the Cambodian Archives, an official publication of the Cambodian Ministry of Information, *Etudes Cambodgiennes,* has published some archival material relating to the rising, accompanied by a commentary prepared by C. M. (Charles Meyer). The material is incomplete without the complementary information to be found in the French archival sources, and the commentary is marked by a strong ideological bias. See *Etudes Cambodgiennes,* 9 (January–March 1967), 20–22 and 36–37; *ibid.,* 10 (April–June), 25–35; *ibid.,* 11 (*July–September*), 32–46; and *ibid.,* 12 (October–December), 20–36.

22. AOM Indochine A-30(67) Telegraphic dispatch from Governor Thomson to the Minister of the Colonies, Saigon, 10 January 1885, Confidential.

23. *Ibid.,* Telegraphic dispatch from Governor Thomson to the Minister of the Colonies, Saigon, 12 January 1885.

24. AC F. 65 12,662 Resident Calan to the Resident General, Kompong Cham, 31 January 1886.

25. AC F. 65 9,867 Resident Calan to the Resident General, Kompong Cham, 19 September 1886.

26. B.–P. Groslier, *Angkor et le Cambodge au XVIe siècle* (Paris, 1958), 11.

27. E. Porée-Maspero, "Traditions orales de Pursat et de Kampot," *Artibus Asiae,* XXIV, 3/4 (1961), 394–396.

28. AC uncatalogued archives Box C. 6 No. 156, personal dossier of Nguon.

29. AAE Asie 71 Indochine 37 "Note sur le Cambodge," prepared by Thomson, Paris, 20 January 1886.

30. AC F. 65 12,657 "Renseignement sur la situation politique de la sous-résidence de Takeo" prepared by Janowski, Takeo, 14 October 1885.

31. For some discussion of this point, see AC provisionally catalogued archives E. O. 67 Resident Fourestier to the Resident Superior, Takeo, 23 February 1898, No. 131, Confidential.

32. A. Leclère, "Histoire de Kampot et de la rébellion de cette province en 1885–1887," *Revue Indo-Chinoise*, 61 (15 July 1907), 939.

33. Dufour (Lieutenant), "Insurrection du Cambodge en 1885," *Excursions et Reconnaissances*, XIII (1887), 23.

34. AC E. 02 7,890 containing a note on Pursat prepared by the *chancelier* of the residence of Pursat, Marguet, in 1905. AOM Indochine A-20(25) Report for the first trimester of 1888 prepared by Resident General de Champeaux and forwarded as an enclosure with his letter to the Governor General of Indochina, Phnom Penh, 1888, No. 144.

35. AOM Indochine A-30(67) Telegraphic dispatch from Governor Thomson to the Minister of the Colonies, Saigon, 6 May 1885.

36. AVN S. L. 1,839 Kingdom of Cambodia, Service of Indirect Contributions, Report on the operations of the first trimester of 1888, Phnom Penh, 20 April 1885.

37. *Lettre commune*, No. 18, Paris, 31 December 1886.

38. "Insurrection du Cambodge en 1885," 18.

39. *Ibid., passim.;* Collard, *Cambodge*, 113–115. See also AOM Indochine A-20(21) "Gouvernement de la Cochinchine, M. A. Filippini, Gouverneur, Rapport général de fin d'année, Situation extérieure et intérieure de la Cochinchine en Mai 1886–1887," Saigon, 4 June 1887.

40. The point is made in Filippini's report noted in the immediately preceding footnote.

41. AOM Indochine A-20(22) Resident General Piquet to the Governor of Cochinchina, Phnom Penh, 25 June 1886.

42. AC G. 87 9,972 Governor Thomson to Resident General, Saigon, 21 April 1885, No. 39.

43. AC G. 87 12,720 "Compte rendu de l'exécution capitale des rebelles Pen et Kong," Phnom Penh, 21 May 1886.

44. AOM Indochine A-20(21) "Gouvernement de la Cochinchine, M. A. Filippini, Gouverneur, Rapport général de fin d'année, Situation extérieure et intérieure de la Cochinchine en Mai 1886–1887," Saigon, 4 June 1887.

45. AOM Indochine A-30(80) Governor Filippini to the Minister of the Colonies, Saigon, 30 July 1886, unnumbered.

46. AC S. O. 3 12,030 "Rapport sur le service de santé du Cambodge pendant le 2e semestre de 1885 présenté par le docteur Maurel," Phnom Penh, 1885.

47. AOM Indochine A-30(74) "Enquête sur les événements du Cambodge," Saigon, 23 July 1885. The report was prepared after Klobukowski had travelled widely throughout Cambodia observing the situation in the country. Unless otherwise identified, the information attributed to Klobukowski in the succeeding paragraphs comes from this report.

48. It is noteworthy, however, that Klobukowski reported that the *obbareach* expressed views about the Vietnamese which were wholly in line with the most truly Cambodian outlook. Describing the Vietnamese, Sisowath used these words: "They are those who pillaged and burnt pagodas, mistreated the women and children, and needlessly burnt whole villages, making a desert of the richest region of Cambodia."

49. On the variety of grievances, see, for instance, AOM Indochine A-30(74) General (Governor p.i.) Bégin to the Minister of the Colonies, Saigon, 20 August 1885, No. 33. This encloses translations of a number of insurgent documents.

50. Bégin recognized this in the dispatch noted in the immediately preceding note. Similar recognition was given by Governor Filippini. AOM Indochine A-30(80) Governor Filippini to the Minister of the Colonies, Saigon, 30 July 1886, unnumbered.

51. AC F. 65 12,645 General (Governor p.i.) Bégin to the Representative p.i. of the Protectorate, Saigon, 18 August 1885, No. 75.

52. AOM Indochine A-30(67) General (Governor p.i.) Bégin to the Minister of the Colonies, Saigon, undated (but clearly from some time in April 1886), No. 29.

53. Aymonier, *Voyage dans le Laos* (Paris, 1895), I, 11.

54. AOM Indochine A-30(74) General (Governor p.i.) Bégin to the Minister of the Colonies, 20 August 1885, No. 33. This dispatch encloses translations of letters that the French authorities were convinced originated from Votha. See the letters dated March and May 1885 addressed to insurgent leaders.

55. AC F. 42 8,588 Chargé de Résidence Collard to Resident Superior, Kompong Thom, 2 May 1890. This letter represents part of the correspondence dealing with Votha's final negotiations with the French.

56. AOM Indochine A-30(74) General (Governor p.i.) Bégin to the

Minister of the Colonies, Saigon, 20 August 1885, No. 33, enclosing translation of a letter from the insurgent governor of the province of Treang, undated.

57. AOM Indochine A-30(80) Governor Filippini to the Minister of the Colonies, Saigon, 19 September 1886, No. 86.

58. AAE Asie 71 Indochine 37 Letter from the Queen Mother to General (Governor p.i.) Bégin, 28 September 1885.

59. AOM Indochine A-30(67) Governor Thomson to the Minister of the Colonies, Saigon, 24 April 1885, No. 12. See also, in the same dossier, General (Governor p.i.) Bégin to the Minister of the Colonies, undated and unnumbered (late April or early May 1886), enclosing a letter from the acting Resident General, Lieutenant Colonel Badens, Phnom Penh, 21 April 1886, which noted that the insurgents had successfully rallied supporters by comparing French treatment of Norodom with that given the Cambodian royal family by the Vietnamese in earlier periods.

60. AOM Indochine A-30(80) Governor Filippini to the Minister of the Colonies, Saigon, 8 August 1886, No. 64. Further evidence for this traditionalist aspect of the revolt occurs in Branda, *Ça et là*, 178–180.

61. AOM Indochine A-11(8) Instructions for the Governor of Cochinchina from the Secretary of State for the Colonies, Paris, 21 May 1886.

62. AOM Indochine A-30(80) Governor Filippini to the Minister of the Colonies, Saigon, 30 July 1886, unnumbered.

63. *Ibid.* and Governor Filippini to the Minister of the Colonies, Saigon, 8 August 1886, No. 64. This encloses a copy of Norodom's proclamation. See also, AAE Asie 84 Indochine 44, which contains, apparently as an enclosure to a letter from Resident General Piquet to the French President of the Council of Ministers, Phnom Penh, 7 August 1886, unnumbered, a copy of the "Concessions demandées par le roi," undated.

64. AOM Indochine A-30(80) Governor Filippini to the Minister of the Colonies, Saigon, 14 January 1887, No. 7.

65. *Ibid.*, Governor Filippini to the Minister of the Colonies, Saigon, 5 September 1886, No. 78.

66. *Ibid.*, 21 October.

67. *Ibid.*, 14 January 1887, No. 7.

68. This estimation is made after consulting a large number of the personal dossiers of Cambodian officials who held senior positions

around the turn of the century. As examples (and the listing is far from exhaustive), see the following dossiers: AC uncatalogued archives Box C. 6 No. 180 Personal dossier of the Minister of War, Mey; uncatalogued archives Box C. 6 No. 206 Personal dossier of Prime Minister Poc; AOM Indochine NF 581 the Secretary General of the Cambodian Council of Ministers, Thiounn, to the Resident Superior, Phnom Penh, 15 November 1900, enclosing Thiounn's *curriculum vitae.*

69. AOM Indochine A-30(67) General (Governor p.i.) Bégin to the Minister of the Colonies, Saigon, 14 October 1885, No. 71.

70. AAE Asie 74 Indochine 40 Governor General Richaud to the Minister of Foreign Affairs, Saigon, 9 March 1889, No. 196, Confidential, enclosing Resident General de Champeaux's report on the last trimester of 1888, Phnom Penh, 15 January 1889.

71. Leclère, *Histoire,* 466. In the records consulted there was no detailed account of deaths inflicted on the Cambodian population either by the insurgents or by the French forces.

72. AOM Indochine H-12(5) Inspector General of the Colonies Verrier to the Minister of the Colonies, Phnom Penh, 10 January 1896, No. 16. This letter notes the continuing importance of slaves for the maintenance of Cambodian revenues.

73. *Ça et là,* 289.

Chapter 11: *The Eclipse of Norodom*

1. AOM Indochine A-20(25) "Rapport—Le Résident Général de France au Cambodge à Messieurs les Ministres des Affaires Etrangères et de la Marine et des Colonies, pour le 1er trimestre de l'année 1888."

2. AAE Asie 73 Indochine 39 "2e Trimestre 1888—Rapport du Résident Général sur la situation du Cambodge."

3. AC E.12 (F.34) 8,358 The Resident of France at Kompong Thom to the Resident Superior, Kompong Thom, 8 May 1894, No. 488.

4. Moura, *Le Royaume,* I, 221–222.

5. AAE Asie 74 Indochine 40 Trimestrial report on Cambodia prepared by Resident General de Champeaux, Phnom Penh, 15 January 1889.

6. AOM Indochine A-30(89) Governor General Piquet to the Minister of the Colonies, Saigon, 4 August 1889, No. 24. In this dispatch, Piquet concluded, "Not to allow succession to the present king would

be imprudent. A few years from now, when the administration has been overhauled and our activity in the interior is exercised directly, annexation will follow quite naturally. The present *obbarach* [*sic*] is neither intelligent nor adroit, but he will lend himself to all our plans."

7. See note 5.

8. AAE Asie 74 Indochine 40 "Cambodge—Rapport du 3ème trimestre 1889" prepared by Resident General de Vernéville, Phnom Penh, October 1889.

9. AAE Asie 73 Indochine 39 "2e Trimestre 1888—Rapport du Résident Général sur la situation du Cambodge."

10. AOM Indochine A-20(32) Trimestrial report on Cambodia prepared by Resident Superior de Vernéville, Phnom Penh, April 1890.

11. According to Vernéville, in the report cited in note 10, Duong Chacr was placed in chains because he had offended Norodom. Dossier AOM Indochine A-30(96), however, contains a letter from Duong Chacr to the Minister of the Colonies, Phnom Penh, 7 May 1891, in which the prince charges that the king acted on one occasion after Vernéville had urged that Duong Chacr should be chained.

12. AOM Indochine A-30(96) The Minister of Foreign Affairs to the Undersecretary of State for the Colonies, Paris, 25 September 1891.

13. AOM Indochine A-30(90) Draft letter from the Undersecretary of State for the Colonies to the Governor General of Indochina, Paris, 6 October 1893, Confidential. AOM Indochine A-30(96) contains correspondence relating to Duong Chacr's exile in Algeria.

14. AC F. 42 8,588 Chargé de Résidence Collard to Resident Superior, Kompong Thom, 2 May 1890.

15. AC F. 42 (F.65) 8,294. This dossier contains a set of confidential reports from the Resident at Kompong Thom on negotiations with Votha. Votha's death was announced in a letter of 13 January 1892.

16. AOM Indochine A-30(103) Personal letter from Governor General Rousseau to the Minister of the Colonies, on board *La Manche*, 7 August 1895.

17. Anon., "Le Cambodge en 1893," *Revue Indo-Chinoise*, 2 (October 1893), 164–173.

18. Collard, *Cambodge*, 136.

19. AOM Indochine NF 587 Resident Superior de Vernéville to the Governor General of Indochina, Phnom Penh, 30 July 1896, No. 123, Confidential.

20. AOM Indochine A-00(36) "Note sur les faits importants par-

venus à la connaissance du département pendant les mois de Janvier et de Février 1897," a summary prepared for the President of the Republic.

21. AOM Indochine NF 585 Telegraphic dispatch from Governor General p.i. Fourès to the Minister of the Colonies, Hanoi, 3 January 1897, and Telegraphic dispatch from the Minister of the Colonies to Governor General p.i. Fourès, Paris, 4 January 1897.

22. *Ibid.,* Telegraphic dispatch from Governor General Doumer to the Minister of the Colonies, Saigon, 23 February 1897.

23. AOM Indochine A-20(48) Governor General Doumer to the Minister of the Colonies, Saigon, 22 November 1897, No. 2,708.

24. AOM Indochine A-20(45) Governor General Doumer to the Minister of the Colonies, Saigon, 22 March 1897, unnumbered, Confidential.

25. AOM Indochine NF 581 contains material relating to the Yukanthor affair, including Um's protestation against Yukanthor's attack upon his character.

26. AOM Indochine A-20(48) Governor General Doumer to the Minister of the Colonies, Saigon, 22 November 1897, No. 2,708.

27. See AC "Ordonnances royales, ordonnances ministérielles, arrêtés ministérielles (en caractères français)," No. 1.

28. AC "Procès-verbaux des séances du Conseil des Ministres (en français et cambodgien)," commencing in 1897. The French text of these manuscript minutes was used throughout. There is no reason to doubt the authenticity by comparison with the Cambodian manuscript text. Indeed, it is far from clear in which of the two languages the original record was made.

29. AC "Conseil des Ministres," No. 4 (1900–1901), 16 March 1900, 12.

30. The text is contained in the *Receuil général permanent des actes relatifs à l'organisation et la réglementation de l'Indochine,* 105–106.

31. AC "Conseil des Ministres," No. 4 (1900–1901), 16 March 1900, 12. The observations in this paragraph are based on a study of all meetings of the council of ministers between 1897 and 1907 inclusive.

32. AC "Conseil des Ministres," No. 1 (1897–1898), 6 April 1898, 471–474.

33. AC C. 02 7,151 Extract from the minutes of the sixth meeting of the council of ministers, 25 September 1897.

34. AC "Conseil des Ministres," No. 1 (1897–1898), 28 October 1897, 196.

35. *Ibid.*, No. 2 (1898–1899), 13 August 1898, 70–71.

36. *Ibid.*, 28 November, 191–192, for the text of the letter.

37. *Ibid.*   38. *Ibid.*, 8 December, 205–206.

39. *Ibid.*, 12 January 1899, 244–246.

40. AOM Indochine NF 581 contains a letter from Thiounn to the Resident Superior, Phnom Penh, 15 November 1900, with this information.

41. AC "Conseil des Ministres," No. 2 (1898–1899), 12 January 1899, 253. The underlined words are French transcriptions of Cambodian terms. *Puthamon* means the "wisdom of Buddha"; *Sayamon* means the "wisdom of the Hindu scriptures"; and *Reach Montrey* is probably a false transcription of *Reachmon,* meaning the "knowledge of government administration." The word *Phendey,* although incorporated with the virtue *Sayamon,* has the sense of earthly as opposed to heavenly wisdom. It is interesting to note the juxtaposition of Buddhist and Hindu wisdom as a necessary ideal. I am indebted to Dr. Frank Huffman for identification of the Cambodian words from the transcription in the original manuscript.

42. AC "Conseil des Ministres," No. 2 (1898–1899), 12 January 1899, 254.

43. *Ibid.*, 29 March, 346–347, for the dismissal of Ouk; and 347–348, for the appointment of Poc; *ibid.*, 26 April, 382–383, for Norodom's refusal to approve Ouk's dismissal; AC uncatalogued archives Box C. 6 No. 165 for discussion of the dismissal of Nguon.

44. AC uncatalogued archives Box C. 6 No. 165 Personal dossier of Nguon, containing a letter from King Norodom to the Resident Superior, Phnom Penh, 18 November 1898, No. 29.

45. *L'Affaire Iukanthor.*

46. *Ibid.*, 233.

47. AOM Indochine A-20(47) Governor General Doumer to the Minister of the Colonies, Saigon, 1 September 1900, No. 1,449.

48. AOM Indochine NF 564 Governor General p.i. Charles to the Minister of the Colonies, Saigon, 10 November 1916, No. 818.

49. The text is contained in *L'Affaire Iukanthor,* 74–86.

50. The question of whether Yukanthor had any right to be considered as heir presumptive is discussed in some detail in AOM Indochine NF 570 Resident Superior Luce to the Governor General of

Indochina, Phnom Penh, 3 April 1906, No. 51, Confidential. Luce was resident superior in 1900. He stated that Norodom had supported Yukanthor's visit since the king had hoped, among other things, that the visit would lead to the king regaining control over some of the Cambodian tax revenues. Luce claimed that only Yukanthor himself and some of his friends regarded his position as being that of heir presumptive.

51. This quotation and the summary of Yukanthor's memorandum in the remainder of the paragraph come from the text quoted in Hess.

52. AOM Indochine NF 581 The Minister of the Colonies to the Governor General of Indochina, Paris, 20 October 1900, No. 361, Confidential.

53. AC "Conseil des Ministres," No. 4 (1900–1901), 3 November 1900, 123–127.

54. *Ibid.,* No. 5 (1901–1902), 27 September 1901, 136–137.

55. Villemereuil, *Explorations,* 400 and *passim.*

56. AC uncatalogued archives Box C. 6 No. 220, Chhun's personal dossier.

57. This information was noted in an extract from the meeting of the council of ministers in 1901 contained in Chhun's dossier.

58. This information comes from Chhun's dossier. There is at least the suggestion that this surveillance was intended to intimidate Chhun.

59. An extract from the minutes of the meeting of the council of ministers of 4 December 1911 is contained in Chhun's personal dossier. Resident Superior de Lamothe had served in Phnom Penh between 1902 and 1904. His views on Chhun's dismissal were recounted to the council of ministers in 1911 by Resident Superior Outrey.

60. AOM Indochine NF 581 Um to the Resident Superior, Phnom Penh, 19 November 1900, containing his *curriculum vitae.*

61. *Ibid.*

62. AC uncatalogued archives Box C. 6 No. 206, Poc's personal dossier. As an illustration of the interlocking nature of the Cambodian elite, it is interesting to find from dossier AC C. 6 7,248 that Poc's elder brother was at one stage *kralahom* and that Poc's nephew, Ui, was a senior provincial official. Poc's son was appointed assistant to the minister of justice in 1902; see AC "Conseil des Ministres," No. 5 (1901–1902), 23 April 1902, 365.

63. AC uncatalogued archives Box C. 6 No. 207, Col de Monteiro's personal dossier.

64. As examples, see AC uncatalogued archives Box C. 6 No. 198, personal dossier of Men, who was appointed acting minister of the navy in 1903; AC uncatalogued archives Box C. 6 No. 180, personal dossier of Mey, who was appointed minister of war in 1893; and AOM Indochine NF 581, which contains a letter from Van (assistant to the prime minister) to the Resident Superior, Phnom Penh, 21 November 1900.

65. AOM Indochine NF 581 Thiounn to the Resident Superior, Phnom Penh, 15 November 1900. In this letter Thiounn gives his father's name as Hui. Tradition holds that Thiounn was of largely Vietnamese descent.

66. AOM Indochine A-20(50) Governor General p.i. Bront to the Minister of the Colonies, Hanoi, 2 August 1902, No. 1,477.

67. These observations are based upon consultation of the personal dossiers of Cambodian officials held in the Cambodian archives. For an instance of a former pupil of the Ecole Coloniale becoming a governor, see the dossier of Ou, AC uncatalogued archives Box C. 6 No. 200. See also, AC uncatalogued archives Box C. 6 No. 219, personal dossier of Douc; and AC uncatalogued archives Box C. 6 No. 222, dossier of Ea-Khan.

68. AOM Indochine G-01(6) Governor General p.i. Bonhoure to the Minister of the Colonies, Hanoi, 13 May 1908, No. 1,237.

69. *Ibid.*

70. AC E. 02 8,932 Report prepared by Stremler, *chancelier* of the residence of Kompong Speu, Kompong Speu, 20 October 1903.

71. AC "Conseil des Ministres," No. 5 (1901–1902), 27 July 1901, 49–53.

72. Examination of the minutes of the meetings of these councils stresses the way in which the resident dominated meetings. See, for instance, AC E. 3 8,868, which contains the minutes of the Svay Rieng council for 1905.

73. The issue of slavery was recognized as delicate, and the French administration accepted that total abolition would have to wait until Norodom's death (AOM Indochine NF 50 Inspector General of the Colonies Piquié to the Minister of the Colonies, Saigon, 3 May 1900). The king's personal slaves had supposedly been liberated in 1897, but there is no evidence that a definitive reform came during Norodom's lifetime. One area in which real change was achieved was amongst the *pols* (slaves) whose duty it was to collect cardamom in the mountains

to the west of Pursat. See A. Rousseau, *Le Protectorat français du Cambodge: Organisation politique, administrative et foncière* (Dijon. 1904), 172–195.

74. AC "Lettres au départ échangées avec le palais," 1905–1909. Resident Superior Luce to King Sisowath, Phnom Penh, 17 June 1907, No. 38. The letter submitted a new code for Sisowath's approval. See also, AC D. 35 3,952 Report on the situation in Cambodia in the month of September 1905 prepared by Morel, Phnom Penh, 6 September 1905, No. 1,150. This report lists reforms achieved following Sisowath's accession.

75. AC "Conseil des Ministres," No. 5 (1901–1902), 13 August 1901, 85–87. This session dealt with the intervention by the resident superior to modify the punishments that Norodom intended to inflict on a princess guilty of illicit sexual relations with a commoner.

76. AOM Indochine NF 581 The Minister of the Colonies to the Governor General of Indochina, Paris, 20 October 1900, No. 361, Confidential.

77. AOM Indochine D-46(1) "Conseil du Protectorat du Cambodge, Procès-verbal," 27 June 1901.

78. AOM Indochine NF 581 Telegraphic dispatch from the Minister of the Colonies to the Governor General of Indochina, received in Hanoi 25 February 1904.

79. Collard, *Cambodge*, 180.

80. The text of Norodom's will is contained in *République Française, Annexe à l'annuaire du Cambodge, Traités, conventions et honneurs militaires* (Phnom Penh, 1905), 63–67. Professor George Coedès discusses the way in which a personal cult was enshrined in religious statues and notes the fact that Norodom did this (*Pour mieux comprendre Angkor* [2nd ed.; Paris, 1947], Chapter 3, particularly 66–67).

81. AOM Indochine NF 581 Telegraphic dispatch from the Minister of the Colonies to the Governor General of Indochina, enclosing a message for King Sisowath, undated (April 1904?).

82. *Ibid.*, Telegraphic dispatch from Governor General Beau to the Minister of the Colonies, Hanoi, 11 May 1904, enclosing a message from King Sisowath.

83. AC provisionally catalogued archives E. O. 67 Resident Fourestier to the Resident Superior, Takeo, 6 April 1899, No. 313. Enclosed with this letter are two letters from Sisowath to the Cambodian officials of Kosthom Province, Phnom Penh, 16 January and 28 April 1898.

84. AC "Lettres au départ échangées avec le palais," 1905–1909; Resident Superior de Lamothe to King Sisowath, Phnom Penh, undated (May 1905), 22–24.

85. A useful summary of the changes that followed Norodom's death is provided in *République Française, Conseil Supérieur de l'Indochine (2ème Commission) Situation politique, économique et financière du Cambodge,* ordinary session 1905, No. 10.

86. The statistics are to be found in *ibid.* A useful summary of the development of the French educational effort is provided by AC provisionally catalogued archives Box 3 (4, 6, 7), No. 321, 14,479 Copy of a report addressed to the resident superior in 1900 prepared by Hamant. In this report, a figure of 140 pupils is given for Cambodians attending the Franco-Cambodian school in Phnom Penh out of a total enrollment of 276 pupils. See also AC R. o 11,868 "Simples Notes sur l'histoire d'enseignement au Cambodge de 1863 à 1890," Phnom Penh, 10 November 1911, unsigned.

87. *République Française, Protectorat du Cambodge, Société d'Enseignement Mutuel des Cambodgiens, Historique* (Phnom Penh, 1905), 7.

88. Moura, *Le Royaume,* II, 147. Moura gives only the briefest note on the cremation, and no account is contained in Doudart de Lagrée's papers.

89. Collard, *Cambodge,* Chapters 15 and 16.

Chapter 12: *Rule and Response*

1. It is of interest to note that there has been a major effort in both North and South Viet-Nam to find nationalist heroes among resistance figures of the past. The interest has been more developed in the north, where rewriting to fit a rigid ideological requirement has been more active. The historical magazine *Nghien Cuu Lich Su* (Historical Research), published in Hanoi, has devoted considerable space to denouncing such figures as Truong-Vinh-Ky (see for instance Nos. 59 and 60 of 1964) and to praising such men as Truong-Dinh (see No. 65 of 1964).

2. A. Rivoalen, "L'Oeuvre française d'enseignement au Viet-Nam," *FA,* Special Number 125, 126, 127 (October, November, and December 1956), 401–402.

3. Leclère, *Les Codes,* I, 1.

4. For a scholarly discussion of the Chinese minority in Cambodia, see W. E. Willmott, *The Chinese in Cambodia* (Vancouver, 1967). Interesting comments on the Vietnamese minority in Cambodia are contained in Jean-Pierre Beauchatard's unpublished study, "La Minorité vietnamienne au Cambodge," Mémoire de stage, Ecole Nationale de la France d'Outre-Mer, 1951–1952.

5. Sarin Chhak, *Les Frontières,* presents this thesis in some detail.

6. AOM Indochine NF 451 Governor General p.i. Bonhoure to the Minister of the Colonies, Hanoi, 4 June 1908, unnumbered.

7. *Quelques Conférences à Paris,* 116 and 118.

8. For a brief discussion of his role, see Philippe Devillers, *Histoire du Viêt-Nam de 1940 à 1952* (Paris, 1952), 40, 41, 66, 69, and 181.

9. *Ibid.,* 32–33, particularly n. 4 on p. 33.

10. Doan-Thi-Do, *Le Journalisme au Viêt-Nam.*

11. See, for instance, extracts from a lecture delivered on 6 March 1907, published in the "Chronique," *BEFEO,* VII, 1–2 (January, June 1907), 155–166.

12. What this meant when Viet-Nam finally emerged from French control is shown in Roy Jumper's "Problems of Public Administration in South Vietnam" (*Far Eastern Survey,* XXVI, 12 [December 1957], 183–190) and "Mandarin Bureaucracy and Politics in South Vietnam" (*Pacific Affairs,* XXX, 1 [March 1957], 47–58).

13. AC G. o 136 Outrey to the Governor General of Indochina, Phnom Penh, 1 December 1911, No. 1,818, and *Projet de création d'une Assemblée consultative indigène: Documents et procès-verbaux* (Phnom Penh, 1912).

14. For some comment on the assembly and its role in the development of Cambodian politics, see P. Preschez, *Essai sur la démocratie au Cambodge* (Paris, 1961), in the section "Rôle dérisoire des institutions représentatives."

15. On discontent within the royal family concerning Sisowath's occupancy of the throne, see AOM Indochine NF 579, in particular Resident Superior Luce to the Governor General of Indochina, Phnom Penh, 18 August 1909, No. 1,018, Confidential, and NF 22 Correspondence for 1912 and 1913. On the prevalence of minor scandals within the royal family, see AC "Lettres au départ éxchangées avec le palais," 1905–1909, Letter 55 of 1905, Letters 15, 21, 27, and 28 of 1907.

16. AOM Indochine NF 579 Governor General Klobukowski to the

Minister of the Colonies, Saigon, 17 March 1909, No. 170, Confidential. This dispatch encloses a letter to Klobukowski from King Sisowath dated 25 February 1909, No. 7, and Resident Superior Luce to Klobukowski, Phnom Penh, 12 March 1909, No. 30, Very Confidential.

17. AOM Indochine NF 570 Governor General Roume to the Minister of the Colonies, Hanoi, 31 March 1916, No. 285.

18. *Ibid.*

19. AC E.O. 4 7,811 Report from Resident Rousseau, Kampot, 5 July 1919.

20. AOM Indochine NF 570 Governor General Roume to the Minister of the Colonies, Hanoi, 31 March 1916, No. 285.

21. Some consideration of this point is contained in my "History and Kingship in Contemporary Cambodia," *Journal of Southeast Asian History*, VII, 1 (March 1966), 1–14.

22. The Vietnamese royal house did retain some residual importance, sufficient, in fact, for the Viet-Minh movement to endeavor to use Bao-Dai as a partial symbol of legitimacy. In general, however, he was a figure who had little appeal for nationalists. See Devillers, *Histoire*, 62–64 and *passim*.

BIBLIOGRAPHY
and INDEX

Bibliography

ARCHIVES

FRANCE

Archives in five locations were used in the preparation of this study. These were: Archives Nationales de France; Archives Nationales de France, Section Outre-Mer; Archives du Ministère des Affaires Etrangères (Quai d'Orsay); Archives de la Marine; and the Service Historique de l'Armée de Terre, Section Outre-Mer.

Archives Nationales de France

Colonies C 1.6 Cochinchine 1819–1863
Marine BB4: reports contained in this series deal, in particular, with the establishment of a French presence in both Cochinchina and Cambodia. The figures following the listing Marine BB4 in the footnotes are for the volume or bundle number in the series.

Archives Nationales de France, Section Outre-Mer

The materials held in this location are from the former Ministère de la Marine et Colonies and Ministère des Colonies. This collection is currently the single most important collection of manuscript documents for the history of Cambodia and Viet-Nam during the colonial period. The archives are classified under "Indochine" by subject, as follows:

Series A. Political Affairs: within this and subsequent series, each subdivision is composed of a varying number of dossiers. Thus, the listing Indochine A-30(67) in the footnotes is of a particular dossier, in this case one entitled "Cambodge—Convention du 17 Juin 1884. Texte, correspondance et ratification. 8 Juin au 31 Décembre."
Series B. External Relations
Series C. Missions [of exploration]
Series D. General and Local Administration

Series E. Administration Disputes, Powers of the Council of State, Powers of the Court of Cassation

Series F. Land, Registration, Labor, Manpower

Series G. Population—Births, Deaths, and Marriages

Series H. Inspection and Control

Series I. Personnel

Series K. Finance

Series L. Customs

Series M. Agriculture, Sericulture, Livestock, Waters and Forests, Fishing

Series N. Commerce and Industry

Series O. Justice

Series P. Police, Security

Series Q. Navy

Series R. Military Affairs

Series S. Public Works

Series X. Education, Fine Arts, Archives, Geographical Society, Meteorology

Series Y. Health and Public Welfare

Series Z. Mémoires and Documents

In addition to the dossiers classified in this subject series, there are a number of dossiers which form part of the "Indochine" holdings but which are classified as *nouveaux fonds*. The abbreviation "NF" has been used in the footnotes. These dossiers will be found catalogued alongside the normal dossiers.

The Section Outre-Mer archives include a "Siam" series. These are not broken down into a subject classification but are listed on a numerical basis in the catalogue.

Apart from the material consulted in dossiers held at the Section Outre-Mer of the French National Archives, reference was also made to the matriculation register of the Ecole Coloniale. The title of this item, which was not classified when consulted, is: Ministère des Colonies, Ecole Coloniale, Registre matricule no. 1, Section indigène: 1885–1913.

Archives du Ministère des Affaires Etrangères (Quai d'Orsay)

At the Quai d'Orsay the archival materials are organized on a volumes system, rather than on a subject basis in dossiers. Materials relating to the Indochinese region form part of the general series

"Mémoires et Documents, Fonds Divers." Within this general series there is a subdivision "Asie Indochine."

Volume 27 of the "Asie" series is the first dealing with Indochina. Following the system used in the footnotes it would be designated Asie 27 Indochine 1. Its full title is "Asie 27 Indochine 1 Cochinchine, Cambodge, Annam et Tonkin (1857–1861)."

All volumes from Asie 27 Indochine 1 to Asie 95 Indochine 57 which have relevance to the present study were consulted.

Archives de la Marine

Part of the series Marine BB4, a portion of which is held in the Archives Nationales, is held at the Archives de la Marine.

Service Historique de l'Armée de Terre, Section Outre-Mer

A limited amount of material relating to the present study was located in the Fonds Tonkin.

CAMBODIA

Archival materials in Cambodia are held in an annex of the National Library. These archives are composed of the residual holdings of what was once the Cambodian section of French Indochinese archives: Archives Centrales de l'Indochine: Résidence Supérieure du Cambodge. A substantial portion of the holdings was removed to France in 1955. Dossiers in the archives are classified on a similar basis to those in the Outre-Mer holdings in Paris, as follows:

A. Official Documents
B. General Correspondence
C. Personnel
D. General Administration
E. Provincial Administration
F. Political Matters
G. Justice
H. Public Works
I. Mines
J. Railways
K. Posts and Telegraph
L. Commerce, Industry, and Tourism
M. Labor, Settlement, Land Regulation

N. Agriculture

O. Navigation

P. Navy

Q. Military Matters

R. Education

S. Health Services

T. Finance

U. Customs Services

V. Archives and Libraries

X. Miscellaneous Matters

Y. Papers Relating to Individuals

Z. Copies of Documents Related to the History of Indochina

Throughout the present study dossiers consulted in the Cambodian archives have been listed with their subject division and a numerical identification. This latter is added since those dossiers which remain are stored on a numerical basis. Thus, a dossier is listed as C. O. 2 7,151. The full title of this dossier is "Dossier concernant les fonctionnaires de l'administration cambodgienne, 1897–1899."

Apart from dossiers which form part of the main body of the archives, there are provisionally catalogued archives and uncatalogued archives. When cited in the footnotes, these have been appropriately identified.

Additional manuscript materials consulted were:

Procès-verbaux des séances du Conseil des Ministres: No. 1 (1897–1898); No. 2 (1898–1899); No. 3 (1899–1900); No. 4 (1900–1901); No. 5 (1901–1902); No. 6 (1902–1903); No. 7 (1903–1906)

Lettres au départ échangées avec le palais: 1905, 1906, 1907, 1908, 1909 (each letter in this manuscript record is in French and Cambodian)

Ordonnances royales, ordonnances ministérielles, arrêtés ministérielles (en caractères français): No. 1, 1897–1898

Ordonnances royales (en caractères français): No. 2, 1899–1904

Circulaires ministérielles (en caractères cambodgiens et français): 1897–1910

VIET-NAM

Archives of the Republic of Viet-Nam

Archival materials relating to Cochinchina (like those in Cambodia, once part of the French Indochinese archives) are conserved in the

Van-Kho Viet-Nam Cong-Hoa (Archives of the Republic of Viet-Nam). For the present study materials in three divisions of the archives were used. The first were those from the Services Locaux classification. These have been noted with the abbreviation S. L. followed by the number of the dossier. Thus, dossier S. L. 172 is Pétrus Ky's dossier, which has as its full title "Dossier individuel de M. Pétrus Truong-Vinh-Ky, Professeur de langues orientales, 1868–1895."

Secondly, dossiers classified on a regional basis were consulted. Such a dossier was Tayninh 15, "Tayninh troubles. 1875, 1876, 1885."

Finally, a series of bound ministerial dispatches from the minister of the colonies in Paris to the governors of the colony of Cochinchina have been used for the present study. Research notes from these volumes were made in 1963. The set could not be located in 1966.

Vien Khao-Co (Institute for Archeological Research)

This institute has a series of papers relating to Pétrus Ky, including some of his own papers, in a series designated Tu Sach Truong-Vinh-Ky (Truong-Vinh-Ky Library).

Pétrus Ky Museum

Now in a state of considerable disrepair, this small museum contains a number of Ky's manuscripts.

UNITED KINGDOM

The following manuscript volume from the holdings of the India Office has some interest for Cambodian contacts with Singapore in the early 1850's: India Office Records. India Secret Proceedings. India Secret Consultations. 25 July to 28 November 1851. No. 170.

UNPUBLISHED MATERIALS

Bain, Chester A. "The History of Viet-Nam from the French Penetration to 1939," Ph.D. thesis, American University, 1957, University of Michigan Microfilm 17,524.

Beauchatard, Jean-Pierre. "La Minorité vietnamienne au Cambodge," Mémoire de stage, Ecole Nationale de la France d'Outre-Mer, 1951–1952, No. 4.

O'Harrow, S. D. "The Growth of Modern Vietnamese Prose Fiction, with Special Reference to the Role of Nhat Linh in the Tu Luc Van Doan and Some Comparisons to the Parallel Development in Modern

Chinese Literary History." M.A. thesis, School of Oriental and African Studies, University of London, 1965.

Sarin Chhak. "Situation politique extérieure du Cambodge de 1863 à 1884." Mémoire pour le Diplôme d'Etudes Supérieures (Sciences Politiques), Université de Paris, Faculté de Droit et des Sciences Economiques, 1964.

Thioum Thiounn. "Le Pouvoir monarchique au Cambodge," Université de Paris, Faculté de Droit, 1952.

Wyatt, David K. "The Beginnings of Modern Education in Thailand, 1868–1910," Ph.D. thesis, Cornell University, 1966.

PUBLISHED MATERIALS

Bibliographies and Guides

Auvade, R. *Bibliographie critique des oeuvres parues sur l'Indochine française.* Paris, 1965.

Barbie du Bocage, V. A. *Bibliographie annamite: Livres, recueils, périodiques, manuscrits, plans.* Paris, 1867.

——. *Bibliographie annamite: Livres, recueils, périodiques, manuscrits, cartes et plans parus depuis 1866.* Saigon, 1880.

Boudet, Paul, and Rémy Bourgeois. *Bibliographie de l'Indochine française 1913–1926: Supplément 1927–1929.* 2 vols. Hanoi, 1929.

Brébion, A. *Livre d'or du Cambodge, de la Cochinchine et de l'Annam, 1625–1910. Biographie et bibliographie.* Saigon, 1910.

——, and A. Cabaton. *Dictionnaire de bio-bibliographie générale, ancienne et moderne de l'Indochine française.* Paris, 1935. Published as Tome VIII of the *Annales* of the Académie des Sciences Coloniales.

Cordier, Henri. *Bibliotheca Indosinica.* 4 vols. Paris: I–III, 1912–1915; IV, Index, 1932.

Doan-Thi-Do. *Le Journalisme au Viêt-Nam et les périodiques viêtnamiens de 1865 à 1944 conservés à la Bibliothèque Nationale.* Paris, 1958.

Ferréol de Ferry. *La Série d'Extrême-Orient du fonds des Archives Coloniales conservées aux Archives Nationales (Registres C.1.1 à C.1.27).* Paris, 1958.

Le-Ngoc-Tru, ed. *Muc-Luc Bao-Chi Viet-Ngu 1865–1965.* Saigon, 1966.

Nguyen The-Anh. *Bibliographie critique sur les relations entre le Viet-Nam et l'Occident.* Paris, 1967.

Truong-Vinh-Ky, Pétrus. *Catalogue des ouvrages publiés et édités jusqu'à ce jour par P.J.B. Truong Vinh Ky à l'usage des écoles indo-chinoises.* Choquan, 1892.

Official Publications (France and French Possessions)

Bulletin Officiel de l'Expédition de Cochinchine
Bulletin Officiel de la Cochinchine Française
Cochinchine Française, Annuaire de la Cochinchine Française
Cochinchine Française, Procès-verbaux du Conseil Colonial
Protectorat Français, Bulletin Officiel du Cambodge
République Française, Bulletin Officiel de l'Indo-Chine Française
République Française, Etat de la Cochinchine Française
République Française, Journal Officiel de l'Indo-Chine Française
The preceding items were published over substantial periods and were consulted for the applicable periods for the present study.

The following items are not serial publications:

Cochinchine Française, Projet de Code civil à l'usage des Annamites par M. Lasserre. Saigon, 1884.

Cochinchine Française, Recueil de jurisprudence en matière indigène, années 1880–1885. Prepared by Lasserre. Saigon, 1884.

Cochinchine Française, Réorganisation de l'instruction publique en Cochinchine. Révision par le sous-commission du projet présenté par M. Rul, Directeur de l'Enseignement. Saigon, 1884.

République Française, Annexe à l'annuaire du Cambodge: Traités, conventions et honneurs militaires. Phnom Penh, 1905.

République Française, Chambre des Députés (session ordinaire de 1885), Documents parlementaires, Annexes aux procès-verbaux des séances, Projets et propositions de loi—exposés des motifs et rapports. Février 1885–Janvier 1886.

République Française, Conseil Supérieur de l'Indochine (1ère commission), Situation de la Cochinchine. Ordinary Session 1902.

République Française, Conseil Supérieur de l'Indochine (2ème commission), Situation politique, économique et financière du Cambodge. Ordinary Session 1905.

République Française, Conseil Supérieur de l'Indochine (1ère commission), Fonctionnement de l'enseignement publique. Ordinary Session 1906.

République Française, Discours prononcé par M. Beau, Gouverneur Général de l'Indo-Chine, à l'ouverture de la session ordinaire du Conseil Supérieur, le 11 décembre 1905. Saigon, 1905.

République Française, Gouvernement Général de l'Indochine, Protecto-rat du Cambodge, Projet de création d'une assemblée consultative indigène au Cambodge, Documents et procès-verbaux. Phnom Penh, 1912.

République Française, Gouvernement Général de l'Indochine, Protec-torat du Cambodge, Recueil des actes du gouvernement cambodgien. Saigon, 1920.

République Française, Protectorat du Cambodge, Société d'Enseigne-ment Mutuel des Cambodgiens, Historique. Phnom Penh, 1905.

Aymonier, E. *Rapport adressé au Sous-Secrétaire d'Etat des Colonies sur le fonctionnement de l'Ecole Coloniale pendant l'année 1890.* Paris, 1890.

Beau, Paul. *Situation de l'Indo-Chine de 1902–1907.* Saigon, 1908.

Doumer, Paul. *République Française, Situation de l'Indo-Chine (1897–1901).* Hanoi, 1902.

Histoire militaire de l'Indochine des débuts à nos jours (Janvier 1922). Etablie par des officiers de l'Etat-Major sous la haute direction du Général de Division Puypéroux, Commandant Supérieur des Troupes du Groupe de l'Indochine. Hanoi, 1922.

Luro, J.-B. E. *Rapport et instruction sur l'administration de la justice indigène.* Saigon, 1870.

Recueil général permanent des actes relatifs à l'organisation et le réglementation de l'Indochine. Hanoi, Haiphong, 1909.

Vial, P. *Cochinchine Française, Rapport sur la situation de la colonie ses institutions et ses finances.* Saigon, 1867.

Official Publications (Cambodia)

Rois de Kampuchea: Ang Duong, Norodom, N. Sihanouk. Ministry of Information: Phnom Penh, 1957.

NEWSPAPERS

Courrier de Saigon (Saigon).
Le Courrier Saigonnais (Saigon).
Le XIXe Siècle (Paris).
Le Figaro (Paris).
Gia-Dinh Bao (The Journal of Gia-Dinh) (Saigon).
L'Indépendant de Saigon (Saigon).
Nam Ky (Southern Region), *quoc-ngu* edition (Saigon).

Nam Ky, French edition (Saigon).

Nong-Co Min Dam (The Tribune of the Old Agricultural People) (Saigon).

Le Saigonnais (Saigon).

NEWSLETTER

Lettre commune (Paris). Published for private circulation by the Missions Etrangères missionary order.

ARTICLES

Anon. "Le Cambodge en 1893," *Revue Indo-Chinoise,* 2 (October 1893), 156–190.

——. "Mot Tram Nam Ngay Mat Cua Truong Dinh" (The Centennial of Truong Dinh's Death), *Nghien Cuu Lich Su* (Historical Research), LXV, No. 8 (1964), 6.

D'Ariès, J. "La Cochinchine française. Son Organisation," *Revue Maritime et Coloniale,* XXXI (1871), 165–202.

Aymonier, E. "Critique du 'Royaume du Cambodge' de M. Moura," *Excursions et Reconnaissances,* XVI (1883), 207–220.

——. "L'Enseignement en Indo-Chine," *Le Temps,* 17 October 1889.

Baudrit, A. "Correspondance de Savin de Larclause, officier d'Infanterie de Marine, concernant les campagnes de Chine et de Cochinchine et les premières années de la Cochinchine française," *BSEI,* n.s. XIV, Nos. 3–4 (3rd and 4th trimesters 1939), entire issue.

Bitard, P. "Les Membres de la famille royale du Cambodge et leurs titres d'après l'ordonnance de S. M. An Duon," *BEFEO,* XLVIII, fasc. 2 (1957), 563–572.

B[onifacy], T. K. Q. "Le *quoc-ngu* et les caractères," *Revue Indo-Chinoise,* 15 (15 March 1904), 265–267.

Boudet, P. "La Conquête de la Cochinchine par les Nguyen et le rôle des émigrés chinois," *BEFEO,* XLII (1942), 115–132.

——. "Chasseloup-Laubat et la politique coloniale du second empire— Le Traité de 1864 entre l'Annam et la France," *BSEI,* n.s. XXII, No. 2 (2nd semester 1947), 17–74.

Boudineau. "De l'Organisation de la justice indigène au Cambodge," *Revue Indo-Chinoise,* 62 (31 July 1907), 977–984.

Bourde, P. "Chronique de l'Exposition," *Le Temps,* 2 October 1889.

Cadière, L. "La Question de *quoc-ngu,*" *Revue Indo-Chinoise,* 9 (15

May 1904), 585–600; 10 (31 May 1904), 700–705; 11 (15 June 1904), 784–788; 12 (30 June 1904), 872–876; 1 (15 July 1904), 58–63.

Camouilly, C. "Le Cadastre en Cochinchine," *BSEI*, 1886 (1st semester 1886), 49–61.

Chesneaux, J. "Stages in the Development of the Vietnam National Movement," *Past and Present*, VII (April 1955), 63–75.

——. "French Historiography and the Evolution of Colonial Viet-Nam," in D. G. E. Hall, ed. *Historians of South-East Asia*. London, 1961.

Coedès, G. "Etudes cambodgiennes XVI—Essai de classification des documents historiques cambodgiens conservés à la Bibliothèque de l'Ecole Française d'Extrême-Orient," *BEFEO*, XVIII, fasc. 9 (1918), 15–28.

Cordier, H. "Pétrus Truong Vinh Ky," *T'oung Pao*, Series II, I (1900), 261–268.

Crémazy, L. "Exposé du droit chinois-annamite," *Revue Indo-Chinoise*, 105 (22 October 1900), 1,022–1,025; 106 (29 October 1900), 1,046–1,049.

Dao-Thai-Hanh, "Son Excellence Phan-Thanh-Gian, Ministre de l'Annam (1796–1867)," *BAVH*, II (April–June 1915), 211–224.

Daudin, P. "Phan-Thanh-Gian 1796–1867 et sa famille d'après quelques documents annamites," *BSEI*, n.s. XVI, No. 2 (2nd semester 1941), entire issue.

Deloustal, R. "La Justice dans l'ancien Annam I," *BEFEO*, VIII, Nos. 1–2 (1908), 177–220. The *préface* by Cl.–E. Maître, Director of the Ecole Française d'Extrême-Orient (pp. 177–181), is of particular interest.

Delvert, J. "L'Oeuvre française d'enseignement au Cambodge," *FA*, Special Number, 125–126–127 (October–November–December 1956), 309–320.

Deschaseaux, E. "Note sur les anciens *don dien* annamites dans la Basse-Cochinchine," *Excursions et Reconnaissances*, XIV, No. 31 (1889), 133–140.

Devillers, P. "Au Sud Vietnam . . . il y a cent ans," *FA*, XX, No. 184 (Winter 1965/1966), 139–156; No. 185 (Spring 1966), 325–347.

Dufour, A. "Insurrection du Cambodge en 1885," *Excursions et Reconnaissances*, XIII, No. 29 (1887), 1–50.

Durand, M. "Alexandre de Rhodes," *BSEI*, n.s. XXXII, No. 1 (1st semester 1957), 5–30.

D[ürrwell], George. "La Commune annamite," *BSEI*, XLIX–L (2nd semester 1905), 67–88.

Dürrwell, G. "Tran-Ba-Loc, Tong-Doc de Thuan-khanh, Sa Vie et son oeuvre, Notice biographique d'après les documents de famille," *BSEI*, XL (2nd semester 1900), 27–60.

Fourès. "Royaume du Cambodge: Organisation politique," *Excursions et Reconnaissances*, XIII (1882), 168–211.

Hanh. "La Mort du Norodom, ses dernier moments," *Revue Indo-Chinoise*, 10 (31 May 1904), 671–674.

Jumper, R. "Mandarin Bureaucracy in South Viet Nam," *Pacific Affairs*, XXX, No. 1 (March 1957), 47–58.

————. "Problems of Public Administration in South Vietnam," *Far Eastern Survey*, XXVI, No. 12 (December 1957), 183–190.

Landes, A. "La Commune annamite," *Excursions et Reconnaissances*, V (1880), 213–242.

————. "Notes sur la langue et la littérature annamite," *Excursions et Reconnaissances*, VIII (1884), 119–130.

————. "Notes sur le *quoc-ngu*," *BSEI*, 1886 (1st semester 1886), 5–22.

Landron, A. "Divisions administratives de la Cochinchine," *BSEI*, n.s. XX (1945), 15–35.

Leclère, A. "Histoire de Kampot et de la rébellion de cette province de 1885–1887," *Revue Indo-Chinoise*, 60 (30 June 1907), 828–841; 61 (15 July 1907), 933–952.

Le-Van-Phat. "La Vie intime d'un Annamite de Cochinchine et ses croyances vulgaires," *BSEI*, LII (2nd semester 1906), 5–142.

————. "Introduction des caractères chinois dans le programme de l'enseignement indigène," *BSEI*, LIV (1st semester 1908), 186–190.

Lewis, M. D. "One Hundred Million Frenchmen: The 'Assimilation' Theory in French Colonial Policy," *Comparative Studies in Society and History*, IV, No. 2 (January 1962), 129–153.

Maître, Cl-E. "L'Enseignement indigène dans l'Indochine annamite," *Revue Indo-Chinoise*, 64 (30 August 1907), 135–148.

Mallaret, L. "La Minorité cambodgienne de Cochinchine," *BSEI*, n.s. XXI, No. 1 (1st trimester 1946), 19–34.

Man Quoc. "Truong Vinh Ky: mot nha bac hoc tru danh da ngang nhien dong vai dac vu tinh bao, lam tay sai dac luc giac Phap" (Truong Vinh Ky, An Eminent Scholar Who Sold Himself Without Shame to the Secret Service of the French Colonialists), *Nghien Cuu Lich Su*, LX, No. 3 (1964), 35–38.

Meyer, C. "Insurrections nationales du siècle dernier," *Etudes Cambodgiennes*, 9 (January–March 1967), 20–22 and 36–37. Further articles on the rising of 1885–1886 appear in *ibid.*, 10 (April–June 1967), 25–35, 11 (July–September), 32–46, and 12 (October–December), 20–36.

Michel, G. "Organisation de la justice en Indo-Chine," *Revue Indo-Chinoise*, 49 (15 January 1907), 3–17; 50 (31 January 1907), 99–111; 51 (15 February 1907), 199–211.

Nel. "Philastre, sa vie et son oeuvre," *BSEI*, XLIV (1902), 3–27.

Nguyen-Huong. "Pétrus Truong-Vinh-Ky (1837–1898)," *Van-Hoa Nguyet-San* (Monthly Cultural Review), XIV, No. 12 (December 1965), 1,709–1,737.

Nguyen-Van-Han. "Une Joute littéraire et politique en 1870," *FA*, IX, 87 (August 1953), 672–677.

Osborne, M. E. "History and Kingship in Contemporary Cambodia," *Journal of Southeast Asian History*, VII, No. 1 (March 1966), 1–14.

———. "Notes on Early Cambodian Provincial History," *FA*, XX, No. 186 (Summer 1966), 433–449.

Passerat de la Chapelle, P. "L'Industrie du décorticage du riz en Basse-Cochinchine," *BSEI*, 1901 (1st semester 1901), 49–85.

Pavie, A. "Excursion dans le Cambodge et le Royaume de Siam," *Excursions et Reconnaissances*, IX (1881), 455–481; X (1881), 99–146.

Perin, J. "La Vie et l'oeuvre de Luro," *BSEI*, n.s. XV, Nos. 1–2 (1st and 2nd semesters 1940), 13–25.

Pinto, R. "Les Assemblées des villages convoquées par l'Amiral Ohier," *BSEI*, n.s. XIX, No. 1 (1st trimester 1944), 9–55.

Porée-Maspero, E. "Traditions orales de Pursat et de Kampot," *Artibus Asiae*, XXIV, 3/4 (1961), 394–398.

Raquez, A. "Norodom de Cambodge avant son avènement," *Revue Indo-Chinoise*, 3 (15 August 1904), 143–156.

———. "Les Fêtes de la crémation de Norodom," *Revue Indo-Chinoise*, 16 July 1906, 1,013–1,024; 30 July 1906, 1,117–1,130.

Reveillère, [Contre Amiral]. "Patriotisme annamite," *Revue Indo-Chinoise*, 190 (9 June 1902), 515–517.

Ricklefs, M. C. "Land and Law in the Epigraphy of Tenth-Century Cambodia," *Journal of Asian Studies*, XXVI, No. 3 (May 1967), 411–420.

Rivière, G. "Une Lignée de loyaux serviteurs, les Nguyen Khoa," *BAVH*, II, 3 (July–September 1915), 287–304.

Rivoalen, A. "L'Oeuvre française d'enseignement au Viet-Nam," *FA*,

Special Number 125–126–127 (October–November–December 1956), 401–422.

Roucoules, E. "Etude sur l'instruction publique en Cochinchine," *BSEI*, 1889 (2nd semester 1889), 25–44.

———. "Le Français, le *quoc-ngu* et l'enseignement publique en Indo-Chine. Réponse à M. Aymonier," *BSEI*, 1890, fasc. 1 (1st semester 1890), 5–17.

Schreiner, A. "Conférence sur l'enseignement en Indo-Chine," *BSEI*, LIV (1st semester 1908), 163–178.

Sogny, L. "Les Familles illustres d'Annam, S. E. Nguyen-Huu-Do," *BAVH*, XI, 2 (April–June 1924), 169–204.

Taboulet, G. "J.-B. Eliacin Luro, Inspecteur des Affaires Indigènes en Cochinchine," *BSEI*, n.s. XV, Nos. 1–2 (1st and 2nd semesters 1940), 27–112.

———. "Emile et Clément Luro, colons en Cochinchine," *BSEI*, n.s. XV, Nos. 1–2 (1st and 2nd semesters 1940), 113–128.

Texier, M. "Le Mandarinat au Viet-Nam au XIXe siècle," *BSEI*, n.s. XXXVII, No. 3 (3rd semester 1962), 325–376.

Thierry, S. "La Personne sacrée du roi dans la littérature populaire cambodgienne," in *Studies in the History of Religions: IV, The Sacral Kingship*. Leiden, 1959.

Thomson, R. S. "The Establishment of the French Protectorate over Cambodia," *Far Eastern Quarterly*, IV, No. 4 (August 1945), 313–340.

To Minh Trung. "Truong Vinh Ky: ten tay sai dac luc dan tien cua chu nghia thuc dan Phap trong lich su ta" (Truong Vinh Ky, The First Lackey in the Service of the French in Viet-Nam), *Nghien Cuu Lich Su*, LIX, No. 2 (1964), 43–46.

Tran-Ba-Loc. "Ce que désirent les indigènes," *Excursions et Reconnaissances*, II (1880), 146–154.

Tran-Ba-Tho. "La Piété filiale (Préceptes de la morale confucéene)," *BESI*, LIV (1st semester 1908), 57–156.

Tran-Tan-Binh. Extracts from a lecture which this mandarin gave on 6 March 1907 are reproduced in "Chronique," *BEFEO*, VII, Nos. 1–2 (January–June 1907), 155–166.

Truong Vinh Ky, Pétrus. "Ecriture en Annam," *BSEI*, 1888 (1st semester 1888), 5–9.

Vial, P. "L'Instruction publique en Cochinchine," *Revue Maritime et Coloniale*, XXXII (1872), 702–718.

Wolters, O. W. "The Khmer King at Basan (1371–3) and the Restoration of the Cambodian Chronology during the Fourteenth and Fifteenth Centuries," *Asia Major*, n.s. XII, No. 1 (1966), 44–89.

Woodside, A. B. "Some Features of the Vietnamese Bureaucracy under the Early Nguyen Dynasty," *Harvard Papers on China*, 19 (December 1965), 1–29.

Wyatt, D. K. "Siam and Laos 1767–1827," *Journal of Southeast Asian History*, IV, No. 2 (September 1963), 13–32.

BOOKS

The following listing includes pamphlets and off-prints which circulated as separate items from the journals in which they were originally published.

Abel, M. H. [A. B.-L. Rieunier]. *Solution pratique de la question de Cochinchine*. Paris, 1864.

Anon. *Etude sur les voies et moyens de la politique française en Cochinchine*. Saigon, 1864.

———. *La Politique indigène en Cochinchine depuis la conquête jusqu'en 1905*. Saigon, 1905.

Aubaret, G., trans. Trinh-Hoai-Duc. *Gia-Dinh Thong-Chi, Histoire et description de la Basse Cochinchine*. Paris, 1863.

———. *Code annamite, lois et règlements du Royaume d'Annam*. 2 vols. Paris, 1865.

Aymonier, E. *Notice sur le Cambodge*. Paris, 1875.

———. *Nos Transcriptions: Etude sur les systèmes d'écriture en caractères européens adoptés en Cochinchine française*. Saigon, 1886.

———. *La Langue française et l'enseignement en Indo-Chine*. Paris, 1890.

———. *La Langue française en Indochine*. Paris, 1891.

———. *Voyage dans le Laos*. 2 vols. Paris, 1895–1897.

———. *Le Cambodge*. 3 vols. Paris, 1900–1903.

Barruel, M. *De La Substitution progressive des tribunaux français aux tribunaux indigènes en Indo-Chine*. Confolens, 1905.

Barthélemy, P. *En Indo-Chine 1894–1895: Cambodge, Cochinchine, Laos, Siam meridional*. Paris, 1899.

Bernard, Paul. *Le Problème économique indochinois*. Paris, 1934.

Betts, R. F. *Assimilation and Association in French Colonial Theory 1890–1914*. New York, 1961.

Boilloux. *Etude sur l'assiette de l'impôt foncier*. Saigon, 1879.

Bonnyman, G. D. *Notices of the Port of Kampot*. Singapore, 1851.

Bouchot, J. *Documents pour servir à l'histoire de Saigon.* Saigon, 1927.

——. *Pétrus J.-B. Truong-Vinh-Ky 1837–1898.* Saigon, 1927.

Bouillevaux, C.-E. *Voyage dans l'Indo-Chine 1848–1856.* Paris, 1858.

——. *L'Annam et le Cambodge: Voyages et notices historiques.* Paris, 1874.

Bouinais, A., and A. Paulus. *L'Indo-Chine française contemporaine, Cochinchine, Cambodge, Tonkin, Annam.* 2 vols. 2nd ed. Paris, 1885.

Boulanger, E. *Un Hiver au Cambodge.* Tours, 1887.

Bourchet, M. A. *Essai sur les moeurs et les institutions du peuple annamite.* Paris, 1869.

Branda, P. [P. Reveillère]. *Çà et là: Cochinchine et Cambodge: L'Âme khmère: Ang-kor.* Paris, 1887.

Briffaut, C. *La Cité annamite.* 3 vols., Tome I "La Fondation," Tome II "Les Sédentaires," Tome III "Les Errants." Paris, 1909–1912.

Buttinger, J. *The Smaller Dragon: A Political History of Vietnam.* New York, 1958.

——. *Vietnam: A Dragon Embattled.* 2 vols. New York, 1967.

Cadière, L. *Croyances et pratiques religieuses des Vietnamiens.* 3 vols. Saigon, Tome I, 1958 reprint; II, 1955; III, Paris, 1957.

Cady, J. F. *The Roots of French Imperialism in Eastern Asia.* Ithaca, N.Y., 1954.

——. *Thailand, Burma, Laos and Cambodia.* Englewood Cliffs, N.J., 1966.

Cao-Xuan-Duc, ed. *Quoc-Trieu Dang-Khoa-Luc* (Register of the National Examinations), Vol. I. Saigon, 1962 reprint.

Caraman, F. T. *Rapport sur le Cambodge présenté le 24 Janvier 1874 au Ministère de la Marine et des Colonies.* Paris, 1874.

Carné, L. de. *Voyage en Indo-Chine et dans l'empire chinois.* Paris, 1872.

Chaigneau, M. D. *Souvenirs de Hué.* Paris, 1867.

——, trans. *Tho Nam Ky, ou Lettre cochinchinoise sur les événements de la guerre Franco-Annamite.* Paris, 1876.

——, trans. *Tho Thiep Theo Tho Nam Ky, Suite de la lettre annamite. Poème sur la conduite des jeunes Annamites après la guerre.* Paris, 1876.

Chenau, H. *Du Protectorat français en Annam, au Tonkin et au Cambodge.* Paris, 1904.

Chesneaux, J. *Contribution à l'histoire de la nation vietnamienne.* Paris, 1955.

La Cochinchine française en 1878. Paris, 1878. Published and prepared by the Agricultural and Industrial Committee of Cochinchina.

Coedès, G. *Pour mieux comprendre Angkor.* 2nd ed. Paris, 1947.

Collard, P. *Cambodge et Cambodgiens: Métamorphose du Royaume Khmêr par une méthode française du Protectorat.* Paris, 1925.

Coulet, G. *Les Sociétés secrètes en terre d'Annam.* Saigon, 1926.

Cultru, P. *Histoire de la Cochinchine française des origines à 1883.* Paris, 1910.

Depierre (Bishop of Benda). *Situation du Christianisme en Cochinchine à la fin du XIXe siècle.* Saigon, 1898.

Devillers, P. *Histoire du Viêt-Nam de 1940 à 1952.* Paris, 1952.

Dinh-Xuan-Nguyen. *Apport français dans la littérature vietnamienne (1651–1945).* Saigon, 1961.

Doumer, P. *L'Indo-Chine française: Souvenirs.* Paris, 1905; 2nd ed. Paris, n.d.

Dürrwell, G. *Ma Chère Cochinchine: Trente années d'impressions et de souvenirs, Février 1881–1910.* Paris, 1911.

D'Enjoy, P. *La Colonisation de la Cochin-Chine: Manuel de colon.* Paris, 1898.

Ennis, T. E. *French Policy and Development in Indochina.* Chicago, 1936.

Franchini, P. *La Genèse de l'affaire de Cochinchine.* Paris, 1952.

Francis, G. [Francis Garnier]. *La Cochinchine française en 1864.* Paris, 1864.

———. *De La Colonisation de Cochinchine.* Paris, 1865.

Garnier, F. *Voyage d'exploration en Indo-Chine, éffectué pendant les années 1866, 1867 à 1868.* 2 vols. Paris, 1873.

De Grammont, L. *Onze Mois de sous-préfecture en Basse-Cochinchine.* La-Roche-sur-Yon, 1863.

Groslier, B.-P. *Angkor et le Cambodge au XVIe siècle.* Paris, 1958.

Heine-Geldern, R. *Conceptions of State and Kingship in Southeast Asia.* Cornell Southeast Asia Program Data Paper No. 18. Ithaca, N.Y., 1956.

Hess, J. *L'Affaire Iukanthor: Les Dessous d'un protectorat.* Paris, 1900.

Huard, P. A., and M. Durand. *Connaissances du Viêt-Nam.* Paris, 1954.

Imbert, J. *Histoire des institutions khmères.* Tome II of the *Annales* of the Faculté de Droit de Phnom Penh. Phnom Penh, 1961.

Isoart, P. *Le Phénomène national viêtnamien.* Paris, 1961.

Jammes, H. L. *Souvenirs du pays d'Annam*. Paris, 1900.

Jobbé-Duval, E. *La Commune annamite d'après de récent travaux*. Paris, 1896.

Jumper, R., and Nguyen Thi Hue. *Notes on the Political and Administrative History of Viet Nam 1802–1962*. Saigon, 1962.

Khong Xuan-Thu. *Truong Vinh Ky 1837–1889*. Saigon, 1958.

Kresser, P. *La Commune annamite en Cochinchine: Recrutement des notables*. Paris, 1935.

Leclerc, J. *De l'Evolution et du développement des institutions annamites et cambodgiennes sous l'influence française*. Rennes, 1923.

Leclère, A. *Recherches sur la législation cambodgienne: droit privé*. Paris, 1890.

——. *Recherches sur le droit public des Cambodgiens*. Paris, 1894.

——. *Les Codes cambodgiens*. 2 vols. Paris, 1898.

——. *Le Buddhisme au Cambodge*. Paris, 1899.

——. *Cambodge: Le Roi, la famille royale et les femmes du palais*. Saigon, 1905.

——. *Histoire du Cambodge*. Paris, 1914.

Lemire, C. *L'Indo-Chine: Cochinchine française, Royaume du Cambodge, Royaume d'Annam et Tonkin*. Paris, 1884.

Le Myre de Vilers. *Les Institutions civiles de la Cochinchine (1879–1881): Recueil des principaux documents*. Paris, 1908.

Le Thanh Khoi. *Le Viêt-Nam: Histoire et civilisation*. Paris, 1955.

Lhomme, H.-F. *Le Gouvernement des amiraux en Cochinchine*. Paris, 1901.

Luro, J.-B. E. *Cours d'administration annamite*. Saigon, 1875.

——. *Le Pays d'Annam: Etude sur l'organisation politique et sociale des Annamites*. Paris, 1878.

Ly-Binh-Hue. *Le Régime des concessions domainiales en Indochine*. Paris, 1931.

Maurain, J. *La Politique écclésiastique du second empire de 1852 à 1869*. Paris, 1930.

Maybon, C. *Histoire moderne du pays d'Annam (1592–1820)*. Paris, 1919.

Meyniard, C. *Le Second Empire en Indo-Chine (Siam, Cambodge, Annam)*. Paris, 1891.

Michel, G. *Répertoire des lois, décrets et ordonnances rendus applicables aux possessions françaises de l'Indo-Chine depuis l'occupation de la Cochinchine jusqu'au 1er janvier 1902*. Hanoi, 1902.

Montaigut, F. de. *La Colonisation française dans l'est de la Cochinchine.* Limoges, 1929.

Morizon, R. *Monographie du Combodge.* Hanoi, 1931.

Mouhot, H. "Voyages dans les royaumes de Siam, de Cambodge, de Laos et autres parties générales de l'Indo-Chine." *Le Tour du Monde,* 1863, 219–352. This text was translated and published as *Travels in the Central Parts of Indo-China (Siam), Cambodia and Laos.* 2 vols. London, 1864.

Moura, J. *Le Royaume du Cambodge.* 2 vols. Paris, 1883.

Mus, P. *Viêt-Nam: Sociologie d'une guerre.* Paris, 1952.

Nam Xuan Tho. *Phan Thanh Gian (1796–1867).* Saigon. 1957.

Nguyen Ba The. *Ton Tho Truong 1825–1877.* Saigon, 1957.

Nguyen Tao, trans. *Dai-Nam Nhat-Thong-Chi* (Geography of the Vietnamese Empire). Vols. 1 and 2 "Luc-Tinh Nam Viet" (The Six Southern Provinces of Viet-Nam) originally prepared post 1865, consulted in Saigon 1959 reprint.

Nguyen-Thanh-Khiet. *La Cochinchine française et son organisation politique.* Montpellier, 1915.

Nguyen Thanh-Nha. *Tableau économique du Viet-Nam au XVIIe et XVIIIe siècles.* Paris, n.d.

Nicolas, P. *Notes sur la vie française en Cochinchine.* Paris, 1912.

Norodom Sihanouk. *La Monarchie cambodgienne.* Phnom Penh, 1961.

Pallu de la Barrière, L. *Histoire de l'expédition de Cochinchine.* 2nd ed. Paris, 1888.

Pannetier, A. *Notes cambodgiennes: Au Coeur du pays khmer.* Paris, 1921.

Pasquier, P. *L'Annam d'autrefois.* Paris, 1907.

Pavie, A. *A La Conquête des coeurs.* New ed. Paris, 1947.

Pham-Quynh. *Quelques Conférences à Paris.* Hanoi, 1923.

Pham-Van-Truong. *Essai sur le code Gia-Long.* Paris, 1922.

Phan Huy Chu. *Lich Trieu Hien Chuong Loai Chi* (Description of the Institutions of all the Dynasties) edited and translated by the Institute for the History of Viet-Nam, Hanoi. 4 vols. Hanoi, 1960–1962, first published 1821/1822.

Phan-Khoang. *Viet-Nam Phap Thuoc Su* (History of Viet-Nam under French Colonialism). Saigon, 1961.

Philastre, P.-L.-F. *Le Code annamite.* 2 vols. Paris, 1876.

Porée, G., and E. Maspero. *Moeurs et coutumes des Khmèrs: Origines, histoire, religions, croyances, rites.* Paris, 1938.

Preschez, P. *Essai sur la démocratie au Cambodge.* Fondation Nationale des Sciences Politiques, Centre d'Etude des Relations Internationales. Paris, 1961.

Reinach, L. de. *Recueil de traités conclus par la France en Extrême-Orient (1648–1902).* 2 vols. Paris, 1902–1907.

Romanet du Caillaud, F. *Histoire de l'intervention française au Tongking de 1872 à 1874.* Paris, 1880.

Rousseau, A. *Le Protectorat français du Cambodge: Organisation politique, administrative et financière.* Dijon, 1904.

Sarin Chhak. *Les Frontières du Cambodge.* Paris, 1966. To date, only one volume of an anticipated two volumes has been published.

Schreiner, A. *Les Institutions annamites en Basse-Cochinchine avant la conquête française.* 3 vols. Saigon, 1900–1902.

Septans, A. *Les Commencements de l'Indo-Chine française d'après les archives du Ministère de la Marine et des Colonies, les mémoires ou relations du temps.* Paris, 1887.

Silvestre, J. *L'Empire d'Annam et le peuple annamite.* Paris, 1889.

Swettenham, Sir Frank. *British Malaya.* Revised ed. London, 1948.

Taboulet, G. *La Geste française en Indochine: Histoire par les textes de la France en Indochine des origines à 1914.* 2 vols. Paris, 1955–1956.

Thai Bach. *Nguyen Dinh Chieu.* Saigon, 1957.

Thomazi, A. *La Conquête de l'Indochine.* Paris, 1934.

Thompson, V. *French Indo-China.* New York, 1937.

Tran-Minh Tiet. *Histoire des persécutions au Viet-Nam.* Paris, 1955.

Tran Trong Kim. *Viet-Nam Su Luoc* (Outline History of Viet-Nam). Saigon, 1964.

Tran Van Trai. *L'Enseignement traditionnel en An-Nam.* Paris, 1942.

Truong Buu Lam. *Patterns of Vietnamese Response to Foreign Intervention: 1858–1900.* Monograph Series No. 11, Southeast Asia Studies, Yale University. New Haven, Conn., 1967.

Truong-Minh-Ky. *Nhu Tay Nhut Trinh: De Saigon à Paris.* Saigon, 1889.

——. *Chu Quac Thai Hoi: Exposition universelle de 1889.* Saigon, 1891.

Truong-Vinh-Ky, P. J. B. *Cours d'histoire annamite à l'usage des écoles de la Basse-Cochinchine.* 2 vols. Saigon, 1875–1877.

——. *Voyage au Tonkin en 1876: Chuyen di Bac-Ki nam At-hoi (1876).* Saigon, 1876.

——. *Souvenirs historiques sur Saigon et ses environs: Conférence faite au Collège des Interprètes.* Saigon, 1885.

Vial, P. *Les Premières Années de la Cochinchine française.* 2 vols. Paris, 1874.

Villemereuil, A. B. de, ed. *Explorations et missions de Doudart de Lagrée.* Paris, 1883.

White, J. *A Voyage to Cochin China.* London, 1824.

Willmott, W. E. *The Chinese in Cambodia.* Vancouver, 1967.

Worsley, P. *The Third World.* London, 1964.

Index